Horton Davies is Putnam Professor emeritus and has taught the History of Christianity in Princeton University since 1956. He is well known for his many publications on various aspects of English church history, including the monumental, 5-volume *Worship and Theology in England.*

D0894075

LIKE ANGELS FROM A CLOUD

Like Angels from a Cloud

THE ENGLISH
METAPHYSICAL PREACHERS
1588–1645

BY HORTON DAVIES

HUNTINGTON LIBRARY • SAN MARINO

1986

BV
4208
.G7
D295
1986

Library of Congress Cataloging-in-Publication Data

Davies, Horton.
  Like angels from a cloud : the English metaphysical
preachers, 1588–1645.

  Bibliography: p.
  Includes index.
  1. Preaching—England—History—16th century.
2. Preaching—England—History—17th century.   3. Church
of England—Clergy—History—16th century.   4. Church
of England—Clergy—History—17th century.   5. Anglican
Communion—England—Clergy—History—16th century.
6. Anglican Communion—England—Clergy—History—
17th century.   I. Title.   II. Title: Metaphysical
preachers.
BV4208.G7D295   1986   251'.00942   86–10613

ISBN 0–87328–088–1

Copyright © 1986
by the Henry E. Huntington Library and Art Gallery
Designed by Ward Ritchie

JESUIT - KRAUSS - McCORMICK - LIBRARY
1100 EAST 55th STREET
CHICAGO, ILLINOIS 60615

For my congenial colleagues,
past and present
in the pioneering Department
of Religion at Princeton
University

Contents

Acknowledgments

The research for this book was facilitated by the award of a National Endowment of the Humanities-Huntington Library Fellowship in 1981–82. The stimulating and congenial presence of the director and the research associates was a sheer delight, and I wish to thank them for it. I have also benefited by the editorial expertise of Dr. Guilland Sutherland of the Huntington.

In the fall of 1982, I directed a seminar at the Folger Shakespeare Library in Washington, D.C. which gave me the chance to try out various chapters of the manuscript and to profit from the lively comments of the faculty and graduate students present. To those also I express my gratitude.

Two earlier versions of my chapters have appeared in print. "A Spur for the Somnolent: Wit in the English Pulpit, 1588–1645" was published in *Thalia. Studies in Literary Humor*, 6 (1983): 32–47. "Ten Characteristics of Metaphysical Preaching" appeared in *Studies of the Church in History*, ed. H. Davies (Pickwick Publications, Allison Park, Pa., 1983), 103–147. I am grateful for the copyright permissions.

H. D.

LIKE ANGELS FROM A CLOUD

Introduction

The researcher knows only too well the gap between intention and achievement. At the outset of my research the project seemed in Milton's words "equal hope and hazard in the glorious enterprise." The first hope was to compare the sermons of the three major metaphysical poets, Donne, Herbert, and Crashaw. What made such a potential comparison fascinating to contemplate was that Donne had been brought up a Catholic and had become a dean of the Church of England, while Herbert had never been anything but an Anglican, and Crashaw, brought up as the son of a determined Puritan moved from the Church of England to the Church of Rome dying as a canon of Loretto. It would have been exciting to see to what extent Herbert and Crashaw imitated Donne in the pulpit as they did in their verse. Furthermore, a second point of comparison and contrast might have emerged in studying the change in Herbert from the eloquent Public Orator of Cambridge University to the rector of bucolic Bemerton who insisted in his *The Country Parson* that the preacher must forego wit, learning, and eloquence to study the humility of holiness. In addition, it would have been intriguing to see if Crashaw's ecstatic sermons did indeed "ravish like poems" as they were reputed to have done in St. Mary's Church, close to Peterhouse in Cambridge. Most of all it would have been stunning to compare the evolution of their Christian paradoxes as they preached festival sermons at Christmas and Easter, to contrast their use of daring images and arcane learning. But those hopes were quickly doomed. For the sad truth is that no sermons of Herbert or Crashaw survive.

The hazard could easily have throttled hope, except for a discovery. This was that in a diligent search I discovered over

1

forty metaphysical preachers whose sermons had survived in print, and there may well be a dozen more. Few of them were of the caliber of Donne—on any comparison he outtops the rest—but some of them deserve consideration not only as homileticians, but as writers of inspired and distinguished prose. The following chapters will introduce these men. Most of them are hardly known in the present day, despite the fact that several were bishops and eminent preachers in the golden age of the English pulpit from the days of the Armada (1588) to the death of Archbishop Laud (1645), and yet others preached metaphysical-style sermons even during the days of the Restoration, although by then they were thought to be quaintly anachronistic.

The chapters of this book are generally presented in the order in which the problems of the research were attempted. It may however be of interest to see how the project developed.

The first task was to isolate the more than forty metaphysical preachers and to deal with them prosopographically. They had to be introduced to the reader in general fashion in order to make the delights and variety of their sermons worth the studying, and samples had to be provided. It was also necessary to indicate why they had not been studied before, and to show how preaching conditions in the seventeenth century differed from modern conditions so that the reader could identify with the preachers imaginatively. The suggestion is made that it was the classical education in the leading English schools, requiring pupils to translate Latin and Greek verse into English verse, that was the single major factor accounting for the metaphysical style in poetry and preaching. Finally, reasons are given why metaphysical preachers in particular were recruited and promoted by the early Stuart monarchs and their advisers. All this became chapter one, "Who are the Metaphysical Preachers?"

Next, it was necessary to determine what the distinctive characteristics of the metaphysical sermon were, in contrast to the plain Puritan sermons which were their competitors. Eleven differentia were determined: wit; patristic learning; classical lore; citations from Greek, and Latin, and occasionally Hebrew originals; illustrations from "unnatural" natural history; allegorical exegesis; plans with complex divisions and subdivisions; a Senecan and staccato style; the use of paradoxes, riddles, and emblems; fondness for speculation; and the relation of doctrinal and devotional preaching to the Christian calendar. This is chapter two of the book.

Since the brilliance of their wit and the display of learning of many kinds were the outstanding features of metaphysical sermons, a chapter had to be devoted to each. Hence chapter three analyzes metaphysical wit in various forms: as conceit, puns and paranomasia, epigrams, paradoxes, extended oxymora, and the use of ingenious texts and titles for sermons. The same chapter indicates the many functions of wit in sermons, and asks why witty preaching was so popular under the early Stuarts and fell so soon out of favor afterwards.

An essential task was to break the stereotype that assumed that all metaphysical preachers were, like Andrewes, Donne, and Laud, of the Arminian type, who glorified hierarchy in both Church and State, esteemed reason highly, and would have nothing to do with the doctrines of election and predestination. This stereotype is shattered in chapter four—"The Metaphysical Calvinists"—which shows that eight bishops were ardent Calvinists and metaphysical preachers, including two of the most popular preachers of the century, John Hacket and Ralph Brownrig. The Calvinist Thomas Adams was even more popular than Donne, at least in terms of the frequency with which his many sermons were reprinted. In avoiding one stereotype, one does not seek to create another, so perhaps naturally, chapter five deals with the Arminian preachers in the metaphysical mode, including Archbishop Laud, Bishops John Cosin, Matthew Wren, and Brian Duppa, and ten cathedral clergy. All of them were characters, and not a few were eccentrics.

Having, in chapters four and five, delineated the *dramatis personae* involved, the next chapter deals with the hotly disputed issue of whether their learning should have been carried from the study to the pulpit, and whether eloquence was appropriate in a pulpit supposedly dedicated to simple Christian testimony. The views of both defenders and critics are explored in chapter six.

The two following chapters (seven and eight) analyze at length the content of the metaphysical sermons, in terms of both "Innovative Themes," and "Traditional Themes." The former were required by the position of a Church of England which lay ecclesiologically midway between Rome and Geneva, and which had to be explained and defended by its leading pulpit apologists. Hence these sermons were often anti-Roman Catholic and anti-Puritan propaganda. They dealt with the continuity between the Church of England and the early Church of the first six centuries, and sought to answer the question: Where was your Church before the Reformation? These sermons defended the threefold ministry of bishop, priest, and deacon, and the liturgy of a Church which borrowed from ancient and reformed forms of worship; and they expressed a concern for decency and reverence in the ritual and ceremonial of the Church of England. "Traditional Themes" records and analyzes the admirable preaching of the metaphysical divines on such orthodox Christian doctrines as the Trinity, the Incarnation, the Atonement, Everlasting Life, the Sacraments, and the Last Judgment.

Following this exploration of the major themes of metaphysical sermons, the next two chapters are concerned with the techniques to be found in them. Chapter nine considers how much the variation in audiences determined the styles of the preachers. Sermons preached before the court, at Paul's Cross, the Hospital (or "Spital") Charity sermons preached annually in Easter week, those preached in cathedrals, in famous parish churches, and before university congregations, are all discussed. Chapter ten recalls how many of the metaphysical preachers were poets, and how important imagery was to their compositions, both as poets and as preachers. Images are analyzed in terms of the functions they fulfilled, such as grasping the wandering attention, or illuminating the abstractions of doctrine and conduct by concretion, or implanting a lesson on the memory. Images used by the most famous preachers are also considered in the light of the range of the experience and reading from which they are drawn.

The final chapter provides an evaluation of the strengths and weaknesses of metaphysical preaching, both in terms of the criticisms made in their own day and during the Restoration, together with their own justifications for preaching as they did.

It should be noted that spelling, except in modern editions, preserves the flavor of the sixteenth and seventeenth centuries. Furthermore, certain citations appear more than once in the text because they are quoted for different analytical purposes.

Finally, our title provides an invitation. Izaak Walton reminds us that Donne preached "like an angel from a cloud, but in none." Like all the metaphysicals his imagination soared to heaven, whose cartographer he was, but his message was meant for the evasive earthbound man in the pew, lost in the labyrinthine mazes of his own heart or the ambush of his excuses. Donne and his fellow divines were profound psychologists too. Like Wordworth's skylark the metaphysical preachers were

> Type of the wise who soar, but never roam;
> True to the kindred points of heaven and home!

Chapter I

WHO ARE

THE METAPHYSICAL PREACHERS?

THIS UNFAMILIAR TERM describes a large and lively group of at least forty-one Anglican preachers who flourished in the last decade of the sixteenth and the first four decades of the seventeenth century, and who were renowned for their wit, learning, eloquence, and loyalty to the Church and Nation. The term "metaphysical" does not imply that they were philosophical preachers; that might be more readily applied to the Cambridge Platonist divines who urged the claims of cool reason and compassionate charity in the embattled times of "apostolic blows and knocks." It is a term extended from its initial reference by Samuel Johnson to the metaphysical poets, the chief of whom employed in the pulpit the same daring wit, esoteric knowledge, colloquial directness, and striking imagery that had marked their verse. Indeed, the chief metaphysical poets, Donne, Herbert, and Crashaw (until the latter's conversion to Roman Catholicism) were outstanding metaphysical preachers in the Church of England. Other minor metaphysical poets, such as Bishop Henry King (author of *The Exequy*—a superbly moving tribute to his dead wife), and Richard Corbet, wag, practical joker, and bishop, as well as several other poet-preachers, also belonged to the metaphysical preaching fraternity. The latter included William Cartwright, William Alabaster, John Hacket, Thomas Goffe, Barten Holyday, and Jasper Mayne.

Why uninvestigated in depth and detail?

The question then arises: why has this group of Anglican divines flourishing in the golden age of Anglican eloquence, the seventeenth century, not been investigated in depth or detail? Three reasons may be given. The first is that it is only within the last quarter-century that scholars have been intrigued by the sermons of John Donne, the greatest of all the metaphysical poet-preachers. The publication, between 1953 and 1962, of the Potter and Simpson critical edition of the sermons in ten volumes made them generally available for the first time; since then there has been a notable series of monographs[1] on the themes, rhetoric, and especially the imagery of his sermons, which indicate the exciting possibilities of further exploration.

Secondly, this would lead us to expect interest in the sermons of two other famous metaphysical poet-priests, Herbert and Crashaw. How intriguing it would be to investigate how far Herbert, the former Public Orator of Cambridge University, had toned down his poetic fertility, ornamentation, and exuberance to meet the needs of his bucolic congregation in Bemerton parish. This can be assumed because Herbert says that while the country congregation needs devices to get and hold attention, yet the parson should be "not witty, or learned, or eloquent, but Holy." Also Herbert is the first to criticize Lancelot Andrewes' distinctive style of text-crumbling.[2] Alas, it is unlikely that we shall ever read a sermon of Herbert's because none has survived in print or is known in manuscript form. Walton states that Lady Cooke (Herbert's widow who had married Sir Robert Cooke of Highnam near Gloucester) "had preserv'd many of Mr. *Herbert's* private Writings, which she intended to make publick; but they and *Hignam* house, were burnt together, by the late Rebels."[3] Aubrey, however, maliciously claims "He writt also a folio in Latin, wch because the parson of Hineham could not read, his widowe, (then wife to Sir Robert Cooke) condemned to the use of good housewifery. This account I had from Mr. Arnold Cooke, one of Sir Robert Cooke's sonnes, whom I desired to ask his mother-in-law for Mr. G. Herberts MSS."[4] We can only assume that Herbert's sermons were used as lining for kitchen pots or for lighting fires.

Nor are there any surviving sermons of Crashaw's. These also would be fascinating to examine, for he had undergone two transitions: from an upbringing as the son of a redoubtable anti-papal Puritan controversialist, to becoming a fellow of the High Church Peterhouse in Cambridge University (whose chapel he had a hand in decorating) until he finally accepted the Roman allegiance. Contemporary accounts of his preaching indicate how serious our loss might be. An early biographer refers to Crashaw's preaching as college catechist and curate of Little St. Mary's, the small parish church adjoining Peterhouse, and to "those thronged Sermons on each Sunday and Holiday [i.e. holy day] that ravished more like Poems . . . the Poet and the Saint . . . scattering not so much Sentences as Extasies, his soul brea[t]hing in each word."[5] A critical Puritan investigator speaks of his idolatrous matter: "Mr. Crashaw fellow of Peterhouse in a speech made in that Colledge Chappell *Die Annunciationis* 1639 is credibly reported to have turned himselfe to the picture of the Virgine Mary and to have used these words *Hanc adoramus, colamus hanc.* [We adore her, we worship her.] That is rather probable because his practises in little St. Maryes, where he is Curat are superstitious."[6]

In the third place, since we have no sermons of either Herbert or Crashaw, we must suppose that there were few, if any, other metaphysical divines whose sermons were worth rescuing from oblivion. It is understandable that ancient sermons find few readers. This, however, is a superficial view: after reading the surviving sermons of forty-one metaphysical preachers I can vouch for the delight of their wit, the breadth and often depth of their knowledge, the interest in their topical allusions, the coruscation of their imagery, and the sustained brilliance of their rhetoric in certain moving passages. Furthermore, they allow attentive readers the greatest privilege of historical literature—to extend their life by three hundred years, and to feel what it was to be God's ambassador in the pulpit in an age of dramatic change in politics, religious beliefs, and science. We see how they meet the challenge to "justify the ways of God to man" (in Milton's phrase) with all the attention-demanding devices of the holy craft of pulpit eloquence with which to satisfy the doubter, quell the caviller, console the bereaved, heal the bruised conscience, and challenge the apostles of alternative versions of Churchmanship, in ways so various that they seemed to be devotees of different religions.

The need for historical imagination

Entering that seventeenth-century world of sermons calls for an exercise of imagination. If we are surprised at the far-flown eloquence, or the far-fetched and artificial nature of the conceits, the improbability of the "unnatural" natural history, the apparent irrelevance of the historical narrations; if the wit seems extremely contrived, and the citation of quotations in the original Latin and Greek, not to mention disquisitions turning on the etymology of proper names in Hebrew, seems unnecessarily pedantic, we have to recall that the congregations being addressed were always an assemblage of prisoners, for attendance at divine worship was compulsory throughout the period. These and other ways of grasping and holding the attention were essential to avoid a proliferation of yawning. Anecdote, fable, psychological insight, and especially wit, were needed to maintain the attention of bored courtiers intrigued only by the possibility of preferment, or of lawyers in the chapels of the Inns of Court. It is hard for us to comprehend the importance of the sermons of that period. Not only the Paul's Cross sermons (preached in the open air in the shadow of the cathedral and attended by the leaders of the state) but almost every sermon in town and country church was an official statement of government policy, since so close was the union of Church and State that bishops and clergy were regarded as officials of the State as well as of the Church. Thus preaching had an official cast for which there is no equivalent in our own time. Furthermore, and this was especially the case in remote villages, the sermons the rustics heard contained almost the only available news of the world outside the parish boundaries.

Chapter I

Special historical factors account for the controversial character of the seventeenth-century pulpit: the breakdown of the medieval Church, together with the fissiparousness of Protestantism, as well as the disputes within Protestantism between Calvinist and Arminian, and the mediating position of the Church of England between Rome and Geneva. All this added to their interest. As Hensley Henson has rightly insisted, "sermons were designed rather to correct popular beliefs than to express them" and as a consequence it was often true that "attention was diverted from the pedestrian duties of normal Christian living to the most exacting requirements of religious revolution."[7] G. N. Clark has pointed out that in the earlier part of the century sermons constituted both in quality and quantity a significant branch of literature, in two ways that did not also hold true of Restoration sermons.[8] In the first place, the sermons were authoritative—the declarations, if not pronouncements, of divinely-inspired and commissioned expositors. In the second place, they could utilize learning, conceits, citations from learned tongues, and the entire "pretentious parade of learning," while their successors after 1660 were on the defensive, confined to the practical aims of explanation and conviction, in the same style as was adopted by the science of the period, plain, clear, and practical. That is why the metaphysical sermons are much more fascinating reading than the pulpit products of the second part of the century.

Three changes in the modern period have weakened the hold of the pulpit on the public, apart from the increasing secularism of our days. The first is the huge reading public which came into existence as a consequence of the spread of national education among all classes of the people in Europe and North America in the nineteenth century. An equally important change has been the arrival of historical criticism of the Bible in the nineteenth and twentieth centuries which has destroyed the older simplicities of exegesis and which has forced the modern preacher to steer a middle and dangerous course between "the Scylla of Orthodoxy and the Charybdis of Modernism."[9] Thirdly, the modern preacher is restricted in time. Far from having an hour in which to preach his regular Sunday sermon, or two hours for the more significant public policy sermons at Paul's Cross, or the annual Easter week charity sermons at St. Mary's Hospital (the so-called "Spital Sermons"), the modern preacher has only a quarter of an hour, or twenty minutes at the most, in a schedule of worship where anthems sung by the choir, voluntaries played by the organist, and the considerable time taken by the liturgy elbow him rapidly in and out of the pulpit. The seventeenth century gave the preacher time to develop several aspects of a worthy topic, but in our rushed days we are not used to such extensive time for directed meditation.

Finally, we have the serious disadvantage of reading what was originally intended to be seen and heard. Bishop John King, in the dedicatory epistle of his *Lectures upon Ionas* delivered at York in 1594 but published in 1611, rued the disadvantage thus: "I . . . have changed my tongue into a penne, and whereas before I spake with the gesture and countenance of a living man, have now buryed my selfe in a dead letter of lesse effectuall perswasion." So for us the congregation is missing, and we can neither hear the preacher in his vehement declamations expressing his *saeva indignatio*, called "deprehension" in those days, nor the gentle and tender wooing voice that was kept for the penitent or the bereaved. We also miss the gestures of his arms and the expressions of his face which reinforced the words. All this argues that if we fully employ our historical imagination we will be able to appreciate the appeal of the greatest of the metaphysical preachers.

In quantity (and often in quality too) there is God's plenty of published sermons. Donne left 160 sermons, Arthur Lake 109, John Hacket his *Century of Sermons upon Severall Remarkable Subjects*, Lancelot Andrewes 96, Ralph Brownrig 65, Thomas Adams 63 (not counting his *Meditations on the Creed*). Another metaphysical preacher of supposedly Puritan inclinations, namely Henry Smith, has 39. Calvinist royal chaplain John Prideaux has 29, John Cosin has 28; there are two volumes of the sermons of witty Thomas Fuller, Daniel Featley's lively and lengthy series in *Clavis Mystica*, the eight-part sermon of

Chapter I

Thomas Playfere called *The Meane in Mourning*, as well as the prolix *Path to Perfection* and another volume of 9 sermons, are, together with a volume of Archbishop Ussher's, the most important collections of sermons of the period. Nor should the work of the late metaphysical preacher, Mark Frank, be forgotten, since his *Course of Sermons for all the Sundays and Festivals throughout the Year* (1672) contained 51. In addition, there are individual sermons of significance preached on important occasions, and a few select ones preached by another twenty-seven preachers whom we have identified as Anglican priests of the metaphysical stripe.

The variety of metaphysical sermons and preachers

Such a listing, however, tells us nothing of the variety of sermons and preachers in the metaphysical pulpits of the era. There are Donne's macabre meditations on the dissolution of the body by worms, equalled only by his transcendent imagining of the state of the blessed enjoying the *visio Dei*, or the damned in their terrified isolation in the unquenchable fires of hell. There are also Donne's brilliant psychological analyses where he follows men and women into the excuses where they have ambushed themselves so as to be hidden from God's mastiffs, the divine preachers—in this respect they are much like the early Anglican sermons of John Henry Newman from the pulpit of St. Mary's, Oxford in the nineteenth century. There are the brilliant paradoxes—apt expression for that Incarnation of the eternal Son of God which transcends human imagination, the Word of God as an unspeaking infant, or the Resurrection where death is itself destroyed—with which Andrewes transfixed his hearers and set a model for all metaphysical preachers following him. There is the immense pity of Thomas Adams for the poor, his omnivorous reading and vivid observation of life in the streets, and his way of describing a "character" which rivals Overbury, Hall, and John Bunyan, a skill which made the sparkling titles of his sermons vie in the stationers' shops with the titles of the latest plays. There is Brownrig, whose Gunpower Treason commemorative sermons are witty in speaking of papal interference in politics, where Peter's fishing boat is transformed into a man-of-war, and the pope, his successor, into a pirate,[10] yet who is also notable for his concentration on the images of God's lovingkindness in his descriptions of Him (with biblical basis) as friend, brother, father, and husband. There is Fuller's sense of humor which he defends by claiming "it is lawfull for them to smile with delightfull language: Always provided that the sweetnesse of the cause spoile not the savouriness of the meat,"[11] and his immense courage. There is John Hacket's profound sense of forgiveness, divine and human, as the repairer of broken relationships, and of the joy and felicity of the Christian life, and his fondness for riddles, emblems, and epigrams. This affable preacher lived out his own epigram: "For we are born in tears, we are preserved with laughter."[12]

If historical lore delights us, then we shall find Heylyn's sermons full of them. For example, one sermon preached in Christ Church, Oxford, in 1643, began with a quotation from Velleius, "rumpit, interdum moratur proposita hominen Fortune," which he paraphrases as "the projects and designes of us mortall men are many times delayed, and sometimes overthrown by a higher Power." He then explains: "Which power, though the Historian being a Courtier, who ascribes all things to good luck, entituled by the name of Fortune; yet the Philosopher, or contemplative man, who had studied in the Government of humane affairs, would have called it Providence."[13] It was a shrewd thrust for, with the downward turn in the affairs of Charles I, Oxford was filled with courtiers. But this particular sermon is even more notable for its exhibition of learning than its shrewdness: it includes fifty-one references to thirty-one different authors, and this is by no means untypical.

If one is intrigued by ingenious but fanciful explanations then not only Donne, but his friend and poetic imitator, Henry King, will be of interest. He is fascinated by the fact that Moses, who would have been stunned by the weight of glory had he seen God on Sinai face-to-face, only just caught a glimpse of

Him from behind. This provides him with an analogy for discerning and accepting the divine will, enlivened with a pun.

> *Moses* cast a Mantle over his head, and would not suffer his eye to meet God comming towards him, or open it selfe at the face of God, but onely to looke after Him being past; so may we, though it be full of hazard to looke on His Will, *à priori*, in the face of it, in the motives or occasions which first induced the operation thereof; we are allowed to survay it, *à posteriori*, in the Backparts, the effects and consequence, for they are visible and unvailed, being the markes and discoveries of His Revealed Will.[14]

A similar capacity for subtle scholastic differentiation is shown in the sermons of another prelate, Arthur Lake, bishop of Bath and Wells. He is discussing in what way God can be said to repent:

> True it is, that God is said to repent; but the Fathers joyntly agree, that his repentance is mutation, not *affectus*, but *effectus:* hee changeth his creatures, unchangeable in himselfe; even as a chirurgeon, who begins with one kind of plaister, when he hath wrought his force, laycth another kind, doth not alter, but pursue his former resolution, which was, by those divers plaisters to cure the sore: even so, whatsoever alteration befalls us, God did eternally decree it, and decree it as befalls.[15]

This would seem more suitable in a university sermon preached by the former warden of New College, Oxford, than for the farming community of Farnham on the borders of Surrey and Hampshire.

Then there is the fascination of Thomas Playfere, Lady Margaret Professor of Divinity at Cambridge, for Plutarch and a whole series of "unnatural" natural histories. We are told that the quail, supposed to be able to rest on the sea, lays one wing upon the water and holds up the other wing towards heaven;

lest he should presume to take too long a flight at the first he wets one wing, but he keeps the other wing dry lest he should despair of taking another flight afterwards.[16] The camelion, he alleges, climbs up into a tree and drops a thread clear as a pearl, which falling upon a serpent's head, kills it immediately. Playfere interprets this as an analogy of Christ climbing into the tree of the Cross, and letting down a thread of blood issuing from his side, which kills the old serpent, the Devil.[17]

Another professor, John Prideaux, proved that a royal chaplain could be a Calvinist throughout the reign of Charles I, and yet still be appointed a bishop. He occupied the Regius chair of Divinity in Oxford. He knew the art of attracting the attention even of courtiers at the very start of a sermon. His title is a witty one, namely *A Plot for Preferment.* The sermon begins: "There is not a *point* more *studied* in *these our dayes,* then to get *preferment:* and *none* there are put in so stifly therein, for a *supremacy,* as those that claim it by St *Peters Title.*"[18] Catching the ambition of the courtier, he deftly turns it to an everlasting preferment, and "the *summe* is A *never fayling Plot, for the surest attaining, of the best preferment.*"[19]

Henry Smith chooses his illustrations from natural history as contrasted with Playfere's preference for "unnatural" history, although he does not wholly avoid the latter. For instance, Smith compares the usurer to ivy. He says that

> the Usurer loveth the borrower as the Ivie loveth the Oke: the Ivie loveth the Oke to grow up by it, so the Usurer loveth the borrower to grow rich by him. The Ivie claspeth the Oke like a lover, but it claspeth out at the iuce and sap, that the Oke cannot thrive after: so the usurer lendeth like a friend, but he covenanteth like an enemie, for he claspeth the borrower with such bands, that ever after he diminisheth, as fast as the usurer encreaseth.[20]

Congregations, he argues, should be as eager for the strong meat of the gospel as young birds for the return of their mothers from foraging for worms. His words have both a compelling tenderness and delicacy:

> As the little birds perke up their heads when their damme comes with meate, and prepare their beakes to take it, striving who shall catch most; now this lookes to be served, and now that lookes for a bit, and every mouth is open untill it be filled: so you are here like birds, and we the damme, and the worde the foode, therefore you must prepare a mouth to take it. They which are hungry will strive for the bread which is cast amongst them, & think this is spoken to me, I have need of this, and I have need of this: comfort goe thou to my feare, promise goe thou to my distrust, threatning goe thou to my securitie, and the *Word* shall be like a perfume, which hath odour for every one.[21]

Another bird simile is used as an analogy for the tentative Christian: ". . . as an Owle peeps at the Sunne out of a barne but dares not come to it, so we peepe at Religion and will not come neere it, but stand aloofe off pinking and winking as though we were more afraid of GOD then the divell."[22] Smith had many other gifts than the selection of illustrations would indicate, for Fuller affirms that he was commonly called "the silver-tongued Smith, being one metal in price and purity beneath St. Chrysostom himself."[23] Indeed, so popular was he that Fuller wittily adds that "persons of quality brought their own pues with them,—I mean their legs to stand there upon in the allies."

Another Calvinist, Archbishop James Ussher, liked learning and vivid metaphors, as well as wit, in his sermons. He shared his gift for conceiving concise and memorable epigrams that flash truths into our minds. Can an abstraction be made more concrete than in the aphorism, "Now faith is the legs of the soul, the feet that carry us to Christ"?[24] The cost of true discipleship is memorably taught: "Thou must account upon thy crosses, losses, and many troubles that will befall thee; for thou must not think to be caried to heaven on a feather bed."[25]

If Anglican sermons of the seventeenth century seem to lack the ecstasy and fervor of continental baroque devotion, then one could turn to the ardor of John Wall. A canon of Christ Church, Oxford, from 1632 until the day he died in 1666, he retained his place despite the cataclysmic changes of religion. We are hardly surprised that he can mix classical and Christian lore to produce an extraordinary image of the Crucifixion: ". . . yet died he like *Seneca* in a bath, not of water, but of blood, and that his owne . . . ,"[26] although it involves the unfortunate linking of Christ with suicide.

Another seraphical divine was William Cartwright, whom David Lloyd described as "an excellent preacher in whom hallowed fancies and reason grew visions and holy passions, raptures and ecstasies, and all this at thirty years of age."[27] So popular was his play, *The Royal Slave,* that in the royal progress of 1636 it was the climax of Oxford University's celebration, and a second performance at Hampton Court for the following year was commanded by the queen. King Charles I, being in Oxford when Cartwright died at thirty-two, wore black and when asked why replied that "since the Muses had so much mourned for such a son, it would be a shame for him not to appear in mourning for the loss of such a subject."[28] Only one of his sermons survives, a Passion sermon, *An Off-spring of Mercy, Issuing out of the Womb of Cruelty,* [29] and, not surprisingly, it fails to live up to the exaggerated evaluation of him by his contemporaries. His other sermons were probably as full of strained conceits as his poem, *The Circumcision,* which includes these lines:

> The Mother's Milk that's now his Bloud,
> Hereafter will become her Food.

and

> When that the Rose it self doth bleed,
> That Bloud will be the Churches Seed.[30]

He can, however, bring the counterbalancing of paradoxes like the contrapuntal music of his era to a glittering conclusion:

> Thus when the Jews by divine foreknowledge had brought the Deity to that despicableness, that they occasioned those miracles, That He should be impleaded and condemned who is Judge of all; He laden with curses, that scatters blessings as Sunne-beams over the face of the world; That health it self languisht, and the very impassible suffered. God (who is wont to take his rise where men stop) was pleased to strike miracles out of these, greater than these. For behold, *An Off-spring of Mercy, issuing out of the womb of Cruelty*; A bundle of new miracles as farre beyond the former, as they are opposite to them; A condemnation that absolves us; A curse that blesseth us; A sicknesse that recovers us; A death it self that quickens us; So much was his love stronger then death, who though He were a son, yet learn'd obedience by the things he suffered; and being made perfect he became the Author of eternall salvation to all that obey Him.[31]

Breathless, Cartwright reaches the brief solemn ending of his sermon: "Among which number, O Lord, write our names, for his sake who this day suffered to blot out that hand-writing that was against us. *Amen.*"

The metaphysical mode continued in the pulpit at least as late as the 1670s, even while South, Glanvill, Arderne, and especially Eachard were making fun of it, and when the admired divines were Tillotson and Burnet. An impressive late exemplar, according to Fraser Mitchell,[32] was Mark Frank, the master of Andrewes's old college of Pembroke and an imitator of his style without some of its quirks.

Our last sample of the delights and fascinations of metaphysical preaching in this section is an excerpt from a sermon preached by Frank on St. Andrew's Day urging the value of renunciation for gaining the Kingdom of Heaven. The sustained quality warrants extended citation:

Regnum Dei tantum valet quantum habes, says St. *Gregory;*
The kingdom of heaven is worth all we have, must cost
us so, be what we will, and alas! what have we the best
and richest of us, as highly as we think of our selves and
ours, more than St. *Andrew* and his *brother,* a few old broken
Nets.

What are all our honours but old Nets, to catch the
breath of the world, where the oldest is the best, and that
which has most knots, most alliances and genealogies, the
most honourable.

What are our Estates but Nets to entangle us? 'Tis more
evident now than ever; to entangle us in strange knots
and obligations, in vexations and disquiets, in fears and
dangers, to entangle silly souls besides in vanities and fol-
lies.

What are all our ways and devices of thriving but so
many Nets to catch a little yellow sand and mud, and if
you will have it in somewhat a finer phrase, a few silver
scaled fishes, in which yet, God knows, there are so many
knots and difficulties, so many rents and holes for the fish
to slip out of, that we may justly say they are but broken
nets, and old ones too, the best of them, that will scarce
hold a pull, all our new projects being but old ones new
rubb'd over, and no new thing under the Sun?

What are all these fine catching ways of eloquence,
knowledge, good parts of mind and body, but so many
nets and snares to take men with? It may be finely spun,
neatly woven, curiously knotted, but so full of holes, vanity and emptiness, that no net is fuller than these things
we take so much pride in, so much delight in. Nay, this
very body it self is but a net that entangles the soul, and
the rational soul it self, too, we too often make but a net
to catch flies, petty buzzing knowledges only, few solid
sober thoughts; at the best but a net for fishes of that
watry and inconstant element, watry, washy, slimy notions
of I know not what, of flitting worldly things; so full of
holes, too, that all good things slip out of them.[33]

Chapter I

Such representative, rather than outstanding, examples of the pulpit discourses of the metaphysical preachers are too few to indicate that many of these divines were extraordinary men, renowned in their times for learning, and wit, as well as for administrative gifts, and, not least, for holiness. Some were also "characters" with all the accompanying eccentricities that mark individuals who dare to differ from their contemporaries—a difficult course for eminent divines who are expected to be conventional.

The three earliest metaphysical divines: Andrewes, Playfere, and Henry Smith

The three earliest metaphysical divines were very different, but each was remarkable. Lancelot Andrewes (1555–1626), whose sermons will be analyzed more fully in chapter five, was the very model of an exemplary metaphysical divine and the most influential of them all. The admiring sermon preached at his funeral by John Buckeridge, then bishop of Ely, concentrates on his great learning and his devout life. He studied late at night and was at his books by four in the morning. His linguistic brilliance was everywhere honored, for "his admirable knowledge in the learned tongues, *Latine, Greeke, Hebrew, Chaldee, Syriack, Arabick,* besides other modern *Tongues* to the number of Fifteene. . . ."[34] He was also a renowned controversialist. In his early days as chaplain to Henry, Earl of Huntingdon, president of the North where there were many of the old faith, he had been most successful in winning back recusants, both priests and laity, to the Church of England; and he was a dexterous foe who twice crossed swords with the redoubtable Cardinal Bellarmine in Latin works.[35] In addition, he was an outstanding patristic scholar and his name stood first in the list of those who in 1607 were appointed to prepare the "authorised version" translation of the Scriptures into English. As a superb Hebraist, he was one of ten scholars responsible for the Pentateuch and the historical books from Joshua to I Chronicles. Although a chaplain to Queen Elizabeth, he twice refused her offers of bishoprics because they were conditional upon his agreement to allow some alienation of the revenues. Without any compromise, he accepted appointment as, successively, dean of Westminster, bishop of Ely, and bishop of Winchester. His devotions were written in Greek and Latin—the classic *Preces Privatae*. These were thumbed by his frequent use of them and even wetted with his penitential tears, for he was a godly man.

As a preacher, whether in Westminster Abbey or in the presence of the sovereign, he was a *stella praedicantium*. His preaching was characterized by two outstanding qualities. The first was his careful preparation, so that when he was vicar of St. Giles, Cripplegate, London, he said that "when he preached twice, he prated once," and the second was the remarkable series of sermons on the great feasts and the chief fast of the Christian year. He instructed the court of James I for a quarter century in the meaning of the Christian faith. For seventeen years he preached the Christmas sermon expounding the doctrine of the Incarnation, for eighteen years at Easter the doctrine of the Resurrection, for fifteen years at Whitsunday the doctrine of the Holy Spirit, and for fourteen years in Lent the doctrine of self-denial.[36] The content of his sermons exhibited a profound and detailed biblical knowledge, an exact knowledge of biblical and ancillary languages, a great reverence for the Fathers of the primitive Church, a deep concern for relating texts to the calendar of the liturgical year, and an almost scholastic division of the text into what critics called "crumbling." He also showed a fondness for wit especially in the beginnings, endings, and transitions of his sermons, which are redolent of unostentatious learning and of holiness.

As Andrewes popularized metaphysical preaching in the court and the cathedrals, Thomas Playfere (1561–1609) exemplified it in the University of Cambridge, where he held the Lady Margaret Professorship of Divinity. He was also a fellow of St. John's College, which, along with Pembroke and Trinity, became the training centers of metaphysical preaching in Cambridge. In addition Playfere was a royal chaplain appointed by King James I, and like many other metaphysical preachers wrote verse in Latin.[37] He preached a learned Latin sermon before the kings of England and Denmark on 27 July 1606. John Chamberlain, writing to Dudley Carlton on 4 November 1602, mentioned the death of the great Puritan preacher and exemplar of the plain style, William Perkins, and added the melancholy news: "another eclipse is befaln that Universitie, for Dr. Plaifer, the Divinitie reader, is lately crackt in the head-peece for the love of a wench as some say."[38]

Playfere's sermons are the product of a rich and occasionally ungovernable fancy. They abound in vivid images, historical narrations and "unnatural" natural history used for illustrative purposes, as well as emblems, fables, riddles, paradoxes, Latin puns, and pithy apothegms. They manifest a tenderness for the status of women and the poor in the two Spital (St. Mary's Hospital) sermons, and an intense sense of the joy of the Christian life. But his aim seems to be to keep our attention perpetually on its toes (to use our own strained conceit). Two concise examples must suffice. He preached a sermon in Exeter Cathedral in 1596 on "The Power of Praier" in which surprise after surprise is created. "*Moses* found Christ," he insisted,

> not in a soft bed, but in a bramble bush. So that the bed is not a fitte place to *finde* him in, who had not where to rest himselfe. But go into the garden among the bramble bushes, and there you shall finde him, not sleeping, but sweating droppes of blood for your redemption, and calling you to him, Come unto me all you that labour, (not you that lye in a bed, and are secure, but you that labour) and are heavy laden, and I will refresh you.[39]

Later in the same sermon he again startles the awakened congregation: "God is taken captive by prayer, and become a prisoner to man, and stands at his curtesie, who sayes, I will not let thee goe, except thou bless me."[40] Yet both statements, however original they appear, are solidly grounded upon Scripture.

The third of the early trio, Henry Smith (1550?–1591), is unusual because he is very different from the expected image of a preacher of the centrist Puritan position. Though a Calvinist, he was a firm supporter of the Church of England as established, and of the state, and only had some hesitations about the ceremonies demanded. A man of independent means he did not take on the entire charge of a church, but was the immensely popular lecturer at St. Clement Dane's Without Temple Bar, London. Wood, no friend of those puritanically inclined, says he was "esteemed for the wonder and miracle of his age, for his prodigious memory, and for his fluent, eloquent, and practical way of preaching."[41] He too was a poet, and, although no poem survives, Thomas Nash related that before Smith entered into "the wonderful ways" of theology, he "refined, prepared, and purified his wings with sweet poetry."[42] He attained some fame in 1582 by curing a visionary who claimed to be the prophet Elijah, and the sermon he delivered after the cure was published as "The Lost Sheep is found." His stepmother was Lord Burghley's sister, and he dedicated his sermons to Queen Elizabeth's chief advisor. Ill health and the illicit dissemination of his sermons by literary pirates, caused him to prepare them for publication, and the collected sermons were issued in 1592. No less than sixteen editions of them appeared in the next thirty years, and as late as 1657 Thomas Fuller reissued them with Playfere's prayers, and other works, and a life of the author. This came out again in 1678— altogether unexampled fame in print for an Elizabethan preacher.

Smith might be thought ineligible for inclusion as a metaphysical preacher because of a certain early Puritan training under Richard Greenham, but although he accepted the articles, liturgy, and the government of the Church of England, he had qualms about its discipline. More to our point however is that, as will be shown, many Church of England metaphysical preachers including bishops were Calvinists (who had no truck with Arminianism's five points). Smith exemplified in a striking way the distinguishing characteristics of metaphysical preaching, including a facile wit, daring metaphors and similes, learning derived from the Fathers and the classical poets, moralists, and historians, as well as the use of historical narrations and "unnatural" natural history by way of illustration. In addition, he delighted in epigrams and paradoxes, and utilized the whole panoply of rhetoric in his eloquence. Moreover, he exhibits a graciousness of manner and a solidity of thought, as well as a profound biblical fidelity, not to be found in every metaphysical preacher. His witty wordplay and daring imagery will be frequently cited later, but one example will do for the present:

> The Hound which runnes but for the Hare, girdes foorth, so soone as he sees the Hare start: the Hawke which flyeth but for the Partridge, taketh her flight so soone as she spyes the Patridge spring: so we should folowe the woord so soone as it speaketh, and come to our Master as soone as he calleth. For God requiring the first borne for his offering, and the first fruits for his service, requireth the first labours of his servants, and as I may say, the maidenhead of every man.[43]

The double analogy drawn from hunting would interest every man in the congregation, even if it temporarily made him wonder what his Sunday dinner would be like, and the conceit of the masculine maidenhead would startle him to attention. One can well imagine Smith's popularity, and wonder just how inappropriate the term of "Puritan" is when applied to him. An even more serious misapplication of the same term will be found in the case of an almost equally popular preacher, Thomas Adams, who was a friend of one of the actor-partners of Shakespeare's dramatic company.[44]

Their status in the English Church

It is worth considering that, in terms of their impact in their own day, of the forty-one metaphysical preachers to be analyzed no less than twenty-one were consecrated as bishops. These include: Andrewes of Chichester, Ely, and Winchester; Barlow of Rochester, and Lincoln; Bowle of Rochester; Brownrig of Exeter; Buckeridge of Rochester, and Ely; Corbet of Norwich; Duppa of Chichester, Salisbury, and Winchester; Field of Llandaff, and Worcester; Cosin of Durham; Gauden of Exeter, and Worcester; Hacket of Lichfield and Coventry; Howson of Oxford; John King of London, and his son Henry King of Chichester; Lake of Bath and Wells; Morton of Chester, Lichfield and Coventry, and Durham; Senhouse of Carlisle; Prideaux of Worcester; Francis White of Carlisle, Norwich, and Ely; and Wren of Hereford, Norwich, and Ely. To these must be added two archbishops: Laud of Canterbury and Ussher of Armagh.

Fortunately for the reputation of the English pulpit in its golden age, many of these prelates had been deans of cathedrals before reaching the topmost rungs of the ladder of ecclesiastical preferment, and not a few had been canons or prebendaries of cathedrals, or ministers of important London parishes, or chaplains of Inns of Court, or heads of colleges in Oxford or Cambridge. All of these involved considerable preaching experience. The following thirteen had been deans: Andrewes of Westminster; Bowles of Chester; Corbet, and Henry and John King, and Brian Duppa, all of Oxford; Cosin of Peterborough, and Durham; Lake of Worcester; Laud of Gloucester; Morton of Gloucester, and Winchester; Senhouse of Gloucester; Francis White of Carlisle; and Wren of Windsor. Only two deans did not become bishops, one the greatest preacher of them all, John Donne, dean of St. Paul's Cathedral. The other was Jackson, dean of Peterborough.

The nine bishops who had not been deans had other preaching experience of a wide variety. Barlow was rector of St. Dunstan's-in-the-East and a prebendary of St. Paul's, and also had a stall in Westminster Abbey. Brownrig was prebendary of Ely, later had a stall in Durham Cathedral, and was master of St. Catharine's Hall in Cambridge. Gauden had been vicar of Chippenham and dean of Bocking (a peculiar, not a cathedral). Hacket was vicar of St. Andrew's, Holborn, a large parish where he was immensely popular, and held a canonry at St. Paul's Cathedral. Howson had been a canon of Christ Church, Oxford, and a prebendary of Hereford Cathedral. Prideaux was a canon of Christ Church and Regius Professor of Divinity at Oxford for twenty-six years. Ussher also served as professor of Divinity, but at Trinity College, Dublin. Buckeridge, who was Laud's tutor at St. John's College, Oxford, became president of his college, and succeeded Andrewes as vicar of St. Giles Cripplegate, London.

What positions did the unfortunate fourteen hold who were neither bishops nor deans? Some had stalls in cathedrals. Such were William Cartwright of Christ Church and Mark Frank. Frank, who had been master of Pembroke College, Cambridge, was also a prebendary of St. Paul's, while Peter Heylyn was a prebendary of Westminster, and Fuller was a prebendary of Salisbury and a popular lecturer at the churches of St. Clement's, St. Bride's, and St. Andrew's in London. Thomas Lushington was prebendary of Salisbury, and became chaplain to his intimate friend, Corbet, the bishop of Norwich. John Wall, according to Anthony Wood, was "a quaint preacher in the age in which he lived" and in 1632 was installed canon of Christ Church, Oxford ". . . which he kept to his dying day, notwithstanding the several revolutions in his time."[45] John White, together with Francis White the bishop, was one of the five clergy sons of the vicar of St. Neots. A royal chaplain and anti-papal controversialist, he was rector of Barsham in Suffolk and died at the age of forty-five. Robert Willan was also a royal chaplain, about whom little is known. Thomas Goffe was rector of East Clandon in Surrey and a woman-hater who deservedly married a harridan. His friend, Thomas Thimble, prophesied an early death for him in consequence, and his final words, aged thirty-eight, were "oracle, oracle, Tom Thimble."[46] Thomas Playfere, equally unlucky in love, which unrequited caused him to lose his mind, was Lady Margaret Professor of Divinity in Cambridge, and a royal chaplain. Henry Smith, although he died at an early age, left a great literary legacy of sermons, and was considered to be in Elizabethan days "prime preacher of the nation,"[47] while he was lecturer at London's St. Clement Dane's. Barten Holyday, also a royal chaplain, was rector of Chilton in Berkshire and, at the Restoration, of Iffley near Oxford. Featley was rector of Lambeth, and later of Acton. Lushington, also a royal chaplain, was canon of Salisbury and Bishop Corbet's close friend. Thomas Adams also won wide fame as a lecturer at St. Gregory's at Paul's Wharf, and was a prebendary of St. Paul's, when Donne was dean.

It is clear that James I valued men of learning and wit, whose plays or poetry or both proved the strength of their imagination. He also required them to be defenders of the *status quo ante* in Church and State. Calvinists he approved, but not Puritans. This could be expected from his famous reproof of the latter at the Hampton Court Conference: "No Bishop, no King." Hierarchy in Church and State were to be mutually reinforcing. Even so James cared little for prelatical pretensions, and on Andrewes's death, his advisor was the Calvinist archbishop of York, Williams. In contrast, Charles I and his favorite Buckingham were advised in ecclesiastical matters by Laud, first as bishop of London and later as archbishop of Canterbury. Only when the royal situation became perilous did Charles I appoint Calvinist bishops and then only to appease his enemies. Thus it was loyalty to and literary defense of the established Church and its royal head, combined with imagination, which were the factors determining ecclesiastical preferment.

Their recruitment

Since the three outstanding characteristics of the metaphysical preachers were their wit, their imagination, and their learning, it is clear that these must have been the qualities which sovereigns and their advisers sought in appointing them. The wit and the imagination would be early evidenced (as well as the reputation for scholarship) in the universities where the wittiest, most inventive writers of plays or encomiastic verses, would be brought to the attention of royal visitors. The most brilliant and learned disputants would also perform before their majesties. Some later appointments would be made because of the reputation they had won for anti-Roman or anti-Puritan polemical writings, making use of the Fathers of the Church of the first six centuries, chiefly to assert the firm doctrinal foundation on which the Church of England was based, but also to demonstrate how the Church of Rome had deviated from its primitive foundations. For our purposes it is worth showing how an early training in poetry, dialectics, the ancient languages, and eloquence helped young divines to achieve preferment, and how it aided the distinctive qualities of metaphysical preaching.

After the Gunpowder Plot, 5 November 1605 in which a Catholic conspiracy, led by Guy Fawkes, to blow up the king in the House of Parliament, was foiled, James I required a stringent oath of loyalty to himself. In doing this, he ran into trouble from Catholic controversialists such as the formidable Cardinal Bellarmine. His newly-found Anglicanism was also under attack from both Papists and Scottish Presbyterians (as well as from English Puritans). To defend his median position he needed good dialecticians and controversialists and to these he gave preferment, as well as to wits. It is unfortunately true that those he preferred to bishoprics and deaneries did not have "a long experience of pastoral service and non-courtly preaching,"[48] but James had much need of apologists, and this factor played a major role in preferments.[49]

Gauden, in his funeral sermon for Brownrig, says "it is not to be expressed how sweet and welcome the very first productions of his most florid and fertile soul were, which had the fragrant blossoms of a most facetious and inoffensive; the fair leaves or ample ornaments of his most eloquent tongue." When King James visited the University of Cambridge, Brownrig was selected to play the part of Jocoserious the *Praevaricator,* which was the equivalent of Oxford's *Terrae filius,* and the king laughed at "the luxuriancy of wit" that "was consistent with innocence." Gauden also adds that "although he had this Magazine of classick and authentick learning, which readily furnished him to speak on the sudden of all things (*apté, ornaté, copiosé*) amply and handsomely, yet as to his sacred Oratory or publick Preaching; He was very elaborate and exact, not only in reading and meditating, but in the compleat writing of his Sermons even to the last; So loth was he to do the work of God negligently."[50]

Fuller had all three qualities needed to be nominated a royal chaplain. Commonly acknowledged the wittiest of men with "quick jocundity of style,"[51] he had contributed to a collection of Cambridge verses celebrating the birth of Princess Mary (4 November 1631). His learning was first revealed in his *History of the Holy Warre* (a study of the Crusades), and his *Holy and Profane State* (1642) and his *Church-History of Britain* (1655) followed. His witty learning brought him to the attention of Charles I who appointed him chaplain to the queen's fourth child, Princess Henrietta born on 16 June 1644, when Charles's fortunes were at a low ebb. Charles II, for Fuller's courageous fidelity to the royal cause throughout the days of the Commonwealth and Protectorate, appointed him a royal chaplain at the Restoration.

Heylyn, a critic of Fuller's history, was a child prodigy, who was elected a demy of Magdalen College, Oxford, at the age of fifteen, on the strength of Latin verses he had written recounting a visit to Woodstock, and he celebrated his election to a fellowship of his college by a Latin comedy, *Theomachia*. He came to the attention of Laud, and therefore of King Charles I, through his defense of the view that the Church of England derived from the Church of Rome, and not from the Wycliffites, the Waldensians, or the Hussites. The latter was the view maintained by the Regius Professor of Divinity, Dr. Prideaux, in a public disputation in 1633 on the subject, in the Divinity School at Oxford. Heylyn was appointed a royal chaplain in 1630.[52]

Howson, educated at those centers of poetry and learning, St. Paul's School and Christ Church, Oxford, like Heylyn drew attention to himself by his loyalty to those anti-Puritan views approved by Elizabeth I and by James, both of whom appointed him their royal chaplain. He pleased Elizabeth by preaching a sermon on Accession Day (17 November 1602) defending the festivities of the Church of England, and delighted James by publicly disapproving of the annotations in the Genevan Bible, and by his vigorous antipapalism. James was mightily pleased by his declaration that he would detach the pope from his papal chair "though he were fastened thereto with a ten-penny nail."[53]

Richard Corbet was educated at Westminster School and Christ Church, Oxford, both institutions that nurtured poets at that time. Wood reports that in 1605 Corbet was "esteemed one of the most celebrated wits in the university, as his poems, jests, romantick fancies and exploits, which he made and perform'd extempore, shew'd."[54] His poetic muse ran to academic satires, congratulatory epistles, tavern-pieces, pasquinades, and he even produced an attack on the loose-limbed Mrs. Mallet, a regular subject for satirists.[55] When he became dean of Christ Church, and shortly afterwards Donne was made dean of St. Paul's, it was observed, "that if Ben Jonson might be made Dean of Westminster, that place, Paul's and Christ Church, should be furnished with three pleasant poetical Deans."[56] It was wit and learning, and the right type of high churchmanship, rather than godliness like that of Andrewes, that gained Corbet his high preferments.

Thomas Morton, bishop of Durham and a nonagenarian, was brought to attention by his success (like Andrewes'), as chaplain to Lord Huntingdon, president of the North, in reclaiming recusants to the Church of England. While chaplain to Lord Eure, the ambassador to the emperor and the king of Denmark, he came to know several learned Jesuits in Mainz and Cologne, and at Frankfurt began his collection of learned books "of the *Pontifican* writers, which became useful in controversies with the Papists."[57] Inevitably he, like Thomas Playfere, became an apologist of the English Church, arguing in the two parts of his *Apologiae Catholicae* (1605–1606) for the fidelity of its doctrine and government to the primitive Church, and writing *A Catho-like Appeale for Protestants Out of the Confessions of the Romane Doctors* (1610), and other similar works.

It was similarly his knowledge of the Fathers of the Church which made Archbishop James Ussher a stalwart defender of the English Church. In order to meet the arguments from antiquity of the Jesuit scholar Stapleton, in *A Fortresse of the Faith* (1565), he began an exhaustive eighteen-year study of the Fathers. Selden, a worthy judge, called Ussher *ad miracula doctus*. [58]

John White, a chaplain in ordinary to James I, gained the royal attention through his popular apology, *The Way to the True Church; Wherein the principal Motives perswading to Romanisme are familiarly disputed and driven to their Issues* (1608), which was re-issued in 1610, 1612, and 1616.

Francis, the brother of John White, reached fame by the same route, except that he was a brilliant oral dialectician. In 1622 James employed him along with Laud as a disputant against John Fisher in an attempt to withstand the Catholic leanings of Mary, Countess of Buckingham.

Richard Senhouse, of the favored St. John's College, Cambridge (which, like Pembroke and Peterhouse in the same university, produced many high church and metaphysical divines) became known early as a good preacher. It was no disadvantage to preferment that he was appointed successively chaplain to the earl of Bedford, Prince Charles, and King James I.

Barten Holyday came to the attention of King James as a dramatist, when his play *Technogamia, or, the Marriages of the Arts* was acted before him at Woodstock. James valued talents such as his, in spite apparently of the fact that either the dullness of the play or the drunkenness of the players bored the king, who twice made signs to leave before the end.

Barlow and Buckeridge were brought to the notice of King James respectively by Whitgift and Laud. They were given their chance, in sermons at Hampton Court, at a foredoomed conference in 1607 which was convened to try to persuade the learned Presbyterian representative of the Church of Scotland of the scriptural and historical superiority of episcopacy as a form of church polity. Melville wrote a short satirical poem against Barlow in elegantly fierce Latin, saying that the image Barlow had given of an episcopal shepherd rather resembled a wolf.[59]

Daniel Featley also attained fame and preferment by his daring to do dialectical battle with the Jesuits in Paris, where he officiated as chaplain to the English ambassador, Sir Thomas Edwardes, from 1610 to 1612. In 1634 both he and Francis White were employed to hold a confrontation with two famous Jesuits, John Fisher (Piercey) and John Sweet. When an account of this was surreptitiously published, Abbot the archbishop requested Featley to produce his own version which was wittily titled, *The Romish Fisher caught and held in his owne Net.* Such was his renown as a controversialist that King James was pleased to fence with him in a "scholastick duell", an account of which Featley published in 1629, entitled *Cygnea Cantio: or, learned Decisions and pious Directions for Students in Divinitie delivered by King James at Whitehall, a few weeks before his death.*

Powerful ecclesiastical patrons

Clearly, it was important to gain the interest of the chief religious, and occasionally secular, advisors to the sovereigns if one was to attain to dignities in the Church of England. Such were, of course, the archbishops of Canterbury, and notably in our period William Laud. Laud wielded great influence even as bishop of London, because Archbishop Abbot, the Calvinist, had accidentally killed a gamekeeper while hunting in Lord Zouch's park. Although James had supported Abbot, at his death the new king was in the hands of Buckingham, and Buckingham was the friend of Laud, who thus virtually ruled the church in England from 1628 to the death of Abbot in 1633, when he succeeded him. Earlier James had been advised by the saintly Lancelot Andrewes in many of his appointments to bishoprics. It is worth noting that Andrewes and Laud were both educated at Merchant Taylors' School. The combination of the influence of Andrewes in Cambridge and of Laud in Oxford was powerful and pervasive in the interests of Arminianism, a high liturgy and ceremonialism, and the support of royal absolutism.

Buckeridge had been Laud's tutor at St. John's College, Oxford, where he had instilled into his pupil anti-Calvinistic principles, and Laud, having gained influence, returned the kindness. Heylyn, in *Cyprianus Anglicanus,* wrote: "It proved no ordinary happiness to the scholar to be principled under such a tutor, who knew as well as any other of his time how to employ the two-edged sword of Holy Scripture . . . brandishing it on the one side against the papists, and on the other against the puritans and nonconformists."[60] The king nominated him to succeed Andrewes as vicar of St. Giles, Cripplegate and on 26 November 1628 he preached the funeral sermon of Andrewes. In the April of the same year he had been appointed bishop of Ely, "by the power and favour of Laud" in the words of Heylyn. His very life indicates, in the preferments he received, the continuity between Andrewes and Laud. Cosin gained the attention of James on the recommendation of Andrewes and was given the delicate task of compiling *A Collection of Private Devotions* (1627). This was to be an English Protestant counterpart of the Catholic Books of Hours, which the queen and her ladies used, but which her Protestant ladies-of-honour had previously lacked. For the punning reply to this work, and for other writings of impudence, the Puritan lawyer Prynne in publishing *A Brief Survey of Mr. Cozens his Cozening Devotions* was eventually to lose his ears.

It is significant that Bishop Lake died after he had made his confession to Bishop Andrewes, and that Laud deliberately imitated the sermon style of Andrewes.[61] It was on the recommendation of Andrewes that Bishop Morton was translated from Chester to Lichfield and Coventry "who was never known to do the like for any other."[62] Another protégé of Andrewes at Pembroke College, Cambridge, when he was master, was Wren who became a fellow of the College; and Andrewes subsequently appointed him his chaplain. In Wren's life too, we can see the Andrewes-Laud influence, for when he was consecrated it was in Laud's chapel in Lambeth Palace, and it was Laud who had him translated from Hereford to Norwich because Laud had found the diocese disorderly at his visitation in 1635. Earlier it was his wit and dialectical skill that had impressed James I, for he had argued that the king's dogs "might perform more than others, by the prerogative."[63] Laud, as archbishop, recommended Brian Duppa to King James as tutor to the Prince of Wales and his brother, afterwards Charles II, and it is interesting to note that he privately ordained priests and deacons during the Commonwealth period, including Thomas Tenison, Tillotson's successor as archbishop of Canterbury. Wood writes of him: "He was beloved of K. *Ch.* I of happy memory, who made use of his pious Conversation during his imprisonment in the Isle of *Wight*, and so much respected by his son K. *Ch.* 2. that when this worthy Prelate laid on his death-bed at *Richmond*, he craved his blessing on his bended knees by his bed-side."[64] Andrewes was always on the lookout for talented scholars, not only in his Cambridge days, but also when he became dean of Westminster, taking a keen personal interest in the pupils of the school there. When one considers the time and trouble he spent to improve the quality of the teaching at that excellent school and the number of old Westminsters who became metaphysical preachers (not to mention those who became poets of distinction) it is difficult not to exaggerate his influence. Bishop Hacket gives a delightful vignette of Andrewes the dean, and his influence on the schoolboys. Hacket informed Bishop Williams that Andrewes strictly charged all the masters that they should give the boys lessons out of only the best classical authors, and that "he did often supply the place of both the head schoolmaster and usher for the place of a whole week together, and gave us not an hour of loitering time from morning to night." Hacket also reported "how he caused our exercises in prose and verse to be brought to him to examine our style and proficiency" and, most impressively of all, "that he never walked to Cheswick for his recreation without a brace of the young fry, and in that wayfaring leisure had a singular dexterity to fill those narrow vessels with a funnel, and which was the greatest burden of his toil." If this was not enough, "sometimes thrice a week, sometimes oftener, he sent for the uppermost scholars to his lodgings at night, and kept them with him from 8 to 11, unfolding to them the best rudiments of the Greek tongue, and the elements of the Hebrew grammar, and all this he did to boys without any impulsion of correction, nay I never heard him utter so much

as a word of austerity among us." As if he thought this encomium was too good to be true, Hacket adds finally, "Alas! this
is but an ivy leaf crept into the laurel of his immortal garland."[65]
Such dedication, devotion to learning and duty, as well as religious devotion, earned for Andrewes the greatest respect as a
moral leader of the highest integrity and generosity, who was
himself an intense foe of simony. The influence of such a man
transcended political considerations.

The influence of Andrewes lived long in Cambridge too, for
in his college (Pembroke) Brownrig, and Wren, and Mark Frank
were all fellows, and Frank became master of the college, as
Andrewes had been. The powerful impact of the Arminian
tradition of Andrewes and Laud is amusingly reflected in a
story attributed to Bishop George Morley. To a country gentleman's question, "What do the Arminians hold?" he is said to
have wittily retorted, "All the best bishopricks and deaneries
in England."[66] And many of them knew, in the words of Francis
Bacon, that a "winding stair" was the way to preferment.

The impact of the classics on the training of preachers

It seems appropriate that this chapter should end by pointing
out the extraordinary success of Westminster scholars (who
usually went on either to Christ Church, Oxford, or to Trinity
College, Cambridge) as preachers of the metaphysical mode
or poets of the same style. There were even some who were
both, like Hacket himself who had written a play *Loiola*, a
Latin comedy, which was twice acted before James I. It is a
play that jeers at Jesuits, who are assisted by a chorus of their
vices: *caeca obedientia, pseudomiraculum, regicidium, Index purgato-
rius*, and *arrogantia*, and in which Machiavelli is depicted as a
precursor of Loyola. Crude in its criticisms of Jesuits, it is no
subtler in deriding friars as immoral and Puritans as total hypocrites. Its importance is that it shows a well-trained student
knowing how to use his imagination to create vividly illustrated
sermons.

The roll-call of distinguished poet-preachers of the metaphysical mode educated at Westminster School is most impressive.

It includes George Herbert, Henry King, John Hacket, William Duppa, Richard Corbet, Thomas Goffe, William Cartwright, Jasper Mayne, and Barten Holyday, four of whom became bishops. There can be no question that the rigorous instruction in the school's curriculum, in Latin and Greek versification and retranslation into English verse, was the training ground of imagination and wit that made the metaphysical mode in verse and prose possible. Westminster School in the seventeenth century alone produced four important poets, Jonson, Herbert, Cowley, and Dryden, and a host of minor poets, including Henry King, Randolph, Strode, Alabaster,[67] Cartwright, Giles Fletcher, Martin Lluellyn, and Jasper Mayne. And it is significant that an old Westminster pupil told Archbishop Laud in 1630 that the boys in the highest forms were sometimes set to turn "Latin and Greek verse into English verse." Margaret Crum, recounting this report, comments: "Perhaps it is not a chance coincidence that so many seventeenth-century poets were Westminster boys. . . ."[68] Nor is it a coincidence that Herbert, King, Corbet, and Alabaster were metaphysical preachers, after such a superb training in the imagination. Merchant Taylors' could boast a Spenser, and St. Paul's a Milton, but Westminster was a nest of singing birds.

Inevitably one turns to the curricula of famous schools to try to learn the secret of such training. The age of the renaissance prided itself on imitation as the highest ideal of literary art, hence it was inevitable that the writing of verse should become a significant discipline in all ambitious schools. The schoolmasters themselves were notable scholars, who had been fellows of their colleges and they tried to persuade their pupils to adopt these vaunted skills. If Latin verses were expected to be produced in all grammar schools, the most famous schools of all expected their pupils to write Greek as well as Latin verses. In the time of Queen Elizabeth boys in the upper forms of Eton wrote verses to demonstrate their loyalty. Sir Henry Wotton, the diplomat who defined his task as "lying abroad for his country" and who later became Provost of Eton in James's time, is reported by Izaak Walton to have encouraged his pupils by setting up two rows of pillars on which were placed the portraits of the most famous Greek and Latin historians, poets, and orators, persuading them "not to neglect rhetoric because Almighty God hath left mankind affections to be wrought upon." Walton adds that he would often say "that none despised eloquence but such dull souls as were not capable of it."[69]

Foster Watson in his authoritative history of English secondary education summarizes the curriculum at Westminster between 1621 and 1628 as requiring exercises each day in forms VI and VII, with prose and verse on alternate days between nine and eleven in the morning. "The verses were in both Latin and Greek upon two or three several themes, and they that made the best two or three of them had some money given by the schoolmaster for the most part."[70] Roger Ascham in *The Scholemaster* had argued for the advantage of changing Latin into Greek, verse into prose, and vice-versa: and, rather than being a novel suggestion, this was in fact the practice in some schools.[71] Brinsley, an educational theorist of the seventeenth century, states that verse-making is "a very great sharpener of the Wit, and a stirrer up of Invention." Most of the English metaphysical preachers were excellent classical scholars, and thus easily able to familiarize themselves with the Greek and Latin Fathers and the Catholic controversialists who, for the most part, wrote in Latin.

Westminster produced a long series of Greek grammars, as for example *Graecae linguae spicilegium* (1575), the work of an early headmaster Edward Grant. Eton on the other hand used Camden's Greek grammar in the period from 1597 to 1647, even though Camden was headmaster at Westminster. At St. Paul's School Greek was a subject of instruction probably ever since William Lily had been appointed its first High Master, and certainly Richard Mulcaster, who had been headmaster at Merchant Taylors' before coming to St. Paul's, emphasized this and even added Hebrew to the curriculum for religious reasons. On 11 June 1596 two students pronounced Greek orations, and four scholars going on to the universities were apposed and examined in Greek and Latin.[72]

Chapter I

Little wonder then that the metaphysical preachers valued epigrams and wit, rhetoric and eloquence; or that their sermons were peppered, or rather salted, with Greek and Latin citations in the original tongues from the Christian Fathers and from pagan poets, moralists, and historians; or that their imagery and figures occasionally mingled biblical histories and classical myths. They were introduced to these treasures in the best schools, and they continued to study them at Oxford and Cambridge, and to hear them used in university and cathedral sermons.

NOTES

1. Among many outstanding works the following: Joan Webber, *Contrary Music: The Prose Style of John Donne* (Madison, Wisconsin, 1963), Gale H. Carrithers, Jr., *Donne at Sermons: A Christian Existentialist World* (Albany, N.Y., 1972), Janel M. Mueller, *Donne's Prebend Sermons* (Cambridge, Mass., 1971), William R. Mueller, *John Donne: Preacher* (Princeton, N.J., 1962), John S. Chamberlin, *Increase and Multiply: Arts-of-Discourse Procedure in the Preaching of Donne* (Chapel Hill, North Carolina, 1976), Winfried Schleiner, *The Imagery of John Donne's Sermons* (Providence, Rhode Island, 1970), and the monumental and revisionary study of Barbara K. Lewalski, *Protestant Poetics and the Seventeenth-Century Religious Lyric* (Princeton, N.J., 1979).

2. Herbert's words from chapter 7 of *The Country Parson* (*The Works of George Herbert*, ed. F. E. Hutchinson [Oxford, 1941], 557) are: "crumbling texts into small parts." A. J. Festugière, the Dominican scholar, in his *George Herbert: Poète, Saint Anglican (1593–1633)* (Paris, 1971), observes that the Calvinist orator John Edwards in *The Preacher*, 1: 202, asserts as late as 1705 that this custom would not have lasted as long as it did if attention had been paid to Herbert.

3. Isaak Walton, *The Lives of Donne, Wotton, Hooker, and Herbert* (London, 1670), 82.

4. John Aubrey, *Brief Lives*, ed. A. Clark, 2 vols. (Oxford, 1898), 1: 309.

5. David Lloyd, *Memoires of the Lives . . .* (London, 1688), 618–619. The flowery account ends thus: he ". . . died of a Feaver, the holy order of his soul over-heating his body, Canon of *Loretto*, whence he was carried to heaven, as that Church was brought thither by Angels, singing." The testimony looks more like Murillo, than El Greco, to use Douglas Bush's pithy evaluation of Crashaw's poetry.

6. See Allan Pritchard's article in the *Times Literary Supplement*, 2 July 1964, 578, "Puritan charges against Crashaw and Beaumont."

7. Bishop H. Hensley Henson's Introduction to *Selected English Sermons, Sixteenth to Nineteenth Centuries* (London, 1939), vi.

8. G. N. Clark, *The Later Stuarts: 1660–1714* (Oxford, 1934), 347.

9. Henson, *Selected English Sermons*, xiii.

10. *Sixty Five Sermons by the Right Reverend Father in God, Ralph Brownrig, Late Lord Bishop of Exceter* (London, 1674), 74.

11. *The Collected Sermons of Thomas Fuller, D.D.* (2 vols., London, 1891), 1: 497.

12. John Hacket, *A Century of Sermons Upon Severall Remarkable Subjects* (London, 1675), 750.

13. Peter Heylyn, *The Parable of the Tares Expounded & Applied in Ten Sermons . . .* (London, 1659), 276.

14. Henry King, *An Exposition Upon the Lords Prayer, Delivered in Certain Sermons in the Cathedrall Church of S. Paul* (London, 1628), 145.

15. Arthur Lake, *Ten Sermons upon Severall Occasions, Preached at Saint Pauls Crosse and Elsewhere* (London, 1640), 130.

16. Thomas Playfere, *The Meane in Mourning. A Sermon preached at Saint Maries Spittle on Tuesday in Easter-weeke, 1595* (London, 1616), 71.

17. Playfere, *The Meane in Mourning*, 33.

18. John Prideaux, *A Plot for Preferment. A Sermon preached at Court* (Oxford, 1636), 1.

19. Prideaux, *A Plot for Preferment*, 4.

20. *The Sermons of Maister Henrie Smith, Gathered into One Volume* (London, 1593), 170.

21. *The Sermons of Maister Henrie Smith*, 655. He repeats the simile in conciser form on 1013.

22. *The Sermons of Maister Henrie Smith*, 932.

23. Thomas Fuller, *The Church-History of Britain* (London, 1655), Bk. IX, 142.

24. *The Whole Works of . . . James Ussher . . . With a Life of The Author . . .* by Charles Richard Elrington, 17 vols. (London, 1847–1864), 13: 217.

25. Ussher's *Whole Works*, 13: 556.

26. John Wall, *Alae Seraphicae* (London, 1627), 56.

27. Lloyd, *Memoires of the Lives*, 423f.

28. *The Plays and Poems of William Cartwright*, ed. G. Blakemore Evans (Madison, Wisconsin, 1951), 10f.

29. Published in London in 1652, but preached in Christ Church, Oxford, at least a decade earlier.

30. *The Plays and Poems of William Cartwright*, 559.

31. William Cartright, *An Off-spring of Mercy, Issuing out of the Womb of Cruelty* (London, 1652), 30–31.

32. W. Fraser Mitchell, in his admirable *English Pulpit Oratory from Andrewes to Tillotson: A Study of its Literary Aspects* (London, 1932), 179, claims that Mark Frank was "the best of the Anglo-Catholic preachers" from the literary point of view and that his *Course of Sermons*

is "the high-water mark of Anglo-Catholic preaching" (176). Apart from the fact that "Anglo-Catholic" is both anachronistic and too narrow a term by which to refer to the metaphysical preachers, who included many Calvinists in both style as well as theological content, the uneven Frank must rank below Donne, Andrewes, Hacket, Adams, and Henry Smith.

33. Mark Frank, *LI Sermons* (London, 1672), 546–547.

34. John Buckeridge, *A Sermon Preached at the Funeral of the Right Honorable and Reverend Father in God Lancelot late Lord Bishop of Winchester. In the Parish Church of S. Saviors in South-warke On Saturday being the XI of November A.D. MDCXXVI.* This sermon was published in 1629 and is an appendix to Andrewes' *XCVI Sermons* (London, 1629). The citation is from p. 18.

35. King James had written a justification for the loyalty oath he had imposed on his subjects after the Gunpowder Plot, to which Bellarmine replied using a pseudonym, "Matthaeus Tortus." Andrewes replied with *Tortura Torti*, and King James wrote another explanation, again replied to by Cardinal Bellarmine in his own name, and to this Andrewes retorted with his *Responsio ad Apologiam Cardinalis Bellarminis.*

36. The biographical information is in J. H. Overton's article in the Dictionary of National Biography, hereafter referred to as DNB.

37. Playfere had contributed as a don of St. John's to the Cambridge University collection of Latin elegies on the death of Sir Philip Sidney (February 16, 1586/7).

38. *The Letters of John Chamberlain*, ed. Norman Egbert McClure, 2 vols. (Philadelphia, 1939), 1: 162.

39. Thomas Playfere, *The Power of Praier* (Cambridge, 1617), 23–24.

40. Playfere, *The Power of Praier*, 33.

41. Anthony Wood, *Athenae Oxonienses* (2 vols., London, 1691–1692), 1: 603.

42. Thomas Nash, *Pierce Peniless his supplication to the divell* (London, 1592), reprint of 1870, ed. J. P. Collier, 40.

43. *The Sermons of Maister Henrie Smith*, 459. The sermon's title is "The Young Mans Taske" on the text, Ecclesiastes 12: 1, "Remember thy Creator in the dayes of thy youth."

44. I owe to the kindness of Gerald E. Bentley the information that Nicholas Tooley, actor and partner in Shakespeare's company, left Adams a legacy of £10, "whom I doe entreate to preach my funerall

sermon." See G. E. Bentley, *The Jacobean and Caroline Stage: Dramatic Companies and Players*, 7 vols. (Oxford, 1941), 2: 649, for a transcript of the will.

45. Wood, *Athenae Oxonienses*, 2: 259.

46. DNB.

47. DNB.

48. Rosemary O'Day, *The English Clergy: The Emergence and Consolidation of a Profession, 1558–1672* (Leicester, 1979), 158. This was demonstrated by Arthur P. Kautz in his essay "The Selection of Jacobean Bishops," in *Early Stuart Studies: Essays in Honor of David Harris Willson*, ed. Howard S. Reinmuth, Jr. (Minneapolis, 1970).

49. The most notorious case of wit winning the highest preferment with King James was the case of Bishop Mountain, who by a happy *mot* gained translation to a more prestigious bishopric, see later, final section of chapter 3, page 125.

50. John Gauden, *The Memorials of the Life and Death of the R. Rd. Father in God Dr. Brownrig . . .* (London, 1660), 147, 155, 209–210.

51. Anon. *The Life of That Reverend Divine, and Learned Historian, Dr. Thomas Fuller* (London, 1661), 69.

52. DNB.

53. DNB.

54. Wood, *Athenae Oxonienses*, 1: 511.

55. *The Poems of Richard Corbet*, ed. J. A. W. Bennett and H. R. Trevor-Roper (Oxford, 1955), xviii.

56. *Letters of John Chamberlain*, 2: 407.

57. Richard Baddiley and John Naylor, *The Life of Dr. Thomas Morton, Late Bishop of Duresme* (York, 1669), 14.

58. DNB.

59. James Melville's epigram against Barlow from *Musae* ends thus: "Pastorem Barlo sculpserat, anne lupum?"

60. Peter Heylyn, *Cyprianus Anglicanus: Or the history of . . . Laud* (London, 1668), pt. I, 44.

61. This is the judgment of William Scott, editor of volume 1 of *The Works of the Most Reverend Father in God, William Laud, D.D., sometimes Archbishop of Canterbury* (Oxford, 1847), vi.

62. DNB.

63. DNB.

64. Wood, *Athenae Oxonienses*, 2: 177–178.

65. John Hacket, *Scrinia reserata: a memorial offer'd to the great deservings of John Williams D. D., who sometime held the places of Ld Keeper of*

*the great seal of England, L*ᵈ *Bishop of Lincoln, and L*ᵈ *Archbishop of York,* 2 pts., (London, 1693), 45.

66. Frederic H. Forshall, *Westminster School: Past and Present* (London, 1884), 160.

67. Alabaster was chaplain to the 1596 expedition of the earl of Essex to Cadiz, whose play *Roxana* (published 1632) was put on in the hall of Trinity College, Cambridge. He turned Catholic and was imprisoned in the Tower of London, escaped, and was incarcerated in the prison of the Inquisition in Rome, was reconverted to Protestantism, and became a prebendary of St. Paul's. No sermons of his survive, but since his *Sonnets* and plays clearly reveal his fondness for metaphysical conceits it would be surprising if they were excluded from his preaching.

68. *The Poems of Henry King,* ed. Margaret Crum (Oxford, 1965), 5.

69. Walton's *Life of Sir Henry Wotton,* cited in Christopher Hollis, *Eton: A History* (London, 1960), 81–82.

70. Foster Watson, *The English Grammar Schools to 1660: Their Curriculum and Practice* (New York, 1970), 471.

71. Foster Watson, *The English Grammar Schools,* 472.

72. Foster Watson, *The English Grammar Schools,* 497–500.

Chapter II

THE CHARACTERISTICS OF METAPHYSICAL
SERMON STYLES

L IKE "WIT," "metaphysical" is a slippery, fugitive term that
has meant different things at different times, especially
to literary and homiletical critics. To Samuel Johnson
the distinguishing characteristic of metaphysical poetry was
that "the most heterogeneous ideas were yoked together."[1] Dryden thought that Donne's poems were marked by wit, and considered him "the greatest Wit, though not the best Poet of
our Nation."[2] He further considered that Donne's use of dialectics and far-fetched conceits was inappropriate in his poems,
for he "affects the Metaphysicks, not only in his Satires, but
in his Amorous Verse, where Nature only should reign; and
perplexes the Minds of the Fair Sex with nice Speculations
of Philosophy, when he shou'd ingage their hearts, and entertain them with the softnesses of Love."[3]

That which distressed the seventeenth- and eighteenth-cen-
tury critics, delighted the twentieth-century. Sir Herbert Grierson, for example, found it was the ingenious speculation and
the intense emotion fused in the imagination, which was the
captivating and distinctive quality of metaphysical poetry.[4] Earl
Miner acknowledged the importance of the conceits in a combination of the "wit of fancy" and the "wit of judgment" (fanciful
resemblances in dissimilar objects or ideas, as opposed to genuine analogical correlations), but claimed that the essential of
metaphysical wit was private not communal.[5] This is, of course,

45

a characteristic wholly unsuitable for a sermon, a public discourse given with the intention of being understood.

The homiletical critics among the Puritans, by contrast, objected to the word-play in quips, puns, and paronomasia as trivializing the encounter between divine communication and human response mediated by the preacher. Gravity rather than levity should characterize sermons. They also deplored the pedantic citation of the Church Fathers in the original Greek or Latin, and the historical narrations and "unnatural" natural history employed, not to mention the elaborate rhetorical ornamentation of style, since all this drew attention to the preacher, not to the treasure (the gospel) in the earthen vessel (the preacher).

What then were the positive virtues of the Puritan plain and not-so-plain styles of preaching as expounded by their leaders? Samuel Clarke, the Puritan hagiographer, writing in 1662, contrasts the plain style of the Reverend Richard Capel with the contemporary fussy, florid, and recondite style of the metaphysical preachers:

> Whereas now adayes, whilest some of our great Divines seem to be too much taken up with quaint and *Historicall* flourishes, there is a terrible decay of the power of God amongst us. An *Exotick,* or strange tongue in the publick Congregation (whatever men think of it) is set out as a sign of Gods displeasure I *Cor.* 14. 21, 22. It feeds such humours as should rather be purged out. It had no good effect in the Church of *Corinth* . . . The Gold upon the Pill may please the eye; but it profits not the Patient. The Paint upon the Glass may feed the fancy; but the room is the darker for it. The Sword of Gods Spirit can never wound so deep, as when it's plucked out of these gaudy Scabbards.

The Puritans objected to the contrived nature of a style which militated against sincerity and conviction. Clarke also cited Sibbes, the famous preacher at Gray's Inn, as being "wont to

say that great affectation, and good affections seldom goe together."[6]

Another Puritan critic, Richard Baxter, thought metaphysical
wit wholly out of place in sermons, disliking its fantastic conceits and rhetorical jingling. He observed, "There's no Jesting
in Heaven, nor in Hell."[7] Sibbes and Baxter (who had read
and admired Sibbes) emphasized the importance of the plain
style, though both were happy to use similitudes for illustrative
purposes. Sibbes felt that the metaphysical preachers were too
often in the clouds, hiding their meanings by their obscurity
of thought and diction. He contrasted the *kenosis,* or self-emptying of Christ, and the humble style which should witness to
Him, with the high-flown language of the metaphysical preachers, in the following appeal to the brotherhood of Puritan ministers: "Christ came down from heaven and emptied himself of
majesty in tender love to souls; shall we not come down from
our high conceits to do any soul good?"[8]

Since the plain (and occasionally not-so-plain)[9] style of the
Puritans, from the time of Perkins onwards, was the direct
opposite of the metaphysical style, it is worth considering what
its practitioners saw as its characteristics and its advantages.
Perkins, in his famous *Art of Prophesying,* claimed that the
preacher's task was: (1) "to read the Text distinctly out of
the Canonical Scriptures" [excluding the Apocrypha]; (2) "to
give the sense and understanding of it being read, by the Scripture it selfe"; (3) "to collect a few and profitable points of doctrine out of the naturall sense" [avoiding allegorical and tropological senses]; and (4) "to apply (if he have the gifte) these
doctrines rightly collected to the life and manners of men in
a simple and plaine speech."[10] The Puritan sermon was clearly
aimed at changing the mind of the congregation with a view
to the improvement of its behavior; hence there was little interest in speculative philosophy or even divinity of that type. Of
paramount Puritan concern was clarity in the task of making
everyone in the congregation understand that form of godliness
which seeks the will of God in order to obey it. Puritan theology, according to Perkins, was "the science of living blessedly
for ever."[11]

Samuel Clarke summed up the characteristics of the Puritan plain style in his eulogy of Dr. Harris, its practitioner: "In those days godly Preachers stuffed not their Sermons with aiery notions, and curious speculations, but sought out profitable matter, which they delivered in *sound words*, and in plain method of Doctrine, Reason, and Use, accommodating themselves to every man's capacity."[12]

Thus the Puritan critics disliked the levity, obscurity, artificiality, pedantry, secularity, pride, and lack of application that, in their view, characterized metaphysical preaching. In brief, they considered that a minister who was not in the pulpit—to use Milton's phrase "ever under my great Task-Master's eye"—was overreaching himself. The servant of the Word otherwise became its master. The preacher's duty was to treat his text, not as a pretext but with respect, since it was God's oracle. After careful study of the Word of God in the original languages, and a pastoral knowledge of the states of the souls of his flock, he was to pray for the assistance of the Holy Spirit, so to light up and apply the message that it would bring a transforming and sanctifying truth to the minds, hearts, and consciences of the congregation before him.

If, however, we ask the metaphysical preachers themselves what they consider the essential components of metaphysical preaching to be, the answer would be a combination of wit and recondite learning. Richard Corbet, poet, practical joker, and possibly the wittiest member of the bench of bishops, included the following lines in his epitaph on John Donne:

He that wood write an Epitaph for thee . . .
He must have wit to spare, and to hurle down
Enough to keep the gallants of the Town.
He must have learning plenty. . .
Divinity great store above the rest,
Not of the latest Edition, but the best.[13]

Both terms, wit and learning, need much fuller elaboration in order to include the subtle and complex apparatus of logic and rhetoric which the prose writers as well as the poets of the late sixteenth and the first half of the seventeenth century employed so brilliantly.

Confining myself to the pulpit in its golden age in England, and leaving aside the elaborate Ciceronian style of Bishop Taylor and the elegant intellectual simplicity of the Cambridge Platonists, I have found the "metaphysical" style of sermon can be distinguished from its major alternative ("Puritan plain") by eleven characteristics.

These characteristics may be listed as follows: (1) wit; (2) patristic citations and references; (3) the use of classical literature and history; (4) illustrations from "unnatural" natural history; (5) quotations in Greek and Latin, and etymology; (6) principles of biblical exegesis; (7) sermon structure and divisions; (8) the Senecan style; (9) paradoxes, riddles, and emblems; (10) speculative doctrines and arcane knowledge; (11) relating doctrinal and devotional preaching to the liturgy and the calendar of the Christian year.

It is however important to recognize that not all metaphysical preachers will adhere to this style throughout their lives, or on all occasions, or even exhibit all of the eleven characteristics in their corpus of sermons. Bishop John King and Dr. Thomas Fuller begin by preaching a series of sermons which expound entire books of the Bible, but discard this approach later. And Fuller changes from doctrine, reason, and use to sermons which, for wit and erudition, are indistinguishable from other metaphysical sermons when he is preaching before the king at Oxford or (after the Restoration) in Westminster Abbey. Similarly John Gauden and Thomas Jackson, as they change allegiances from the Puritan to the cavalier side, switch from moderately Puritan plain to metaphysical–ornamental—that is, to the correct party style of preaching. Further, the degree to which a preacher uses wit and erudition will depend in part on the circumstances of place and time. A sermon at court, cathedral, university church or college chapel, or in a fashionable London parish, would obviously use more wit and erudition than one preached in a country chapel of ease. Similarly, whether the preacher was officiating on a church festival such as Christmas, Easter, and Whitsun, or on a fast-day or black-letter day, would determine the elaboration of learning, conceits, and other ornaments in the style and diction of his sermon.

1. Wit

The first distinguishing mark is of course wit, which is analyzed in detail in the following chapter in all its copiousness and variety. It exhibits itself in a multitude of ways: in a great fondness for puns and paronomasia in English and ancient languages; in abstruse and often paradoxical expressions of thought; in memorable epigrams and striking imagery, deliberately intended to elicit curiosity or to shock, and drawn from unexpected quarters (science, hermeticism, rabbinics, voyages of discovery); in an admiration for antitheses; and in a combination of the lyrical and the satirical, such as in the brilliant contrast between the adoration of God and the ironical flaying of human beings.

2. Patristic citations and references

The many citations from the Fathers served a double purpose. They enabled the preachers to gain the respect of both learned and illiterate for the lore expounded in those large folio volumes, whose meaning was wrapped in the obscurity of Greek, Latin, and Hebrew. This was also the kind of knowledge learned at the two universities, whose graduates, in contrast to the early days of Elizabeth's reign, now filled the pulpits.

The second function which citations from the Fathers fulfilled was more significant: it attempted to prove that the Church of England was the direct descendant of the undivided Church of the first five centuries. This served as an important controversial ploy in showing the Puritans of Presbyterian or Independent leanings that the liturgy and polity of the Church of England kept faith with the worship and government of the earliest Church. It provided an apologetical armory of arguments and examples for the defense of the claim that it was the Roman Church not the Anglican which was the innovator, and which had departed from the central tradition in East and West. Thus the politicization of the papacy, the development of the doctrine of purgatory and indulgences as means of commutation of its punishments, the intercession of the saints and the veneration of their relics, could all be claimed to be idolatrous deviations from orthodox faith and practice. An additional value of patristic quotations (though subordinate to the other two functions they fulfilled) was that such theologians as Ambrose, Augustine, Gregory the Great, Gregory of Nyssa, John Chrysostom, Bernard of Clairvaux, as well as Tertullian (despite his Montanist heresy), and others provided the preachers with tropes and figures which they were happy to borrow for exegesis and illustrations.

For example, Bishop Henry King wisely cites Calvin when he is opposing the Puritan dislike of Latin citations and patristic references, and when asserting that there is no necessary quarrel between eloquence, and integrity, and simplicity in religion. He is most critical of the denial of the value of learning in sermons and worship on the part of those men "that have such an unlearned conceit of Gods service that they think it a trespasse of high nature to staine their Discourses with a Latine sentence, or authority of Fathers quoted in their own Dialect, or that make it a nice case of Conscience to present God with a studied Prayer, or any other forme of speech than . . . what comes into their heads whilest they are speaking."[14] But it is intriguing to see how ready King himself is to use patristic citations in the very book from which he made the criticism of unlearned preaching, a series of eleven sermons titled *An Exposition Upon the Lords Prayer* (1628). In over 360 pages he has 160 citations from the Greek and Latin Fathers (58 from Augustine, 15 from Ambrose, 12 from Chrysostom, and 10 from Aquinas), 8 from Reformed divines, and 49 references to Roman Catholic commentators and apologists (15 from Hales, 13 from Biel, and 3 from Bellarmine). Classical authors are referred to 25 times (Seneca 6 times, and Plutarch twice), and there are also references to Erasmus, Rabbi Jehuda, and the Qu'ran. Thus we have a grand total of 245 citations or references, amounting to an average of 22 per sermon. Moreover, this is not untypical of the metaphysical preachers.

It should not be assumed that each of the Jacobean or Caroline divines read the patristic theological treatises throughout. In fact, several kept commonplace books in which they noted such citations compiled by or quoted by contemporary writers. In yet other cases they simply borrowed them from contemporary printed sermons. The famous sermon of St. John Chrysostom on the Magi, used at Epiphanytide, was borrowed by both Andrewes and Donne, and their treatments of the same subject were borrowed by Bishop John Cosin. Hacket and Frank both borrowed as well from Andrewes.[15]

The real scholars, such as Andrewes, Adams, and Hacket, have a profound and detailed knowledge of the Fathers. This can be demonstrated in a single sermon by Andrewes. In his fifteenth Easter Day sermon he indicates that Christ's rebuke to Mary Magdalene, *noli me tangere*, is interpreted in three different ways by the Fathers Chrysostom, Gregory, and Augustine. The first, says Andrewes, suggests the Magdalen was too forward. The second declares that "her touch was [was] no Easter-day touch; her *tangere* had a *tang* in it (as we say)."[16] The third, Gregory the Great, understands it as a way of saving time "so that Jesus might hasten the message, *Vale et dic.*"[17]

It is significant that Andrewes usually summarizes briefly the content of the citations, rather than citing them fully, as most of the other metaphysical preachers do. It was typical of his modesty, and of Bishop Buckeridge's[18] too, who followed the example of Andrewes in this and other ways. Occasionally, however, Andrewes was given to citing snippets of Greek and whole passages of Augustine's Latin.[19]

Donne, too, quotes copiously from the Fathers and does not in the least mind differing from their interpretations, especially when they differ among themselves. In his Easter sermon of 1622, he chooses the difficult text from the First Epistle to the Corinthians 15:51, which reads "We shall not sleep, but we shall all be changed." This, says Donne, is delivered by St.

Paul as a mystery, but the commentators "have multiplied mystical clouds upon the words." Some Fathers, he continues, interpret this as meaning we shall not all sleep, and therefore we shall not all die (thus Chrysostom). The Vulgate reads this passage differently: *omnes resurgamus,* we shall all rise again, but we shall not all be changed. St. Augustine concludes that both meanings are orthodoxly Catholic and acceptable. It is then only Chrysostom's reading that Donne denies, since it contradicts the Apostle's assertion that "it is appointed once to every man to die."[20] Early in his preaching career Donne insisted that it was important to go *ad fontes,* that is, to the Fathers in the original languages, and not to rely on chrestomathies or commonplace collections. He said, "we steale our Learning, if we forsake the Fountaines, and the Fathers and the Schooles [scholastics], and deal with the Rhapsoders, and Commonplaces, and Methodmongers."[21]

It is intriguing to note where Donne's own preferences among the Fathers lie. In an analysis of three of the ten volumes that comprise the Potter and Simpson edition of *The Sermons of John Donne* (volumes 3, 6, and 9), the editors find that Donne has 226 citations from Augustine, 86 from Jerome, 58 from Chrysostom, 38 from Gregory the Great, and 37 each from Ambrose and Basil.[22]

Thomas Adams admires the Fathers, but he, on one occasion among several, dares to dissent from the interpretations of Ambrose, Augustine, and Jerome. They regard the struggle of Esau and Jacob in the womb of their mother to be the first-born as merely playful, but Adams believes it to be warlike.[23] Oddly enough, apparently none of the authorities stopped to consider how any of them could possibly *know* the fact, but that was typical of patristic as of Jacobean and Caroline speculation.

In general, however, the Fathers are cited frequently and respectfully. Bishop William Barlow, for example, was invited by King James to preach at Hampton Court in the presence of the Melville brothers, stout Presbyterians, to try to convince them of the authority and superiority of a church government by bishops. In this single sermon he cited twenty-seven different authors in seventy-six references, and eighteen of the authors were Fathers of the Church.[24]

The peculiar authority of the Fathers was thought to derive from their closeness in time to the days of the promulgation and canonization of New Testament Scripture, as distinct from apocryphal writings. Fuller, who in his later days made a greater use of the Fathers, indicates the varied attractions which some of the more popular Fathers supplied:

> Indeed we Modernes have a mighty advantage of the Ancients: Whatsoever was theirs by Industry may be ours, The Christian Philosophy of *Justin Martyr*; the constant Sanctity of *Cyprian*; the Catholick faith of *Athanasius*; the Orthodox Judgment of *Nazianzen*; the manifold learning of *Jerome*; the solid Comments [Commentaries] of *Augustine*; the excellent Morals of *Gregory*; the humble Devotions of *Bernard*: All contribute to the edification of us who live in this later age.[25]

3. The use of classical literature and history

The metaphysical preachers also delighted in studding their sermons with references to the pagan poets, philosophers, and historians of Greece and Rome. Their aim was fourfold. The poetical citations provided fancy in the midst of the ardors of argument, the philosophers inculcated moral lessons, the historical narrations supplied exempla, while the "unnatural" natural history gave illustrations that elicited wonder. In all this the preachers were making use of the Renaissance rediscovery of the classical world.

So many of the metaphysical preachers were minor poets, or at the lowest estimate versifiers, that it is astonishing how relatively few of them cited poetry in their sermons, and then only rarely. Thomas Playfere quotes Homer's *Odyssey* in one sermon and Martial in another.[26] Adams cites Horace and Ovid in his sermons.[27] In one of them he paraphrases the Latin in colloquially witty fashion: "Many a Pope sings that common ballad of Hell: *ingenio perii qui miser ipse meo:* Wit whither went thou? woe is me; my wit hath wrought my misery."[28] These jingling translations, uniquely his own, were admirable aids to the memory. Bishop Henry King, in his series of eleven sermons, *An Exposition Upon the Lords Prayer,* has two references to Homer, two to Horace, and one each to Virgil, Ovid, and Juvenal.[29] Among other preachers quoting Latin poetry were Bishops Gauden[30] and Howson,[31] and the Reverend Thomas Goffe.[32]

The impact of classical poetry, whether epic, satire, or ode, was not as great as might be expected, considering that it was taught in almost every English grammar school. It was more clearly seen in intriguing mixtures of classical mythology and Christian story, where the combination is often striking. Thomas Playfere, for example, borrows from Ambrose the figure of Christ as "our heavenly Ulysses," to whose Cross the faithful must fasten themselves for safety.[33] He also draws a parallel between the retrospective look of Lot's wife, and of Orpheus looking back longingly at Eurydice, in his Spital sermon of 1593.[34] In a third use of classical mythology, Playfere likens the Puritans, troubled as he thinks with trivia, to Atalanta, distracted by the golden apples.[35] And he can even find a parallel to Rahab's red thread which guided the Hebrew spies into Canaan in Ariadne's thread which led Theseus through Dedalus's labyrinth.[36] John Wall draws an inexact parallel between Telemachus saved by a dolphin, and Christians carried through deep waters on the back of the Lamb of God, Christ.[37] The image of a lamb carrying a fully grown person on its back through dangerous waters is ludicrous, and provided legitimate grounds for complaint against far-fetched analogies.

Occasionally the correlations between classical and Christian references are casual, but all the more significant for revealing how natural it was to make such analogies. Andrewes slips into saying that to follow the Anabaptist idea that all men can be prophets would result in "a *Cyclopian Church,* [which] will grow upon us where all were *Speakers,* no body heard another."[38] Similarly Josiah Shute, not a metaphysical preacher, speaks of the first sin of Adam and Eve as "the Trojan horse."[39] Henry King points out that the Lord's Prayer has seven parts, like Minerva's shield, or the targe of Ajax.[40]

Bishop Hacket can use a classical story to provide a Christian lesson. This leads us to the subject of the value of classical historical narrations in metaphysical preaching. One of his sermons was on the Temptation of Christ in the wilderness, when Satan requested him to turn the stones into bread, and it begins with the following narration:

> A *Roman Orator* in the days of *Tiberius* the *Emperour, Afer* by name, had so often taken in hand the worst part of every Plea to defend it, that at last his credit was prejudicated, and it was enough to say, *Afer* pleads on this side, therefore the justice of the cause is on the other side.

The moral is that if Satan propounds anything, the opposite must be true. Also, Hacket points out that the Devil's proposal, though appearing good, actually contained two sins, gluttony and infidelity.[41]

The use of historical exempla was far more common than the use of classical poetry or drama for the purposes of illustration. They were chiefly used as ethical examples, and, from the time of Aquinas at least, to illustrate the four cardinal virtues common to paganism and Christianity. Exempla of the virtues would be drawn from such historians as Herodotus, Xenophon, Livy, and Plutarch, and stories of wonderful beasts would be culled from such "unnatural" naturalists as Pliny, or Physiologus, not forgetting the fables of Aesop. Historical narrations continued to be employed throughout our period with unabated zeal, but the interest in "unnatural" natural history weakened considerably. This diminishment may be attributed to two factors. The first is the advance of the scientific spirit. This can be seen in the activities of a group of experimenters in the 1620s at Wadham College, Oxford under the wardenship of Dr. Wilkins. The membership, who were later to found the Royal Society, included the young mathematical and architectural genius, Christopher Wren. This sceptical spirit rightly challenged the credibility of stories which seemed too good to be true. Further, this type of illustration had been in use ever since the Middle Ages, and was simply worn out.[42]

Andrewes rarely used historical illustrations, but Donne, Adams, Playfere, and Hacket used them frequently. Also, it was not unusual for narrative examples to be taken from the history of countries other than Greece and Rome, and from postclassical times. Some examples must now be given.

Adams wishes to demonstrate how important it is to safeguard time. Hence he chooses Vespatian as a good exemplar: "The good Emperour *Vespatian*, if he had heard no causes, or done no charitable act, would complaine to his courtiers at night, *Amici, diem perdidi:* my friends, I have lost a day, I feare too many may say of the whole day of their lives, *I have lost my day.* "[43] In another sermon Adams takes Julius Caesar's moni tion as his own, when he appeals for charity towards the needy: "*Iulius Caesar* seeing women carry Dogges under their armes, asked if they had no children. God asketh you, that give your bread to dogges, if he hath no children for your charitie."[44]

Andrewes uses a historical narration in a Gowrie Day sermon. Gowrie Day was August 5, and recalled the deliverance of James, when king of Scotland, from attempted assassination by the earl of Gowrie and his brother, at their ancestral house where they were entertaining the king. He parallels David's sparing the life of his enemy King Saul, because it was inconceivable to kill the Lord's anointed ruler, with the somewhat different treatment afforded to King James:

It calls to my minde, what long since I read in *Herodotus:* that at the taking of *Sardi,* when one ranne at *Croesus* the *King,* to have slaine him, that a little boy borne dumbe, that had never spoken word in all his life, with the fright and horror of the sight, his *tongue* loosed, and he broke forth, and cried, *O man, destroy not the King,* and so saved his life. So writeth he, as of a wonder: and see if this were not like it.[45]

Both Playfere and Hacket retell the story of the first Christian Roman emperor, Constantine, honoring a courageous bishop who had suffered for his Christian convictions. Hacket's is the briefer version, from an Easter sermon dealing with the women who ran to tell the disciples of the empty tomb:

> They that held him by the feet had had the occasion to honour those parts of the body which had been pierced with Nails for our sakes upon the Cross. And I doubt it not, but to shew themselves thankful for his death, they did offer to lay their modest lips upon his wounds. As when *Paphnutius* his right eye was pluck'd out for being a constant *Christian*, the *Emperour Constantine* kissed the hollow pit from whence the eye was taken in reverence to his sufferings.[46]

Donne uses a military narration from classical history. This was of an unnamed general, who was threatened by the prediction that the arrows of his enemies would be so plentiful that they would block out the sun. He replied, "*In umbra pugnabimus;* All the better, says he, for then we shall fight in the shadow." Donne then makes the application: "Consider all the arrows of tribulation, even of *tentation,* to be directed by the hand of God, and never doubt to fight it out with God."[47] The aptness of the illustration is clear when the text is considered. It is from Psalm 38:22: "For thine arrows stick fast in me, and thy hand presseth me sore."

A comprehensive use of historical narration is exemplified by Cosin in a sermon of 1632 on the first commandment, in which he gave a minatory account of the horrific deaths of several ancient and modern atheists, including Machiavelli, drawn from the works of Diogenes Laertius, Sozomen, and Camden.[48]

4. Illustrations from "unnatural" natural history

The metaphysical preachers were particularly fond of using "unnatural" natural history as well as straight historical exempla. Christ represented as the self-wounding pelican feeding her young with her own flesh and blood was a famous medieval image of the Eucharist (to be seen to this day in the courtyard of Corpus Christi College, Oxford, and its copy outside the chapel of Princeton University).[49] So also was the phoenix re-born from its own ashes, symbolizing the Resurrection of Christ after three days in the grave. Thomas Playfere uses an intriguing reference to a panther as an image of godliness: "A panther hath foure clawes and no more on each hind foote; but five clawes and no lesse on each fore foote: so the godly, though they be bee weake to the worldward, yet they are strong to Godward."[50]

Bishop Barlow, wanting to vivify a situation in which every man would be master and all men bishops, recalls Pliny's *Amphisbaena*, "a *Serpent* which hath a head at each end of his body, both striving which should be the *maister-head*, in the meantime toiles the body most miserably, and in the end returns and tears it self most lothsomely."[51] Brownrig is captivated by the salamander, a cold-blooded creature which supposedly cannot be warmed by the flames that surround it, and applies it to persons who respond coldly to the flames of God's love.[52] Henry Smith uses the unicorn in typically brief form: "As the Unicorne dippeth his horne in the fountaine, and maketh the waters which were corrupt and noisome, cleare and wholesome upon the sodaine: so, whatsoever state Godlines comes into, it saith like the Apostles, *Peace be to this house*, peace bee to this heart, peace be to this man."[53] Smith also uses the old favourite, the harpy.[54] Robert Willan says it is reported that the birds of Norway fly more rapidly than the birds of all other lands, not because of any superior natural agility, "but by an instinct they know the dayes in that Climate to bee very short, not above three houres long, and therefore they make more haste unto their nests: Strange that birds should make such use of their observation, and we practically knowing the shortnesse of our lives, yet make no haste to our home, *the house appointed for all living*."[55] The theme of *carpe diem* is an old one, but the attempted rational explanation for the unfamiliar is new in the use made of "unnatural" history. This may be because it appears late in a sermon of 1630.

Donne has several exempla of this type. Snakes fascinate him, especially the kind that knows its skin is useful to humans suffering from the falling sickness, and so "out of Envy, they hide their skin when they cast it."[56] He is also intrigued by the *Lithospermus*, which he calls the greatest wonder of nature, which produces a very hard stone as its fruit. His application is strained, namely "that temporal affliction should produce spiritual stoniness, and obduration, is unnaturall, yet ordinary."[57] And Hacket, as one might imagine, has a farfetched example, necessary to illustrate the fact that God's eye is on the evil even when they are unaware: "Wherefore one says of the Crocodile, that the Egyptians in the vain Idol did resemble a *God, Quia ex omnibus aquaticis habet oculos obtectos ut cernat, ne cernatur;* It hath both eyes so befilmed that perceives afar off, and is not perceived."[58] Another Egyptian tale is used by Henry King to illustrate the danger that comes from those whose ears strain after too much preaching: "A man may heare so much that he may stone the sense, and bee like the *Catadupes*, whom the continuall fall of Nile makes deafe. Cisternes that have more powred into them then they can hold, must needs run to wast; and men that affect to learne more then they have braine to comprehend, waste their Pastors labour, and their own patience."[59]

John White, the controversialist, is not the only one to perceive the value of an example drawn from "unnatural" history. He likens the Jesuits to birds which, when men are away at a sacrifice, burn their houses—a clear allusion to the Gunpower Plot.[60] It is interesting that, in contrast, Andrewes dislikes anti-Roman references in his sermons, rarely uses historical narrations, and even rejects using a natural historian like Pliny to learn the functions of the dove, feeling that Scripture is sufficient.[61]

I have dealt at some length on the parallel use of the Fathers in Greek and Latin with classical learning in general. Preachers acquired their classical learning at school and university, and used it to enliven their discourses. Poetical references were chiefly included for delight, and moral maxims for instruction. They were also used to urge Christians to go further than the pagans, who had not received the special revelation peculiar to Christianity. Historical narrations were intended to produce both variety of material and to illustrate the four cardinal virtues of fortitude, temperance, prudence, and justice. The function of the fantastical accounts of strange creatures was to elicit wonder and to prepare the listeners for the transcendent *gesta Dei*, the wonderful works of God.

It was for the latter purpose that classical riddles were retold, since riddles certainly held the attention. Thomas Playfere, one of the earliest metaphysical preachers, wished to illustrate a neuter, that is a Christian who goes backwards and forwards and makes no real progress in belief or behavior, and so he uses a quadruple riddle borrowed from Athenaeus's *Deipnosophistai* ("The Learned Banquet"):

> *Panarches* riddle was this, how a man and no man, can with a stone and no stone, kill a bird and no bird, sitting upon a tree, and no tree? *Athenaeus* makes the answer, That an Eunuch, is the man, and a Pumeise is the stone, a Batte is the bird, and fennell is the tree. After the same sort a *Newter* is a very hard riddle. You cannot tell what to make of him. For going backward and forward, he is a Christian & no Christian.[62]

Hacket, who like Donne always delights in the curious and arcane, combines a riddle with a historical narration. Philip of Macedon was at a banquet when he propounded the question: what was the greatest thing in nature? Various answers were given including the servile one, Philip himself, and others such as Olympus, the ocean, and the sun, all of which were wrong. Philip answered: "*Sed cor quod res maximas despiceret;* the greatest of all things was an heart that despises the greatest things which are in this world beneath."[63]

5. *Quotations in Greek and Latin, and etymology*

This fifth characteristic of metaphysical preaching need not occupy us long, since it has been touched upon in our consideration of historical narrations, which often included maxims in the original classical languages. And it will be seen again in some of the witty wordplay of our following chapter. An interest in etymology was, of course, not only an echo of the schooling of the preachers, but a necessity for a learned biblical expositor. The best of the preachers were familiar with the Hebrew of the Old Testament, the Greek of the Septuagint (the translation of the Hebrew of the Old Testament), and the Latin of the Vulgate (for understanding the Roman Catholic commentators of which the Jacobean and Caroline divines made good use). Further, Greek was essential for exposition of the New Testament. Greek tags (and less frequently, citations), and frequently Latin tags and citations, and etymology were used without exception by all the metaphysical preachers from Andrewes and Adams to Gauden and Goffe, and from Hacket and Holyday to Willan and Wren.

Andrewes was the ablest scholar of the group in biblical languages, but it is Barten Holyday, the archdeacon of Oxford, who uses them more often, and who positively revels in semantic history. He gives the usual translation of Proverbs 7:9 as *"in the black and deep night,"* telling us that "it is in the original באישוכ כוכה, as if we should say, *in the apple of the eie of the night.* " His application is "Yet out of the darkest sorrow, God will at last raise the most cheerful light."[64] Andrewes is less pedantic and more practical in his semantic illustration: *"Sinceritie* (that is) *cleanesse of life:* (a word thought to be taken from *honie,* which is then *mel sincerum,* when it is *sine cerâ,* unmingled, without wax, or any baggage."[65] It was typical of him also to illustrate hypocrisy, by deriving it from its Greek original and pointing out that that a hypocrite is essentially a stage-player, an actor or pretender.[66]

6. Principles of biblical exegesis

Another distinctive aspect of metaphysical preaching was its type of biblical exposition. From the days of the early Church there had been two tendencies: the Alexandrian which favored allegorical, and the Antiochene which preferred literal or historical interpretation. Ambrose and Augustine combined both, and it was Cassian who schematized for the Western Church the four senses of Holy Writ.[67] Each passage of Scripture could be interpreted in a literal or historical sense; in an allegorical sense, strictly so-called when it was applied to Christ and the Church Militant; in a tropological or moral sense, in which it was to be understood to relate to the soul and its virtues; or in an anagogical or mystical sense, when it was applied eschatologically to the heavenly realities. Protestantism, especially in its Calvinist form, had virtually rejected all allegory, except where the sense was plainly metaphorical, as for example in the Johannine discourses, when Jesus says, "I am the door"[68] and "I am the vine: ye are the branches."[69] Medieval Catholics, especially the schoolmen, had used the four senses, and many of the sixteenth-century Roman Catholics continued to do so. This approach had two advantages: it enabled apparent contradictions within the Scriptures easily to be resolved, and it allowed preachers to exercise considerable ingenuity in interpretation. It was the latter characteristic, which often led to digressions and even deviations from the primary historical meaning of Scripture, that led Protestants to emphasize the literal sense and virtually to exclude the other senses. On the other hand, while Protestant commentators made significant contributions to biblical studies in their zeal to understand the Bible in the original languages, they also sometimes fell into the very error for which they criticized the Roman Catholics. An emphasis on the interior illumination of the Holy Spirit did not always save them from the perils of subjective interpretation. The wilder sectaries of the Commonwealth period sometimes took the short step from the inner light to the outer darkness.

The distinctive contribution of the metaphysical preachers was that they were truly of the *via media* in choosing neither to use all four senses of the Roman way, nor the dominant single sense of the Genevan or Puritan way. This we might expect of Donne, because he had been brought up as a Catholic, and because of the brilliant opportunities polysemous interpretation provided for his imaginative and rhetorical genius. But it also proved invaluable for Andrewes and his followers. It enabled them to use the Old Testament in their typological exegesis, so that they found anticipations of the New Testament in the Old Testament, as Origen and Augustine had done before them. This approach gave them the opportunity, especially in court sermons, to use the Psalms historically. They were able to refer to their authorship by a king (David), then to apply the text to the circumstances of another king (James or Charles), and, finally, to see in it a reference to the King of Kings, Christ.

Among a multitude of possible exemplars three must suffice for the present. Dr. John Cosin preached a sermon to the Protestant members of the exiled English queen's household in Paris, whose chaplain he was, on the Octave of the Resurrection, 16 April 1651, using the text John 20:9: "For as yet they knew not the Scriptures, that he must rise from the dead." He provided a thoroughly typological exegesis of Abraham's willingness to sacrifice Isaac at God's command as a foretelling of Christ's Passion and Resurrection. He found no less than seven parallels between Isaac and Jesus. Both were the only beloved sons of their fathers, who were determined to put them to death. Both accepted their lot obediently. Both were bound up for sacrifice. The wood for that sacrifice was laid on their shoulders. Both were led to a mount, and Calvary and Mount Moriah are the same mountain. The ram that was caught in the thornbush and was offered up to save the life of Isaac is seen "as the figure and pledge of Him that came forth with the crown of thorns, and offered up himselfe to save ours." Finally, each was released in three days for a new life.[70] Cosin followed this by adducing all the Old Testament passages, from the Psalms to the Prophecies, thought to point to the Resurrection.

Calvinist though he was, Thomas Adams could use an Old Testament text as a text for embroidering those of his fancies which were only partly determined by the Bible. He takes a text from Hebrews 6:7, "For the earth which drinketh in the raine that commeth oft upon it, and bringeth forth Herbes meet for them by whom it is dressed, receiveth blessings from God." The sermon is entitled "A Contemplation of the Herbes." So far, so good. Then he starts allegorizing with a pun on "*Herbes* of our *graces*" and glosses "meete for the dresser" as "contentfull to God" and then refers to "the *Garden* of our hearts" and says God will require four virtues in them: "*Odour, Taste, Ornament, Medicinall Vertue.*" Then he proceeds to allegorize without limit, speaking successively of Hyssop (Humility), Bulapathum (Patience), Balsamum (Faith), St. John's Wort (Charity), and several others, until he reaches the Holy Thistle (Good Resolution).[71] Similarly, Adams has a sermon entitled "Heaven-Gate: Or, The Passage to Paradise." The text, Revelation 22:14, is allegorized with the Gate having the foundation of faith, the two sides of patience and innocence, and the roof of charity.[72]

John Donne can use an Old Testament text with a multiple typological reference, so that its context is Babylon at the time of Ezekiel, Jerusalem at the time of Christ, and England at the time of the Reformation. In each case he shows how God's people were under the tyranny of Church and State in collusion to oppress them. What makes it interesting is that Donne uses the correct exegetical terminology to introduce these different applications. He says of the text Ezekiel 34:19, "And as for my flock, they eate that which yee have troden with your feet, and they drinke that which yee have fouled with your feet," that their deepest distress was "that their own *Priests* joyned with the *State* against them," translating this very aptly in a sermon before the court to ". . . the *Church* joyned with the *Court* to oppress them." On that very context he comments: "This is the *literall* sense of our text, and context, evident in the letter thereof." Then his next comment is: "And then the *figurative* and *Mysticall* sense is of the same oppressions and the same deliverance over againe in the times of *Christ*, and of the Christian Church." Then he declares a paragraph later that it concerns "the oppressions and deliverances of *our Fathers*, in the *Reformation of Religion* and the shaking off of the yoak of *Rome*, that *Italian Babylon*, as heavy as the *Chaldaean.*"[73] In similar fashion, Hacket can preach a Gowrie Conspiracy sermon before King James. It starts with the text from Psalm 41:9, "Yea, mine own familiar friend, in whom I trusted, which did eat of my bread, hath lifted up his heel against me," which he takes as a reference to Achitophel's treachery against David. He then applies it to Judas' betrayal, and finally to the rebelliousness of the Earl of Gowrie and his brother.[74]

The distinction between metaphysical use of allegorical and typological exegesis, in contrast to the almost exclusive adherence to the literal-historical sense to be found in Puritan sermons, is striking in our period.

7. Sermon structure and divisions

Another striking difference between metaphysical preachers and Puritan preachers was the preference of the former for sermons with complex divisions in the plan, sometimes seeming almost a recovered scholasticism. In this they can be compared with the simplicity of Puritan exegesis according to the text. There was also a further difference in structure. Some of the metaphysicals, like Andrewes and Cosin, structured their sermons so that the text was followed by a general introduction which might be contextual or refer to the special liturgical occasion for which the congregation had met, followed by a bidding prayer, and succeeded by the division and the exposition. All of them in the early days used the scholastical plan, with its complex divisions and sub-divisions, but these became increasingly simpler as time went on. The preferred Puritan structure of sermons, which for example Fuller used in his pre-cavalier days and which was standardized in the Westminster Assembly of Divines, was that of doctrine, reason, and use.[75]

Thomas Playfere's lengthy sermon, *The Meane in Mourning* (1595), is so ludicrously elaborate in its eight-fold division that it would almost justify the Puritan determination to keep sermons simple, if not, occasionally, even simplistic. The division of the text, which is brief enough (Luke 23:28; "Weep not for me, but for yourselves"), proceeds as follows:

In which sentence we may observe, so many wordes, so many parts, Eight wordes, eight parts. The first, *Weepe not*; the second, *But weepe*; the third, *Weepe not, But weepe*; the fourth, *For mee*; the fifth, *For your selves*; the sixth, *For Mee, For your selves*; the seventh, *Weepe not for mee*; the eighth, *But weepe for your selves*. [76]

The seventh and eighth divisions alone would be an adequate division of this twofold, contrasting text.

A relatively simple example of scholastic division, with the major points made in Latin, is provided by Andrewes as the structure for his Christmas sermon before the king and court in 1611. The text is John 1:18: "And the WORD was made Flesh, and dwelt among us: (and we saw the Glorie thereof, as the Glorie of the Onely-begotten SONNE of the FATHER) full of Grace and Truth." The division of the text is given thus: "All reducible to these three: *Quod Verbum Caro; Quid Verbum, Carni; Quid Caro, Verbo*. That the *Word became flesh*; the *Mysterie*: What the *Word* did for *flesh*; the *Benefit*: And, what flesh is to doe to the *Word* againe; the *Duety*."[77]

It is perhaps most instructive to compare the changes from a Puritan to a cavalier sermon structure in the life of one preacher, namely John Gauden, whose Commons text is Zechariah 8:19, "Thus saith the Lord, The fast of the tenth moneth, shall be to the house of Iudah, joy and gladnesse, and cheerfull feasts; therefore love the Truth and Peace." The division is as follows: "In the words consider three things: First, the inference, *Therefore*; Secondly, the objects propounded, *Truth* and *Peace*. Thirdly, the dutie required: *Love*."[78] Nothing could be simpler or more directly derived from the text, nor patterned more clearly on doctrine, reason, and use, with a strong concluding emphasis on the application to the affections, called "the patheticks." With this should be contrasted the future bishop's sermon preached in 1659 to "the Lord Mayor, the Lord General, Aldermen, Common Council and Companies of the honorable City of London." He took his text from Jeremiah 8:11: "For they have healed the hurt of the Daughter of my people slightly, saying, Peace, peace, where there is no peace." It was an apt text for the day of thanksgiving appointed for the return of the secluded Members of Parliament to the House. Now a cavalier parson, he not only shows off his knowledge of Latin, but expands his division to a sixfold analysis, and the printed sermon balloons to 112 pages. Here is the clear but cluttered division:

1. *Persona laesa, icta, afflicta*, the *Patient* or *afflicted;* whom the Prophet, yea God himself *deplores* and owns; she is called the *daughter of my people;* 2. *Plaga* or *laesio;* the *grief* or *malady*, the *hurt* or *lesure*. 3. *Ficta medela*, or *insana sanatio*, the pretended cure or verbal *healing;* they have *healed, with saying, Peace, peace*, slightly and superficially. 4. Ψευδε or *mendacium;* the fallacy and cheat, when there is no *peace*. 5. *Medicorum turba;* the *Physitians or Empericks; They*, great Statists, grave Polititians, formal pretenders to do great feats, and miraculous cures in *Church* and *State*, when really they are no other than *imperious Hypocrites, magniloquent Mountebanks*, cruel and covetous, confident and careless *Boasters* of their skill; but no way *Effecters* of a real cure. 6. *Vera medendi Methodus;* the true way of *curing a diseased Nation*, a distressed Country, a sick and languishing Church, which is implied. . . .[79]

While the division is clearly derived from the text, and the sermon is a declamation, the fifth section of the division ran away with the rest. This is precisely what the London congregation wished to hear at this critical juncture in their history, since Monk, who was to engineer the Restoration of the monarchy, was among their number on this occasion.

8. The Senecan style

Another distinguishing feature of the metaphysical preaching mode was the preference for a Senecan *pointed* as compared with a Ciceronian *periodic* style, though the distinction is far from absolute.

Chapter II

The mode is Senecan in a double sense. First, its form is
marked by directness, terseness, even occasional roughness, vividness, controversial nimbleness, and a love of epigram and
antithesis. The Ciceronian style, in contrast, prefers the copiousness, smoothness, and branching, exfoliating style of long
paragraphs and periods.[80] It is also, in a way that became increasingly true of the later Puritan style, Senecan in content
and emphasis. By this I mean that the Caroline divines do not
only quote Seneca, but that their emphasis is also strongly
moral, which makes it approximate to the third element in
the Puritan schema of doctrine, reason, and use, that is, the
application. But the Puritans abominated the Ciceronian style
generally. They mistrusted its copiousness and smoothness, to
say nothing of its display of esoteric learning, which they felt
was suspect in drawing attention to the eloquence of the
speaker. The Puritan divines were ever mindful of the strictures
of St. Paul against Apollos and his smoothly seductive style
in the church at Corinth.[81]

The Ciceronian style was admirably exemplified by Richard
Hooker as well as by Jeremy Taylor. Donne combines both,
but he is dominantly Senecan, as are Andrewes and his followers. Donne's Ciceronianism in its superb balance is seen in
the "Sermon of Valediction" preached to the benchers of Lincoln's Inn, when leaving for Germany in 1619. In this moving
farewell the vivid anthropomorphic image "the ears of God"
is the pearl in the context of his superlative prose:

In my long absence, and far distance from hence, remember me, as I shall do you in the ears of that God, to whom
the farthest East, and the farthest West are but as the right
and left ear in one of us; we hear with both at once; and
he hears in both at once; remember me, not my abilities;
for when I consider my Apostleship that I was sent to
you, I am in St. Pauls *quorum, quorum ego sum minimus*,
the least of them that have been sent; and when I consider
my infirmities, I am in his *quorum* in another commission,
another way, *Quorum ego maximus;* the greatest of them;

but remember my labours, and endeavours, at least my desire to make sure your salvation. And I shall remember your religious cheerfulness in hearing the word, and your christianly respect towards all them that bring that word to you, and towards my self in particular far [a]bove my merit.[82]

With this may be compared Donne's Senecan style, with its colloquial idioms and interrogatories, in an intriguing sermon reconciling contradictory texts. He speaks of God's *judicium detestationis:*

and hence he knows and therefore detests evil, and therefore flatter not thyself with a Tush, God sees it not, or, Tush, God cares not, Doth it disquiet him or trouble his rest in heaven that I breake his Sabbath here? Doth it wound his body, or draw his bloud there, that I swear by his body and bloud here? Doth it corrupt any of his virgins there, that I solicit the chastity of a woman here? Are his Martyrs withdrawn from their Alleagance, or retarded in their service to him there, because I dare not defend his cause, nor speak for him, for fight for him heare?[83]

The jerkiness of the Senecan style, not an amble but a series of stops and starts, can be seen in the balanced antitheses and terseness of the form and the practicality of the substance in the following citation from Brownrig:

Popery is a Religion for the Eye; Ours for the Ear . . . A Christian is described, *In auditu Auris.* At the Hearing of the Ear they shall obey. Hearing it is that breeds Faith. It is a comfort to have these Visions, Tastings, Feelings; but if all these fail us, or be denied us; yet if we can Hear, and Believe, it sufficeth. We must stick to this. In this sense, *All the Body must be an Ear. Miracula, muta sine voce;* but Seals to a Blank.[84]

The directness of the Senecan manner, with a vivid simile, is shown in Bishop Morton's defense of the Book of Common Prayer against the charge that it has passages taken from the Roman liturgy: "Let us understand that truth is truth wherever it soundeth, even as a Pearle is a Pearle of price, although it be taken out of the head of a toade."[85]

How suitable a style it was for controversy can be seen in an anti-papal citation of Morton on the text of Romans 13:1, "Let every soul be subject to the higher powers, &c." Morton questions:

> Every soul subject? Not I, saith the Pope, and so all Popes of after-times, for we have power over all *Powers*, be they *Emperours* themselves, to kick off their Crowns with our feet; to depose their persons, and to dispose of their kingdoms.[86]

Thus the Senecan style succeeded in achieving vividness and ingenuity by a variety of devices. These included rhythmical word play, alliteration, hyperbole, antithesis, and, of course, paradox. Senecan brevity and epigrammatic concision, as well as abruptness, were victorious over Ciceronian periodic expansiveness and smoothness.[87]

9. Paradoxes, riddles, and emblems

Another distinguishing characteristic of metaphysical preaching was a fondness for paradoxes, riddles, and emblems. They are, of course, interrelated. Each demands a teasing concentration on the meaning of what appears to be mysterious and thought-provoking. They also represent a continuation of the medieval delight in allegorization which also intrigued Renaissance minds until the middle of the seventeenth century.

It belonged to the Platonic inheritance in which individual objects were viewed as members of a class, rather than seen in their individuality and particularity, the *haeccitas*, or thisness, that the opposing Nominalists had stressed. It seemed possible to see objects, and to see through them to the divine pattern or idea in the mind of the Creator God. Hence allegorical symbolization was built on the conviction, equally flattering to the philosopher and the mystic, that symbolic thinking penetrated the external nut to reach the inner kernel of thought or union, and the harder the nut was to crack the more valuable and esoteric was the meat within. What Huizinga says of medieval understanding was still true of much of the epistemology of those preparing sermons in the Renaissance. He wrote:

> The Middle Ages never forgot that all things would be absurd if their meaning were exhausted in their function and their place in the phenomenal world, if by their essence they did not reach a world beyond this. About the figure of Divinity a majestic system of correlated figures crystallized which all have reference to Him. The world unfolds itself like a vast whole of symbols, like a cathedral of ideas. It is the most richly rhythmical conception of the world, a polyphonous expression of eternal harmony.[88]

Such a conception lingered on in the Church after it had been given up by the world. Paradoxes are found throughout our period. Indeed, at the very time that contradictions, or apparent contradictions, in Scripture were acutely felt by the preachers, two such collections of paradoxes appeared. To use Rosalie L. Colie's fascinating title for her book, the contagion of paradoxitis had led to *Paradoxia Epidemica*. The two most popular exponents of paradox were Herbert Palmer and Ralph Venning.

Both flourished in the middle decades of the seventeenth century. Palmer was an honored member of the Westminster Assembly of divines and Master of Queen's College, Cambridge. He was the author of *Memorials of Godliness & Christianity* which appeared in 1644, and its second part, *The Character of a Christian in Paradoxes and seeming Contradictions*, appeared in 1655. This latter work was attributed to Lord Bacon, presumably because it seemed to be better at demonstrating biblical contradictions than in resolving the difficulties it had disclosed. It was a compilation of eighty-five paradoxes. Many of them dealt more with scriptural inconsistencies than doctrinal paradoxes, though the latter were included.

Venning's *Orthodoxe Paradoxes, Theoreticall and Experimentall, or, a Believer clearing truth by seeming Contradictions* appeared in 1647 and ran through five editions in the next five years. It is better than Palmer's works, both because it expounds a complete system of theology and because it has clearer and more rational definitions. Palmer's first paradox reads: "A Christian is one who believes things which his reason cannot comprehend." Venning's first reads: "He [the Christian] believes *that* which reason cannot comprehend, yet there is reason enough why he should believe it." Here we have displayed all the difference between the contra-rationalistic fideism of Tertullian, who said *credo quia impossibile est* (I believe because it is impossible), and the illuminating faith of St. Anselm, *credo ut intelligam* (I believe in order to understand).

The strength and weakness of the over-paradoxical approach is revealed in Venning's final paradox, number 127. This reads: "He is one who lives *in another and for another*; He seeks not himself when he aims most at his good: God is his all, and his *all* is God's; he aims at no *end* but the glory of God, of which there is no end."[89] The strength is in the echo both of Christ's teaching, that one must lose the world to win one's soul, and of the definition of man's true end in the Westminster *Shorter Catechism.*[90] Its weakness is that it depends upon a verbal quibble on the two meanings of "end," namely aim and terminus, and thus sounds more profound than it is.

Doctrinal paradoxes (as our chapter on metaphysical wit and its many examples will try to make clear) are integral to Christian doctrine and life. Some of the more familiar are the paradoxes inherent in the idea of the Holy Trinity, the Incarnation, the Atonement of the holy for the unholy and love for the loveless, and the Resurrection as the death of death.

The value of the paradox to the preacher was that it helped him to elicit a sense of wonder in the listeners. George Puttenham called the genre itself "the Wondrer,"[91] and in the preaching of Andrewes and his followers the use of the paradox became orthodox.

The intellectual function of the paradox, from the days of Parmenides onwards, was to force contemplation, while rhetorically, to quote Rosalie Colie, it has the "double aim of dazzling—that is, of arresting thought altogether in the possessive experience of wonder."[92] Its other function is to encourage further question and possibly even contradiction on the part of the teased audience.

Two examples only will be given of a single paradox: that God immutably wills mutability. Dean Jackson's theme for his entire third sermon on Jeremiah 26:19 is to ask the question, In what sense is God said to repent? The answer he gives is, "God immutably willeth mutability."[93] Bishop Lake, however, shows himself to be a true scholastic in his illustrated explication of this paradox:

> True it is, that God is said to repent; but the Fathers joyntly agree that his repentance is mutation, not *affectus*, but *effectus:* hee changeth his creatures, unchangeable in himselfe. Even as a Chirurgeon who begins with one kind of plaister when that hath wrought his force, layeth another kind, doth not alter, but pursue his former resolution, which was, by those diverse plaisters to cure the sore: even so, whatsoever alteration befalls us, God did eternally decree it, and decree it as befalls.[94]

The metaphysical preachers also used riddles, but more frequently in Elizabethan than in Caroline days. It is interesting to observe two of them using the famous riddle of Samson, recounted in the Book of Judges. The riddle is: "Out of the eater came forth meat, and out of the strong came forth sweetness." The answer is almost equally obscure: "What is sweeter than honey? and what is stronger than a lion?"[95] The mystery clears when it is realized that Samson is referring to a honeycomb found in a lion's carcass. In an Easter sermon Bishop Brownrig, following Augustine, applies the riddle as another proof of the transformation effected by the grace of God: ". . . the devouring Lyon shall bring hony in his mouth; the Church's cruel persecutours shall by the Gospel be made affectionate foster-fathers."[96] Thomas Fuller applies the riddle in an entirely different fashion: ". . . part of *Samsons* Riddel shall be fulfilled in your ears: *Out of the Devourer came meat: Gluttony,* that vice which consumeth and devoureth food, the discourse thereof by Gods assistance shall feed us at this time."[97]

Emblems became popular in the 1630s and later, when the emblem books of Quarles and Wither appeared. Quarles's work *Emblemes* (1635),[98] and Wither's *A Collection of Emblemes* of the same date, were made up of symbolic pictures and explanatory words, as was the earliest emblem book in English, Geoffrey Whitney's *A Choice of Emblemes and other Devises,* published in 1586 in Leyden.

Mario Praz has rightly stressed the link between the emblem and the conceit, maintaining that seventeenth-century man needed the assurances of the senses, and wished "to externalize it, to transpose it into a hieroglyph, an emblem."[99] The aim of the device associated with the emblem was, like the paradox, to produce a sense of the marvelous, as its great exemplifier, Marino, had affirmed.[100] A further link between the brilliant analogy, or witty conceit, and the emblem is M. W. Croll's discovery that Lyly used seventeen of Alciati's emblems as the basis of similes in his *Euphues.*[101]

The great attraction of the emblem, as Rosemary Freeman has shown in her admirable *English Emblem Books,* is the wit, "the apparent lack of any relation between the two ideas [of the analogy] and the subsequent establishment of an intellectually convincing link between them that pleases."[102] She claims that it is the same delight as is found in the Elizabethan drama and the modern English music–hall for puns, a delight experienced no matter how arbitrary the link appears to common sense or the feelings. Of direct interest to this study is the claim of Thomas Beachcroft that the emblem is simply a metaphysical conceit in miniature.[103]

The function of the majority of English sacred emblem books

was to help Protestants to learn Christian doctrine through visual education and to enable them to meditate as Catholics had been taught to do. Louis L. Martz[104] has shown how Catholic meditation techniques assisted Donne, and certainly Crashaw, though it now seems unlikely that Donne ever had a Jesuit tutor, since Jesuits were so few in England and their work so dangerous. Also it seems improbable that Herbert was unduly influenced by Catholic techniques. On the other hand, the Ignatian technique of "composition"—visualizing biblical events, and the struggle of the *miles Christianus* to gain victory— had a powerful effect on the religious imagination of Europe both in art and architecture, and the development of meditation. As complement and partial correction of Martz, Barbara K. Lewalski[105] has shown how important Protestant meditation techniques, aided by emblem books, were in their impact on the English religious lyric. If such ideas were influential on the English metaphysical poets, they must have been equally influential on the English metaphysical preachers.

For Protestants emblems were derived from the natural world (God's Picture Book since it was his creation), and from the Scriptures (His living and transforming Word), and from other emblem books, chiefly Catholic, which they borrowed and amended. Furthermore, history itself was seen by the eyes of faith as the saga of the *gesta Dei per sanctos*, themselves illuminated by the Holy Spirit. Barbara Lewalski rightly sees that the major types of emblems are three: natural, historical, and moral, presumably including the scriptural as part of the historical.[106]

Space only allows us to illustrate the variety of homiletical emblematic usage with concise examples taken from the late Elizabethan and late Caroline periods. Playfere, in his Spital sermon of 1593 using Philippians 3:14 as his text, illustrates progress towards the high calling in Christ by referring to the emperor's motto thus: "Hereupon Charles the 5. gave this Embleme, Stand not stil, but go on Further."[107] In a sermon on the duties of marriage Henry Smith maintains that wives should stay at home, for homes are not prisons but paradises, and continues: "Phidias when he should paynt a woman, painted her sitting under a Snailes shell, signifying, that she should go like a snaile, which carrieth his house upon his backe."[108]

Daniel Featley combines a natural symbol with a strong moral meaning in a funeral sermon for a mercer named Benet. Ending the sermon by saying that they will strew a few flowers on the hearse, he emphasizes that these are emblematic flowers: "The first flower is a Rose, the embleme of charity. For a Rose is hot in nature, it spreadeth it selfe abroad, and after it is full blowne scattereth both leaves and seeds; so charity is hot in the affection; spreadeth it selfe abroad by compassion, and scattereth seeds by almesdeeds." Similarly, the lily is the emblem of purity, and the violet of humility.[109] Another late sermon in our period represents a fiery heart as an emblem of a consecrated soul, a commonplace of its time. This is from Bishop Hacket's sixth sermon on the Baptism of Christ. He reports: "Truly did one say that the Emblem of a pious was, *Carbo ignitus divini amoris flamma absorptus*; a fiery coal wasting away all the gross and earthy parts of it with the flame of divine love."[110]

John Donne, according to Joan Webber, obtained many of his images from emblem books.[111] A common emblem, that he uses on at least three occasions, is that of a balance. Here is the use he makes of it in a Lincoln's Inn sermon:

If you value God, weigh God, you cannot give him halfe his weight; for you can put nothing into the balance, to weigh him withall, but all this world; and there is no single sand in the sea, no single dust upon the earth, no single atome in the ayre, that is not likelyer to weigh down all the world, then all the world is to counterpose God.[112]

10. Speculative doctrines and arcane knowledge

A fuller consideration of this characteristic distinction of metaphysical preaching will be given in chapter VI, "The Uses of Learning and Eloquence." Only the briefest consideration will be given in this section to speculative thinking and the scope of arcane learning.

Metaphysical preachers, especially those like Donne[113] familiar with and fond of the medieval schoolmen, were far more inclined to speculation than the strict Calvinist divines. But even Donne, like any staunch Calvinist, warned against prying into the secret counsels of God[114] though he himself often failed to take this advice. Convinced Calvinists contrasted the exclusiveness and profundity of divine knowledge with the superficiality of merely human guesses. For them *sola Scriptura* was the authority for doctrine, whereas in general for the metaphysical preachers nature, reason, and history, as well as the Scripture, were pointers to God.

Already we have mentioned the fondness of the metaphysicals for knowledge ancillary to the Scripture: patristic and classical scholarship and parallels uniting their insights; historical narrations and natural history of the legendary type such as Pliny provided. They also enjoyed recounting the Aesopian type of fable with moral application. Moreover, they read the many biblical commentators, ancient, medieval, and contemporary, in which the hermeneutical cruxes of the Bible were illuminated. They tried to reconcile them when possible, or to select the most appropriate option when the interpreters differed. The learned Puritan divines were equally familiar with these sources in exegetical illumination, and conveyed the insights to be culled from them in their sermons. They served the strong meat of the Gospel sauced with illustrations, without dragging their lexica, concordances, commonplaces, and patristic folios into their sermons.

When thinking of excursive speculation in sermons, one inevitably turns to Donne for his Faustian curiosity, even if, after his ordination, this was confined to scripture, patrology, hermetics, and the schoolmen. For example, he is fascinated by the guesses, from three sources in turn, on how to interpret "the messenger of Satan" in the Pauline letters. The possibilities include headache, gout, stomach-ache, heretics, and diabolical temptations.[115] On another occasion, he cites Origen to try to describe what is meant by the eternal generation of Christ, the Son of God.[116] On yet a third and typical occasion, using a suggestion of Justin Martyr's elaborated by Athenagoras, he wants to know what happens at the General Resurrection to a man's body which has been swallowed by a fish which, in its turn, is eaten by another man.[117]

There was considerable guessing about the nature of life after death and not only by Donne, whose morbid interest in death and vermiculation was equaled by a permanent fascination for "ouranology," as Hacket called the geography and architecture of heaven. Indeed Hacket himself says he rarely ventured into this area because of its difficulty. "It is," he said, "one of the most difficult tasks in Divinity to understand the several quarterings and mansion–places of heaven. I confess I am not skilled in Ouranography."[118]

Yet Barten Holyday outreaches even Donne in his speculations on eternal life. He delivered a remarkable Easter sermon, preached in St. Mary's Church, Oxford in 1623, on the text "Now is Christ risen from the dead and become the first-fruits of them that believe," (I Corinthians 15:20). After a description of how he thinks the Resurrection was experienced by Christ, he insists that souls and bodies will be reunited although there will be no marriage of the sexes. He suggests that critics will consider it impossible to gather the bodies of those eaten by cannibals who descended from ancestors similarly nourished, "for by this wild reckoning there will bee such a Genealogie of debt, that the bodie of the Nephew must peradventure be paid to the great Grand-father." He concludes that God has decreed there will never be a human body consisting wholly of other human bodies. The eager soul will be renewed in an adorned body: "Mankind shall feel and expresse a youthfull spring: the walking-staffe and the wrinkle shall bee no more the helpe and distinction of age."[119]

The other set of theological questions which led to uncertainty and therefore to some speculation was common to both metaphysical preachers and strict Puritans: those of Calling,

Election, Predestination, and Assurance. The Calvinist Fuller had a "travelling" sermon preached again and again to help the serious Christian decide whether he was truly called and elected by God, a problem which John Downame addressed in *Christian Warfare*. He offered ten "signes and infallible notes of our election."[120] Fuller's sermon on 2 Peter 1:10, "Give rather diligence to make your calling and election sure" provides a syllogistic answer to the problem:

> . . . a Christian thus collecteth this *Assurance* of his *Calling* and *Election* by composing this practicall *Syllogisme* in his soule.
>
> The Major : *He that truly repenteth himselfe of his sinnes, and relyeth with a true faith on God in Christ, is surely called, and by consequence Elected before all Eternity to be a vessel of honour.*
>
> The Minor : *But I truely repent myselfe of my sinnes, and rely with a true faith on God in Christ.*
>
> Conclusion : *Therefore I am truly Called and Elected, &.*[121]

Donne's fondness for philosophical and theological subtleties, many of which had been propounded and answered by St. Thomas Aquinas in the *Summa Theologica*, is well known.[122] His curiosity provides a natural bridge to arcane learning.

Thomas Goffe uses St. Paul's example as the authority for considering extra-biblical knowledge as being of value to Christians. He claims that Paul was "able to cite their owne Poets among the then learned Athenians, and to apply a Satyricall Verse out of *Epimenides*, to reprehend the lying, gluttonous and bestiall manners of the *Cretians*." He continues, "his powerfull language so ravish't the Lystrians, in the 14 of the *Acts*, that hee gain'd the repute of *Mercury* among them: and questionlesse, the sitting so long at the feet of Gamaliel, made him *vas electionis*. . . ."[123] Hacket too, according to his biographer, Dr. Thomas Plume, followed Origen in that "he made use of all Heathen Learning to adorn the Doctrine of Christianity."[124]

Andrewes insisted, paradoxically, on the biblical authority

for using the Apocrypha, simply because the Epistle of Jude uses information from the Book of Enoch.[125] Andrewes,[126] Donne, and Henry King among others, were glad to use rabbinic lore. John Chamberlin's *Increase and Multiply*[127] shows how Donne, in his fascination with the Divine Names, was intrigued by cabalistic studies derived from Notarikon in the *Essays in Divinity*.[128] Donne also alludes to the cabalistic device of Gematriya, in which not only words but syllables, letters, and points reveal mysterious meanings to the instructed, in a sermon preached as late as 1626.[129]

Henry King gladly acknowledges in the conclusion of his series of sermons on the Lord's Prayer that Rabbi Jehudah "thought the pronouncing of *Amen* so meritorious that hee who said *Amen* in this world, was worthy to say *Amen* in the next."[130] Other rabbis thought it so effectual when devoutly uttered that it would accelerate the time of their redemption.

The inexhaustibly curious Donne even refers to the Qu'ran to contradict its teaching:

> It was the poor way that *Mahomet* found out in his Alchoran, that in the next life all women should have eies of one bignesse, and a stature of one size; he could finde no means to avoid contention but to make them all alike: But that is thy complexion, that is thy proportion which God hath given thee.[131]

Hacket also provides Muslim lore, about which he raises some doubts. He believes, however, that on completing their pilgrimage to Mecca, the zealots "presently draw hot burning steel before their eyes to put them out, that they may never see any other spectacle after they have been honoured to see that Monumant [Tomb] of their Prophet."[132]

Donne, from the wealth of his travelling experience and his visually acute imagination, can provide much recondite geographical and marine information. He uses images indicating his knowledge of the North Sea passage,[133] and even of how whales are caught.[134]

11. Liturgical-devotional preaching

The final distinguishing characteristic of metaphysical preaching is the way in which Christian doctrine was related to the liturgical calendar, and the way this served to stimulate Christian devotion.

There are striking differences between the calendar[135] of the Roman Catholic Church, the Church of England, and the Puritan calendar of the Westminster Assembly days. For both Catholics and Anglicans, the calendar had a retrospective look: it was a permanent Christological reminder. Year after year, the calendar of these Churches renewed the remembrance of the mighty acts of the triune God in Creation, Redemption, and Sanctification. It centered on the climax of the Christian dispensation, the Incarnation. Preparation at Advent (with a brief prospective glance at the second Advent), the Nativity of Christ (God-as-Man), the Epiphany (Wise Men bringing their triple tribute), Lent (the Temptations of Christ) and climactic Holy Week, from the hollow triumph of Palm Sunday, through the Agony and Bloody Sweat of God on Good Friday, to the full triumph of Easter Day and the Resurrection. Then followed the Ascension at which the parabola of Christ's going "from God to God"[136] is completed by Pentecost, with the gift of the purifying, illuminating, and inspiring Holy Spirit, and Trinity Sunday. Thus the revelation of the Triune God, Father, Son, and Holy Spirit, was consummated.

The major calendric difference between the Church of Rome and the Church of England was that the former had many saints days celebrating the imitators of God in many lands and centuries, whereas the English Church celebrated exclusively the New Testament saints. This was amusingly reflected in a casual fashion by the observation: "One said to another that his face was like a popish almanack all holydayes because it was full of pimples."[137]

Continuing the same analogy, the Anglican's calendric complexion was clearer, while the Puritan's face was unspotted except for a blush. At the time of the Westminster Assembly, the Puritan calendar was prospective rather than retrospective. This sabbatarianism celebrated the Creation in which God rested on the seventh day, and looked forward to the Christian's future well earned rest in eternity. It also meant that each Sunday (changed from the Jewish sabbath to the day commemorating Christ's Resurrection) the devout would maintain a firm family and personal discipline of prayer, attendance at worship, and hearing the oracles of God preached. This would be followed by the master of each household testing the servants and the children on their recollection of the expository sermon (with its emphasis on doctrine, reason, and use); and the Lord's Day would conclude with family prayer and private spiritual account–taking. All this was appropriate for those who believed they were called to be saints in the New Testament sense of sanctification—a process, not an achievement.[138] The Puritan calendar was also contemporary in its insistence upon days of judgment and thanksgiving to acknowledge nationally, locally, or privately, the criticisms or comforts of God's providence, so strong a feature of Puritan diaries of this period.[139]

What were the contextual consequences for preaching? The Puritans could preach entire series of sermons, from individual books of the Bible or upon major Christian doctrines and their practical import, whenever they chose, and unhampered by the liturgical cycle. They disliked the official Anglican calendar because of the immoderate merriment that took place at the Christmas season—ending only on the twelfth night after the Nativity—and on May-day and -night. They loathed the beery buffoonery, bawdiness, and profanity that characterized such occasions. In particular, they disliked the profanation of the Lord's Day which, in their view, the royal Book of Sports (issued by James I in 1618 and renewed by Charles I in 1633) encouraged. Royalist Anglicans considered them occasions of jollity and harmless fun: Puritans as occasions of triviality if not worse.[140]

The Puritan system of lectureships[141] enabled the "silver-tongued" Henry Smith and others like him, denied the ceremonies of the Church of England, to supplement the leaner spiritual fare offered in many pulpits with the strong meat of the gospel, conveyed with all the power of their considerable eloquence.[142] Similarly the Puritan chaplains at the Inns of Court, like Preston and Sibbes, were not circumvented by ecclesiastical calendric conventions, because the lawyers' terms excluded the feast days.

On the other hand, the Christological cycle of the Church of England provided the opportunity for the metaphysical preachers to ring the changes on the great festivals. So we have Andrewes, Brownrig, Donne, and Hacket—to mention only the most outstanding metaphysical preachers—producing masterpieces of eloquence, doctrine, and devotion at Christmas, Easter, and Whitsunday (Pentecost), when their cathedral churches or the court chapel at Whitehall were filled with joyful listeners and communicants.

There were secular feast days also to commemorate. These included the accession days of the sovereigns, and days of thanksgiving for the deliverance of King James—the fifth of August (Gowrie Day), and the fifth of November when the king and Parliament were saved from the Gunpowder Plot. And the cavaliers, both during the Commonwealth and in the Restoration, kept January 30th as a sacred day, that of the "martyrdom" of Charles I in 1649.

Both Andrewes and Cosin almost always linked the liturgical lesson with the calendric context in their sermons. Most metaphysical preachers made much of the great Christological occasions of Christmas and Easter. Cosin regularly followed a method which Andrewes occasionally used.[143] He began by connecting the sermon matter with the calendar year; he then introduced the bidding prayer, and then gave out the text. This indissolubly united the feast or fast, the appropriate devotion, and the apt text. Even in a marriage sermon, Cosin remains liturgically loyal by expanding a passage from the Gospel lection for the day, the second Sunday after Epiphany.[144]

Donne's contribution to observing the Christian year, claims a modern Methodist minister, was massive.[145] As dean of St. Paul's Cathedral, he was required each year to preach on Christmas Day, Easter Day, and on Whitsunday for almost ten years. He also preached extra sermons on Candlemas, Lent, Trinity Sunday, and the day commemorating the conversion of St. Paul; nor should the prebendary sermons on the Psalms be forgotten, which he was also required to preach.[146] Donne records his grave sense of responsibility in a letter to Mrs. Cockain towards the end of his life:

> I was under a necessity of preaching twelve or fourteen solemn sermons every year, to great auditories at Paul's, and to the judges and at Court . . . You know the ticklishness of London pulpits.[147]

Donne used the term "complication," to describe the linking of the preacher's meditation on the text to the sacred occasion of the day.[148]

The contrast between the Calvinist ministers on the one hand, whose chief employment was as lecturers in parish churches or chaplains of the Inns of Court, and on the other hand the parish priests who became prebendaries, or deans, and in most cases Calvinist or Arminian bishops, is striking; and nowhere more so than in the number of calendric sermons in their total output. It can be most succinctly indicated by providing a comparative table. Henry Smith and Thomas Adams have been chosen to represent the first category; Andrewes, Brownrig, Cosin, and Hacket, the second. Broadly speaking, the first category averages less than 15% of calendric sermons, the second closer to 70%.

Henry Smith, it must be remembered, had "Decalogue Dod" as his mentor, a strict sabbatarian[149] who therefore objected to the Christian year but not to such topics as the Incarnation, the Atonement, and the Resurrection. Smith also had doubts about some of the ceremonies of the Church of England. While this did not prevent him from being ordained, as a lecturer he ran less risk than a parish incumbent who could have fallen

Table of the use of the Christological calendar in sermons

Total of collected sermons in print	Nativity or Epiphany	Lenten Passion	Easter	Ascension	Whitsun	Trinity (a) Transfiguration (b) All Saints (c) Candlemas (d) Conversion of St. Paul (e)	Total %	
Thomas Adams	63	4	1 + 2	1			1 (a)	9	14.3
Lancelot Andrewes	96	17	14 + 3	18		15		67	69.8
Ralph Brownrig	65	7	1	7	1	4	7 (b)	27	41.5
John Cosin (no Restoration sermons survive in print)	28	5	11	1	1	1		18	64.3
John Donne	160	8	11	10		10	7 (a) 1 (c) 5 (d) 4 (e)	56	35
Mark Frank	51								51
John Hacket	100	15	27 + 5 (6 Baptism, 21 Temptation)	9		5	7 (b)	70	70
Joseph Hall	42	2 Advent	6 + 1	1		4	2 (d)	16	26.25
Arthur Lake	109	14	1	2		3	1 (a)	21	19.2
Henry Smith	37	4	5			2	1 (a)	12	32.4

foul of his bishop despite his influence with Cecil. However, his wealth saved him from the necessity of a parochial charge.

Thomas Adams, as a lecturer for much of his life and as preacher at St. Gregory's near Paul's Wharf, London, only had parochial responsibility for part of his life and was sequestered by Cromwell's Triers. Adams however did say, as a clear indication of his approval of the Church of England calendar, that Faith, Hope, and Charity correspond to the three festivals of the Christian year.[150] Oddly enough, though, he linked Faith (not Hope) with Easter, Hope with Whitsun (because of the transformation possible), and Charity with Christmas (although Augustine had taught that the Holy Spirit was the bond of Charity—*vinculum caritatis*—in the Holy Trinity).

All that requires comment on the part of the others is the great importance attached by Bishops Brownrig and Hacket to the Transfiguration, presumably because it links Old and New Testaments, and anticipates the glory that will be Christ's on the other side of his Passion and Death. It also shows his sacred servant role in descending to the Valley of Humiliation from the Mount of Transfiguration.

Finally, we note that Andrewes, Cosin,[151] and Hacket preach more calendric than other sermons, amounting to approximately two-thirds of their total output. Their eloquence rose to its highest peak on these great festal occasions. A sense of their mid-century importance is conveyed by Davenant in the preface to his play *Gondibert,* where he writes:

> Divines . . . are the Tetrarchs of Time, of which they command the fourth Division, for to no less the Sabboths and Daies of Saints amount, and during these daies of spiritual Triumph Pulpits are Thrones, and the People oblig'd to open their Eares. . . .

In conclusion, the eleven characteristics we have isolated did not distinguish all of the sermons, of all of the metaphysical preachers, all of the time. They were exemplified, however, by most of them, most of the time. Taken together, they provide an index to the theological breadth of reference during this period; the biblical, patristic, and classical learning; the controversial zest; the imaginative brilliance in wit and illustration; and the devotional spirit and sense of charity that marked the golden age of the English pulpit.

NOTES

1. Samuel Johnson, *The Lives of the Poets*, ed. G. B. Hill, 3 vols. (London, 1903), 1: 20.

2. Epistle Dedicatory to *Eleanora*, third paragraph.

3. "Discourse concerning Satire," *The Poems of John Dryden*, ed. James Kinsley, 4 vols. (Oxford, 1958), 2: 604.

4. H.J.C. Grierson, *Metaphysical Lyrics and Poems of the Seventeenth Century* (Oxford, 1922), xvi. Here Grierson speaks of "the peculiar blend of passion and thought, feeling and ratiocination, which is their greatest achievement."

5. Earl Miner, *The Metaphysical Mode from Donne to Cowley* (Princeton, N.J., 1969), 47. Here Miner writes: "The chief literary radical of metaphysical poetry is, whatever the qualifications, its private mode."

6. Samuel Clarke, *A Collection of the Lives of Ten Eminent Divines* (London, 1662), 253–254.

7. Richard Baxter, *The Saints Everlasting Rest* (London, 1650), 368. One may contrast this with Luther's assertion that if there were no laughter in heaven, he would not wish to go there.

8. Richard Sibbes, *The Bruised Reede and the Smoaking Flax* (London, 1630), 1: 53–54, quoted in J. K. Knott, Jr., *The Sword of the Spirit: Puritan Responses to the Bible* (Chicago, 1980), 185.

9. See Laurence Sasek, *The Literary Temper of the English Puritans* (Baton Rouge, Louisiana, 1967) for the range from plain to moderately ornamental in Puritan pulpit styles.

10. William Perkins, in *The Workes of that famous and worthie Minister of Christ, in the Universitie of Cambridge, M. W. Perkins . . .* 3 vols., (London, 1613), 2: 673. Perkins says the minister "may, yea and must privately use at his libertie the arts, Philosophy and variety of reading, whilest he is framing his sermon: but he ought in publike to conceal all these from the people, and not make the least ostentation. Artis etiam est celare artem: it is also a point of art to conceal art." He ruled out the use of Greek or Latin phrases because they distract the minds of the auditors, and the telling of stories and reciting of profane or ridiculous speeches. The most suitable style for a preacher,

89

said Thomas Cartwright, was "a speech both simple and perspicuous, fit both for the peoples understanding, and to expresse the Maiestie of the Spirit," (*A Dilucidation or Exposition of the Apostle St. Paul to the Colossians*, ed. A. B. Grosart, 6.) Perkins, however, approved of illuminating (not obfuscating) metaphors and exempla as sermon illustrations.

11. William Perkins, *A Golden Chaine* (London, 1600), 1. Perkins, according to Thomas Fuller's *The Holy State* (London, 1681), 81, was said to have preached so that "his sermons were not so plain but that the piously learned did admire them, nor so learned but that the plain did understand them."

12. Clarke, *A Collection of the Lives of Ten Eminent Divines*, 285.

13. Quoted in Izaak Walton, *The Life of John Donne* (London, 1658), 145.

14. Henry King, *An Exposition Upon the Lords Prayer. Delivered in certaine Sermons in the Cathedrall Church of S. Paul* (London, 1628), 46.

15. See P. G. Stanwood, "Patristic and Contemporary Borrowing in the Caroline Divines" in *Renaissance Quarterly*, 23 (1970): 421–449.

16. Andrewes, *XCVI Sermons* (London, 1629), 547.

17. Andrewes, *XCVI Sermons*, 551.

18. For example, in *A Sermon preached at Hampton Court 23 Sept. 1606* (London, 1606), he has thirty-eight brief patristic references.

19. As in the 1588 Spital sermon of twenty-six pages, which has twenty-one patristic references. There are thirteen references to Augustine (chiefly citations), two Greek citations from Chrysostom, and single references or brief citations from Jerome, Cyprian, and Gregory, and two to unnamed Fathers. The sermon is among those bound in with the *XCVI Sermons* at the end.

20. *The Sermons of John Donne*, eds. George R. Potter and Evelyn M. Simpson, 10 vols. (Berkeley, 1953–1962), 4: 74–75.

21. Donne, *Sermons*, 1: 259.

22. The statistics will be found in 10: 367. There is also the estimate that Donne has about 2200 biblical citations and 700 citations or references to Augustine, by far the most popular Father for Donne, who resembles him in his wild youth, and in his mastery of rhetoric and imagination.

23. *The Workes of Tho: Adams* (London, 1629), 123.

24. William Barlow, *One of the Foure Sermons Preached before the Kings Maiestie at Hampton Court in September last. This Concerning the Antiquitie and Superioritie of Bishops. Sept. 21, 1606* (London, 1606). His sermon

Christian Libertie, preached prior to his consecration but printed in 1606, has thirty-three references in all, Calvin having the lion's share with fourteen extensive citations from the *Institutes.*

25. *The Collected Sermons of Thomas Fuller, D.D.,* eds. J. E. Bailey and W.E.A. Axon, 2 vols. (London, 1891), 1: 311. It comes from *A Sermon of Reformation Preached at the Church of the Savoy, last Fast day, July 27, 1643.*

26. Homer is cited in "Christs Wounds Our Health" (1598), and Martial in "God be with you" (1604), both court sermons.

27. Horace is cited in "The Sacrifice of Thankfulnesse" (1616) and Ovid in "Heaven and Earth Reconciled" (1613).

28. *The Workes of Tho: Adams,* 50.

29. Henry King, *An Exposition Upon the Lords Prayer.* The references to Homer will be found on 314 and 340, those to Horace on 157 and 229, and the references to Ovid and Virgil on 314, and to Juvenal on 114.

30. John Gauden, *Three Sermons Preached upon Severall Publike Oaccasions* (London, 1642), 63, 77, and 130. There are several references to Homer in Gauden's *Kakouroi* (London, 1659).

31. John Howson has two references to Juvenal in *A Sermon preached at Paules Crosse the 4 of December 1597* (London, 1597), which was a criticism of simony, and two further references to Juvenal in *A Sermon preached at St. Maries in Oxford the 17. Day of November, 1602* (second impression, London, 1603). Virgil, Juvenal, and Horace, as well as Plautus and Pindar, are each cited once in *A Second Sermon preached at Paules Crosse the 21 of May, 1598* (London, 1598). This particular sermon has a total of ninety-four references in fifty-two pages.

32. Thomas Goffe has a reference to Virgil in a Spital sermon, *Deliverance from the Grave* (London, 1627).

33. Thomas Playfere, *The Whole Sermons* (London, 1623), 8. It is from "Hearts Delight," a Paul's Cross sermon of 1603.

34. Thomas Playfere, *The Pathway to Perfection. A Sermon preached at Saint Maries Spittle in London on Wednesday in Easter-Weeke* (London, 1593), 6.

35. Also from "The Pathway to Perfection" in Playfere, *The Whole Sermons,* 177.

36. Yet again from "The Pathway to Perfection" in Playfere, *The Whole Sermons,* 185.

37. From John Wall, *The Lion in the Lambe, Or, Strength in Weakness* (Oxford, 1628), 48–49. See also Wall's *Christ in Progresse* (Oxford, 1627),

34–35, for a parallel between Telemachus in Athens and Christ in Jerusalem.

38. Andrewes, *XCVI Sermons*, 717, from a sermon preached at Holyrood Castle, Edinburgh, on Whitsunday, 1617 before King James.

39. Josiah Shute, *Sarah and Hagar: Or, Genesis the sixteenth Chapter opened in XIX Sermons* (London, 1649), 180, and from a sermon originally delivered on 19 January 1641/2.

40. Henry King, *An Exposition Upon the Lords Prayer*, 32, 33.

41. Hacket, *A Century of Sermons Upon Severall Remarkable Subjects* (London, 1675), 273.

42. See G. R. Owst, *Literature and Pulpit in Medieval England* (rev. edn., Oxford, 1961), 186–190. Pliny's *The Natural History* (in thirty-seven books) was ably Englished by Philemon Holland in 1601.

43. *The Workes of Tho: Adams*, 420. It is from the sermon, "The Spiritual Navigator Bound for the Holy Land."

44. *The Workes of Tho: Adams*, 869.

45. Andrewes, *XCVI Sermons*, 793. From "A Sermon preached before the Kings Maiestie at Holdenbie, 5. Aug. 1608."

46. Hacket, *A Century of Sermons*, 618. Playfere's exemplum comes from "Christs Wounds our Health" in *Nine Sermons* (London, 1621), 111–112.

47. Donne, *Sermons*, 2: 69. For other examples see 5: 233, 6: 85, and 10: 161.

48. *The Works of the Right Reverend Father-in-God John Cosin*, Volume 1: *Sermons* (Oxford, 1843), the conclusion to the Ninth Sermon.

49. See Owst, *Literature and Pulpit in Medieval England*, 202.

50. Playfere, *The Sermons* (London, 1616), 162. From the 1593 sermon, "The Pathway to Perfection."

51. William Barlow, *One of Foure Sermons Preached before the Kings Maiestie* (London, 1606), sig. C1.

52. Brownrig, *Sixty Five Sermons* (London, 1674), 247.

53. *The Sermons of Maister Henrie Smith* (London, 1593), 225–226.

54. *The Sermons of Maister Henrie Smith*, 593.

55. Robert Willan, *Eliahs's Wish: A Prayer for Death. A Sermon preached at the Funerall of the Right Honourable Viscount Sudbury, Lord Bayning* (London, 1630), 2.

56. Donne, *Sermons*, 10: 186.

57. Donne, *Sermons*, 7: 55. Other examples of Donne's "unnatural" history can be found in 9: 299, and 4: 339.

58. Hacket, *A Century of Sermons*, 749.

Chapter II

59. Henry King, *A Sermon Preached at Pauls Crosse, the 25 of November, 1621* (London, 1621), 4.

60. *The Workes of that learned and reverend Divine, John White, Doctor in Divinitie* (London, 1624), 13. From a Paul's Cross sermon delivered 24 March 1615.

61. Andrewes, *XCVI Sermons*, 680. From a Whitsunday sermon preached before the king at Greenwich in 1615.

62. Playfere, *The Sermons*, 175. From the Spital sermon, "The Pathway to Perfection."

63. Hacket, *A Century of Sermons*, 448.

64. Barten Holyday, *Motives to A Good Life in Ten Sermons* (Oxford, 1657), 52. See 24 for another example. In the fourth sermon on "God's Husbandry" Holyday uses Greek etymology (97, 103), Latin (97), and Hebrew (103).

65. Andrewes, *XCVI Sermons*, 455. From an Easter sermon before king and court, 1612. Other examples can be found on 36, 46, 77, 200, 404, 635, and 960–961.

66. Andrewes, *XCVI Sermons*, 455. From a sermon on Ash Wednesday, 1622, preached before the king and court.

67. Cassian, *Collationes*, XIV, 8.

68. John 10:5.

69. John 15:7b, 9.

70. *The Works of . . . John Cosin*, Volume 1: *Sermons*, 255.

71. *The Workes of Tho: Adams*, 1036–1045.

72. *The Workes of Tho: Adams*, 656f. Among several allegorical sermons see "Loves Copie" (815), "Eirenopolis: The Citie of Peace" (995–1015), and "Mysticall Bedlam, Or, The World of Mad-Men" which includes a series of nineteen "characters" from Epicure to Vain-glorious (478–514).

73. Donne, *Sermons*, 10:141–142.

74. Hacket, *A Century of Sermons*, 731–741. This was evidently the pattern of court preachers, since, in similar fashion, Andrewes preached the ninth of his Gunpowder sermons (before King James and the court on 5 November 1617) from the Benedictus, applying the text first to salvation in Christ—Simeon's confession of the messiahship of the infant Jesus—but went on to apply it to the king and the nation's temporal salvation from the Gunpowder Plot (*XCVI Sermons*, 983–996.)

75. The Puritan structuring of sermons is analyzed by William Perkins in his influential *The Arte of Prophesying*, contained in the

complete *Workes*, 2: 673. Perry Miller has attributed it exclusively to Ramist influence in his *The New England Mind: the Seventeenth Century* (New York, 1939), 338f, but there are some likenesses to the classical rhetoric of the modern modified kind also.

The Westminster *Directory* offers the following triple *schema* for preachers: "In raising doctrines from the text, his care ought to be, First, that the matter be the truth of God. Secondly, that it be a truth contained in, or grounded on, that text that the hearers may discern how God teacheth it from thence. Thirdly, that he chiefly insist upon those doctrines which are principally intended, and make most for the edification of the hearers" (*Reliquiae Liturgicae* [Bath, England, 1848], vol. 3: *Directory*, 37.)

Thomas Fuller's earlier style is described by his anonymous biographer thus: "But the main frame of his publique SERMONS, if not wholy, consisted (after some briefe and genuine resolution of the Context and Explication of the Termes, where need required), of Notes, and Observations with much variety and great dexterity drawn immediately from the Text, and naturally and without restraint, issuing or flowing either from the maine body, or from the several parts of it, with some useful Applications annexed thereunto . . ." (*The Life of that Reverend Divine, and Learned Historian Dr. Thomas Fuller* [London, 1661], 79–80.)

76. Playfere, *The Whole Sermons*, 3. Although the sermon was preached in 1595, it was published posthumously in 1623.

77. Andrewes, *XCVI Sermons*, 45.

78. John Gauden, *The Love of Truth and Peace. A Sermon Preached before the Honourable House of Commons Assembled in Parliament Novemb. 29, 1640* (London, 1641), 5.

79. John Gauden, *KAKOYRIOI, sive Medicastri: Slight Healers of Publick Hurts set forth in a Sermon Preached in St. Pauls Church, London . . . Febr. 28, 1659* (London, 1660), 9–10.

80. See the descriptions of the styles of Cicero and of Seneca on 236 and 975 of *The Oxford Classical Dictionary*, 2nd edn., ed. N.G.L. Hammond and H. H. Scullard (London, 1970).

81. See I Corinthians 1:17: "For Christ sent me not to baptize, but to preach the gospel: not with wisdom of words, lest the Cross of Christ be made of no effect." See also I Corinthians 2:4.

82. Donne, *Sermons*, 2: 248.

83. Donne, *Sermons*, 2: 315.

84. Brownrig, *Sixty Five Sermons*, 83. From the fifth Transfiguration sermon.

85. Thomas Morton, *The Presentment of a Schismaticke* (London, 1642), 15. Preached at St. Paul's Cathedral on 19 June 1642.

86. Thomas Morton, *A Sermon Preached before the Kings Most Excellent Majestie, in the Cathedrall Church of Durham* (London, 1639), 3. The sermon was preached on 5 May 1639, when King Charles was on his way to Scotland.

87. For the pointed Senecan style of the Latin Silver Age, see Michael Grant, *Greek and Latin Authors, 800 B.C.-A.D. 1000* (New York, 1980), 388.

88. J. Huizinga, *The Waning of the Middle Ages* (New York, 1944), 203.

89. Ralph Venning, *Orthodoxe Paradoxes* (5th ed., London, 1650), 24.

90. The Westminster Assembly's *Shorter Catechism* goes: "What is the true end of man?" and answers: "To glorify God and to enjoy him for ever."

91. G. Puttenham, *The Arte of English Poesie*, eds. Gladys D. Wilcock and Alice Walker (Cambridge, 1936), 225–226.

92. Rosalie L. Colie, *Paradoxia Epidemica* (Princeton, 1956), 22.

93. Thomas Jackson, *Three Sermons preached before the King upon Ier. 26.19* (Oxford, 1637).

94. Arthur Lake, *Ten Sermons upon Severall Occasions, Preached at Saint Pauls Crosse and elsewhere* (London, 1640), 130–131.

95. Judges 14:14 and 14:18.

96. Brownrig, *Sixty Five Sermons*, 281.

97. *The Collected Sermons of Thomas Fuller*, 1: 198.

98. Francis Quarles, *Emblemes* (London, 1635), sig. A3, defines an emblem as "but a silent Parable," using a pointedly religious term.

99. Mario Praz, *Studies in Seventeenth-Century Imagery*, 2nd edn., revised and enlarged (Rome, 1964), 17.

100. Praz, *Studies in Seventeenth-Century Imagery*, 55.

101. *Euphues*, eds. M. W. Croll and R. Clemens (London, 1916), *passim*.

102. Rosemary Freeman, *English Emblem Books* (London, 1948), 3–4.

103. The article, referred to by Rosemary Freeman in *English Emblem Books*, is "Quarles and the Emblem Habit," in *Dublin Review*, 188, (1931): 80–96.

104. Louis L. Martz, *The Poetry of Meditation: A Study in English Religious Literature of the Seventeenth Century* (New Haven, 1954).

105. Barbara Kiefer Lewalski, *Protestant Poetics and the Seventeenth Century Religious Lyric* (Princeton, N.J., 1979).

106. Lewalski, *Protestant Poetics*, 184f. This was the triple classification adopted by Georgette de Montenay's *Emblèmes ou Devises Chrestiennes* (1571), the first French Protestant book of sacred emblems, and of George Whitney's *A Choice of Emblemes and other Devises* (London, 1586), the first English book of its kind.

107. Playfere, *The Whole Sermons*, 155. Other emblems in Playfere are found on 161 ". . . a Crabfish and a Butterflie, with this Mot, Soft pace goes farre"; a *festina lente* warning(131); and in "God be with you," a royal sermon of 1604 (54).

108. *The Sermons of Maister Henrie Smith*, 51.

109. Daniel Featley, *Clavis Mystica: A Key opening divers difficult and mysterious texts of Holy Scripture, handled in Seventy Sermons* (London, 1636), 290. He rather improbably derives the humility of the violet etymologically *ab humo*, from the earth.

110. Hacket, *A Century of Sermons*, 199.

111. Joan Webber, *Contrary Music: The Prose Style of John Donne* (Madison, Wisconsin, 1963), 81.

112. Donne, *Sermons*, 3: 95. The balances emblem image is explicit in 3: 95; it is implicit in 9: 135 and 137.

113. See Donne, *Sermons*, 8: sermon 1, and 6: sermon 3.

114. Donne, *Sermons*, 5: 298.

115. Donne, *Sermons*, 5: 374.

116. Donne, *Sermons*, 1: 293.

117. Donne, *Sermons*, 3: 96–97.

118. Hacket, *A Century of Sermons*, 1000.

119. Barten Holyday, *Three Sermons upon the Passion, Resurrection and Ascension of our Saviour, preached at Oxford* (London, 1626), 55, 65–66.

120. The signs of the assurance of election will be found in John Downame's *Christian Warfare* (London, 1604), 235–247.

121. Thomas Fuller, *A Sermon of Assurance. Foureteene yeares ago Preached in Cambridge, since in other Places. Now by the importunity of Friends exposed to publike view* (London, 1647). It was first preached in St. Benet's, Cambridge, later at St. Clement's, London where Fuller was lecturer. It was reprinted in *The Collected Sermons of Thomas Fuller, D.D.*, 1: 475.

122. For example, how angels recognize one another, whether they were created before the world or after it, if they age or not, and what their hierarchical orders are. These are discussed in Donne, *Sermons* 8: sermon 1, 94f., and in 6: sermon 3, 331f, among other places.

123. Thomas Goffe, *Deliverance from the Grave*, a Spital sermon preached on 28 March 1627.

124. Hacket, *A Century of Sermons*, biographical introduction, xiii.

125. Andrewes, *XCVI Sermons*, 31. From a sermon preached at St. Giles, Cripplegate, London in 1592, on the Second Commandment.

126. See also Andrewes, *XCVI Sermons*, 31.

127. The full title is *Increase and Multiply: Arts-of-Discourse Procedure in the Preaching of Donne* (Chapel Hill, N.C., 1976), 106f.

128. Donne's *Essays in Divinity*, ed. E. M. Simpson (Oxford, 1952), 91.

129. Donne, *Sermons*, 9: sermon 2.

130. Henry King, *An Exposition Upon the Lords Prayer*, 361.

131. Donne, *Sermons*, 2: 243.

132. Hacket, *A Century of Sermons*, 93. This is from Hacket's tenth sermon on the Incarnation.

133. Donne, *Sermons*, 6: 212.

134. Donne, *Sermons*, 5: 199–200.

135. See H. Davies, *Worship and Theology in England*, 5 vols. (Princeton, N.J., 1961–1975), 2: chapter 6, 215–252, "Calendary Conflicts, Holy Days or Holidays." See also Howard Happ, "Calendary Conflicts in Renaissance England," (Ph.D. dissertation, Princeton University, 1974) for a more comprehensive study of the same topic.

136. John 13:3: "Jesus knowing that the Father had given all things into his hands and that he was come from God, and went to God, took a towel and girded himself" to wash the feet of the disciples.

137. R. Chamberlain's collection of *Conceits, Clinches, Flashes and Whimsies newly studied* (London, 1639), No. 38. The reference to this volume I owe to Professor Paul Zall of California State University at Los Angeles.

138. See Edmund Morgan, *Visible Saints; the History of an Idea* (New York, 1963). See also Winton Udell Solberg, *Redeem the Time: the Puritan Sabbath in Early America* (Cambridge, Mass., 1977).

139. *Two Puritan Diaries, by Richard Rogers and Samuel Ward*, ed. with an introduction by M. M. Knappen (Chicago, 1933).

140. See Christopher Hill, *Society and Puritanism in pre-Revolutionary England*, 2nd edn. (New York, 1967), 160f., for proof that the establishment preferred the common man to disport himself at a tavern than to attend a Puritan religious lecture (shown by the case of the Somerset ales).

141. *The Activities of the Puritan Faction of the Church of England, 1625–*

1633, ed. Isabel M. Calder (London, 1957), and John D. Eusden, *Puritans, Lawyers and Politics in Early Seventeenth Century England* (New Haven, 1958).

142. For Puritan sermons, see William Haller, *The Rise of Puritanism; or The Way to the New Jerusalem as Set Forth in Pulpit and Press, from . . . 1570–1643* (New York, 1938). For "political" sermons, see John F. Wilson, *Pulpit in Parliament* (Princeton, N.J., 1969). For Puritan exegesis, see J. S. Coolidge, *The Pauline Renaissance in England: Puritanism and the Bible* (Oxford, 1970).

143. Andrewes' sermons which follow this pattern of interruption of the sermon by a bidding prayer are nos. 2 and 3, in his *XCVI Sermons*. Heylyn and Basire also did so on rare occasions. See also *The Works of . . . John Cosin,* 1: introduction, vii.

144. *The Works of . . . John Cosin*, 1: 44.

145. F. A. Rowe, *I Launch at Paradise* (London, 1964), 173.

146. See Janel Mueller, *Prebend Sermons* (Cambridge, Mass., 1971).

147. In Izaak Walton's *Life of Donne*, 75.

148. Donne, *Sermons*, 9: sermon 5, lines 74–76, as noted by J. S. Chamberlin in *Increase and Multiply*, 17.

149. Smith at least sympathises with sabbatarianism. See *The Sermons of Maister Henrie Smith*, 841:

he which will not allowe men to prophane the Saboth, but saith, that Cardes & dice, & stage plaies, & Maigames, & May poales, & May-fooles, and Morris-dauncers are *vanitie*, is a pratler, a disturber, an Arch-pustan, by the lawe which the Iewes had to kill Christ, the reason is, because men cannot be controlled of their pleasures.

150. *The Workes of Tho: Adams*, the sermon entitled, "The Three Divine Sisters."

151. We have part of Cosin's sermons only, including those he delivered in Paris during the Commonwealth and Protectorate, *coram Duce Iacobo*. We can confidently guess this distinguished liturgiologist would have continued to preach liturgical sermons during the Restoration.

Chapter III

METAPHYSICAL WIT

A CYNIC MAY DEFINE PREACHING as talking in other people's sleep. The English metaphysical preachers were determined that their congregations, captive as they were, should not be bored, whether in the chapel at Whitehall with the king and courtiers making up the congregation, or in the college chapels at the universities of Oxford and Cambridge, or in the cathedrals and larger London parish churches. Hence their delight in and full employment of wit in the pulpit. The term, it need hardly be stressed, had a wider reference than our modern usage. It meant both intelligence in general, as well as fanciful ingenuity—the ability to instruct, delight, and amuse; and its equivalents were εὐφυΐα, *ingenium*, *bel ingegno*, and *bel esprit*. In writing of wit, it will not be possible to deal with the subject without reference to recondite learning, to imagery in general and to conceits in particular.[1] The following sections give some indication of the types of wit to be found in the metaphysical sermon.

The conceit

The most dominant type of wit was the farfetched conceit, intended as a mind-expanding and imagination-stretching analogy. It was, as Spingarn points out, a European-wide fashion, probably originating in Spain, immensely popular in Italy and indeed known there as the *concetto predicabile*, and the *conception théologique* in France.[2] It was a transference of euphuism to the pulpit[3] and it continued in England for some sixty years from the 1580s to the late 1630s, with a few die-hard practitioners surviving into the Restoration.

From the outset it was recognized that comparisons could become too bizarre. Henry Peacham, in *The Garden of Eloquence*, already by 1593 felt it necessary to warn against possible absurdity—of seeing unfit likenesses, as for example saying "the barking of a bull," or of using comparisons too farfetched and strange, "as if one should take the Metaphors from the parts of a Ship, and apply them among husbandmen which never came at the sea."[4] And Francis Meres, in the second part of *Wits Commonwealth* (1634), wanted to see "Truthes soundnesse in Sentences, her elegancie in Similitudes."[5]

Examples of farfetched conceits are easy to find. Here is Thomas Adams, misnamed by Southey the "Puritan prose Shakespeare." He was no Puritan, as his exposition of the words of the Canticles, "Stay me with flagons, and comfort me with apples, for I am sick of love," indicates:

> Come to this Wine, *Bibite & inebriamini . . . drinke and be drunke with it.* God will be pleased with this (and no other but this *Drunkennesse*). The vessel of our heart being once thus filled with grace, shall hereafter bee replenished with glorie.[6]

In another sermon Adams is again determined to shock us. He uses the image of God's Word as a Balm tree. "We finde the *eternall Word* so compared. He is a *Tree,* but *arbor inversa:* the roote of this tree is Heaven."[7] He also provides a double and contrary conceit in his sermon entitled, "The Black Saint, Or, the Apostate":

> The *White Devill,* the *Hypocrite* hath been formerly discover'd, and the sky-colour'd vaile of his *dissimulation* pulled off. I am to present to your view and detestation, a sinner of a contrary colour, swarthy rebellion and besmeared *Profaneness:* an *Apostate* falling into the clutches of eight *uncleane spirits . . .* If *Hypocrisie* there were iustly called the

White Devill; Apostacie here may as iustly bee termed the
Black Saint. [8]

Thomas Jackson, dean of Peterborough, uses the daring image
of a polygamous Christ, which he sees typologically fore-
shadowed in the multitude of David's wives. In the same sermon
he continues:

> *Howsoever, as the desolate hath more children then she that hath
> an husband,* so are the spouses of this chaste and *holy one,*
> more in number, then the wives and concubines of luxuri-
> ous *Salomon.* Hee is that everlasting bridegroome whose
> Courts no multiplicitie of consorts can pollute: there is
> no sowle, so it bring faith for its dowrie, but may be as-
> suredly espowsed to him.[9]

Thomas Playfere has a very farfetched conceit when he is expounding the cloven tongues of fire that descended upon the
disciples at Pentecost. His racy and colloquial speech must be
cited:

> They had cloven tongues. Cloven tongues? What's that?
> I'le tell you. Doe you not see how our hands are cloven
> and divided into fingers? They (in a manner, if I may so
> say) had fingers upon their tongues, as well as we have
> upon our hands.[10]

And Henry Smith, another of the earliest metaphysical preachers, and a Calvinist, preached a sermon entitled, "The Young
Mans Taske," which has this startling conclusion: "For God
requiring the first borne for his offering, and the first fruits
for his service, requireth the first labours of his servants, and
as I may say, the maidenhead of every man."[11]

It seems significant to me that I have cited these examples
of exotic conceits from two High Church and two Low Church
or Puritan Anglicans. It makes it abundantly clear that W. F.
Mitchell's description of the Anglo-Catholic preachers is doubly
erroneous. First, it is anachronistic to describe any seventeenth-

century group of Anglicans as Anglo-Catholics; and second, the assumption that hardly any Anglican Calvinist ministers use the metaphysical mode of preaching is not tenable.[12] Ralph Brownrig, John King, Henry King, John Hacket, Henry Smith, and Thomas Adams—to mention some renowned Calvinist examples—all do so.

Puns and paronomasia

The second type of wit was wordplay, either punning or paranomasia, of which metaphysical sermons are full. They can be found amongst the learned preachers in Latin commonly, Greek rarely, and most frequently in English. Donne was particularly fond of the pun he made on the second person of the Trinity, whom he called both "Son" and "Sun," which enabled him to make Christ's Incarnation the Dawn, and his Crucifixion the Setting, and his Resurrection the re-Rising of the Son.[13] Another favourite pun of Donne's was the ordinance of God, preaching, which is also the divine artillery, or ordnance.[14] A third pun, common in metaphysical preaching, played upon the contrast between those who prayed and those who preyed upon others; this third pun was employed by both Andrewes and Adams. It is interesting to compare the treatment of the pun by the two divines. Andrewes is discussing hypocrisy, which he derives from the Greek word which means a stage-player, and makes another pun in saying "It is a very fitt *resemblance* for them, that are nothing but *resemblance*."[15] On Ash Wednesday 1619 he asks his congregation (which included James I) to consider Matthew, chapter 23: "Will you see *Prayer* playd? Looke upon the *Players* . . . that under the colour of a *long prayer*, now and then *prey upon the houses and goods* of a sort of seduced *widowes*: and make as good gaine of their Prayers, as *Iudas* would have done of his *Almes*."[16] Adams makes a less subtle use of the pun: "There be many that pray in the Temple, who yet also prey on the Temple."[17]

Classical sources, that is the Latin Fathers such as Augustine, or Ambrose, or Gregory, or Bernard, were full of examples of Latin puns or paranomasia. Bishop Brownrig, the Calvinist, explains the failure of Peter to walk upon the Sea of Galilee by saying it wasn't his feet but his faith that failed him, contrasting *pedes* with *fides*.[18] Bishop Barlow preached at Paul's Cross on the first Sunday in Lent, 1600, immediately after the execution of the Earl of Essex. Of Essex's written and verbal confession to him, he says that he has only to inform the congregation of what he has seen with his own eyes, and heard with his own ears; and he manages to be witty in Latin. He declares that his aim was "onely to declare what I have eyther *ex occulo*, or *oraculo*, as Bern. [ard] speaketh, from his owne writing, and confession to us."[19] A happy example comes from Andrewes, who contrasts the worldling's hope with that of the Christian thus: "The carnall man, all he can say is, *dum spiro spero:* his hope is as long as his breath. The Christian aspireth higher . . . and saith, *dum expiro spero:* his hope fails him not, when his breath failes him."[20] Again the same pair of Latin tags is used by Adams—borrowed from Andrewes presumably, more pithily but without the pun of "aspireth" which Andrewes employed. Here is the brief version of Adams: "Therefore *dum spiro, spero,* says the Heathen: but *dum expiro, spero,* sayes the Christian. The one, whilest I live, I hope; the other also when I dye, I hope. . . ."[21]

Andrewes, the multilingual scholar, is, as we might expect, an expert in Greek paranomasia. One example must suffice. He is playing with three Greek words: λατρεῦσαι, to serve; λύτρον, delivery or ransom; and λάτρον, recompense or reward. He becomes excessively pedantic when he says:

And so I returne now to the word of our *service,* the word of our Text, λατρεῦσαι. In λατρεῦσαι there is λάτρον: And λάτρον, is a recompense or reward. Gods service is λατρεία. *Delivered* we are, by Covenant: of His great bountie, Rewarded we shall be beside. It is in the very body of the Word (this.)

So heer is λύτρον and λάτρον: λύτρον in our delivery,

and λάτρον in our recompense. Let one of them, λύτρον or λάτρον: or, if not, one of them, both of them prevaile with us, to see *Him served.* [22]

From Andrewes being pedantic and periphrastic, we turn to him using a pun with great subtlety and substance. In a sermon for Christmas Day he recalls that the term "mystery" means both a trade and a divine revelation concentrated in a sacrament. His text is "And without controversie, great is the Mysterie of Godlinesse . . ." (I Timothy 3:16). He begins in this way: "The Mysterie . . . is the *Mysterie* of this *Feast;* and this *Feast,* the *Feast* of this *Mysterie:* for, as at the *Feast, GOD was manifested in the flesh.* In that it is a great *Mysterie,* it maketh the *Feast great.* In that it is a *Mysterie of Godlinesse,* it should make it likewise a *Feast of Godlinesse.*" Then Andrewes draws the further consequence in the pun: "For, hearing that it is so *great,* & of so *great* availe *rising* by it, . . . a trade so beneficial, it makes us seek, how to incorporate ourselves . . . how to have our *part* and fellowship in this *Trade* or *Mysterie.*" Finally, he insists that the real purpose of a mystery is its operation and effect: "And *work,* it doth; els *Mysterie* it is none . . . If you ask what it is, to *work?* . . . It is to make that, it workes on, like it selfe."[23] Clearly the pun is a ligature in the logic, and in using it Andrewes has been able to provide an entire theology of the sacraments, apt on one of the three Sundays of the year when the reception of Holy Communion was mandatory.

Since Andrewes has been quoted so often to the disadvantage of Adams, fairness dictates that we give a sustained example of the latter's paronomasia as wordplay. He is explaining how God, who has already attempted to reach the heedlessly opulent person by sermons, judgments on himself, and crosses on others, will finally catch him by the words, "This night thy soul shall be required of thee":

He will be understood, though not stood under. *Vociferat, vulnerat: per dictum, per ictum.* This is such a Sermon as shall not passe without consideration. So he preached by *Pharaoh*, by frogs, flies, locusts, murraine, darknesse: but when neither by *Moses vocall*, nor by these actuall lectures he would be melted, the last Sermon is a *Red Sea*, that drowns him and his Armie.[24]

There is a more succinct and useful double example provided by John King, bishop of London, usually a joyful man compared with his lugubrious son Henry, author of one superb metaphysical poem, *The Exequy*. The elder Bishop King is reflecting on the meaning that can be given to pain:

My sufferings, grievous though they are, are my lessonings, which *Lipsius* well rendred, *nocumenta, documenta*; and Gregory not worse then he, *detrimenta corporum, incrementa virtutum*; paine to the body, gaine to the soule.[25]

Puns were also used for satirical effect. John Donne, for example, wisecracks in this way about Bellarmine's cardinal's hat: ". . . as a Cardinal *Bellarmine* hath changed his opinion that he held before he was hood-wincked with his Hat."[26]

The love of puns became so overwhelming that it was even thought appropriate to include one in a funeral discourse. The preacher was John Bowle, future bishop of Salisbury, and the deceased was Henry, Earl of Kent. In a concluding encomium, the preacher allowed himself the mild liberty of referring to the earl's private devotions as being "performed without a Trumpet: I will not make them more by *Arte* then they were in *heart*."[27] What is even more astonishing is that Archbishop William Laud, preaching his own courageous funeral sermon on the scaffold, has the spirit for a witticism: "I am going apace, as you see, towards the Red-sea, and my feet are upon the very brinks of it. . . ."[28]

Maxims

The third medium for the expression of wit in the pulpit was the epigram, apophthegm, or memorable maxim. The sermons of the metaphysical preachers coruscate with such gems.

Donne is the author of the most vivid and least forgettable of the maxims. Here are four of his most sparkling examples of wit, wit that also happens to be wise. "In poverty I lack but other things: In banishment I lack but other men; But in sickness I lack myself."[29] A rebuke to uncharitableness follows: "Do not make God's Rheubarbe thy Ratsbane, and poyson thine owne Soule with an uncharitable misinterpretation of that correction which God hath sent to cure his."[30] And here are my two favorites: "Christ beats his Drum, but he does not Press men; Christ is serv'd with Voluntaries"[31] and "The Devill is no Recusant; he will come to Church, and he will lay his snares there."[32]

Donne is hard to match because of his wide experience of life and his originality and terseness of expression, but other metaphysical preachers can also mint thoughtful and memorable sayings. Andrewes does not have the necessary concision, but as early as 1588 he makes a pointed reference to charity: "And there shall never be a rich man with *Lazarus* in his bosome in heaven, unless he have had a *Lazarus* in his bosome on earth."[33]

Bishop Corbet laments, "pews are become tabernacles with rings and curtains to them: there wants nothing but beds to hear the Word of God on."[34] More serious are the appeals to conscience. The Calvinist bishop, Ralph Brownrig, observes, "He that means to fish for Souls, let him bait his Hook with this Worm of *Conscience*, and he will take them presently."[35] But Brownrig offers consolation as well as condemnation in a maxim on the work of the Holy Spirit: "He ministers Corrosives to make way for Cordials."[36] With equal brevity, Charles I's favorite bishop, the Arminian Brian Duppa, can say it all in four words: "Sorrow is sin's eccho."[37]

Another Calvinist bishop, John Prideaux, preaching on humility warns, "A *hoppe* will soon start up, to *overlooke* the pole by which it climb'd."[38] Another Calvinist, Henry Smith, has a characteristically sensitive and monitory maxim in a sermon on marriage, directed at husbands and urging them to cherish their wives: "Her cheeks are made for thy lippes and not for thy fists."[39] Smith can also revitalise the old theme of human transience, apt in a New Year sermon: "We are not lodged in a castell, but in an Inne, where wee are but guests."[40] Edward Willan, an obscure chaplain of Charles I, has a maxim that tolls the same melancholy bell to start with but ends with a peal: "Earth is but a turfe to trample on, heaven is our home."[41]

One might expect a learned Calvinist like Archbishop James Ussher to wish to push St. Peter aside at heaven's gate to keep the reprobate out. In fact, he believed Peter excluded himself. So I particularly admire his welcoming maxim, "Christ keeps open house."[42] I conclude this section with a characteristically Arminian Anglican aphorism, pragmatically concerned with motives. It is Bishop Lake's maxim, ". . . for God loveth not adjectives, but adverbs; that is, considereth not so much what we do, but how."[43]

Paradoxes

From conceits, puns and paranomasia, and maxims, we turn to paradoxes, another striking characteristic of metaphysical thought and expression. At the outset it is worth recalling G. K. Chesterton's definition of a paradox: "Truth standing on her head to draw attention."[44] That might well have been part of Donne's justification for the frequency with which he used them in poetry as well as prose. But both he and Andrewes would also have argued that paradoxes are the only fitting ways of trying to express mysteries of divine revelation which transcend human reason,[45] and therefore can only be apprehended by faith. It was neither obfuscation nor deliberate mystification that led the metaphysicals to stress the importance of paradoxes. On the contrary, they were characteristic of the central dogmas of the orthodox Christian faith, affirmed in the first five oecumenical councils of the early Church in the East and West. These high mysteries of the *creatio ex nihilo*, of God as man in the Incarnation, of the Trinity in Unity, of the death of Death in the Resurrection, and of the *felix culpa* or fortunate Fall of mankind, and of the freedom of the will bound in the *imitatio Christi,* all these were the commonplaces of Christianity affirmed by the early Fathers, with whom the divines of the Anglican Communion maintained fealty. The heretics were those who chose half-truths chopped off the Procrustean bed of common sense. Moreover, these paradoxical doctrines of the Trinity and Incarnation were anchored to the liturgical calendar of the Church of England and renewed with the cycle of the year; and they led to adoration in worship, and imitation in ethics.

Paradox is by no means used only by Arminian High Church divines. Thomas Adams, accepting the Augustinian notion that time and creation were coeval, for God was before time, says quite naturally, "Loe, I begin with him, that hath no *Beginning. . . .*"[46]

The Incarnation of the Son of God is, of course, the best known source of paradox, especially in Andrewes, but others followed his example, such as Adams, Brownrig, and Cosin. Adams, on the humility of God as man, observes: "If your understandings can reach the depth of this bottome, take it at one view. The Sonne of God cals himself the *Sonne of man.* The omnipotent Creator becomes an impotent creature."[47] Brownrig is more interested in the impact of Christ's coming than in adoring the child in the stable at Bethlehem. He delights in a Christmas sermon on the potential universality of salvation: "Every place as Bethlehem, and the Cities of the Aliens shall be as holy as Ierusalem. A full moon makes a full Sea; and the full exhibition of Christ makes an enlarged Church."[48] In a remarkable meditation on the humility of the eternal Son of God at his earthly nativity, Cosin sees four steps in a descending ladder: to be born, in insignificant Bethlehem like a brute beast in a stable, on a cold winter's night, in the days of the bloodthirsty tyrant Herod.[49]

Andrewes is staggered by the ultimate self-emptying of the Son of God in the Crucifixion. Here is the paradox of the physician slain so that the patient might recover: "*Quis audivit talia?* The Physitian slaine; and, of his flesh and blood, a receipt made, that the patient might recover!" It is also the occasion of another paradox for Andrewes when he is preaching on the words of Jesus, "Dissolve (or Destroy) this Temple, and within three days I will raise it up again" (John 2:19): ". . . and they cryed, *Crucifige*, at the time (that is) *fasten; fasten* Him *to the Crosse;* but that *fastening* was His *loosing;* for it lost Him and cost Him his life."[50] In this case the paradox is a matter of style not of doctrine, as happened in other metaphysical preachers all too frequently.

The Resurrection as the death of Death was a favorite doctrinal paradox. Goffe expounds the Resurrection as follows: "*Uteri nova forma,* saith a Father, for the Tombe to become a womb to take in a dead man, and bring him forth alive; for the Grave to swallow up, not a dead Corps, but Death it selfe."[51]

Brownrig, one of the finest of the Calvinist metaphysical preachers who became bishops, sees the whole of history summed up between the first and second comings of Christ in a splendid paradox. As he views the eschatological skyscape he makes out both mercy and judgment, light and darkness; "Here is the shining of a Star pointing out his first appearing and then there is a dismal Comet in the Text fore-running his second: both *vagitus Infantis* and *rugitus Leonis:* or, as St. *John* puts them together, *ira agni,* the fiercest wrath from the meekest Lamb."[52]

Some of the paradoxes seem designed to get both preacher and congregation tied up in mental knots, as for example when John Wall speaks of Christ "that created his mother when he was begot of his Father, and glorified his Father, when he was borne of his mother."[53] Yet the same preacher can effectively use a paradox to point out the disunity of the church as the broken body of Christ: "*Persecutor non fregit crura, Donatus rupit Ecclesiam,* (saith learned *Austin*) the souldiers would not break the legs of Christ, but Donatus teares the Church of Christ. As long as his body hung upon the crosse among theeves and malefactors, it remained whole: but when it was received by Christians, it was rent and torn into many parts and sections."[54]

Other paradoxes are startling, but they are more concerned with style than doctrine. This is true of Barten Holyday's comment on David trying to escape from Saul: "... but David in the extremitie of wit and banishment disguises himselfe in a false madnesse, making it the best use of his reason to seeme to have lost the use of his reason."[55] Donne's paradoxes have generally both doctrinal validity and devotional utility. Donne is lost in wonder at the Passion of Christ in his final sermon, "Death's Duel." Paradox is the only suitable style for miracle, and Donne piles paradox on paradox:

That *God,* this *Lord,* the *Lord of life could dye,* is a strange contemplation; That the *red Sea* could bee *drie,* That the *Sun* could *stand still,* That an *Oven* could be *seaven times heat* and *not burne,* That *Lions* could be *hungry* and *not bite,* is strange, *miraculously strange,* but *supermiraculous* that *God could dye;* but that *God would dye* is an *exaltation* of that. But even of that also it is a *superexaltation,* that *God shold dye, must dye,* and *non exitus* (said S. *Augustin*) *God* the *Lord had no issue but by death,* and *oportuit pati* (says *Christ* himself) all this *Christ ought to suffer,* was bound to suffer.[56]

Reverses of thought, or extended oxymora

Paradoxes were thought daring because what appeared at first to be contradictions of thought or experience were ultimately resolved. At a more popular level riddles fulfilled the same function, except that they almost always turned out to be only verbal tricks; not sleights of hand, but sleights of tongue. The rarest examples of wit seem close to paradoxes. They are what might be termed reverses of thought, or extended oxymora in which what is expressed is the exact opposite of what the hearers expect. Three examples will be given. In each case suspense is succeeded by surprise.

In a Lenten sermon Donne states that the Latin Fathers, Lactantius and Augustine, found it hard to believe in the roundness of the earth, since they thought that the inhabitants of the Antipodes—*homines pensiles,* "those men that hang upon the other cheek of the face of the earth"—must fall off. He continues:

> But whither would they fall? If they fall, they must fall
> upwards, for heaven is above them too, as it is to us. So
> if the spirituall Antipodes of this world, the Sons of God,
> that walk with feet opposed in ways contrary to the sons
> of men, shall be said to fall, when they fall to repentance,
> to mortification, to religious negligence, and contempt of
> the pleasures of this life, truly their fall is upwards, they
> fall towards heaven.[57]

The brilliance of Donne's reversal is that he has been speaking
of the Sons of God, the associates of Lucifer, the fallen angels,
a fall downwards from their high home in heaven, and this is
totally reversed in the speculation that they may repent and
fall upwards.

Similarly Bishop John King, Donne's diocesan and friend,
assumes our knowledge of the first miracle of Christ in Cana,
and then reverses it unexpectedly. This sermon, preached at
Whitehall before King James, celebrates the marriage of King
James' daughter, the Lady Elizabeth to Frederick, the Elector
Palatine in 1614. It is a brilliant allegorical analysis of its theme,
the Palatine Vine.[58] Its title is *Vitis Palatina* and its text (or
pretext) is Psalm 28:3: "Thy wife shall be a fruitful Vine by
the sides of thine house." King insists that "They must marry
in Domino, in the Lord; not *in Pluto* the God of riches, nor *in
Venere*, the goddesse of lust: and Christ must be a bidden guest,
or else the Wine of this *Vine* will turn into Water, into Vinegar,
into the wine of dragons."[59]

The third example has the playful humor characteristic of
witty Tom Fuller, whose later sermons are studded with ornament and learning, in contrast to his earlier, plainer, and strictly
expository discourses. His main concern is to demonstrate the
dangers of heresy in the contemporary Church, a danger worse
even than schism. Heresy, he avers, "Sinnes against Faith" and
Schism "against Charity" and "though those two Graces be

sisters and twins, yet Faith is the eldest and choycest." Then follows this charming domestic illustration: "However, as children used to say, they love Father and Mother both best. So let us hate Heresies and Schisms both worst."[60]

Ingenious titles and texts

Peter Heylyn, in a dedicatory epistle to a book of ten sermons, points out that the usual excuses for printing sermons are three: the pressures of friends, the requests of superiors, and the prevention of pirated copies. He says the motives also are three: "protection, profit, or preferment."[61] Thomas Adams was the preacher whose sermons were most frequently reprinted in the early Stuart period. Their popularity accounts for thirty-three items in the Short Title Catalogue, including two editions of his complete sermons in 1629 and 1630, yet they brought him no preferment. This popularity is at least partly due to the ingenious titles he gave them. It seems as if he deliberately tried to compete with the titles of the plays which sold so well in stationers' shops in London, for he comments, "the Stationer dares hardly venture such cost on a good *Sermon*, as for an Idle Play: it will not sell so well, wicked dayes the whiles."[62]

Two of his sermon titles evoke popular plays of his time: one, "The White Devill" appeared soon after Webster's play of the same title, and another "The Taming of the Tongue" recalls Shakespeare's *The Taming of the Shrew*. Other striking sermon titles of his are "Mystical Bedlam: Or, The World of Mad-men"; "The Three Divine Sisters" suggesting the three graces of classical culture and the three Christian graces or theological virtues, Faith, Hope and Charity; "Lycanthropy, Or, The Wolfe worrying the Lambe"; "The Spirituall Navigator Bound for the Holy Land"; "Politicke Hunting"; "The Fatal Banket" [Banquet]; "The Black Saint"—a complement to "The White Devill"; and "Eirenopolis: The Citie of Peace." They were arresting titles, guaranteed to evoke the curiosity of the reader. They also have a commendable brevity.

Other intriguing titles were Thomas Jackson's "The Woman a True Helpe to Man, Or, Mankinds Comfort from the weaker sexe," and three of Daniel Featley's sermons, "The Lambe turned Lion"; "Pandora her box, or, *Origo omnium malorum*"; and "The Salters Text." This last was a sermon preached to the Company of Salters from the text Mark 9:40: "For everyone shall be salted with fire, and every sacrifice shall be salted with salt." Prideaux preached before the court a sermon aptly called "A Plot for Preferment." In the 1620s and 1630s the more elegant preachers were described as "ecstatic," "enraptured," and even "seraphical," so stratospherically airborne had their rhetoric become. Duppa's title, "Angels Rejoicing for Sinners Repenting," is therefore no surprise, and one is prepared for John Wall's set of sermons named *Alae Seraphicae. The Serafins Wings to raise us to Heaven,* or even William Cartwright's sermon on the Passion of Christ, titled "An Off-Spring of Mercy, Issuing out of the Womb of Cruelty." Then, in a class by itself for title and content, is Donne's own climactic funeral sermon, "Deaths Duell."

Wit and ingenuity were also displayed in the selection of appropriate texts for discourses. One particularly witty sermon was preached by Matthew Wren before a congregation of judges, at a time when the dons of Cambridge University were threatened by the loss of water from the impending draining of the Fens—Wren chose to preach on Amos 5:24, "But let judgment run down like waters, and righteousness as a mighty stream." Equally apt was his text from Psalm 42:7, after the failure of the negotiations for a marriage between Charles, Prince of Wales, and the Infanta of Spain, negotiations which had the whole of England tottering on the edge of a nervous breakdown. Wren had accompanied Charles and Buckingham on their diplomatic mission to Spain, and his text for a sermon preached soon after was "Deep calleth unto deep at the noise of thy waterspouts: all thy waves and billows are gone over me."[63] The reference was doubly apt since Prince Charles was nearly drowned at Santander on 12 September 1623, when the rowing boat carrying him from ship to shore was tossed like a cork on the mountainous waves. Other texts were also picked for their topical relevance. Donne, preaching his first sermon after the devastating plague of 1625, took Exodus 12:3 as his text: "For there was not a house where there was not one dead." Andrewes, preaching as the Earl of Essex's expedition was ready to leave port, used Deuteronomy 23:9, "When thou goest out with the host against thine enemies, keep thee from wickedness." Playfere, at the commemoration of the death of the young Prince Henry, heir to the throne, preached on Psalm 6:6, "I water my couch with my tears."

The preachers who had the greatest difficulty in finding texts, and who seemed to ransack the Bible before settling on one, were those invited to preach on August 5 and November 5. These were annual commemorations of the Gowrie and Gunpowder Plot conspiracies. To find texts appropriate to these events required much ingenuity. Three successive preachers on Gowrie Day took three differing texts. Andrewes used II Samuel 18:32, having in his mind the image of the dead Absalom who had treacherously revolted against his father and was found spreadeagled and hanging by his hair from a tree. The text read thus: "And Cushi answered, The enemies of my Lord the King and all that rise against thee to doe thee hurt, be as that young man is." Hacket and Featley chose their texts from the Psalms, with King David supposedly their royal author as spokesman. Hacket's text taken from Psalm 41:9 was, "Yea, mine own familiar friend in whom I trusted, which did eat my bread, hath lifted up his heel against me." Featley picked Psalm 63:9, "But those that seek my soul to destroy it, shall goe into the lower parts of the earth."

Equal ingenuity was exhibited in finding texts commemorating the deliverance from the Gunpowder Plot. Donne chose Lamentations 4:20: "The breath of our nostrils, the Anointed of the Lord, was taken by their Pits." Barlow used Isaiah 59:5: "They hatch cockatrice' egges, but weave the spiders webbe." Hacket preached twice on this commemoration. The first time he chose to use "Though they dig into Hell, there shall my hand take them," a text from Amos 9:2a. The second text came from the Acts of the Apostles 28:5 and read "And he [the Apostle Paul] shook off the beast into the fire, and he took no harm."

Chapter III

Jasper Mayne, one of the many poet-preachers among the metaphysicals, in a diatribe against uneducated and self–ordained preachers among the sectaries in Commonwealth days, chose an appropriate text from Ezekiel 22:28, which went: "And her prophets have daubed them with untempered morter [sic], seeing vanity, and divining lyes unto them, saying, Thus saith the Lord God, when the Lord hath not spoken."

Other choices of texts were made for personal reasons. The rigorously upright Morton's farewell sermon as dean of Winchester challenged the cathedral congregation to question his integrity and honesty, employing I Samuel 12:3 as his text. It thundered, "Whose Oxe have I taken? Or whose hand have I taken any bribe to blind mine eyes therewith?" One supposes that the answer was silence. Certainly that was a risk which Dr. Theophilus Field, a Jacobean bishop of St. Asaph, could not have taken. This former chaplain to Bacon, when he was Lord Chancellor, was accused of brokerage and bribery, and, while his defense was accepted, he was reported to the archbishop of Canterbury that he might admonish him for conduct unbecoming a bishop.[64] Bishop Senhouse also awakened his congregation with a challenging text from Galatians 4:16: "Am I therefore become your enemie, because I tell you the truth?"

Bishop Hacket, the convinced Calvinist, surprised his congregation in Lichfield Cathedral by refusing one Christmas day to take the usual Nativity accounts as the basis of his sermon. Instead he wished to stress the primary role of Jesus and the secondary role of his mother. Hence he took as his text the incident narrated in Luke 11:27 and 28: "And it came to pass, as he [Jesus] spake these things, a certain woman of the company lifted up her voice and said unto him, Blessed is the womb that bare thee, and the paps which thou hast sucked. But he said, Yea rather, blessed are they who hear the word of God and keep it."

The functions of wit in sermons

The general function of wit is clear. It is to keep the congregation on its toes, intrigued, delighted, amused, and, hopefully, instructed. But the metaphysical preachers found that it helped in quite specific practical ways too.

For example, it made an excellent start to a sermon. Thomas Adams' text is "Now abideth Faith, Hope, Charitie, these three; but the greatest of these is Charitie," (I Corinthians 13:13). He begins:

> When those three Goddesses, say the Poets, strove for the golden ball, *Paris* adiudged it to the Queene of *Love*. Here are three celestial graces, in an holy emulation, if I may so speake, striving for the chiefedom; and our Apostle gives it to Love. The greatest of these is Charity.[65]

Donne, of course, is the master of the striking opening. In a Lenten sermon at Whitehall, he chose a melancholy text from Ecclesiastes 5:12, 13: "There is an evil sickness that I have seen under the sun: riches reserved to the owners thereof, for their evill. And these riches perish by evil travail: and he begetteth a son, and in his hand is nothing." Donne begins: "The Kingedome of heaven is a feast; to get you to a Stomach to that, we have preached abstinence. The kingdom of heaven is a treasure too, and to make you capable of that, we would bring you to a just valuation of this world. He that hath his hands full of dirt, cannot take up Amber; if they be full of Counters, they cannot take up gold."[66]

A second practical purpose that wit could serve was as an apology for not going deeply into all aspects of a text and its context. This is the approach Adams uses in his sermon "The Spirituall Navigator Bound for the Holy Land." Here he uses Revelation 4:6, which reads, "Before the Throne there was a Sea of Glass like unto Chrystal." He apologizes for not diving into the apocalyptic depths and darkness of the Book of Revelation: "For my owne part, I purpose not to plunge to the depth with the *Elephant*; but to wade with the *lambe* in the shallowes: not to be over-ventrous in *Apocalypse*, as if I could reveale the *Revelation*: but breifely to report what expositions others have given of this branch: and then gather some fruit from it."[67]

Theophilus Field, perhaps the worldliest and laziest of the bishops, offers the same excuse for not going deeply into how the senses (which he wittily calls "The Cinque Ports") can lead the soul astray. He apologizes, "I might heere blocke up the other Ports, and pursue the rest of the *Traytors:* but let it suffice that as in the suppression of a great Rebellion, I shew the heads of the chief Rebels (as it were) upon stakes."[68]

Wit also allowed a preacher to apologize for the prolixity or brevity of his sermon, as the case may be. Copious Donne offers this aside, looking at the hourglass besides his pulpit: "But we are now in the work of an houre and no more. If there be a minute of sand left, (There is not) If there be a minute of patience left, heare me say, This minute that is left, is that eternitic which we speake of; upon this minute dependeth that eternity. . . ."[69] Laud, preaching on Psalm 21:6–7, "For Thou hast set him as blessings for ever   ", makes the apologetical aside, "If you think I have staid too long in this circumstance, I hope you will pardon me. You should be as loth as I to go from amidst the 'blessings': but I must proceed."[70]

A fourth practical purpose is served by wit. It can be used to fasten the divisions or parts of the sermon more firmly on the mind. Andrewes preached before King James at Romsey on Gowrie Day, 1607. He argued that kings stand in God's stead, and after providing one biblical reason for cursing God's enemies as the king's enemies, he mentioned two more. Then he says, "But there are three darts in *Absolons* heart, one would have served the turne; so this one would suffice, but I will cast yet a second, and third at them."[71] Theophilus Field has a wittily sinister excuse for providing no division, since his text is a brief summons, from Deuteronomy 4:9, "*Attende tibi.* Take heed to thy selfe." Here it is: "For our orderly proceeding, rather in *dispersing* than *dividing* the Text, not long enough for a division (for a watch-word must be carried entire:) let your attention go along with me, and by the guidance of Gods holy Spirit I shall shew you three *Watches* and *Wards* implyed in *Attende tibi.*"[72] John Cosin, preaching an Epiphanytide sermon in 1621, says: "The text would do well to have no division to-day because it is a day of union, wherein they that were divided before were made one under Christ; and therefore I might only call it the Epiphany, one general head and so away."[73] He then went on to enumerate five parts to his sermon, probably disappointing his congregation who thought there would be only one. John Hacket preaching on Luke 2:7, "And she brought forth her first born Son, and wrapped him in swaddling cloths, and laid him in a Manger, because there was no room for him in the Inn, &c.," says he will insist on five points in his sermon: "these are the parts of my Text: With great reverence be it spoken, I may call them the swadling clouts wherewith I must wrap my Saviour."[74]

A fifth practical use for wit is in providing a transition in a sermon. Hacket wishes to turn from considering Achitophel to the case of Judas. Achitophel, "ambitious of nothing but to seem wise, disposeth his house in prudent order, and hangs himself. And," says the bishop, "because I cannot leave such a miscreant in a better place, here ends my treatise of *Achitophel*. . . ." He continues: "And as *Achitophel* left himself hanging between heaven and earth for all men to gaze upon, so likewise hath *Judas* in the second part of the Text. I am now come from the complotting Statesman to the Apostaticall *Churchman*; from him that dealt perfidiously with *David*, to him that was the traitor against *Davids Lord*."[75] A briefer transition was provided by Henry King in a series of sermons on the various clauses of the Lord's Prayer. He says: "I have held you too long upon these first words *Our Father*, indeed beyond a *Pater noster* while. But shall quickly dismisse you, for my speech is now arrived at the end and period of our Prayers iourney, Heaven. *Which art in Heaven*."[76]

A very effective sixth use of wit is made in satirical references which act as dissuasion. Fuller, for example, wishes to show that a literal interpretation of Scripture can be ludicrous, though it is normally to be preferred to allegorical interpretations, often not so much exegesis as eisegesis. He observes: "Besides, Christ at his death spake no other language than what his tongue and his Disciples were used to in his life time: *I am the Vine, I am the Way, I am the Doore.* Hee who is so sottish as to conceive that Christ was a materiall Doore sheweth himselfe to be a Post indeed."[77] It is, as it happens, part of an anti-Roman tirade, as many Protestant witticisms are, since he denied that the phrase, "This is my body," could be literally interpreted and used as a justification for Transubstantiation. Brownrig and Adams provide the most amusing anti-Roman references. Bishop Brownrig is critical of the political pretensions of the papacy, "that the Pope should be an univeral Monarch; Emperours and Kings subject to his controul." He derides the notion "that *Peter's* Fisher-boat should become a man of War, and scour the main Ocean, and his Succesour, the Pope turn Pirate."[78] Adams too explodes in fireworks of anti-Roman wit: "The *Inquisition* is their *Grammer*, fire and fagot their *Rhetoricke*, fleet and fetters their *Logicke*, the Cannons rore their *Musicke*, and poysoning their *Physicke*. Whose Priests have such almighty power, that they can make their Maker. . . ."[79] It is a relief to turn from such facetiousness to the quieter wit of Andrewes who hardly ever made an anti-Catholic gibe. A satiric reference of his is to those who scruple to kneel at Holy Communion (implying a belief in Transubstantiation) by which he means, but does not name, the Puritans. He sums the matter up thus: "They in the Scripture, They in the Primitive Church, did so, did *bow.* And verily, He will not have us worship Him like Elephants, as if we had no ioynts in our Knees."[80]

A final practical, wakening use of wit is in the conclusion of a narration, or of a sermon itself. Donne provides an example of the former use. He has been describing the way in which Potiphar's wife tried to beguile Joseph in Egypt: when, in the dean's own words, "she had found her opportunity when there was none in the house but they, he came into an inward *Eripe me Domine,* O Lord take hold of me now, and she caught, and God caught; She caught his garment, and God caught his soule; she delivered him, and God delivered him; She to Prison, and God from thence."[81] Henry Smith was courageous enough to preach a series of sermons against usury in London, where the sin was notorious. His conclusions to two such sermons are shrewd as well as witty. One ends with these words: "Now I may conclude with Paul, *I have not spoken, but the Lord*: and therefore as the Lord said to Saul that he persecuted him; so they which resist this doctrine, do contemne him, and not me."[82] The second sermon ended with a warning and a prayer for paradisal profit-making:

> Now seeing you may not be Usurers to men, let everie man hereafter be an usurer to God, which promiseth; If thou leave father or mother, or wife, or children, or house, or land, for him; not ten in the hundred, but an hundred for ten, nay an hundred for one, and in the world to come life everlasting: that is, a thousand for one. That wee may receive this usurie, let us pray that the words which we have heard out of this Psalme, may dwell with us till we dwell in heaven.[83]

The decline of wit

Fashions in prose, whether in or out of the pulpit, change and the Puritan plain style began to win from 1640 onwards. The first objection to metaphysical wit in the pulpit was to its strained artificiality. The comparisons of the conceits were judged too farfetched, the language too tortuous, even tortured. The metaphysical demand for increasingly "seraphical" language led to "angelism," that is, to an exaggeration of the feelings beyond what was considered normally human. The use of recondite lore drawn from "unnatural" natural history, or from supposed philological researches, repelled by its obscurity not to say its utter incredibility. No wonder that a bishop of the Restoration, secretary and first historian of the new Royal Society, expressed the growing demand for a "naked" and "natural" style.[84] Those very adjectives repudiated their opposites, the convoluted artificiality, the brocaded and over-ornamental style of metaphysical expressions in poetics and in the pulpit. Thus Dr. Sprat, Bishop of Rochester, in expressing what was felt to be the suitable style for scientific discourse, by extension caught the exponents of religious discourse in the net of a new popularity.

Consider the sheer reiteration of the puns in the following excerpt from Andrewes in a Spital sermon of 1588, not to mention the staccato, alarm-clock effect of his style, and how soon it becomes wearisome. His text is I Timothy 5:17f., "Charge them that are rich in this world, that they be not high-minded, etc." He declares: "It is a *Charge* then, and consequently to be discharged. To be discharged? Where? *Charge* (saith he) the rich."[85]

A criticism more serious than artificiality was irreverence, laughing at holy things, where wit slipped into slickness and profanity. Brownrig, a Calvinist and himself one of the wittiest prelates, produced a ludicrous comparison that becomes unintentionally a mockery of Holy Communion in his fifth sermon on Christmas Day, a sermon which will be followed by the reception of the Eucharist. The proper preparation is repentance and the preaching of repentance, a repentance which he says is more apt for fasts than festivals. Then follow the words: "yet these sowre Herbs of Penitentiall sorrow will quicken our appetite, to feed more savourly on this lamb of God."[86] This conceit was bound to suggest cannibalism, offensive in itself and amazing given that its inventor believed in virtualism not in the corporal presence. Even Donne can slip into ludicrousness, as when he imagines Christ to be like a hen: "He sits upon his Church, as a hen upon her eggs; He covers all our sinners, whom he hath gathered into that body, with spreading himselfe and his merits upon us all there."[87]

A third criticism of metaphysical wit was its occasional tendency to degenerate into vulgarity, as when the grave supposedly expelling Christ on the first Easter Day is likened to vomiting. Brownrig, in his use of this foul analogy, could at least claim St. John Chrysostom as a precedent for it.[88] Donne also speaks of vomit, less offensively, in relation to confession, and purging the soul. He knew it was vulgar, for he says: "It is but a homely Metaphor, but it is a wholesome and a useful one, *Confessio vomitus*, Confession works as a vomit; It shakes

121

the frame, and it breakes the bed of sin; and it is an ease to the spirituall stomach, to the conscience, to be thereby disburdened."[89] More vulgar, I judge, is to speak of the circumcision of Christ as anticipating the greater blood-shedding of the Crucifixion, as Andrewes, usually meticulous in such matters, nevertheless does: "The Tabernacle of GOD was with *men*. He might not stay eight dayes in the campe, but He must take the *Sacramentum militare:* So He did. And the ceremonie of it was to be *stroken,* and to *bleed* some small quantitie: So He was, at his *Circumcision:* And after He performed the battaile at his *Passion.* . . ."[90] Even Archbishop Laud made use of circumcision as a common metaphor.[91]

A fourth charge, which could equally well be levelled at orthodox Calvinists as at the Commonwealth sectarians, and which applied to the metaphysical divines, was speculative curiosity. If the orthodox divines in the Westminster Assembly speculated about predestination, election, reprobation, and who were saved, and who were damned, and what were the signs, and whether you could fall from grace or not if you were one of the elect—the unorthodox Puritans of the left speculated about when the Kingdom of God would be established upon earth, how soon, and for how long, and who would be its subjects and who its enemies. For such metaphysicals as Donne there was great speculation as to the nature of life after death, and what the resurrection body was like, especially in the case of those who had had accidents to parts of themselves: "What cohaerence, what sympathy, what dependence maintaines any relation, and correspondence, between that arm that was lost in Europe, and that legge that was lost in Afrique or Asia, scores of yeeres between?"[92] Others wanted to know how you would get your body back at the Resurrection if you were a sailor swallowed by a shark, or a soldier eaten by a cannibal. Such speculations, dogmatically answered, had created a phenomenal disorder during the English Civil War, not to mention the Thirty Years War between Catholics and Protestants, with all parties engaging in private interpretation and treating Scripture as a "nose of wax." Therefore there was a general determination at the Restoration to keep to an unspeculative, common–sensible, pragmatic theology and style of preaching, which was soon distinguished for its tolerant, urbane, easy-going practicality. This became known as Latitudinarianism.[93]

In this changed mental climate one can easily imagine how laughable the following image would seem, where Donne speaks of the net of the promises of the Gospel:

> This is the net, with which if yee be willing to bee caught, that is, to lay downe all your hopes and affiances in the gracious promises of his Gospel, then you are fishes reserved for that great Mariage-feast, which is the Kingdome of heaven; where, whosoever is a dish, is a ghest too; whosoever is served in at the table, sits at the table.[94]

Why was witty preaching so popular?

If the decline of witty preaching was so complete after about fifty years of the fashion, one is forced to ask, why was witty preaching so popular for so long?

First, the object of wit, as we have seen, was to surprise, even to shock, to elicit wonder, admiration, delight, and laughter in the congregation. This, we should remember, was essential to gain and to maintain the attention of the legally captive congregations of Elizabethan and early Stuart times. The ultimate enemy of monotony and boredom is wit if one lacks religious motivation. For the hearers it was the necessary sugar-coating on the pill of theology, while, for the preachers, it was the Christian doctrine, ethics, and worship that were (to use the Pauline phrase) the strong meat of the Gospel.[95]

In the second place, this was a period of great turbulence and transition in England: from Catholicism to Protestantism; from an international to a national Church; from the Petrine pope to the paper pope of the Bible; from a geocentric to a heliocentric universe, in which the heavens had grown very far off; from a position where religion had once been a widely accepted tradition, and was now a matter of acute controversy.

Donne had appraised the problem, as only a profound sceptic who later turned to faith could, in these lines from "An Anatomy of the World" in *The First Anniversary:*

> And new philosophy calls all in doubt,
> The element of fire is quite put out;
> The sun is lost, and th'earth, and no man's wit
> Can well direct him where to look for it.
> And freely men confess that this world's spent,
> When in the planets and the firmament
> They seek so many new; they see that this
> Is crumbled out again to his atomies.
> 'Tis all in pieces, all coherence gone;
> All just supply and all relation.

And in Satyre III, even when he knows where truth is to be found, on a huge, cragged, and steep hill, he also knows that one must travel round and round in circles to find her.[96]

Even the daily news in those perplexing days was theologically interpreted, as at the beginning of Dr. Lushington's scandalous sermon in Christ Church, Oxford, speaking of the progress of the Thirty Years War:

> What's the best News abroad? So we must begin: 'Tis the *Garb* (*les novelles*) the grand salute, and common *Preface* to all our talk. And the news goes not as things are in themselves, but as mens fancies are fashioned, as some lust to report, and others to believe: The same relation shall goe for true or false, according to the key wherein mens minds are tuned; but chiefly as they stand diverse in Religion, so they feign and affect different News. By their *News* ye may know their *Religion*, and by their *Religion* fore-know their *News*. This week the *Spanish match* goes forward, and *Bethleem Gabors* troups are broken; and the next week *Bethleem Gabors* Troups goe forward, and the *Spanish Match* is broken. The *Catholique* is of the *Spanish match*, and the *Protestant* of restoring the *Palatinate*; and

each party think that the safety of the *Church* and the success of *religion* depend upon the event of one or other. . . .[97]

In such controversial and changing circumstances, where the sovereign of England was also the head of the English Church, it became essential for the official representatives of that Church to be able to challenge both papists to the right, and Puritans to the left, by their learning, their illustrations, and their memorable ingenuities, where strong guidance from the pulpit was a political as well as a pastoral necessity.

Finally, like Emperor Constantine (who called himself "the thirteenth Apostle") King James considered himself a good theologian, and needed theologians to battle against the great learning and acute dialectics of such men as Cardinal Bellarmine. James delighted in learning, the more esoteric the better, and above all he enjoyed wit. He demanded and rewarded wit, as Thomas Fuller reported: "His wit was passing sharp and piercing, equally pleased in *making* and taking a *smart* jest, *His Majestie* so much stooping to *His mirth*, that He never *refused* that *coine* which he paid to other folk."[98] It was his special pleasure to take note of those students at the universities who showed wit in the public disputations, or imagination in the comedies they devised for his and his queen's pleasure. One famous anecdote shows how a careerist bishop gained translation to the archdiocese of York simply by a witticism. George Mountain (or Montaigne), whom Milton classified among the "swan-eating and canary-sucking" prelates,[99] was apparently consulted by James as to whom the king should appoint to the see of York. After various names were mentioned, Mountain could no longer contain his patience, and the *bon vivant* delivered himself of this carefully prepared *bon mot*: "Sire, if you had faith even as a grain of mustard-seed, you would say unto this mountain, Go and be removed into the See!"[100] James was so delighted by the remark that he gave instructions there and then that Mountain's wish should be granted.

With a king and a court that delighted in wit; with senior

common rooms in Oxford and Cambridge colleges that prized
wit then as now; in a London where the gallants of the city
loved to be called wits; and in the theatres where witticisms
were memorized, for repetition in the taverns and at the tables
of the elite, it became essential for the official representatives
of the Established Church to have a reputation for having all
their wits about them.

NOTES

1. See William C. Crane, *Wit and Rhetoric in the Renaissance* (New York, 1937), 9–12, for the changing and overlapping meanings of "wit."

2. Joel E. Spingarn, *Critical Essays of the Seventeenth Century*, Volume 1: 1605–1650, (Oxford, 1908), xxx and xxxviii.

3. Euphues, as we read in John Lyly's *Euphues: The Anatomy of Wit* (London, 1578) sig. Bii, was a young gallant who "gave himselfe almost to nothing, but practising of those things commonlie, which are incident to these sharpe wits, fine phrases, smooth quips, merrie taunts, using iesting without meane, and abusing mirthe without measure." Lyly clearly thought true wit required judgment.

4. Henry Peacham, *The Garden of Eloquence, Conteining the most Excellent Ornaments, Exornations, Lightes, flowers, and formes of speech, commonly called the Figures of Rhetoricke* (London, 1593), 14.

5. Francis Meres, *Wits Commonwealth. The Second Part. A Treasurie of Divine, morall, and Phylosophicall similies and sentences, generally usefull* (London, 1634), Preface, sig. Λ2–Λ2v.

6. "A Divine Herball, Or, Garden of Graces" in *The Workes of Tho: Adams* (London, 1629), 1026.

7. *The Workes of Tho: Adams*, 272. The sermon is "Physicke from Heaven."

8. *The Workes of Tho: Adams*, 351.

9. Thomas Jackson, *Nazareth and Bethlehem, or, Israels Portion in the Sone of Jesse. And, Mankinds Comfort from the weaker sexe. Two Sermons preached in St. Maryes Church in Oxford* (Oxford, 1617), 65.

10. Thomas Playfere, *The Whole Sermons* (London, 1623), 141.

11. *The Sermons of Maister Henrie Smith, Gathered into One Volume* (London, 1593), 459.

12. W. Fraser Mitchell, *English Pulpit Oratory, From Andrewes to Tillotson, A Study of its Literary Aspects* (London, 1932), 148–194.

13. The Sermon on Easter Day 1622: "This day both Gods Sons arose; the Sun of his Firmament and the Son of his bosome," *The Sermons of John Donne*, eds. George R. Potter and Evelyn M. Simpson, 10 vols. (Berkeley, 1953–1962), 4: 65.

14. "Preaching then being *Gods Ordinance*, to beget Faith, to take away preaching were to disarm God and to quench the spirit; for by that *Ordnance*, he fights from heaven," Donne, *Sermons*, 4: 195; the same pun had been used already in the same sermon, at 4: 192.

15. Andrewes, *XCVI Sermons* (London, 1629), 233.

16. Andrewes, *XCVI Sermons*, 232.

17. Adams, *The Collected Sermons*, ed. Thomas Smith (Edinburgh, 1861–1862), 972.

18. *Sixty-Five Sermons of the Right Reverend Father in God, Ralph Brownrig* (London, 1674), 217.

19. William Barlow, *A Sermon preached at Paules Crosse, on the first Sunday in Lent, Martij.I, 1600* (London, 1601), sig. [C1v].

20. Andrewes, *XCVI Sermons*, 395. Adams also uses this citation, see next note.

21. *The Workes of Tho: Adams*, 137, dealing with Hope in a sermon entitled "The Three Divine Sisters."

22. Andrewes, *XCVI Sermons*, 995. "A Sermon preached before the Kings Maiestie at Whitehall on Nov. 5, 1617."

23. Andrewes, *XCVI Sermons*, 21–22. "A Sermon before the King in Whitehall on Christmas Day, 1606."

24. *The Workes of Tho: Adams*, 677.

25. John King, *A Sermon at Publicke Thankes-giving for the happy recovery of his Maiesty from his late dangerous sicknesse. Preached at Pauls-Crosse the 11 of Aprill, 1619* (London, 1619), 42.

26. Donne, *Sermons*, 7: 196.

27. John Bowle, *A Sermon preached at Flitton in the Countie of Bedford, at the Funerall of . . . Henrie, Earle of Kent, the sixteenth of March, 1614* (London, 1615), 26–27.

28. William Laud, *The Archbishop of Canterbury's Speech: or, his Funerall Sermon, preacht by himself on the Scaffold on Tower-Hill on Friday the 10 of January, 1644* (London, 1644), 7.

29. Donne, *Sermons*, 2: 80.

30. Donne, *Sermons*, 5: 285.

31. Donne, *Sermons*, 7: 156.

32. Donne, *Sermons*, 10: 58.

33. Lancelot Andrewes, *A Sermon preached at Saint Maries Hospital, on the X of April being Wednesday in Easter-Weeke, AD. MDLXXXVIII* (London, 1588), 20.

34. State Papers Dom. Carl. I, 266, no. 58. This is an excerpt from

Corbet's charge to his clergy delivered in Norwich Cathedral on 29 April 1634, begging them to give generously towards the rebuilding of St. Paul's Cathedral.

35. Brownrig, *Sixty Five Sermons*, 150.

36. Brownrig, *Sixty Five Sermons*, 260.

37. Brian Duppa, *The Souls Soliloquy and Conference with Conscience preached before the King at Newport, 25 Oct. 1648* (London, 1648), 9.

38. John Prideaux, *The Patronage of Angels. A Sermon preached at Court* (Oxford, 1636), 10. Prideaux has previously told the fable of the gardener who accepted the briar which insolently prevented all the other bushes entering his garden.

39. *The Sermons of Maister Henrie Smith*, 44.

40. *The Sermons of Maister Henrie Smith*, 552.

41. Edward Willan, *Conspiracie against Kings, Heavens Scorne. A Sermon preached at Westminster Abbey before the Iudges, upon the fift of Novemb. 1622* (London, 1622), 34.

42. *The Whole Works of the Most Rev. James Ussher, D.D., Lord Archbishop of Armagh and Primate of all Ireland*, 17 vols. (Dublin and London, 1847–1864), 13: 321.

43. *Sermons, with some Religious and Divine Meditations. By the Right Reverend Father in God, Arthur Lake, late Lord Bishop of Bath and Wells* (London, 1629), 113.

44. G. K. Chesterton, *The Paradoxes of Mr. Pond* (London, 1937), 71.

45. Winfried Schleiner, in *The Imagery of John Donne's Sermons* (Providence, Rhode Island, 1970), 183, points out that in dealing with the images of the Spirit's descent at Pentecost Donne "draws his analogies from the natural world less in order to explain the divine than to infer by his carefully worked out paradoxes the supernatural quality of the event."

46. *The Workes of Tho: Adams*, 83. From the sermon, "The Sacrifice of Thankfulnesse," first published in 1616.

47. *The Workes of Tho: Adams*, 879. From the sermon, "The Lost are Found."

48. Brownrig, *Sixty Five Sermons*, 91.

49. *The Works of the Right Reverend Father in God John Cosin, Lord Bishop of Durham*, Volume 1: *Sermons* (Oxford, 1843), 10.

50. Andrewes, *XCVI Sermons*, 59. A sermon preached before the king in Whitehall on 25 December 1612.

51. Thomas Goffe, *Deliverance from the Grave. A Sermon preached at Saint Maries Spittle in London on Wednesday in Easter Weeke last, March 28, 1627* (London, 1627), 33.

52. Brownrig, *Sixty Five Sermons*, 94. The second sermon for Christmas Day.

53. John Wall, *Alae Seraphicae. The Seraphins Wings to raise us unto Heaven. Delivered in Six Sermons, partly at St. Peters in Westminster, partly at St. Aldates in Oxford. 1623* (London, 1627), 219.

54. Wall, *Alae Seraphicae*, 137.

55. Barten Holyday, *A Sermon preached at Pauls Crosse, August the 5, 1623* (London, 1626), 8.

56. Donne, *Sermons*, 10: 243.

57. Donne, *Sermons*, 4: 59. This Lenten sermon was preached at Whitehall on 8 March 1621.

58. John King, *Vitis Palatina. A Sermon appointed to be preached at Whitehall upon the Tuesday after the Mariage of the Lady Elizabeth her Grace* (London, 1614). The characteristics of this fruitful vine are its flexibility and tractability, its tenderness, its refreshing shadow for a weary husband, its smell which drives away serpents and noxious things, its frailty which requires a husband's support, and the liquor and blood of the grape which are the compensations for its weakness (17–18).

59. John King, *Vitis Palatina*, 13.

60. *The Collected Sermons of Thomas Fuller, D.D., 1631–1659*, eds. John E. Bailey and William E. A. Axon, 2 vols. (London, 1891), 1: 118.

61. Peter Heylyn, *The Parable of the Tares Expounded and Applied in Ten Sermons Preached Before his late Majesty King Charles the Second Monarch of Great Britain* (London, 1659).

62. *The Workes of Tho: Adams*, 191.

63. Thomas Fuller, *The History of the Worthies of England* (London, 1662), 2: 208. See also S. R. Gardiner, *Prince Charles and the Spanish Marriage: 1617–1623*, 2 vols. (London, 1869), 2: 413.

64. See DNB, Theophilus Field.

65. *The Workes of Tho: Adams*, 134. The title of the sermon is "The Three Graces."

66. Donne, *Sermons*, 3: 47.

67. *The Workes of Tho: Adams*, 393.

68. Theophilus Field, *A Watch-Word, Or, the Allarme, Or, A Good Take Heed. A Sermon preached in the open Preaching place at Whitehall last Lent before King Charles* (London, 1628), 21.

69. Donne, *Sermons,* 7: 368.

70. *The Works of the Most Reverend Father in God, William Laud, D.D., sometimes Archbishop of Canterbury* (Oxford, 1847), 1: 39.

71. Andrewes, *XCVI Sermons,* 779.

72. Field, *A Watch-Word, Or, the Allarme, Or, A Good Take Heed,* 9.

73. *The Works . . . of John Cosin,* 1: 9. The sermon was preached in St. Edward's Church, Cambridge, 6 January 1621, and at Coton Church on the Second Sunday after Epiphany.

74. Hacket, *A Century of Sermons Upon Several Remarkable Subjects* . . . (London, 1675), 2.

75. Hacket, *A Century of Sermons,* 737.

76. Henry King, *An Exposition Upon the Lords Prayer. Delivered in certaine Sermons in the Cathedrall Church of S. Paul* (London, 1628), 59.

77. *The Collected Sermons of Thomas Fuller,* 1: 144.

78. Brownrig, *Sixty Five Sermons,* 75. This is from the third sermon, on the Gunpowder Treason.

79. *The Workes of Tho: Adams,* 509. This is from the sermon, "Mysticall Bedlam: Or, The World of Mad-Men."

80. Andrewes, *XCVI Sermons,* 475–476. This is from a sermon preached before King James at Whitehall on Easter Day, 1615.

81. Donne, *Sermons,* 5: 376.

82. *The Sermons of Maister Henrie Smith,* 185.

83. *The Sermons of Maister Henrie Smith,* 202.

84. Thomas Sprat, *The History of the Royal-Society of London, For the Improving of Natural Knowledge* (London, 1667), 112–113. Sprat says the stylistic enemy is "this vicious abundance of *Phrase,* this trick of *Metaphor,* this volubility of *Tongue,* which makes so great a noise in the world." As a result the members of the Royal Society determined to "reject all the amplifications, digressions, and swellings of style" and instead "they have extracted from all their members, a close, naked, natural way of speaking; positive expressions; clear senses; a native easiness; bringing all things as near the Mathematical plainness as they can: and preferring the language of Artizans, Countrymen, and Merchants, before that of Wits, and Scholars."

85. Andrewes, *XCVI Sermons,* first of the section near the end, entitled "Certaine Sermons Preached at Sundry Times." It is from "A Sermon Preached at Saint Maries Hospital, on the X of April, being Wednesday In Easter-weeke, AD. MDLXXXVIII," 1.

86. Brownrig, *Sixty Five Sermons,* 128. From the Fifth Sermon on Christmas Day.

87. Donne, *Sermons,* 9: 263.

88. See Brownrig, *Sixty Five Sermons,* 192.

89. Donne, *Sermons,* 9: 304.

90. Andrewes, *XCVI Sermons,* 48. From a Christmas sermon preached before the king at Whitehall in 1611.

91. *The Works of . . . William Laud,* 1: 72–73.

92. Donne, *Sermons,* 8: 98.

93. See my analysis in *Worship and Theology in England, From Watts and Wesley to Maurice, 1690–1850* (Princeton, N.J., 1961), 175–195.

94. Donne, *Sermons,* 2: 309–310. For speculative considerations see also 3: 96–97, and 8: 98f. *inter alia.*

95. Hebrews 5:12, 14, is the New Testament reference.

96. The lines referred to are:

. . . On a huge hill,

Cragged and steep, Truth stands, and he that will

Reach her, about must, and about must go.   (lines 79–81)

97. *The Resurrection Rescued from the Soldiers Calamities, in Two Sermons Preached at St. Maries in Oxon.* (London, 1659), 1. Attributed to a pseudonymous author, "Robert Jones, D.D.," it was the work of Thomas Lushington, and was preached on Easter Monday, 1624, according to Antony Wood (*Athenae Oxonienses,* 2 vols. [London, 1691], 2: 171–173).

98. Thomas Fuller, *The Church-History of Britain* (London, 1655), Bk. 10, 114.

99. The context of the phrase is in Milton's comparing primitive bishops with the prelates of his day: "swan-eating and canary-sucking palat, let old Bishop Mountain judge for me," (*Of Reformation,* in *The Works of John Milton,* ed. F. A. Patterson, 21 volumes in 18, [New York, 1931], 3: Pt. 1, 19).

100. DNB, and cited in H. R. Trevor-Roper, *Historical Essays* (London, 1964), 139. The biblical citation comes from Matthew 17:20, which reads rather differently: "If ye had faith as a grain of mustard-seed, ye might say unto this mountain, Remove hence to yonder place, and it shall remove." But it is probably a combination of the Synoptic parallels. In fact, the anecdote cannot refer to Mountain's translation to York, since this occurred on 24 June 1628, when James had been dead for three years, but it could have happened in 1617 or 1620 when he was preferred respectively first to Lincoln and then London by James I.

Chapter IV

THE METAPHYSICAL CALVINISTS

O UR FIRST CHAPTER considered the reasons for the relative neglect of the metaphysical preachers, the delights they have to offer the modern reader, the differences between the conditions and the status of seventeenth- and twentieth-century preachers as an opportunity to exercise our historical imagination, and how they were recruited for preferment. Finally, we saw how their schooling had prepared them to develop the wit, imagination, classical and patristic learning, and ingenious eloquence that we looked at more closely in chapters two and three.

In this chapter we intend to fracture the stereotype that the witty or metaphysical preachers were exclusively Arminians, by showing that several of them were in fact Calvinists. Indeed, our first eight profiles will be those of eight bishops of the Church of England who held the Calvinist tenet of predestination. This was their way of safeguarding the essential Protestant doctrine of justification by faith and not merely by good works, which went along with a recognition of the exclusive role of God's grace in Christ in effecting human salvation, and the supportive comfort it brought in piety. This was, indeed, the *rule* in the Protestant Church of England from the very beginning. It was reaffirmed in the Thirty-Nine Articles, and confirmed by the English Church in 1618, when it sent representatives to the Synod of Dort, with James I's strong backing, to refute the implicit Pelagianism of Arminianism. Arminians denied a limited atonement, and made salvation depend upon God's rewarding of a foreseen and foreknown human response to his election. This was not the official doctrine of the English Church; so it was the Arminians who were the *exceptions* to the rule. For this reason we begin with Calvinist profiles, rather than with Andrewes, the Arminian forerunner of them all. Andrewes was reluctant even to consider predestination, since it seemed to him only a speculative doctrine, while for the episcopalian Calvinists this was the doctrine that safeguarded grace and gave assurance of salvation, and did so because it was wholly the work of God, and not dependent upon fallible human cooperation.[1]

There were three stages in the development of the Arminian and Calvinist battle in the seventeenth century. First, Calvinism counterattacked Arminius at Dort in Holland, by rejecting the famous Five Articles of the Remonstrants. Arminius, as professor of divinity in the University of Leyden, had in 1603 charged the holders of the Calvinist interpretation of predestination, included in the *Confessio Belgica*, with making God the author of sin. He accepted election but claimed that its basis was God's foreknowledge of human merit, not a divine arbitrary decree. Second, the battle, with learned episcopalian supporters, spread to England. Third, it re-emerged during the Commonwealth in the polemics of left-wing Puritans and Separatists, at which point it goes beyond our present concern.

Returning to Dutch Arminianism, its supporters affirmed five major points which are stated in summary form. (1) That God by an eternal decree means to save those who believe in Him through Christ steadfastly to the end, and will damn those remaining contumacious and unbelieving. (2) Christ died to gain reconciliation and remission of sins for all, but only believers obtain salvation. (3) Man cannot find saving faith in himself; it is only through the Holy Spirit that he can know and do God's will. (4) The grace of God precedent, awakening, and following, is the sole cause of goodness in mankind, but the operation of grace is not irresistible. (5) Those who are engrafted into Christ by faith and share the powers of the Holy Spirit can overcome Satan, the world, and their own flesh, if they call on and rely on Christ; but whether it is possible through sloth or negligence to lose grace, is left for further consideration.[2]

The Calvinists argued for the divine decree as the sole determinant of salvation and damnation, irrespective of human merit. They also argued for reprobation, for the certainty election offers of salvation (as contrasted with the uncertainty of depending upon fallible human beings and their cooperation), for the irresistibility of grace, and for the final perseverance of the elect. This gave all the glory and the grace to God. Arminianism's God might seem less arbitrary than Calvinism's; Arminians also placed a higher value on the strength of will and reason, which according to the Calvinists had been first shattered then blinded in the Fall, with the consequent effects of original sin.

The battle on the Netherlands front was soon joined in England. The first important anti-predestinarian shots were fired in Cambridge, in a sermon preached in April 1595 by William Barrett before the university. In this sermon he declared that perseverance in grace was dependent on the effort of the individual, and criticized the Reformers who affirmed the opposing viewpoint, namely, Calvin, Peter Martyr, Beza, and Zanchius. Although Calvinist leaders in the university insisted that Barrett recant, the result of this storm was the formulation of the Lambeth Articles, themselves the fruit of discussion between Archbishop Whitgift, Whitaker the Cambridge theologian, and others. The Lambeth Articles assert in the strongest terms the predestinarian theology of grace. The next shot in the quarrel was fired by Peter Baro, Lady Margaret Professor of Divinity in Cambridge University, who criticized the predestinarianism of the Lambeth Articles. He argued in a sermon that God died for all, not only for the elect, and hence God only reprobated those who rejected the grace in Christ. Other Cambridge dons who held the same views as Barrett and Baro, but more discreetly, were Lancelot Andrewes, master of Pembroke, Samuel Harsnett, who succeeded Andrewes at Pembroke

when the latter was consecrated bishop in 1605, and John Over-
all, who succeded the Calvinist Whitaker as Regius Professor
of Divinity. All three became bishops, which is curious, in
view of James's attachment to the Calvinism in which he was
reared, if not to the Presbyterian polity of parity among ministers. One can only suppose that he preferred this trio, apart
from their learning and loyalty to the established Church of
England, because they were unfaltering supporters of the divine
right of kings.

There is no need to follow the widening battle front in the
reign of Charles I, but we can observe that, however many
and powerful the Calvinist episcopalians were, they received
the highest preferment only if they turned Arminian, or when
Charles had to make concessions to gain some support from
Parliament. For example, as a rearguard action, he appointed
Prideaux and Henry King to the sees of Worcester and Chichester only in 1641. Prideaux had waited twenty-six years as Regius
Professor of Divinity in Oxford for this preferment to Worcester. King, son of a bishop of London, had been a royal chaplain
for twenty years before being appointed dean of Rochester,
and was promised the see of Chichester on the day after the
House of Lords had agreed to pass a bill depriving the bishops
of their votes (6 February, 1641/2).[3]

Arminianism's most powerful ecclesiastical backer was William Laud, who became bishop of London in 1627 and archbishop of Canterbury in 1633, but was the power behind the
primatial throne long before he ruled in Canterbury. Moreover,
he was in high favor with the duke of Buckingham, who was
in high favor with Charles I. Buckingham, as Chancellor of
the University of Cambridge, and Laud, as Chancellor of the
University of Oxford, were able to control preferments while
in these key positions.

This all too rapid summary of history is necessary to indicate
how deepseated the antagonisms were between Calvinists and
Arminians. This polarity would eventually be one of the causes
of the English Civil War.[4] It also explains why the Calvinists
were bitterly disappointed when it seemed the Arminians were

not only turning their back on the gains of the English Reformation, but also, in the matter of supporting the proposed Spanish marriage of Prince Charles to the Infanta of Spain, appeared to be appeasing European Roman Catholic sovereigns. All the same, the Arminians in England remained Protestant, although accused of flirting with Rome.[5]

Our first profiles are of the eight Calvinist bishops whose sermons survive. They include two who were unyielding Calvinists, Brownrig and Prideaux, the scourge of Arminians at Oxford. The others, more moderate, were Hacket, John King, Morton, Barlow, Bowle, and Henry King. Of these Hacket was unquestionably the most stellar preacher.

Ralph Brownrig

Ralph Brownrig (1592–1659), bishop of Exeter, was sufficiently strict a Calvinist to be elected to the Westminster Assembly of Divines in Commonwealth days, yet remained unswervingly loyal to the English Church. So great was his reputation as a preacher, that when Tillotson first came to London he sought out Brownrig to make him his model. He was courageous enough to preach a royalist sermon before the University of Cambridge in 1645, even though it cost him the headship of St. Catharine's Hall. In his funeral sermon on Brownrig, Gauden, his successor at Exeter, spoke of the fame of his wit from his undergraduate days, and observed: "Nor did any man make a more ample dedication of the gems and rarities of wit to good use then did this excellent person."[6] His advantages as a preacher, apart from his learning and his ready wit, were, according to Gauden, "the majesty of a goodly presence," careful preparation, the power to move the religious affections, the "power and warmth of his delivery," and "the blessing of a very happy historick memory."[7] We have substantial examples of his work, since sixty-five of his sermons were posthumously published, although in his modesty he had requested that none be published during his lifetime.

The two volumes contain seven sermons for Christmas Day,

seven for Easter, one Ascension Day sermon, four Whitsunday sermons, seven on the Transfiguration, twenty sermons on individual texts, five sermons on Proverbs 30:7–9, two on St. Luke 12:4, four on II Corinthians 4:3–4, one sermon to the clergy, one funeral sermon, two sermons for the inauguration of Charles I, three Gunpower Treason sermons, and one Lenten sermon. This Calvinist's use of the Christian year is unremarkable, with two exceptions. The one is that there is a single Lenten sermon, presumably because he believed that the Christian life should be a continuing Lent. The other remarkable fact is his choice to preach seven times on the Transfiguration.

He seizes on the practical benefits of revelation for the Christian life. The result of the Incarnation is "Every place as Bethlehem, and the Cities of the Aliens shall be as holy as Ierusalem. A full Moon makes a full Sea; and the full exhibition of Christ makes an enlarged Church."[8] Preaching on St. John 3:19, "This is the Condemnation, that Light is come into the World, and men loved Darknes rather then Light," in his second Christmas sermon, he sums up the meaning with reference to both mercy and judgment:

> Here is the Mercy of his Incarnation, if we have Grace to make use of it; and here is the Vengeance for his Rejection at the day of Retribution. Here is the sound of the Harp, and the Song of the Angels at the day of his Birth; and then there is the sound of the Trumpet, the voice of the Arch-Angel at the day of Judgment. Here is the shining of a Star pointing out his first appearing; and then there is a dismal Comet in the Text fore-running his second; both *vagitus Infantis,* and *rugitus Leonis:* or, as St. John puts them together, *ira agni,* the fiercest wrath from the meekest Lamb.[9]

Perfect antithesis, pictorially reinforced, reaches the climax of a single firework, cascading into a brilliant paradox. The same sermon quotes a racy proverb to exemplify how light detects, and darkness hides, shady deeds: "Dark Shops fit best bad Wares."[10] The same vigorous vividness enables him to counter

Pelagianism: "We all set out to Sea in a Leaking Vessel, that still lets in Water; we must always be Pumping."[11] Abstract concepts—the working of the Holy Spirit, for example—are made memorably concrete: "He ministers Corrosives, to make way for Cordials,"[12] where the alliteration makes the apt Pentecostal message memorable.

His sermons are remarkable for the absence of standard anti–Catholic tirades, since in two hundred consecutive pages I was able to find none. Usually the divisions are clear, as for example the first sermon on the Gunpowder Treason, on the text Daniel 6:21–22, "This Chapter upon a Summary View represents, and relates unto us, a malitious Conspiracy, and a miraculous Delivery."[13] His images are brief and to the point, as this of the Gospel: " 'Tis not like some Drug that Apothecaries will venture on, if it will do not good, it will do not hurt but like strong Physick, it will either mend us, or end us."[14] There is wit in Latin as well as in English, as in: "When he was risen, *umbra Petri* did more then *fimbria Christi*; the shadow of *Peter* healed more diseases, then the touch of his garment before the Resurrection. His Death purchased it; his Resurrection performed it."[15] He uses historical narrations sparingly to give the Scriptures their due. Unlike Donne, he is not interested in doctrinal speculation. He cites the Fathers in moderation, but always translates them into English. As the editor of his sermons, William Martyn, Preacher of the Rolls, says: "So great was his care to keep himself close to the Texts [Brownrig] preach'd upon, that . . . His study and Endeavour was to bring Matter out of the Text (they were his own words) and not Matter to the Text, as is the manner of too many of the great and popular *Sermocinatours* of these loose Times."[16] He would have thought it overreaching, not to be under the discipline of the Word of God. That was his strength as a Calvinist.

John Prideaux

The other rigorously Calvinist bishop was John Prideaux (1578–1650) of Worcester, who as Regius Professor of Divinity in Oxford was a veritable hammer of the Arminians, as Heylyn (among many others) came to know. He was another strongly biblical preacher, as one might guess from the title of his book on preaching, *Sacred Eloquence: or, the art of Rhetorick, as it is laid down in Scripture* (1659), and his theology was eminently practical. Prideaux was chaplain to Prince Henry, and on his death, to James I. In 1612 he became Rector of Exeter College, Oxford, and three years later was appointed Regius Professor of Divinity, a chair he held for twenty-six years. He wrote occasional verse, contributing poems to *Iusta Funebra* in 1613 on the death of Sir Thomas Bodley, and to *Epithalamia* on the marriage of Charles I in 1625. Anthony Wood says of him: "In his professorship he shew'd himself a stout champion against Socinus and Arminius."[17] He had to wait until 1641 to become a bishop, only because Charles wished to appease his Calvinist and Puritan opponents.

His wit is a little strained but not excessively so. Here is an example of his wordplay on tenses: "It is the *fashion* of the *world*, to be so ill *Grammarians*, that they bee all for the *present*, but little for the *praeter-perfect*, or the *future* tense. Though S. *Paul* tell us that the *fashion* of this world *passeth away*, and wisheth us, not to *fashion* our *selves*, according to this world."[18] He is better at maxims than wit, as in the following example, an encouragment to humility. He had previously told the story of the gardener who accepted a briar which prevented all others from entering the garden, and then continues with: "A *hoppe* will soone start up, to *overlooke* the *pole*, by which it climb'd."[19]

His qualities as a preacher were many. His sermons usually have arresting beginnings. Each text is placed fully in its narrative context. His sermon titles are either lively or intriguing. His divisions are relatively simple and rarely run to elaborate sub-divisions. He commonly compares the views of many biblical interpreters, including the major Fathers, medieval schoolmen, and modern Catholic and Protestant interpreters, especially when illuminating cruxes. He uses historical narrations to great effect, though not as frequently as most metaphysical preachers. Those that he does use are often polemically anti-Catholic, as the following shrewd example:

Chapter IV

Pius Quintus (that Pope who excommunicated Queene *Elizabeth*) was wont to say (I should not *relate* it, but that I have a *Iesuit* for my *author*, and that is *Cornelius a Lapide* upon the 11th of *Numbers*, at the 11th verse) *Cum essem religiosus*, when I was a *religious* man (he meant, I thinke a *plaine Monk*, without any *Ecclesiastical degree*, or *dignity*) I had a very good *hope*, of the *salvation* of my *soule*. Being made *Cardinall, Extimui*, I was much afraid of it; *Nunc Pontifex creatus*, but now being *Pope*, what now? *Pene despero*, I almost despaire of it."[20]

Like most metaphysical preachers, he makes effective use of Greek and Latin sources and words, and even of Syrian and Arabic words, so that their etymology clarifies a dark or obscure text. In a sermon on *Heresies Progresse* he points out that "heresy" has nothing to do with the Latin *haereo* (meaning "to stick,") but, in various places in the New Testament, can mean an indifferent opinion, or a sect, and elsewhere an infamous division, or an adulterous and unfaithful character.[21]

His style is one of great oratorical ease, occasionally almost conversational in its naturalness. He can use simple oratorical appeals: "When may a *Captaine* better approve himselfe, then in a fight? Or a *Sea-man* then in a *storme?* Or a good *Physitian*, then in a time of *sicknesse?* Or a resolute *Souldier* of *Christ*, but where *schismes* and *heresies*, are most *tumultuous* and *dangerous?*"[22] He is also capable of making a fine ending to a sermon, as in an Easter discourse, which ends with the concision of a collect:

O thou therefore that of *stones* canst raise up children unto *Abraham*, and revived'st *Lazarus* when he stanke in his grave, make our dead hearts sensible of the vertue of thy *Resurrection*, that seconding thy *first fruits* with a serious awakening to righteousnesse, we may triumphantly meete death in the face with this happy 'ἐπινίκιον, *O death where is thy sting: o grave where is thy victory?*[23]

141

John Hacket

The greatest of the eight Calvinist bishops as a metaphysical preacher was undoubtedly John Hacket (1592–1670). His brilliance marked him out at the start. Andrewes, then dean of Westminster, encouraged him at Westminster School; and at Trinity College, Cambridge he was chosen Fellow immediately on graduating as a B.A.[24] His promise was brilliantly fulfilled. He preached more than eighty times at court and left one hundred sermons in print, his *Century of Sermons Upon Several Remarkable Subjects,* published posthumously in 1675. He was also a man of great courage—anything but a trimming and compromising Vicar of Bray. His early backer was Bishop John Williams, later archbishop of York and James I's Lord Keeper, who invited him to become his chaplain in 1621. Shortly afterwards the king appointed him to St. Andrew's, Holborn and to Cheam, the former for wealth and the latter for health.[25] At Holborn he had many famous lawyers in his congregation, including Sir Julius Caesar, as well as the severe Judge Jones. On Sundays his church was crowded, such was the fame of his sermons, and "well attended upon all occasions of weekly Prayer, and Sacraments celebrated Monthly, besides at other times, at which, especially upon the *Churches* Festivals, not only the whole Body of the Church, but the Galleries would also be full of communicants."[26] Plume, his biographer, considered Hacket to be in the first rank of preachers "if we consider his acute Wit, deep Judgment, flowing Elocution, singular Learning, and great Reading, whereby (as *Porphiry* complained of *Origen*) he made use of all Heathen Learning to adorn the Doctrine of Christianity." The same writer adds that sometimes that "nothing but *Honey* and *Milk* lay under his *Tongue:* At other times he seemed (like St. *Basil*) to be a *strong Hailshower,* bearing down all before it" and wounding the "most obstinate and insensible mind."[27]

His courage was seen during one Sunday while he was reading the Prayer Book service in his church. Interrupted by a soldier of the earl of Essex, who pushed a pistol against his breast and commanded him to stop reading the liturgy, "the *Doctor* smiled at his insolency in that *sacred* place, and not at all terrified, said *he* would do what became a *Divine*, and he might do what became a *Souldier*, so the Tumult was for that time quieted, and the *Doctor* permitted to proceed."[28] Hacket's dialectical skill was equal to his courage. Called upon, at only a day's notice, to defend the work of deans and cathedral chapters before an iconoclastic Parliament, he performed his task so skillfully and tactfully—stressing the importance of divine worship and preaching, the training in music, the contribution they made to education in schools and libraries, the employment they offered the laity, and the prizes for clerical scholars they provided—that a delay was conceded before their eventual removal.[29] One example of his wit can be seen on the death of Oliver Cromwell, when he enquired of General Monk "whereby he should be a *Benedictine* Monk, or a Blessing to the Nation, and not a *Dominican, Dominari in exercitu.* "[30]

At the Restoration he was reappointed to his resident canonry at St. Paul's Cathedral, and soon afterwards offered the see of Gloucester which he turned down. Later, however, he accepted the "ruined Cathedral, City, and Diocese of Lichfield and Coventry." 2000 shot and 1500 granadoes had been discharged against the cathedral and had smashed the steeple. He managed to raise £20,000 in eight years to finance the rebuilding. He would preach up and down his diocese three out of every four Sundays, and was exemplary in rectifying disorders in churches.

Calvinist he was, but he did not follow Musculus' way of preaching by doctrine, reason, and use, as did so many Puritans. His practice was rather the contrary, for he thought that the clerk of every justice of the peace could do that, as well as any minister. In his view, a good preacher needed "*Logick* to divide the Word aright, *Rhetoricke* to perswade, *School Divinity* to perswade Gainsayers, knowledge of many Tongues to understand *Originals* and learned Authors." But he firmly believed that all learning "without a good Example and innocency of life was but *a jewel of gold in a Swine's snout.* "[31]

As to his appearance and voice, we are told that he was "small and slender" but "of a serene and comely countenance, vivid eyes, with a rare alacrity and suavity of aspect, representing the inward candour and serenity of his mind." His voice "was ever wonderful sweet and clear, so that Dr. *Collins* would say, *he* had the finest Bell in the University. . . ."[32]

The outstanding characteristics of his sermons are many. Doctrinally, there was a profound emphasis on worship as the central act of the Christian life. He had many sermons on the adoration of God and the need for reverence, and, subordinately, he stressed that the sacraments and memorial days were reminders of God's unfailing graciousness. He was fond of the beauty of holiness and the holiness of beauty; and appreciated the English Church as the *via media* between Rome and Geneva, and its fidelity in doctrine and polity to the undivided Church of the first five centuries. He expressed a profound understanding of the Cross and the Resurrection of Christ, because they won forgiveness and eternal life for the penitent and faithful Christian. Also, he felt the Christian life to be marked by true joy and unending felicity.

Rhetorically, his sermons are marked by a great fondness for emblems and riddles, a liking for evoking the curiosity of his listeners by the choice of unusual texts, a fondness for witty transitions, a delight in epigrammatic citations (especially from poets such as Homer, Sophocles, Euripides, Virgil, Ovid, and Horace), and a pleasure in narrations from Greek and Roman history through Plutarch and Pliny, and for ecclesiastical history from Josephus and Eusebius.

Expositorily, his sermons show a fondness for series of disquisitions exfoliating from a single text or narrative passage of Scripture. He exhibits a delight in citing several authorities when weighing up a crux, and a liking for polemical references to Roman Catholicism, while, contradictorily, feeling the scandal of Christian disunity.

Some of his qualities deserve to be sampled. Ingenious text choice is exemplified for his Gowrie Sermon preached before King James. On that occasion his text was Psalm 51:9. "Yea, mine own familiar friend . . . hath lifted up his heel against me." Equally ingenious was his text for the commemoration of the deliverance from the Gunpower Plot. This was Amos 9:2: "Though they dig into Hell, there shal my hand take them." The first of fifteen sermons on the Incarnation exhibits his fondness for paradoxes and his wit—when he mentions his five divisions, he refers to them as follows: ". . . these are the parts of my Text: With great reverence be it spoken, I may call them the swadling clouts wherewith I must wrap my Saviour."[33] The fifth sermon on the Incarnation begins with Andrewes' paradox of the infant and unspeaking Word of God in the cradle, but continues with great originality: "He that bears up the pillars of the earth was born in the arms of *Joseph*, and carried into Egypt. The Infinite Majesty that hath made the bounds of heaven and earth, being himself without limits or circumscription, was bound with swadling clouts, and laid in a manger."[34] The eighth sermon on the Incarnation has a striking and appropriately Protestant start: "This is the *Sons* day, and not the *Mothers*: This is Christs own day, and not *Maries*. Therefore it is not for the Wombs sake, but for the fruit of the Womb; not for the Paps of a mortal Woman, but for the Infants sake, an *immortal* God that I have chosen this Text."[35] This opening was all the more striking in a Christmas sermon, since he chose to preach on the unusual text, Luke 11:27–28, telling of the woman who admired Jesus, saying, "Blessed is the Womb that bare thee, and the Paps that gave thee suck," whom Jesus rebuked with, "Yea, rather blessed are they that hear the Word of God, and keep it."

His maxims and his images are memorable: "Happy is the man . . . who will not come near the suburbs of sin" is one. Another is this: ". . . folly and melancholy make some men suck at the Dugs of hope, and fill themselves with wind and vanity. Luther expresseth this madness in this phrase, that every man hath a *Pope* in his belly."[36] A third maxim goes: ". . . a blessing is soon forgotten which is but tackt on with joy; when fear drives a nail in, it stays the faster in the memory."[37] He can borrow an image from Augustine but make it his own, as in the following analogy of the Devil as a mastiff, that if you "beat him, thrust him away, stave him off, break his teeth in his head, yet he flies upon you, till he have torn and devoured you."[38] He can combine wit and imagery, when he describes the Puritans who wish to change the liturgy as chess players trying to checkmate the king or remove the bishop.[39]

He can delight his auditory with humor, shrivel them with irony, and move them to compassion, such was his command of what that century called "the religious affections." He joyfully reports that it was not the male apostles that first learned of the Resurrection but the women, humorously playing with colloquial verbs such as "gad" and "lackey" and "gallop." He jokes about their going to and fro to tell the disciples the good news, and how Eastern observers would be scandalized "for women to gad openly from place to place."

> But these holy Matrons had a clear conscience in them, that it could be no blemish to their honour to lackey up and down in so good an occasion, and upon the Errand of an Angel. Nay, whereas undoubtedly all will say that a sober gate, without too much acceleration, doth best become that Sex, and especially in Publick, yet no pace would best serve but a gallop. In the verse immediately before my Text they did run to bring his Disciples *word*. The Heathen paint *Mercury* with wings at his heels: The Messenger of good tidings should make haste. *Nescit tarda molimina spiritus sancti gratia.* God loves quick despatch in his business.[40]

His irony is seen in contrasting the distance traveled by the three Magi who came to offer gifts to the new-born Christ, with the reluctance of his modern disciples to go out of their way to church: "If it be far from Church from our own home, 'tis too common to mutter at it, and to maunder at a little way, every one would have a Chapel of Ease at his next door: as if it were fitter for Christ to come to them, then for them

to come to Christ."[41] How ironical, too, is his denunciation
of the vanity of women's hairstyles:

> Will you be stiff in your opinion that you may paint, and
> powder, and crisp, and clip hair, and use all those Island
> dog tricks about your head, because the Bible doth in no
> place by name condemn these things? *Beloved,* if the Spirit
> of *God* had penn'd a thousand Bibles more, they could
> not have contain'd the Catalogue of all those Peacock fash-
> ions, into which you transform yourselves from time to
> time.[42]

As for his compassion, it is fully revealed in brief in this
citation from his Spital sermon, before the mayor and aldermen
of the City of London and the orphans of several hospitals,
"these Penons [Pennants] and Triumphs of your charity, which
are placed before mine eyes; wearing their blue cassocks," and
"the *Blew Coat*[43] wherewith you cloath the fatherless is more
precious in God's sight than our own Scarlet. Your *Halls* for
several Companies set out with all magnificence and cost, are
not such stately buildings in Gods eyes as your Hospitals and
Bethlems, and such pious house for the crasie and the diseased."[44]

Far more impressive than the wit, humor, irony, compassion,
and the learning of these sermons is their Christological direction. It transcended his capacity to express it, but his devotion
to Christ finds almost adequate expression in this tribute:

> When I call him the *Glass* in which I see al truth, the
> *Fountain* in which we taste all sweetness, the *Ark* in which
> all precious things are laid up, the *Pearl* which is worth
> all other Riches, the *Flower* of *Jessai* which hath the favour
> of life unto life, the *Bread* that satisfies all hunger, the
> *Medicine* that healeth all sickness, the *Light* that dispelleth
> all darkness; when I have run over all these, and as many
> more glorious Titles, as I can lay on, this description is
> above them, and you may pick them all out of these Sylla-
> bles, our salvation.[45]

John King

John King (?1559–1621), bishop of London, was a great-nephew of Robert King, the first bishop of Oxford, and the father of Henry King, who was belatedly consecrated bishop of Chichester. Both father and son were educated at Westminster School and Christ Church, Oxford, and both were appointed deans of Christ Church. John King was appointed a royal chaplain by Queen Elizabeth. He had also been rector of the important London parish of St. Andrew's, Holborn, and a prebendary of St. Paul's Cathedral. James I retained him as royal chaplain, calling him "a King of preachers." So lugubrious was the son's preaching compared with his father's that—to perpetrate the kind of pun the seventeenth-century preachers delighted in—one is tempted to call him the Prince of Wails.

John King received rapid preferment at the hands of King James, who appointed him dean of Christ Church in 1605, one of the four learned preachers at the important Hampton Court Conference, and bishop of London in 1611, when George Abbot was translated to Canterbury. While he was a bishop, according to Fuller, he preached every Sunday in a pulpit in or near London.[46] According to Anthony Wood he had so excellent a "volubility of speech that Sir Edward Coke would often say of him that he was the best speaker in the Star Chamber of his time."[47]

His first and most extensive set of printed sermons was *Lectures upon Ionas delivered at Yorke,* where he had been the chaplain to Archbishop Piers. They were dedicated to Sir Thomas Egerton, Lord Keeper of the Great Seal, whose chaplain he became on the death of Piers—this at a time when Donne was also a member of Egerton's household. In the preface King laments the disadvantage for any preacher of having his animated words frozen in print: "I . . . who have changed my tongue into a penne, and whereas before I spake with the gesture and countenance of a living man, have now buryed my selfe in a dead letter of lesse effectual perswasion." This suggests the liveliness of his demeanor in the pulpit.

148

Like a good Protestant he makes the literal and historical sense of the Scriptures primary, and he is critical of allegorization, the fault of the schoolmen who, as he wittily puts it, "take the Scriptures by the neck and writhe them from the aime and intention of the holy Ghost."[48] There is, however, a considerable amount of etymological wordplay in his own exegesis, some of it farfetched. For example, he plays on the meaning of the Latin words for man and woman, respectively *vir* and *mulier*, suggesting that the former means strength and the latter softness, citing Varro's improbable derivation of "*Mulier quasi mollior*, of niceness and tendernesse, one letter being changed and another taken away."[49]

He provides an impressive defense of learning in the pulpit:

> So all things are yours, whether the Scripture, or nature, or art, all is yours. Yours are Philosophers. Orators, Historiographers, Poets, Iewes, Grecians, Barbarians, Fathers, new-writers, men, angelles, that you may be saved, this onely is the ende, whereunto our knowledge and learning of what kinde soever is directed.[50]

The erudite references in his lecture-sermons show that, in this respect at least, he practices what he preaches. In addition to a variety of patristic sources cited, the fourth sermon quotes Horace and Cicero twice, the fifth Juvenal and Theocritus, the sixth summarizes part of Ovid's *Metamorphoses*, and the seventh translates Hadrian's poem, *Anima vagula blandula*.

The Calvinist doctrine of predestination is clearly and unflinchingly expounded in reference to the betrayal of Judas:

> Iudas was not yet formed, nor any member of his body set together or fashioned when they were *all written in the booke of God*. He saw the treason in the glasse of his foreknowledge, and *understood his thoughts afarre off.*[51]

King argues that God foreknows good and evil, but only predestinates the good, yet is able to turn Judas's treachery into an act of salvation for others. He faces objections honestly and directly. For example, he is ready to defend the necessity for martyrs in the Church to become the seed of future growth. When he is asked whether this benefit could not have been attained by good means, he replies in Augustinian terms that it seemed better to the wisdom of God to work good out of evil, than to permit no evil at all.[52]

King, in true metaphysical fashion, can shock his congregation by reversing their expectations. He preached a sermon to commemorate King James's daughter's wedding to the ruler of the Palatinate, *Vitis Palatina*, shortly after the ceremony itself. Here he makes the point that Christ must be a wedding guest at this marriage as he was at Cana in Galilee when he performed the first miracle of turning the water into wine, otherwise the wine of the Vine (the potentially fruitful Lady Elizabeth) will only turn into bitter vinegar.[53] Similarly, he can surprise his congregation by the resolution of a paradox, when pointing out that, without the creation of children, there can be no creation of saints:

> *The wife* is the mother of virgins that are no wives; (*Laudo connubium quia generat virgines*, saith Hierome, γυναικομάσις) no generation, no multiplying beneath, no multiplying above, no filling the earth, not so much filling the heavens: if not *filii seculi*, nether will there be *filij coeli*. [54]

The last sermon of Bishop John King's to be published was preached at Paul's Cross in 1620 in the presence of King James, on behalf of the necessary repairs to St. Paul's Cathedral. The text was Psalm 102:13: "Thou shalt arise and have mercy upon Sion, for the time to favour her, yea the set time is come. For thy servants take pleasure in hir stones, and favour the dust thereof." King ingeniously employs an historical narration from Eusebius, the church historian, to create a sense of pity in the vast crowd for the ruined cathedral, the windows of which are like empty eyesockets:

Chapter IV

Thus did that great *Constantine* kisse the eye of *Paphnutius* which the tyrant had caused to be digged out. He tooke no pleasure in the wound and deformity of it *cui lumen ademptum*, but because it had been the orb and circle of so glorious a Confessor, as *Paphnutius* was . . . *Miserentur pulveris*, they so take pleasure in the stones, that they *pittie the dust of Sion.* [55]

King calls upon the pride of the citizens of London in their capital city, in a marvellously sustained encomium. He begins by claiming that England is Europe's ring and London is its gem, if England is the eye, London is the apple of its eye. Then he surveys the great Thames-side city below St. Paul's:

When I behold that forrest of masts upon your river for trafficke and that more than miraculous bridge, which is the *communis terminus*, to joyne the two bankes of that river; your Royall Exchange for Merchants, your Halls for Companies, your gates for defence, your markets for victualls, your aquaeducts for water, your granaries for provision, your Hospitalles for the poore, your Bridewells for the Idle, your Chamber for Orphans, and your Churches for holy Assemblies; I cannot denie them to be magnificent workes . . . But after all these, as Christ said to the young man in the Gospell, which had done all and more, *Unum tibi deest, si vis perfectus esse, vade, vende:* So may I say unto you, if you will be perfit, perfit this Church: not by parting from all, but somewhat, not the poore, but God himselfe.[56]

With resounding prose like this we can agree with King James, that John King belonged to the royal race of preachers.

Thomas Morton

Bishop Thomas Morton (1564–1659) lived longer than any of the other metaphysical preachers. He was a Calvinist, educated under Whitaker, the head of St. John's College, Cambridge, where he became a fellow, and gained his D.D. with great distinction in 1606. Meanwhile he had served as chaplain to Lord Huntingdon, Lord President of the North, where he was employed in reclaiming recusants to the Church of England. One of them, Herbert Croft, later became bishop of Hereford. Morton later accompanied Lord Eure as a chaplain on the embassy to the emperor of Germany and the king of Denmark in 1602. And in 1605 he published the first part of his *Apologia Catholica,* in which it is supposed that he was helped by his friend, John Donne. This work was a defense of the Church of England against the calumnies of the Jesuits, arguing that the English Church bore all the marks of a true church. Partly as a result of this public defense of the Church he was quickly advanced. First he became royal chaplain, then dean of Gloucester in 1606, dean of Winchester in 1609, was consecrated bishop of Chester in 1615, translated to Lichfield and Coventry in 1618, and in 1632 to Durham.

Morton was remarkable for his asceticism: he was celibate, slept on a straw bed, rose at four, retired at ten, rarely drank wine, and ate only one meal a day. He was a patron of scholars, and a refuge for the poor and the troubled. It was characteristic of him that, when the plague raged in York in 1603, he looked after the inmates of the pest-house regardless of the risk of contagion. His biographer provides the details:

> Mr. *Morton* often repaired unto them from Marston [where he was Rector] to *preach* unto the World of God, and to minister consolation to their languishing soules: having withall provisions of meat carried with him in Sacks, to relieve the poorest sort withall. But, as often as he went thither, he suffered not any servant to attend him, but himselfe sadled and unsadled his horse, and he had a private door-stead made through the wall of his study (being the utmost part of the house) for prevention, lest he might bring the contagion with him, and indanger his whole Family.[57]

This man of great integrity gave as the text of his farewell sermon at Winchester, the words of Samuel (I Samuel 12:3):

"Whose Oxe have I taken? or whose Asse have I taken? or whom have I defrauded? whom have I oppressed? or of whose hand have I taken any bribe to blind mine eyes herewith?" He died at the age of ninety-five, having been a model bishop for fifty-four years. The poor were much in his thoughts: it was at his request to the king that the trunkmakers' houses, which were to be demolished to repair St. Paul's Cathedral, were allowed to remain untouched.

He left several apologetical books, but only two printed sermons. One was preached in Durham Cathedral on 5 May 1639, when King Charles visited the city on his way north. His text was Romans 13:1, "Let every soul be subject to the higher Powers, &c.," and his theme was "that arms are not to be taken up by Subjects for defence of Religion." By this he insinuated that the papacy had no right to intervene in political matters, and he has the pope saying, "*Every soul subject?* Not I, saith the *Pope,* and so all Popes of aftertimes, for we have power over all *Powers,* be they *Emperours* themselves, to kick off their Crowns with our feet. . . ."[58] It is not surprising to find him, in a sermon preached four years later, opposing the extreme Puritans, especially the sectaries, and here his wit aids him, as he points out their contradictions:

> But in these times the hand and foot both mutine because they are not eyes, and except our Coblers and Weavers be allowed for Ministers, they will acknowledge no head nor member; how these should receive tolleration anywhere within this Church I know not, except men thought themselves worthy to bee led by blind guides: when as there might be as true Doctrin some time expected from Bedlam, whereof some examples might be given, if such Doctrines were not fitter for a Stage than a Pulpit.

A little later he adds that these enthusiasts inveighing against the papacy are popish, because they constitute themselves supreme and infallible judges of doctrine.[59]

He insists upon the need for passive obedience, except when earthly government countermands the demands of the immortal

God, and pleads that Christians ought, in defense of their Christian profession, "to imitate Christ their General in *Passive Obedience*, in resisting the wicked world, by dying for the Christian Faith and Religion, whensoever the *Alarme* for Martyrdome shall be heard."[60]

This sermon cites Calvin to show that obedience is due to princes even when government degenerates into tyranny, and has references to twenty-one other writers, including contemporary Roman Catholic apologists, such as Parsons, Creswell, Garnet, Thuanus, Barelaius, and Bellarmine, as well as to Luther, Beza, Peter Martyr, and Calvin (thrice quoted) on the Protestant side. He also refers to nine Fathers of the Church, and has a moving reference to the ancient Church:

> The ancient *Catholike Church*, and *Mother* of all Churches Christian, ought also to be acknowledged our blessed Nurse, from whom we may suck the most pure and *wholesome milke*, which the innumerable multitudes of *Martyrs*, *Confessors*, and Professors did; who, notwithstanding the 300 yeeres persecution for Religion, never used, or professed any *forcible defence*.[61]

Clearly, this noble man was a better controversialist and apologist than a preacher, for all his fidelity to Scripture, useful images, and ironical humor.

William Barlow

The sixth bishop, a moderate Calvinist, was William Barlow, who by the time of his death in 1613 had been bishop of Rochester and afterwards of Lincoln. The Calvinist archbishop of Canterbury, Whitgift, made this former fellow of Trinity Hall, Cambridge, his chaplain, and in 1597 presented him to the rectory of St. Dunstan's-in-the-East, near the Tower of London. During his career he was also prebendary of Chiswick in St. Paul's Cathedral, given a canon's stall at Westminster Abbey (which he retained with his episcopal preferments until his death), and dean of Chester for three years before being consecrated as bishop of Rochester. He played his part in producing the King James's translation of the Bible, as one of the scholars who were given the responsibility for translating the apostolic epistles "from Romans to Jude inclusive." Queen Elizabeth thought highly of his preaching, and at the opening of Convocation in 1601 he was chosen to preach the Latin Sermon. This may well have been the one that so displeased the Puritans that they contemptuously termed it "the Barley Loaf."[62] The term punned on his name and denied that his loaf was good wheaten bread.

Bishop Barlow was called upon to preach at times of national crisis, which argues his great soundness of judgment. His two sermons preached at Paul's Cross, the first in 1601, the Sunday after the execution of the earl of Essex, and the second in 1605, the Sunday immediately after the discovery of the Gunpowder Plot, must have been listened to with unusual attention. Apart from these two, we have only four other sermons extant in print. One, "The Eagle and the Body," was a Lenten disquisition preached before Queen Elizabeth in 1601; a second was a Hampton Court sermon on the antiquity and superiority of bishops, in the presence of King James and that unyielding Presbyterian, Melville, a sermon which earned the preacher a pasquinade from Melville. The third was a commemoration of the Gunpowder Treason preached before the Lords of the Privy Council and the chief judges in 1607. Its title was *A Brand, Titio Erepta.* The fourth sermon, entitled *Christian Liberty*, was delivered in Westminster Abbey. Its preface supplies the curious information that this censure of liberty will not please the conventiclers who muddy the city, but adds, "when this Sermon was preached, applause ensued."[63]

His qualities as a preacher are exemplified in the sermon preached at Paul's Cross, on the Sunday following the execution of the earl of Essex. In the gloomy context of the threat of possible civil war, he can still be witty. He had been given the briefest time in which to prepare this sermon, so, as he puts it, the auditory may say that "this was but like the growth of Tadstoole, *Oritur, Moritur.*"[64] Moreover, he was suspected of being a propagandist, so he shrewdly indicates that his aim is "onely to declare [of the earl of Essex] what I have eyther *ex occulo,* or *oraculo,* as Bern.[ard] speaketh, from his owne writing, and confession."[65] Anticipating the crowd's objection that he is not only a time-server but a preferment-seeker, Barlow counters criticism with the statement that, in this very place, he had previously celebrated the victory at Cadiz won by the earl. Inevitably he spoke of the danger of inordinate pride and overweening ambition in the earl of Essex, which he likened to a fire, for the potential good and harm it can do:

> . . . for could he in any moderation have carried himselfe, and have been contented with his great state, what good might he have done to this church and realme, to men of state, of religion or learning, of war? but as fire, if it be well and rightly used, burneth in the house to the profit of the familie; but if mistayed or abused, burneth the house to the undoing of the inhabitants: so had he beene contented to have beene τις μεγαι, a certaine great man, great among the rest; and not affected with *Magus,Act. 8.* to be ὁ μεγας, the onely great man, and none to be great but he; in honour he might still have lived and preferred others.[66]

In this passage, he has not only provided a simple but apt image, but also a pun in Greek, reminding us that he was, in fact, a distinguished Greek scholar.

In the same sermon he uses an example of "unnatural" natural history to illustrate the many-bodied character of a rebellion: "This rebellion is a compound of many rebellions, just as the *Nabis* in *Egipt* is a beast shaped of many beasts."[67] Barlow uses two historical narrations to parallel Essex's dastardly insurrection. One was Friar Clement who assassinated Henry III of France and used the act of a biblical murderer as both example and justification, as Essex himself had done.[68] The other was the rebellion of Henry, Duke of Lancaster, against Richard II of England.[69]

Chapter IV

Then follows a careful analysis and summary of the earl's crime derived from his own confession in writing and by word of mouth. It indicates how the conspiracy was hatched, how the contagion spread, how it cried to God for vengeance, how bloody the execution would have been if effected, how it endangered the queen's life had he remained alive, so that "Himselfe a surfet to the realme, to be spewed out iustly."[70] Details are then given: the articles propounded against the state, the surprising of the court with armed power, the imprisoning of the queen, the summoning of Parliament, the chief places at court to be at the command of the papists. Then Barlow finishes with two final sentences to defuse the crowd's admiration for Essex, when he notes the earl's ambitions for "The command of the tower, as bridle to you of this citie," and "His hard opinion and censure of your basenesse and unfaithfulnesse to the Queene."[71]

It is only fair to Barlow to give an example of a different type of sermon, namely a court sermon, "The Eagle and the Body," preached before Queen Elizabeth during Lent of 1601, just a year after the execution of Essex. The text is unusual, from Luke 17:37, "He [Jesus] said unto them, Wheresoever the Body is, there will be the Eagles be gathered together." He begins by indicating the variety of interpretations possible: "Which words may bee handled, either as a *Parable* in Scripture, or as a *Text* of Scripture; as it is a *Proverbe* at randome applied, the use is manifold and generally *Morall*: as it is a *Text*, ioyned to the Precedents, the doctrine is comfortable and properly *Spirituall*."[72] In fact, he chooses a very allegorical interpretation, firstly with Christ as the Body, secondly the eagles are the elect, thirdly their flocking is their affection, and fourthly the place is Christ's unlimited residence. This allows him to produce a fine passage on the Communion of the Saints:

> The third followeth συναχθήσονται, thcy will *flocke* or be *gathered together*; wherein many things are worth observation, if time would suffer. First, in the praeposition συν the *ioint* resort and the *Communion of Saints*, both in their

inward man; for howsoever they bee, either *triumphant* in heaven, or *militant* on earth; or *disperst* in place; or *unequall* in condition; or *aliens* in nation; or differing in some circumstance of opinion; yet *congregabuntur*, there will be among them a *unanimous coalition*, aswell mutuall betweene themselves, in charitable affection, as also in a concurrent desire of this *one* BODIE, which is their head, *Christ*; professing the same *Faith*; resting upon the same *hope*; holding the unitie of the of the same *spirit* in the bond of peace: So, for their outward man also, even these bodies which whether consumed by fire; or suncke in the seas; or devoured of beasts; or rotted in their graves; or quartered (yea minsed by tyrants;) yet *congregabuntur*, they shall all be gathered in one place, and bee ioyned with the same Christ, to sit with him in his *Throne*. [73]

Earlier Barlow had another fine passage, telling of the power of faith and the sharp eaglelike sight of the elect, which transcends reason. But the very sermon which speaks of the inadequacy of reason in matters of religion is crammed with learned references. There are thirty-eight of them in thirty-six pages, citing sixteen different authors, including (in order of frequency) Bernard, Chrysostom, Philo, Gregory the Great, Gregory Nazianzen, Plato, Basil, Augustine, Isidore Pelusiot, Origen, Clement of Alexandria, Ambrose, Theophrastus, Aristotle, Jerome, and Hilary.

The end of the sermon, which is an admirable summary of its theme, also describes the progress of the Christian pilgrimage:

Wherever *he* is, his chosen will *Flocke* unto him, in his *word* they *beleeve* him, in *Baptisme* they *indue* him, in the *Eucharist* they eate him, in the poore they *releeve* him, in his *life* they followe him, in his *death* they *trust* in him, in his *Temple* they *glorifie* him, on *earth* they *affect* him, in *heaven* they *inioy* him. *They will follow the Lambe wheresoever hee goeth.* To him with the Father, etc. [74]

Wit and learning he had in plenty, but Barlow's sermons had other qualities which we have not illustrated. One is the use of intriguing texts and mottoes—in a commemoration of the Gunpowder Plot his motto was, "They match Cockatrices egges but weave the Spiders Webbe."[75] Another of his qualities is the gift for vivid narrative writing. Again in a sermon describing the Gunpowder Plot he tells of the brutish inhumanity of the manner of death planned, "not *man-like to kill,* but beast-like to discorpe and teare parcell meale, the bodies of such personages," a manner of death intended also as death of the soul "by taking away many, so suddenly in their sinnes unrepented, with their mindes unprepared."[76] He also had the capacity to make abstract doctrines vivid and practical. He deals, for example, with the danger that an exclusive emphasis on the doctrine of salvation by faith alone might produce, in its possible neglect of good works.[77] Incidentally, that was an indication that the bishop who preached so powerfully on the doctrine of election, could also warn of the dangers of solefideism, and was thus genuinely a moderate Calvinist.

John Bowle

John Bowle (d. 1637), the seventh Calvinist bishop, can be rapidly considered since only two English sermons of his survive. A former fellow of Trinity College, Cambridge, he became household chaplain to Sir Robert Cecil, then dean of Salisbury, and, in 1629, bishop of Rochester. He delivered a Latin sermon to the clergy of the Province of Canterbury gathered in Synod in London in 1620, which was published in the same year. One surviving English sermon was preached at the funeral of Henry, Earl of Kent. Another, preached at Maple Durham in Oxfordshire in 1616, shows his Calvinism in its concern to link the *ordo salutis* to Christ at every stage. Only the funeral sermon will be analyzed.

His text is Luke 2:20, "Lord now lettest thou thy servant depart in peace." He has a fondness for Latinisms, as when indicating that the incarnate Christ was accompanied by four voices (Latin *Voces*):

> *At his Baptisme, Voce proclamantis. . .*
> *In his Preaching, Voce acclamantis. . .*
> *At his Death, Voce exclamantis. . . .*[78]

The division of the sermon is complex: the present time, the fervent desire, the dutiful servant, the powerful servant, the infallible promise, and the comfortable condition offer six separate themes. His wit is revealed in a pun already quoted on the deceased: "His private devotions were performed without a Trumpet: I will not make them more by *Arte* then they were in *heart*,"[79] and in the following instance of psychological insight:

> We may tell you, that one thiefe went from the gallowes to glory: but we must not conceale, that God opened the mouth of one Asse, which is no priviledge for common Asses. And yet I will be liberal on Gods part; I will promise heaven assuredly to the sinner, that doth repent but *one day* before he dies. You heare this mercy with greedinesse; turne not the grace of God into wantonnes: be sure you repent *one day* before you dye, *whereof you cannot be sure except you repent every day.* [80]

He is also fond of biblical exempla, patristic citations, and historical narrations. An intriguing example of the latter makes the point of the democracy of the dead, as medieval a theme as one could wish to find:

> *Mennippus, the Satyricall Philosopher,* meeting *Mercurie* in the *Elizian* fields: amongst all the ghosts, would needs know, which was *Philip the great King of Macedon.* Hee (quoth *Mercurie*) is *Philip* of *Macedon,* that hath the *bald head. Mennippus.* I know not him by this, for *all* their skuls are bald. *Mercurie.* Hee which hath a *flat nose.* is *Philip* of *Macedon.* (*Mennippus.*) Why, all have *flat noses.* (*Mercurie*) Hee with the *hollow eyes,* is King *Philip* of *Macedon.* (*Menippus.*) Why, all have *hollow eyes, bare teeth, naked ribs, open pores,*

disionted members, all are carkasses. Mercurie. Why then, *Men-ippus,* in death there is no *difference* betwixt a King and a Beggar. [81]

The margin indicates that the source was Lucan, and this is a clue to the learning of this man who, in a forty-five page sermon has thirty-nine references to sixteen different Fathers, and ten references to nine different classical authors. If not one of the greatest preachers of the century, he is still a very able one.

Henry King

The last of our octet is Bishop Henry King (1592–1669), and he is mentioned last because his Calvinism is milder than that of the others, although he is not averse to quoting Calvin, nor to affirming that there are limits to human freedom. The son of John King, bishop of London, he was educated at Westminster School, and Christ Church, Oxford. He was both a metaphysical poet and preacher. A close friend of John Donne (and a prebendary of St. Paul's when Donne was dean), he was an executor of his will, and counted Ben Jonson, George Sandys, and Izaak Walton among his friends. His father unwisely pushed him to make his first sermon at St. Paul's Cross on 8 November 1617, on which Chamberlain reports that "he did reasonablie well, but nothing extraordinarie . . . beeing rather slow of utterance, *orator parum vehemens.*"[82] On 25 November 1621 he was asked to preach again at Paul's Cross, in order to repudiate the rumor that his father had died as a convert to Roman Catholicism.

Possibly because of the uncertainty of his theological allegiance or a feeling that he lacked rigor in administration, preferment came slowly. He had been a canon of Christ Church some five years before he was appointed dean of Rochester, and he was only elevated to the see of Chichester, on the day after the Lords had consented to pass a bill depriving bishops of their votes, because the king needed to palliate the opposition.

At the Restoration he returned to Chichester, but he only lived to enjoy his see for six years.

Many of his sermons, like many of his poems, were published, but they are not among the finest products of the golden age of the English pulpit. However, between the rather monotonous passages of his many sermons, there are to be found some foothills and even an occasional peak of eloquence. He is capable of the occasional lively metaphor, as when he defends the integrity of his father's reputation with this effective image: "If any should labour to perswade that Snow were black, his foule report could not sully it; and though you might thinke him shamelesse that would averre it, you would take him to be mad that should beleeve it."[83] He can use classical parallels for Christian terms neatly, as in dealing with the seven petitions of the Lord's Prayer. First he likens the seven parts to the seven turrets of the landscape of Jerusalem for the Psalmist, and then to the shield of Minerva made of many parts yet it is "but one Christian Buckler," and is like "the Targe of *Aiax* this is *Oratio Septemplex* (as his was a sevenfold *Clypeus Septemplex.*)" Finally he adds, "that Buckler was Dart-proofe, impenetrable and this prayer an impenetrable shield to *resist the fiery darts of Satan.*"[84]

He is capable of a daring expression in the metaphysical manner, when expounding the "Amen" of the Lord's Prayer: "In a Commonwealth it would be thought a Forgerie for a Party to Seale his owne Passport; but in the Church tis Religion, and an Indulgence given by Christ, that each man may promote not only his Prayers, but his passage to Heaven, and contribute something to the Sealing of his owne Passport."[85] Hardly less audacious are his words on Prayer:

> It is our scaling ladder, *Oratio iusti penetrat nubes,* our Engine of Battery, by which Heaven is beseiged and suffers violence (as Christ said). 'Tis our Weapon with which we would our enemies, nay, *Telum est quo vulneramus cor Dei;* with it even God himself is wounded, as the Spouse in the *Canticles* cryes, *Charitate vulneror.* [86]

162

Chapter IV

As late as 1662, King was still meditating on death in the meta-physical manner, not only in the maxim "There is no gluttony like *Death*"[87] but in an extensive passage reminiscent of Donne:

> The Grave is commonly as powerful an Oratour as the Pulpit, and by presenting the Fears of an ill Death instructs us in the Rules of a Good Life: My assurance is that as the winding Sheet fits every Body by dilating or contracting it self to every Hearer, so my discourse will suit it self to every Hearer. Like *Philipps* Boy, it holds out to Youth a Skull, to Age, a Coffin.[88]

King can coin fresh maxims, too, with a touch of wit, as the following, urging his hearers to confession: "Thus you may perceive, there are no Arrerages left in Gods Audit; he forgives both the *Guilt* of the sin, and the *punishment*; both the suit and the damages."[89] The place where wit was expected in meta-physical sermons was at the beginning or end, but chiefly in the divisions, and King is no exception. One sermon ends thus: "I have held you too long upon these first words *Our Father*, indeed beyond a *Pater noster* while, But shall quickly dismisse you, for my speech is now arrived at the end and period of our Prayers journey, Heaven, *which art in Heaven*."[90] In his funeral sermon for Bishop Duppa, he says that he will not trouble his auditory with any curious division, and that "The First Joint whereof is (that which disjoins Nature, and must Divide us from one another, Yea makes a Division of us from Ourselves by Disuniting Soul and Body . . .) *Death*."[91] He can also employ his wit for an anti-Roman Catholic squib, referring to the political interference by the princes of that Church, arguing that if the cardinals had only lived within their cloisters, "many Princes had gone downe to their Graves, *Sicca morte*, with white winding sheets, not stained or discoloured with their own bloud."[92]

He is a most learned man, as can be seen from an analysis of the citations of the eleven sermons in his *An Exposition Upon the Lords Prayer*. Of the Fathers he cites Augustine fifty-eight times, Ambrose fifteen, Chrysostom twelve, Aquinas ten, Cyprian nine, Tertullian and Jerome eight, Peter Lombard seven, Bernard six, Minutius Felix, Leo, and Gregory the Great four, and Origen, Eusebius, and John of Damascus twice. Reformed divines cited are Calvin and Chemnitz thrice. Fifteen classical authors are cited, Seneca six times, Homer, Plutarch, Petronius, and Horace twice, Aristotle and Plato once each. In addition, he refers to fifteen Roman Catholic commentators on the Bible, whether late medieval or contemporary, including Biel thirteen times, Alexander of Hales fifteen, and Cajetan and Bellarmine respectively four and three times, and there is a single reference each to Rabbinics and to the Qu'ran.

At the Restoration Henry King tried to find the middle way between the over-ornamental Donne and the simplicity of the Andrewes method, which he called the "clothed" and the "naked." He refused the "naked" manner because it rejected culture, but became dissatisfied with "clothed" rhetoric because wit was uncontrolled by judgment. His preference is expressed in a sermon of 1663:

> As Judgment is the Ballast of Wit, so Matter is of Words. A Vessel at Sea, which bears more Sail than Ballast, is ever apt to over-set: so they whose Phantasie is stronger than their Religion, whose words more full of sound than devout sense, for want of just poise lose their own Adventure and endanger others.[93]

James Ussher

No account of Calvinists in the Anglican hierarchy would be complete without a profile of the learned Calvinist archbishop of Armagh in the Protestant Church of Ireland. Archbishop James Ussher (1581–1656) was nurtured by and nurtured Trinity College, Dublin, of which he was graduate, fellow, and first professor of divinity, when its earliest provosts were distinguished Puritans. Before he entered the college at thirteen, he had already read William Perkins in manuscript and Augustine's *Meditations*. Before graduating he had prepared a biblical chronology in Latin, and later became famous for proposing B.C. 4004 as the date of the Creation.

It became his early ambition to answer a controversial work by Stapleton the Jesuit, *A Fortresse of the Faith* (1585), where the claims of the Roman Catholic Church were powerfully reinforced from antiquity. To this end he spent eighteen years studying the Fathers. In 1621 he was consecrated Archbishop of Armagh and Primate of the Anglican Church in Ireland, a counterpart (and correspondent) of William Laud, Archbishop of Canterbury. He was a Calvinist who shared the theology of the Puritans, without their ceremonial scruples, liturgical ideals, or wish for a more egalitarian church polity.

Although Ussher and Laud belong to opposing theological schools, yet they shared a love of learning, respect for antiquity, veneration for constituted authority (though Ussher was not as rigid as Laud in his demand for uniformity), and a belief in the divine right of kings. Burnet, the Latitudinarian bishop, said of Ussher: "No man had a better soul" and "He had a way of gaining people's hearts and touching their consciences that look't like somewhat of the apostolical age reviv'd."[94]

Ussher's sermons are a cross between metaphysical and Puritan preaching. That is, he can be elegant and witty, epigrammatic and metaphorical, and use Latin and Greek tags and proverbs. He does not, however, employ paradoxes, complex divisions, historical narrations, riddles, and his learning is never ostentatious or obscure. His teaching is consistently and faithfully biblical and, starting from the contexts of his texts, always ends with practical "uses" or applications. He is especially good at raising objections and answering them, and at developing theological doctrines in logical sequence with concision and clarity.

For all his delight in the whole logically interrelated system of Calvinist theology, he was nevertheless extremely tolerant and argued strongly for the avoidance of name-calling in the Church and of party politics in religion, because of the disruptive dangers of the *odium theologicum*. The most remarkable parts of his discourses from the pulpit are vivid descriptions of the confusion of the naked soul facing divine judgment,[95] the horrors of hell,[96] and, especially, the terrible pain of the Crucifixion.[97]

His elegant wit is seen in the opening of a sermon preached before the House of Commons at St. Margaret's Church, Westminster in 1620. Here he engages his auditory by citing the verse but one before his text, "I speak to wise men" (I Corinthians 10:15). He adds that, however unwise he feels himself to be, he is cheered by the following thought: "no great blame can light herein upon me, but that some aspersion thereof must reflect upon yourselves, who happen to make so evil a choice: the more facile I expect you to be in a cause wherein yourselves are someways interested."[98] At another time his wit will pillory ignorant ministers: "What sincere milk of the Word can we draw out of such dry-nurses, who had need of instruction themselves, and to be set to school again."[99]

For a vivid image of a merely superficial and transient faith, he turns to the wine-taster

who sips, but does not drink a deep draught of the wine: He that can take a full draught of Christ crucified, he shall never thirst . . . but it shall not be so with him that doth but taste. The vintner goes round the cellar, and tastes every vessel; he takes it into his mouth, and spits it out again, and yet knows by the tasting whether it be good or bad; the wine goeth but to his palate, it reaches not to the stomach. So a temporary believer tastes and feels what an excellent thing it is to have communion with Christ, and to be made partaker of his glory; but he does not taste it.[100]

On the great divisive theological issue of Calvinism or Arminianism, Ussher preached a courageous sermon before King Charles at Greenwich in 1627, when he advised that "all opprobrious terms be suppressed" and defended the Calvinists now going out of favor. He shrewdly pointed out that the king's learned father was a Calvinist:

I see that those who will not yield to that new doctrine [Arminianism] which hath disturbed the low countries, there is an odious name cast upon them, and they are accounted puritans, which is a thing tending to dissension; we know who are esteemed by Christ, and were it not a vile thing to term him a puritan? And King James maintained the same; and shall those be accounted so, who confess the points which he maintained?[101]

He is bold enough to add that, since the majority of English churchmen are Calvinists, if he were an Arminian himself he would feel bound to keep the knowledge of it to himself "rather than by unseasonable uttering of it, to disturb the peace of the Church."[102]

As for his powers of description, I know of no parallel passage which, refusing to play with paradoxes, reveals the agony of the Cross as memorably as Ussher in his sermon on the text of Philippians 2:8, "And being found in fashion as a man, he humbled himself and became obedient to the death of the cross." He asks the congregation to consider its accursedness and shame, and, finally, its pain. He insists that placing Christ on the beams of this instrument of barbarous torture was such a stretching of his limbs as on the rack. He claims that the depiction of the event by painters is misleading: "Believe not the painters: Our Saviour had four nails. Not one through both feet as they describe it, but two through his hands, and two through his feet."[103] Then Ussher describes the raising of the Cross with Christ on it: "As when a man is stretched to the full length, and should be with a jerk put up; it is like a strapado, as it were the unjoining of a man."[104] And Christ hung there for six interminable hours. Ussher has resisted all impertinent attempts at rhetorical effect; he is concerned only with the unvarnished horror of the cruelty of men and the anguish of the eternal Son of God. This was the vertebral quality of his Calvinism which saved him from baroque or rococo theatricality.

It is intriguing, if not unexpected, to discover that his answer to the taunting Roman Catholic question: Where was your Church before Luther? is virtually the same as Laud's:

In all places of the world, when the ancient foundations were retained, and these common principles of faith, upon the profession whereof men have ever been wont to be admitted, by baptism, into the Church of Christ; there we doubt not but our Lord had his subjects, and we our fellow-servants. For we bring in no new faith no new Church.[105]

Leaving the eight bishops and one archbishop, we now turn to the better known of the Calvinist minor clergy, most of whom were royal chaplains, and two of whom were redoubtable controversialists: Daniel Featley and Thomas Fuller.

Daniel Featley

Daniel Featley, or Fairclough, (1582–1645) was appropriately trained at Corpus Christi College, Oxford, the alma mater of England's two earliest apologists for the Church of England, Jewell and Hooker. His godfather, John Rainolds, was president of the college, and the leader of the Calvinists in the university. He proved his mettle as a controversialist as chaplain to Sir Thomas Edmondes, British ambassador in Paris, when he disputed with Jesuits from 1610 to 1612. The twenty-one sermons he preached in the embassy chapel are included in his *Clavis Mystica* (1636). Later he was appointed domestic chaplain to the Calvinist archbishop of Canterbury, Abbott, and he was rector of Lambeth, and rector of Acton.

He came to national attention as a controversialist on two occasions. On 27 June 1634 he and Francis White (then dean of Carlisle) held a famous conference at the house of Sir Humphrey Lynde with the Jesuits, Fathers John Fisher and John Sweet. When an account of this was published favorable to

Rome, Abbot asked Featley to prepare a report favorable to Canterbury, which was titled, *The Romish Fisher caught and held in his owne Net; or, a True Relation of the Protestant Conference and Popish Difference. A Justification of the one, and a Refutation of the other, &c.* The second occasion was when James I was pleased to fence with him in a "scholastick duel." Featley published an account of this as *Cygnea Cantio: or learned Decisions . . . and pious Directions for Students in Divinitie, delivered by . . . King James at White Hall, a few weeks before his death* (1629).

He ran into trouble with Laud, for refusing to move his communion table at Lambeth against the east wall altar-fashion, and several philippics against Roman Catholics were ordered to be eliminated before his *Clavis Mystica* could be printed. The atrabilious Heylyn said that Featley, who served as a member of the Westminster Assembly but who scrupled taking the Solemn League and Covenant, was "a Calvinist always at heart."[106] At that time Featley was a royal chaplain. He retired from the Assembly at the royal request, but always maintained his belief in the divine right of kings and in the liturgy and discipline of the Church of England. His reputation was so high as a scholar that he was offered the chair of divinity in the University of Leyden in 1643.[107]

The only time he refrained from controversial writings was in 1625 and 1626 when the plague was ravaging England. It was then that he wrote his *Ancilla Pietatis.* This had reached its sixth edition by 1639 and was a favorite of Charles I in his troubles. His most famous book recorded his verbal jousting with the Baptists, Denny and Kiffin, and was entitled, characteristically, Καταβαπτισταὶ Καταπτυστοί. *The Dippers dipt: or, the Anabaptists duck'd and plung'd over head and eares at a Disputation at Southwark* (1645). The year before he had published *Roma Ruens; Romes Ruin; being a succinct Answer to a Popish Challenge concerning the antiquity, unity, universality, succession, and perpetual visibility of the true Church.* This work was written at the request of Parliament while he was imprisoned by Parliament for association with Ussher and the king. In January 1633/4 he published the third part of his *Gentle Lash* which vindicated the articles, discipline, and liturgy of the Church of England against contemporary Puritan divines. He was an honest and coura- geous, as well as a learned and witty man.

Like Thomas Adams, Featley, had a gift for inventing intrigu- ing sermon titles, such as "The Lambe turned Lion," "Pandora her boxe, or *Origo omnium malorum,*" and "The Salter's Text" for a sermon preached before the company of salters.[108] He also uses unusual texts, as Psalms 63:9–11, which speaks of those who wish to destroy the Psalmist's soul going down to the lower parts of the earth, and ends by declaring that "the King shall rejoice in God . . . but the mouth of them that speak lies shall be stopped." It was an apt choice for a commemoration of the king's deliverance from the conspiracy of the Gowrie brothers.

Calvinist though Featley was, he meditated on the paradoxes of the Christian revelation in the authentic Andrewes manner, a manner which we shall explore in the next chapter. The following meditation on the Incarnation is moving:

> *O King of glory,* who hadst no Palace in this world, but an Inne; no Chamber of Presence, but a *Stable;* no Tapestry, but *Straw;* no Chaire of estate but a *Cratch;* no Scepter but a *Reede;* and no *Crowne* but a wreath *of thornes;* worke in me an holy high-mindednesse to *despise this world* which so despised thee. Make the *worldly greatnesse* seeme small, honour base, estimation vile, and pompe vaine unto me.[109]

In this same sermon he balances paradoxes perfectly, in meditat- ing on the Passion. This section incidentally, is interesting in that the extended image tells us that he preached from notes, and gives us an idea of how he made his points:

> Let others goe on forward if they please; I will stay still at the *Crosse,* and take no other Lesson, for I desire no other *Pulpit* then that *tree;* no other *Preacher* then thy *Cruci- fied body;* no other *Text* than thy *death and passion;* no other *parts* then thy *wounds;* no other *amplification* then thy *exten-*

sion; no other *notes* then thy *markes;* no other *points* then thy *nailes;* no other *booke* then thy opened *side.* [110]

The conceits are brilliantly maintained. His wit is even found as a *concordia discors* in the beginning of a prayer: *"Faithful Creator, and preserver of all men,* especially of thine Elect, whom thou smitest in mercie and *chastenest* in love, and *correctest* in tender compassion, and *wounding and healing againe.* . . ."[111]

His other distinguishing characteristic as a metaphysical preacher is a fondness for emblems. The last two lines of his *Ancilla Pietatis* offers us "The Hand-Maide's Posie," again a paradox:

In *heaven* with thee, Lord, let me be;
On *earth* my heaven's alone in thee.[112]

He ends another sermon, preached at the funeral of a mercer in the Mercers' Chapel in London, by saying that he will strew a few flowers on the hearse: the first is a rose, emblematic of charity which "hot in the affection; spreadeth it selfe abroad by compassion, and scattereth seeds be almes-deeds." The second flower is the lily, the symbol of purity and chastity, "for the Lilly is perfect white in colour, and cold in operation, and therefore representeth pure chastity, which cooleth the heat of lust." The last flower is the violet, because it is small and grows near the ground, "from whence the humble taketh his name, *humilis ab humo,* and of all other flowers it yeeldeth the sweetest savour, as humility doth in the nostrils of God and man."[113]

Thomas Fuller

Our second jovial controversialist, also a Calvinist, was Thomas Fuller (1608–1661), preacher and also a chronicler. He was the most amiable and humorous of men, without a trace of malice. Educated at Queens' College, Cambridge, where his uncle, John Davenant (later to become bishop of Salisbury) was the president, he never attained the preferments his wit, erudition, devotion, and conscientiousness warranted. He contributed to a collection of Cambridge poems on the birth of the Princess Mary (4 November 1631) while he was perpetual curate of St. Benet's Church in Cambridge. His uncle's influence gained him the rectory of Broadwindsor in Dorset. So popular was he there that four of his parishioners accompanied him at their own cost when he journeyed to Cambridge to be examined for his B.D. degree. From 1635 onwards his fame as lecturer at the Savoy Chapel in London was so great that his biographer asserts that "he had in his narrow Chappel two Audiences, one without the pale, the other within; the window of that little Church, and the sextonry so crowded, as if Bees had swarmed to his mellifluous discourse."[114]

In the tempestuous days of the Commonwealth he lectured occasionally in several other London churches, notably at St. Clement's, St. Bride's, and probably at St. Andrew's, Holborn. Before this, although a moderate Calvinist, he had been ejected from two livings by Parliament, despite Heylyn's accusation that he was a crypto-Calvinist. Retiring to Oxford in 1643, he found employment as chaplain to the royalist regiment commanded by Lord Hopton. He lived in great poverty until the Restoration, when he was appointed a chaplain to King Charles II, and resumed his curacy at the Savoy chapel, and his prebend at Salisbury. This distinguished historian of the Crusades, of the "Worthies" of England, and of the lives of the modern divines of the English Church, deserved better recognition than he got.

He still continues to fascinate by the jocundity of his style, its unfailing playfulness and kindliness, integrity, shrewdness, and sound commonsense, the perfect index to his character. No one can tell a story as well as he can because, as Charles Lamb said, he so enjoys himself in telling it. His favorite virtue, in a century that exhibited so little of it, was moderation.[115]

In appearance he was corpulent, ruddy, cheerful, and "his Head adorned with a comely Light-Coloured Haire, which was so by Nature exactly Curled."[116] His attire was careless, and like many antiquaries he was absentminded. But his memory was astonishing—it is said that he could repeat five hundred unfamiliar names after hearing them only once or twice, not to mention an ability to recollect all the road signs after walking through London from one end to the other.[117]

His collected sermons run to two considerable volumes. His earlier Calvinist sermons do not cite the Fathers in Greek or Latin, or use historical narrations with anything like the frequency they do in his court sermons, and they employ the Puritan structure of doctrine, reason, and use. But their wit is a far departure from the so-called "plain Puritan style." His method, generally, was to be so careful a biblical expositor in his "observations," that he required very few ancillary and corroborative scriptural citations.

One notices first the naturalness of his wit. A rather abrupt end to a sermon is explained thus: "These things deserve larger Prosecution; but this is none of Joshua's day, wherein the Sunne standeth still; and therefore I must conclude with the time."[118] Occasionally he makes an ironical aside, as this against the Puritans: "I never knew nor heard of an Army all of Saints, save *the holy Army of Martyrs*; and those, you know, were dead first."[119] A single memorable phrase castigates the Puritans' forced conversions of Indians in New England as "rather watered than baptized, driven into the Church, as the money-changers out of the Temple."[120] And he defended the use of wit in sermons, provided that "the sweetnesse of the sauce spoile not the savourinesse of the meat."[121]

His sermons are marked by the most careful biblical exposition with corroborative instances, an imaginative use of puns, aphorisms, riddles, and wit in starts and divisions. The latter tend to be simple and unstrained. So vivid were his illustrations that John Spencer's *KAINA KAI PALAIA. Things New and Old*, a collection of "similies," cites eighty-three examples from his sermons—more than any other of the preachers, including Adams, Featley, Lake, and Burroughes. As an historian, he makes abundant use of historical narrations. His favourite topics are faith, the assurance of the divine calling and election, and the necessity of peace. He often insists upon the mistake of making secondary matters seem important, a mistake which he felt caused so much feuding in the English Civil War.

There is so much deserving of quotation in Fuller that it requires discipline to resist the temptation. One double metaphor and a fine passage on the need to recognize the varied gifts of different ministers must be our simple sample. In preaching on the text I Corinthians 1:12, "Now this I say, that every one of you saith, I am of Paul, and I am of Apollo, and I am of Cephas, and I am of Christ," (a text which was highly applicable to divisions in the English Church) he observes: "Heare is such doting on the Dish, there is no regarding the Dainties: Such looking on the Embassadour, there is no notice taken of the King that sent him."[122] The extended citation which follows is a vivid appreciation of the variety of ministerial gifts in the pulpit:

> As in comparing severall handsome persons, one surpasseth for the beauty of a naturally painted face; a second, for the feature of a well-proportioned body; a third, for a grace of Gesture and Comelinesse of carriage: so the Iustice it selfe may be puzled, and forced to suspend her Verdict, not knowing where to adjudge the Victory: So may it bee betwixt several Pastors. One Excellency may consist in the unsnarling of a known controversie; an other in plaine expounding of Scripture, to make it portable in the weakest memory. One, the best *Boanerges*; an other, the best *Barnabas*. Our Iudgements may bee best informed by one; our Affections moved by a second; our Lives reformed by a third.[123]

Thomas Adams

The very best Calvinist wine has been kept until last. No other preacher can rival Donne for popularity or rhetorical gifts unless it be Thomas Adams (1583?–1652). The entry in the *Dictionary of National Biography* is singularly spare for so distinguished a preacher. Since that entry appeared, it has been learned that Adams was educated at Trinity and Clare Colleges,[124] Cambridge (not at Sidney Sussex as Thomas Fuller indicated),[125] and it is interesting that the racy preacher Bishop Latimer and the devout mystic Ferrar were Clare men, for Adams had affinities with both. We also know that he had links with men of the theatre, as his dramatic titles might indicate. Gerald E. Bentley thinks it is likely that he was familiar with Shakespeare, since an actor-partner in Shakespeare's company, Nicholas Tooley, left £10 to "my good freind Mr. Thomas Adams preacher of Gods Word whom I doe entreate to preach my funeral sermon. . . ."[126]

The facts about him are that, like Bunyan, he was a Bedfordshire preacher: he was to be found at Willington in that county in 1612. Two years later he was vicar of Wingrave in Buckinghamshire. From 1618 to 1623 he was preacher at St. Gregory's under St. Paul's Cathedral, and an associate of Donne's for some of those years. As a notable Calvinist he may well have lost this post soon after King James's *Instructions regarding Preaching* appeared in 1622, for these forbade all preaching on such cardinal points of Calvinism as predestination, election, and reprobation. During the same years he preached occasionally at Paul's Cross and at Whitehall. He was also either vicar, or lecturer, at St. Benet's church near Paul's Wharf. His friends included several of the nobility, who must have found him to be a witty and learned companion. He was for a time "observant chaplain" to Sir Henry Montague, Lord Chief Justice of England.

A. B. Grosart has a judicious evaluation of him: "Thomas Adams stands in the forefront of our great English preachers. He is not so sustained as Jeremy Taylor, nor so continuously sparkling as Fuller, but he is surpassingly eloquent and brilliant, and much more thought-laden than either."[127] This encomium indicates the difficulty of offering a few samples to indicate the breadth, depth, and variety of this man who exhibited "God's plenty," as Dryden said of Chaucer. It is probably best to cite a few passages of sustained eloquence, rather than a few scraps, to indicate his wealth of wit, aphorisms, characters, images, proverbs, emblems, paradoxes, historical narrations, conversations, "unnatural" natural historical illustrations, riddles, and the rest of his armory of eloquence.

The elaborateness of his eloquence can be illustrated by quotation from a sermon explaining the perils and powers of the ministry, and its temptations:

> Compare the Minister with his Charge, and thinke the difference. 1. One man to a multitude. 2. One without pompe, to many wise, rich, noble. 3. A weake man with a few leaves of Paper, to those that are armed with a prejudiciall opposition of Nature against it. 4. The Message not promising liberty, ease, incouragement to lustes; but threatning persecution, crosse, rodde, trouble; yet to binde Kings in Chaines, Nobles in Fetters of Yron: to recover the Heathen from their ancient and nationall Idolatries, and prostrate them to the name of *Iesus:* to make the drunkard sober, covetous mercifull, malicious charitable; *Hic digitus Dei,* This is the Finger of God.

Yet the difficulties are great because of the attachments to the values of this world; hence Adams warns,

> We may as well preach to these materiall Walles, and move the Seates, as your cauteriz'd and nummed consciences . . . You come before the Pulpit, but your Faith and Conscience is left behind you: Your Closets, Shoppes, Fields, nay, perhaps Taverns and Tap-houses plead possession of your affections: and all the Law that comes out of the Chaire of *Moses* cannot give the Devill a *Defeasance.* [128]

He is acutely aware of the temptations of the ministry. These include playing to the gallery which he calls "catching at popular applause," or flattery which is molding sermons "with Court dough,"[129] or laziness, or covetousness, which is the disease of "the pearl in the eye."[130] He counterbalances these temptations with the arrogance of the laity towards ministers, for "there is scarce a man that can read English, scarce a woman that can make herselfe ready to Church, but will presume to teach the Minister; and either wee must preach what you will heare, or you will not heare what wee will preach."[131]

He can produce metaphysical conceits to grab our attention as well as any poet. At the beginning of a sermon on "The Taming of the Tongue," expounding the text James 3:8, he says: "Goe lead a Lyon in a single haire, send up an Eagle to the skie to peck out a starre, cope up the thunder, and quench a flaming City with one widdowes teares: if thou couldest doe these, yet *nescit modo lingua domari: the Tongue can no man tame.*"[132] He can produce a startling analogy, as in the case of the guest of the Devil who "was madder than *Nero* in delights, *feare compasseth him on every side.* He starts at his own shaddow, and would not change firmnesse with an *Aspen leafe.*"[133] Equally, he can provide a memorably beautiful image for the wounded Conscience which

> runnes, like the stricken Deare with the arrow of death in the ribbes, from thicket to thicket, from shelter to shelter, but cannot change her paine with her place. The wound ranckles in the soule, and the longer it goes on the worse still it festers. Thus sinne that spake thee so faire at her inviting to the *Banket,* now presents to thy waked soule her true forme. . . .[134]

He can also use a simple farmyard image to illustrate Christ's parable of the two sons and the vineyard, on the text Matthew 21:28, illustrating the idea of a promise not followed by performance:

> The Hen, when she hath laid an egge, straight cackles it, which causeth it instantly to be taken from her. But heres one cackles when hee has not laid; and God comming findes his nest empty. This is to fry in words, freeze in deeds: to speak by elles, and work by inches: to promise mountaines, and bring forth ridiculous mole-hills. A bad

course, and a bad discourse agree not. Words are but vocall interpreters of the minde, actions reall.[135]

The aphoristic language and the alliteration repeat the lesson without wearying the auditors.

Although Adams has rightly been described as "hell's local colorist,"[136] he was much happier, to use his own phrase, "stroking than striking." His compassion for the poor was outstanding in an age of covetousness.[137] His joy in Christianity is the chief bell that he rings, which is why his wit is so merry, rather than melancholy or ironic. His famous "Mysticall Bedlam" sermon is whimsical in its wordplay: "It is our happinesse, not to be borne, but to be *new borne.* It is not the seed of man in the wombe of our mother; but the *seede of Grace* in the wombe of the *Church,* that makes us blessed. Generation lost us; it must be regeneration that recovers us."[138] His theme can be serious, such as the primary need of humility in the Christian life, yet he can be playful in discussing it:

> *Zaccheus* climes up into a Sycamore tree to behold *Iesus:* but when *Iesus* beheld him got up so high, he said, Come downe, *Zaccheus,* Luke 19. Whosoever will entertaine *Iesus,* must come downe. The haughty *Nebuchadnezzar,* that thinkes with his head to knock out the starres of heaven, must stoop at the *gate,* or he cannot enter. Be you never so lofty, you must bend. Gods honour must be preferred before your honours. It is no discredit to your Worships to worship God.[139]

Our last and lengthy citation is a marvellous passage on the way in which God draws men to Himself through their delights, as magnets. In an Epiphany sermon he parallels this with the way in which the stargazing Magi were led from their superstition to true wisdom:

> Here let us observe, that God doth sometimes draw men to him *suis ipsorum studijs;* by their owne delights and studies. No doubt these *Magi* were well acquainted with

dreames: it being among the Ethnickes and Peripatetickes a speciall obiect of divination. Therefore there is a booke bearing the name of *Aristotle; De divinatione per somnium.* Many errors these men had swallowed by dreames; now behold in a dreame they shall receive the truth. So God Called them by a *Starre,* whose profession was to relie too much on the *Starres. Quare per Stellam? ut per Christum, ipsa materia erroris, fieret salutis occasio.* Why by a *Starre?* that through *Iesus* Christ, the very matter of their error might be made a meanes of their salvation. *Per ea illos vocat, quae familiaria illis consuetudo fecit.* God calls them by those things which custome had made familiar to them. They that are stunge with Scorpions, must be cured by the oyle of Scorpions. Thus God allures men to him, as Fishermen fishes, with such baites as may be somewhat agreeable to them. *Paul* is occasioned by the *Altar to the unknowne God,* to make knowne the true God, the everliving *Iesus.* Doth *David* love the Sheepe-folds? hee shall be a Shepheard still. *From following the Ewes great with young, hee brought him to feede Iacob his people, and Israel his inheritance.* Doth *Peter* love fishing? hee shall goe a fishing still, though for more noble creatures; to catch soules . . . *Iudaei signa quaerunt? Do the* Iewes *seeke a signe?* Why Christ will there even among them worke his Miracles. Doth *Augustine* love elo-quence? *Ambrose* shall catch him at a Sermon. *All things shall worke to their good,* that are good: *Omnia, etiam peccata.* All things, even their very sinnes, saith *Augustine.* Mount-aigne in his *Essayes* writes, that a libidinous gentleman sporting with a Courtezan in a house of sinne, chanced to aske her name; which shee said was *Mary.* Whereat he was stricken with such a remorse and reverence, that he instantly not only cast off the Harlot, but amended his whole future life.[140]

The application follows:

Wel-beloved, since this is Gods mercy, to allure us by our owne delights, let us yeeld ourselves to be caught. What scope doth thy addiction levell at, that is not sinnefull, which Gods word doth not promise and affoord? what delight can you aske, which the Sanctuarie gives not? Love you hunting? learne here to hunt *the Foxes, the little* Cubbes, those crafty sinnes sculking in your bosomes. Would you dance? let your hearts keepe the measures of Christian ioy; and leape, like *Iohn* the Baptist in *Elizabeths* wombe, at the salvation of *Iesus* . . . What should I say more? what can winne you? Which way soever your desire stands, God doth allure you.[141]

No fishermen ever prepared their lures of fly or worm with more astuteness and finesse than the metaphysical fishers of men used in their rhetorical bait.

NOTES

1. For a thoroughgoing analysis of the importance of the doctrine of predestination as a doctrine of grace, the sense of security it gave to the elect, its orthodoxy in early English Protestantism until the advent of Arminianism, the difference between Dutch and English Arminianism (ceremonialism, the absolutism implicit in the divine right of kings, and the patristic learning manifest in sermons), and a general discussion of the cultural and political impact of the doctrine, see Dewey D. Wallace, Jr., *Puritans and Predestination: Grace in English Protestant Theology 1525–1695* (Chapel Hill, North Carolina, 1982).

2. See Philip Schaff, *The Creeds of Christendom*, Volume 3: *Evangelical Creeds* (New York, 1878), 554f.; and *Documents of the Christian Church*, ed. Henry Bettenson (London, 1943), 374–376.

3. DNB.

4. For a cogent, comprehensive, and concise analysis of its theme, see Lawrence Stone, *The Causes of the English Revolution, 1529–1642* (London, 1972).

5. See David B. McIlhiney, "The Protestantism of the Caroline Divines," *Historical Magazine of the Protestant Episcopal Church*, 44 (1975): 143–154.

6. John Gauden, *The Memorials of the life and death of R. Rd. Father in God, Dr. Brounrig* (London, 1660), 149.

7. Gauden, *Memorials*, 210.

8. *Sixty Five Sermons by the Right Reverend Father in God, Ralph Brownrig* (London, 1674), 91. Brownrig is contrasting the ancient Church of God restricted to the Jews with the New Testament Church open to both Jews and Gentiles.

9. Brownrig, *Sixty Five Sermons*, 94.

10. Brownrig, *Sixty Five Sermons*, 104.

11. Brownrig, *Sixty Five Sermons*, 303.

12. Brownrig, *Sixty Five Sermons*, 260.

13. Brownrig, *Sixty Five Sermons*, 35.

14. Brownrig, *Sixty Five Sermons*, 4.

15. Brownrig, *Sixty Five Sermons*, 189.

16. Brownrig, *Sixty Five Sermons*, Epistle "To the Reader."

17. Anthony Wood, *Athenae Oxonienses*, 2 vols. (London, 1691–1692), 2: 68. See also Wood's full account of the theological struggle between Prideaux and Heylyn, 2: 183–213.

18. John Prideaux, *The Christians Expectation. A Sermon Preached at the Court* (Oxford, 1636), 12.

19. John Prideaux, *The Patronage of Angels. A Sermon Preached at Court* (Oxford, 1636), 10.

20. John Prideaux, *Idolatrous Feasting. A Sermon Preached at Court* (Oxford, 1636), 21.

21. This sermon was preached at court, and published in Oxford in 1636. Its text was I Corinthians 11:9: "For there must also be Heresies among you, that they which are approved may be made manifest among you."

22. John Prideaux, *Heresies Progresse* (Oxford, 1636), 23.

23. John Prideaux, *The First Fruits of the Resurrection. A Sermon Preached on Easter Day, at St. Peters in the East, in Oxford* (Oxford, 1636), 31.

24. The "Epistle Dedicatory" to Hacket's *A Century of Sermons Upon Several Remarkable Subjects*, (London, 1675), sig. A2ᵛ states: "in his ordinary attendance upon your Majesty, Charles [II], your Royal Father, and Grandfather, [Hacket had] the Honour to preach more than Eighty times at Court."

25. John Plume, editor of the *Century of Sermons*, in the preliminary biography, viii.

26. Plume, biography, x.

27. Plume, biography, xiii.

28. Plume, biography, xxvi.

29. Plume, biography, xviii–xxv, includes the text of the speech Hacket gave to Parliament.

30. Plume, biography, xxix.

31. Plume, biography, xxxviii.

32. Plume, biography, li.

33. Hacket, *A Century of Sermons*, 2.

34. Hacket, *A Century of Sermons*, 41.

35. Hacket, *A Century of Sermons*, 79.

36. Hacket, *A Century of Sermons*, 336–337.

37. Hacket, *A Century of Sermons*, 462.

38. Hacket, *A Century of Sermons*, 332.

39. Hacket, *A Century of Sermons*, 819.

40. Hacket, *A Century of Sermons*, 616.

41. Hacket, *A Century of Sermons*, 123–124.

42. Hacket, *A Century of Sermons*, 174.

43. To this day the pupils of Christ's Hospital School wear the traditional blue cassocks referred to in this sermon, "The Second Sermon upon the Coronation." The scarlet refers to the color of the ceremonial robes of the Lord Mayor and aldermen of the City of London.

44. Hacket, *A Century of Sermons*, 718.

45. Hacket, *A Century of Sermons*, 110–111.

46. Fuller, *The Church-History of Britain*, ed. J. S. Brewer, 6 vols. (Oxford, 1845), 5: 500.

47. Wood, *Athenae Oxonienses*, 2: 488.

48. John King, *Lectures upon Ionas delivered at Yorke, In the yeare of our Lord 1594* (London, 1611), 12.

49. John King, *Lectures upon Ionas*, 161.

50. John King, *Lectures upon Ionas*, 553.

51. John King, *Lectures upon Ionas*, 248.

52. John King, *Lectures upon Ionas*, 258.

53. John King, *Vitis Palatina. A Sermon appointed to be preached at Whitehall upon the Tuesday after the mariage of the Ladie Elizabeth her Grace* (London, 1614), 13.

54. John King, *Vitis Palatina*, 6.

55. John King, *A Sermon at Paules Crosse, on behalf of Paules Church. March 26, 1620* (London, 1620), 29–30.

56. John King, *A Sermon at Paules Crosse*, 42–43.

57. *The Life of Dr. Thomas Morton, Late Bishop of Durham* (York, 1669). It was begun by Richard Baddiley and finished by John Naylor. The citation is from 16–17.

58. Thomas Morton, *A Sermon Preached before the Kings Most Excellent Maiestie, in the Cathedrall Church of Durham. Upon Sunday, being the fifth day of May, 1639* (London, 1639), 3.

59. Thomas Morton, *The Presentment of a Schismaticke. A Sermon Preached at the Cathedrall Church of Saint Pauls the 19 June, 1642* (London, 1642), 23–24.

60. Morton, *A Sermon preached before the King*, 30.

61. Morton, *A Sermon preached before the King*, 35.

62. The information in this paragraph was derived entirely from the DNB.

63. William Barlow, *Christian Liberty Described in a Sermon Preached in the Collegiate Church at Westminster, by a Minister of Suffolke* (London, 1606), preface.

64. William Barlow, *A Sermon preached at Paules Crosse, on the first Sunday in Lent, Martij. I. 1600. With a short discourse of the late Earle of Essex his confession, and penitence, before and at the time of his death* (London, 1601), sig. D2v.

65. Barlow, *Essex Sermon*, sig. Clv.

66. Barlow, *Essex Sermon*, sig. Ciii.

67. Barlow, *Essex Sermon*, sig. D5.

68. Barlow, *Essex Sermon*, sig. Cvr.

69. Barlow, *Essex Sermon*, sig. Dv.

70. Barlow, *Essex Sermon*, sig. D8v.

71. Barlow, *Essex Sermon*, sig. Ei.

72. William Barlow, *The Eagle and the Body Described in One Sermon Preached before Queene Elizabeth of precious memorie, in Lent. Anno 1601* (London, 1609), sig. Bi.

73. Barlow, *The Eagle and the Body*, sig. E4v–F1.

74. Barlow, *The Eagle and the Body*, sig. F2r–F2v.

75. Isaiah 59:5.

76. William Barlow, *The Sermon Preached at Paules Crosse, the tenth day of November, being the next Sunday after the Discoverie of this late Horrible Treason* (London, 1606), sig. C3–C3v.

77. William Barlow, *Christian Liberty Described in a Sermon Preached in the Collegiate Church at Westminster, by a Minister of Suffoke* (London, 1606), sig. D1.

78. John Bowle, *A Sermon preached at Flitton in the Countie of Bedford, at the Funerall of the Right Honourable Henrie Earle of Kent, the sixteenth of March, 1614* (London, 1615), sig. A2.

79. Bowle, *A Sermon preached at Flitton*, sig. F3.

80. Bowle, *A Sermon preached at Flitton*, sig. D3–D3v.

81. Bowle, *A Sermon preached at Flitton*, sig. C4.

82. *The Letters of John Chamberlain*, ed. N. E. McClure, 2 vols. (Philadelphia, 1939), 2: 114.

83. Henry King, *A Sermon preached at Pauls Crosse, The 25 of November, 1621 Upon occasion of that false and scandalous Report (lately Published) touching the supposed Apostasis of the right Reverend Father in God, Iohn King, late Lord Bishop of London. By Henry King, his eldest Sonne* (London, 1621), 60.

84. Henry King, *An Exposition Upon the Lords Prayer. Delivered in certaine Sermons, in the Cathedral Church of S. Paul* (London, 1628), 30.

85. Henry King, *An Exposition Upon the Lords Prayer*, 13–14.

86. Henry King, *An Exposition Upon the Lords Prayer*, 361. The same audacious conceit is to be found in Herbert's poem on Prayer.

87. Henry King, *A Sermon preached at the Funeral of the R. Reverend Father in God Bryan* [Duppa] *Lord Bp. of Winchester. At the Abby Church in Westminster. April 24. 1662* (London, 1662), 9.

88. Henry King, *A Sermon preached at the Funeral*, 2. See also the extensive meditation on death, 16f.

89. Henry King, "Davids Enlargement," in *Two Sermons* (Oxford, 1625), preached at St. Mary's Church, Oxford, 10 July 1625, 32.

90. Henry King, *An Exposition Upon the Lords Prayer*, 59.

91. Henry King, *A Sermon preached at the Funeral*, 3.

92. Henry King, *An Exposition Upon the Lords Prayer*, 100.

93. Henry King, *A Sermon preached at Lewes in the Diocese of Chichester* (London, 1663), 18.

94. DNB.

95. *The Whole Works of the Most Rev. James Ussher, D.D., Lord Archbishop of Armagh and Primate of all Ireland* (London, 1857–1864), 17 vols., in which the sermons are contained in vols. 2 and 13. For the soul before judgment, see 13: 105.

96. Ussher, *The Whole Works*, 13: 115–116.

97. Ussher, *The Whole Works*, 13: 151–155.

98. Ussher, *The Whole Works*, 2: 417.

99. Ussher, *The Whole Works*, 13: 563.

100. Ussher, *The Whole Works*, 13: 235.

101. Ussher, *The Whole Works*, 13: 348.

102. Ussher, *The Whole Works*, 13: 350.

103. Ussher, *The Whole Works*, 13: 153.

104. Ussher, *The Whole Works*, 13: 154.

105. Ussher, *The Whole Works*, 13: 493.

106. Peter Heylyn, *Aerius redivivus: Or, the History of the Presbyterians* (London, 1679), 464.

107. *Featlaei Παλιγγενεσία: or, Doctor Daniel Featley revived* (London, 1660), pt. ii, 37, put together by his nephew.

108. Daniel Featley, *Clavis Mystica* (London, 1636), 196. The sermon was preached at St. Mary's, Bread Street, London and the text was

Mark 9:49: "For every one shall be salted with fire, and every sacrifice shall be salted with salt."

109. Daniel Featley, *Ancilla Pietatis, or the Handmaid to Private Devotion* (London, 1626), 208–209.

110. Featley, *Ancilla Pietatis*, 302.

111. Featley, *Ancilla Pietatis*, 530.

112. Featley, *Ancilla Pietatis*, 610.

113. Featley, *Clavis Mystica*, 290.

114. Anon., *The Life of that Reverend Divine, and Learned Historian, Dr. Thomas Fuller* (London, 1661), 15.

115. *Life of . . . Fuller*, 16.

116. *Life of . . . Fuller*, 66. "His exhortations to peace and obedience were his constant subjects in the Church; (all his Sermons were such Liturgies)."

117. DNB.

118. *The Collected Sermons of Thomas Fuller, D.D., 1631–1659*, ed. J. E. Bailey and W. E. A. Axon, 2 vols. (London, 1891), 1: 220.

119. Fuller, *Collected Sermons*, 1: 250.

120. Fuller, *Collected Sermons*, 1: 448.

121. Fuller, *Collected Sermons*, 1: 497.

122. Fuller, *Collected Sermons*, 1: 224.

123. Fuller, *Collected Sermons*, 1: 227–228.

124. J. and J. A. Venn, *Alumni Cantabrigienses*, 10 vols. (Cambridge, 1922–1954), 1: 6.

125. Thomas Fuller, *The Church-History of Britain* (London, 1655), Bk. 10, 154.

126. G. E. Bentley, *The Jacobean and Caroline Stage. Dramatic Companies and Players*, 7 vols. (Oxford, 1941–1968), 2: 649. Bentley's educated guess that Adams probably made the acquaintance of Shakespeare through Tooley was made in a conversation in the Henry E. Huntington Library, San Marino in February of 1982.

127. DNB article on "Thomas Adams."

128. *The Workes of Tho: Adams. Being the Summe of his Sermons, Meditations, and other Divine and Morall Discourses. Collected in one intire Volume* (London, 1629), 63. This volume contains sixty-three sermons, excluding the Meditations on the Creed.

129. *The Workes of Tho: Adams*, 65.

130. *The Workes of Tho: Adams*, 66.

131. *The Workes of Tho: Adams*, 76.

132. *The Workes of Tho: Adams*, 143.

Chapter IV

133. *The Workes of Tho: Adams*, 234.

134. *The Workes of Tho: Adams*, 241.

135. *The Workes of Tho: Adams*, 428.

136. See William Mulder, "Style and the Man: Thomas Adams, prose Shakespeare of Puritan Divines," *Harvard Theological Review*, 48 (1955): 148. For three vivid descriptions of the torments of hell, see *The Workes of Tho: Adams*, 242, 650, and 1061.

137. *The Workes of Tho: Adams*, 37, 134, 324, 590, 802, for outstanding examples of Adams's compassion for the poor.

138. *The Workes of Tho: Adams*, 480.

139. *The Workes of Tho: Adams*, 655.

140. *The Workes of Tho: Adams*, 844.

141. *The Workes of Tho: Adams*, 844–845.

Chapter V

THE METAPHYSICAL ARMINIANS

THE CALVINIST-ARMINIAN POLARITY reached its apogee in the Civil War. Its impact is strikingly clear in our second group of profiles of metaphysical preachers. First we shall sketch the biographies and sermon styles of notable Arminians, including archbishop William Laud their dedicated and disciplined leader, whose policy of "thorough" cost him his head in 1645 and contributed to the death of his beloved sovereign, Charles I, in 1649. Our profiles will also include the two outstanding Arminian metaphysical preachers, Lancelot Andrewes and John Donne (the latter contrasted with another dean, Thomas Jackson), then other Caroline bishops, and, finally, significant royal chaplains and prebendaries.

William Laud

Archbishop William Laud (1573–1645) was educated at St. John's College, Oxford, where his tutor was John Buckeridge, the leader of the opposition to Puritanism in Oxford. In 1601 he was ordained deacon and priest, and in 1604 he defended two theses for his B.D. degree: the necessity of Baptism, and the necessity of diocesan episcopacy for a true Church. He first preached before King James in 1608, and was elected president of St. John's College in 1611. In 1616 he was appointed dean of Gloucester. Thereafter preferments followed one another in rapid succession: the sees of St. David's in 1621, Bath and Wells in 1624, London in 1628, and the primatial see of Canterbury in 1633.

His ideal for the Church of England was Hooker's, that it must recover the spirit that had inspired the undivided early Church of Christ before it was almost strangled by an imperialistic political system. His most important theological work is his *Conference with Fisher the Jesuit.* There he argued that the Roman Church is a true Church in its acceptance of the Scriptures as the rule of faith, together with the creeds and the sacraments, but that it is not a "right" Church. This because it is not reformed from its misinterpretation of Scripture, its superstition, and popular image-worship; and, in addition, it defrauds the people in not giving them the wine with the bread at Communion, in accordance with the institution of Christ. Furthermore, it does not recognize the Greek Church as a true Church, although it was the Catholics themselves who added the procession of the Holy Spirit from the Son (the so-called *filioque* clause) to an ecumenical creed, and then accused the Greeks of being doctrinally incomplete. Moreover, it is the Catholics who are the schismatics, because they unchurch all others except themselves.

The "Epistle Dedicatory" to his *Conference* volume states his position with concise clarity: "The Catholic Church of Christ is neither Rome nor a conventicle. Out of that there is no salvation, I easily confess it. But out of Rome there is, and out of a conventicle too; salvation is not shut up into such a narrow conclave."[1] In reply to the charge that the Church of England did not exist before the Reformation, Laud answers that

> there is no greater absurdity this day stirring in Christendom than that the reformation of an old corrupted Church, will we, nill we, must be taken for the building of a new. And were this not so, we should never be troubled with that idle and impertinent question of theirs: "Where was your Church before Luther?" for it was just there, where theirs is now. One and the same Church still, no doubt of that; one in substance, but not one in condition of state and purity: their part of the same Church remaining in

corruption, and our part of the same Church under reformation. The same Naaman, and he a Syrian still; but lep-
rous with them, and cleansed with us.[2]

Laud's major difference from the Puritans, apart from his
emphasis on the freedom of the will and the potential universality of salvation, was in his insistence that episcopacy was of
the *esse,* not the *bene esse* of the structure of the Church. The
Puritans, by contrast, preferred presbyterian or independent
forms of Church polity, forms which they too claimed to
find in the New Testament. Laud believed episcopacy was
Christ's own ordinance, even if it was formalized by the Apostles.[3]

Laud had one other significant difference from the Puritans.
This was over ceremonies and the liturgy. The more radical
Puritans rejected any formal liturgy, believing that the minister
must be free, under the inspiration of the Holy Spirit and a
knowledge of the needs of his congregation, to form his own
prayers *ex tempore.* Laud, however, preferred the order and uniformity of a liturgy, and considered it significant that the most
primitive churches of the East and West had their own historic
liturgies. The Puritans also differed from him in their attitude
to ceremonial. Since the early days of Elizabeth they mounted
a strong criticism of the three ceremonies which they found
noxious: crossing in Baptism, kneeling for the reception of Holy
Communion, and the use of the ring in marriage. They also
objected to the use of the surplice as copying the garb of Rome.[4]

Laud, for his part, was readier to recognize that we worship
through the gateway of the senses, and that a beautiful church,
rich with biblical symbolism, using ceremonies which were
an outward indication of an inward reverence towards God,
fulfilled several purposes. In the first place, this was to meet
the apostolic requirement that all things should be done "decently and in order." Secondly, a beautiful external worship
strengthened the inner worship of the heart. Thirdly, such worship fosters unity among Christians, as well as preventing profanity and sacrilege. His arguments went as follows:

No external action in the world can be uniform without some ceremonies; and these in religion, the ancienter they be the better, so they fit time and place. Too many overburden the service of God, and too few leave it naked. . . . ceremonies are the hedge that fence the substance of religion from all the indignities that profaneness and sacrilege too commonly put upon it. And a great weakness it is, not to see the strength which ceremonies—things weak enough in themselves, God knows—add even to religion itself.[5]

Furthermore, Laud believed that it was the slovenliness of much contemporary worship in the Church of England that caused former Catholics to return to recusancy.[6]

His mistake was that he was unable to allow for the differences of human temperaments, and that he tried to enforce his ecclesiastical laws with what seemed to be a vengeful rigor. The Puritans could never understand that he sincerely believed that there was a higher ordinance than preaching—the sacrament of Holy Communion. Nor could they understand that, for him, the altar was more important than the pulpit since, as he expressed it, "a greater reverence, no doubt, is due to the Body than to the Word of the Lord."[7]

In spite of his lack of emphasis on preaching, the seven sermons of his which survive are surprisingly good. They were all delivered on public occasions and so, unfortunately, we have no indication of what his parochial type of preaching was. They appear to have been carefully prepared from a study of what the Fathers and the modern Roman and, to a lesser degree, Protestant commentators have to say on controversial passages. He is fond of texts from the Psalms, and especially loves the Church-State unity in Jerusalem as a model for Anglican Erastianism. He analyzes the texts word by word, like Andrewes, but unlike him not syllable by syllable. His divisions are relatively simple, and the style is concise, pellucid, and even monosyllabic in stretches. He uses few metaphors and those are conventional. His citations from the Fathers or recent commentators are brief and to the point, and neither pedantic nor ostentatious. He is capable of interesting openings to his sermons, and his preaching is more concerned with duty than doctrine. His favorite themes are the unity of Church and State, duty to God and the king, belief in the divine right of kings, and the stability of life as dependent upon obedience to superiors. From so serious and grave a man it is intriguing to discover his penchant for wit: this alone would qualify him as a metaphysical preacher, especially a wit linked with patristic scholarship. In other respects, his earnestness and simplicity of style and structure resemble Puritan models of preaching.

His wit is occasionally Latin, as when He declares that, if the Temple was not built in David's time, he did at least foresee it: "For it is evident, *qui non videbat, praevidebat.*"[8] In a sermon on a text from Psalm 21:6, "For Thou hast set him as blessings for ever," Laud makes a witty aside, apologising for his prolixity: "If you think I have staid too long in this circumstance, I hope you will pardon me. You should be as loth as I to go from amidst the 'blessings': but I must proceed."[9] But the most remarkable example of his wit comes in the sermon he preached on the threshold of his execution. His final words and actions deserve the kind of poetic accolade that Marvell gave to Laud's master, King Charles. Preaching on the text of Hebrews 12:1, 2, he said:

I have been long in my race, and how I have looked unto Iesus the Author and finisher of my Faith, is best known to him: I am now come to the end of my race, and here I find the Crosse, a death of shame, but the shame must be despised—the shame for me, and God forbid that I should despise the shame for him; I am going apace, as you see, towards the Red-sea, and my feet are upon the very brinks of it, an Argument, I hope, that God is bringing me to the Land of Promise, for that was the way by which of old he led his people.[10]

193

He finishes by claiming that he never tried to introduce popery into England: "this is no time to dissemble with God, least of all in matter of Religion, and therefore I desire it may be remembered; I have always lived in the Protestant Religion established in *England*, and in that I now come to die."[11]

Typical in its theme, as in the simplicity and burning sincerity with which it was uttered, is the following passage from a sermon preached at the opening of Parliament in 1625 when Laud was bishop of St. David's: "For these three, God, the King, and the Church, that is, God, His Spouse, and His Lieutenant upon earth, are so near allied,—God and the Church in love, God and the King in power, the King and the Church in mutual dependence upon God, and subordination to Him,— that no man can serve one of them truly, but he serves all three."[12] The same sermon contains a criticism of the Jesuit Lorinus for reducing Catholicism to Roman Catholicism,[13] and a criticism of Presbyterian Puritans who desire parity for their ministers. While it echoes the famous remark of James I at the Hampton Court Conference, "No Bishop, No King," it already envisions that the toppling of hierarchy in the Church will bring the monarchy tumbling down too: "they that would overthrow *sedes Ecclesiae . . .* will not spare, if ever they get power, to have a pluck at 'the throne of David'."[14] This same sermon includes thirty-four references to twenty-one different authors in twenty-six octavo pages. They range from Caesar to Calvin, from Tacitus to Theodoret, and from Aristotle to the English Ainsworth.

His usual manner is that of the grave pedagogue; but he is also capable of irony, as when he describes millenarians as mere "men in the Moon,"[15] or declaims against those who break the unity of the Church: "A thing so good, that it is never broken but by the worst men. Nay, so good it is, that the very worst men pretend best when they break it. It is so in the Church: never heretic yet rent her bowels, but he pretended that he raked them for truth."[16] The irony of it is that the same words could equally well have been spoken by the Calvinist archbishop, James Ussher, a man equally concerned for the peace of the Church.

Lancelot Andrewes and John Donne

Inevitably we turn to the bishop of bishops and the dean of deans, the prototypical metaphysical preachers and the most renowned of them all, Bishop Lancelot Andrewes and John Donne, dean of St. Paul's Cathedral. Although they had much in common in their styles, yet each was very much his own man. They shared a love of wit, patristic learning, paradoxes, maxims, the introduction of Latin tags from the Vulgate, a profound respect for the Scriptures, and each had uncommon psychological penetration. The differences between them are equally significant. Donne had been a Roman Catholic, dissolute, skeptic, and a twice-born Christian, where Andrewes remained consistently ascetical, scholarly, and spiritual. Donne does not crumble the text as Andrewes does, and although he has a far more magisterial imagination, yet he cannot command fifteen languages as Andrewes does. Although he is greatly intrigued by philological research it is not for the same reason as Andrewes. As Janel M. Mueller shrewdly observes, "Donne's philological research has, in fact, the opposite objective [to Andrewes']: to open many possibilities of nuance and meaning, not to settle upon one."[17] Andrewes went to the Hebrew and Greek originals of his texts, and to Chaldee and Arabic parallels, always to illuminate the most reliable meaning rather than to exfoliate multiple meanings from many texts. Yet Andrewes' sermons, taut in argument, lack the fecundity of images that makes Donne's a veritable kaleidoscope of changing colors and impressions.

If Andrewes is less dramatic than Donne, he is more intellectual. Donne relied on memory, since for him his task was to remind the congregation vividly of the traditional truth,[18] while Andrewes relied more on the power of logic. Andrewes, as an apologist and controversialist, had good grounds for valuing the powers of reason highly. He had first come to prominence as chaplain to the earl of Huntingdon who had employed him in the Catholic north of England in reclaiming recusants to the English Church. Buckeridge, in his funeral sermon for Andrewes, says that Secretary Walsingham wished to make him "Reader of Controversies in Cambridge."[19] The characteristics of his sermons are a profound and detailed biblical knowledge, an exact grammatical knowledge of the biblical and ancillary languages, a grasp of alternative readings of obscure texts and cruxes, and a great respect for the Fathers of the primitive Church. He conveys the substance of their thought rather than parading his knowledge with detailed and extensive citations as most other metaphysical preachers did. He was concerned to relate texts to the calendar of the liturgical year, as evidenced by the frequency of his saying, "This Text for this day" (out of the lections appointed for the day in the Book of Common Prayer). His wit is noticeable specially in the beginnings, endings, or transitions of his sermons, but he lacks the poet's facility for memorable tropes and dazzling metaphors, though he can etch a striking maxim on the memory. Although he defends the use of classical references and Jewish lore, he rarely used extra-biblical sources, as does Donne or Hacket. Almost every historical narration he uses as an exemplum, or in a series of exempla, is biblical in origin, and again in this respect he differs from most of the other metaphysical preachers. Further, his spirit is less contentious than that of many other preachers, especially when dealing with dissent from Roman Catholicism.

There are two defects in the style of his preaching: one is scholastic divisions and subdivisions into which he fractured his texts; the other is the breathless, staccato effect of his chopped sentences, especially when he is excitedly dealing with those paradoxes of the Christian faith beyond the possibility of human understanding—the Divine creation *ex nihilo*, the descent of the eternal Son of God in the Incarnation and the Virgin Birth, and the death of Death in the Resurrection of Christ. They so stagger the imagination that his style staggers in sympathy with the paradoxes.

What did his contemporaries think of his preaching? Sir John

Harington remarked on his ability "to raise a joint reverence to God and the Prince, to spirituall and civill Magistrate" and his concern to lead his congregation to the fruits of true repentance, "the amendement of life, and to good works." The same witness also testified to the impact of a sermon before Queen Elizabeth on the text, *Thou leddest thy people like sheep by the hands of Moses and Aaron,* "Which Sermon, (though courteous ears are commonly so open, as it goes in at one ear, and out of the other) yet it left an *Aculeus* behind in many of all sorts. And *Henry Noel* one of the greatest Gallants of those times, sware as he was a Gentleman, he never heard man speak with such a spirit."[20] Certainly, as T. S. Eliot said of him, he is a contemplative who is more interested in God than in his own reactions, which Eliot thought was the defect in Donne.[21] Without subscribing to Eliot's view that Donne's sermons are shadowed by impure motives, one can readily agree with Eliot that Andrewes has "the *goût pour la vie spirituelle.*"[22]

Andrewes should be heard on the greatest of paradoxes:

> The *Word, by whom all things were made,* to come to be *made* it selfe . . . what *flesh?* The flesh of an *infant.* What, *Verbum Infans,* the *Word* an *Infant?* The *Word* and not able to speak a word? . . . How borne, how entertained? In a stately *Palace, Cradle* of *Ivorie, Robes* of *estate?* No: but a *stable* for his *Palace;* a *manger* for his *Cradle;* poore *clouts* for his array. This his beginning . . . Is His *end* any better, (that Maketh up all:) what *flesh* then? *Cujus livore sanati, blacke* and *blew, bloudie* and *swolne; rent* and *torne;* the *thornes* and *nayles* sticking in his *flesh:* And *such flesh* He was made . . . *Love* respects it not, cares not, what flesh he be *made,* so the *flesh* be made by it.[23]

Another sermon preached before the king and the court on Easter Day, 1607 begins with wit and ends with wit. Andrewes startles the courtiers into attention by beating them at their own game—but with a higher prize in mind, heavenly preferment. "The carnall man, all he can say is, *dum spiro spero:* his

197

hope is as long as his breath. The Christian aspireth[24] higher; goeth further (by vertue of this verse) and saith, *dum expiro spiro:* his hope fails him not, when his breath fails him."[25] The closing provides another pun: "*Atque hic est vitae finis, pervenire ad vitam cujus non est finis:* This the end of the Text, and of our life, to come to a life, whereof there is no end."[26]

Here is a rare and cheerful geographical image, preached on Easter Day, 1616: "Heer then is a *third Cape of good hope:* that, though one had been downe as deep in the entrailes of the spirituall Great *Liviathan,* as ever was *Ionas* in the *Sea-Whale's,* yet, even there also, not to despaire."[27] Who can teach a lesson with the laconic brevity of Andrewes, pointing out that the Holy Spirit came thrice in the *Acts of the Apostles,* and each time significantly for our practice: at Jerusalem, at Caesarea, and at Ephesus, respectively at occasions of prayer, preaching, and the Sacraments?[28] If we look for unforgettable maxims, here are two. The first urges us to good practice: "Our wish hath *lipps,* but no *leggs.*"[29] The second comes in a Spital sermon, preached before many notabilities, where he refuses to be a flatterer of the great: "We will not sett up for *Upholsterers,* and stuffe *cushions* and *pillows,* to lay them under their *elbowes . . .*"[30]

His greatest achievement was to have been the preacher on the great occasions of the Christian and the secular year before the court. His *XCVI Sermons* appropriately include seventeen sermons preached on Christmas Day, eight sermons on Repentance and Fasting, preached on Ash Wednesday, six other Lenten sermons, three sermons on the Passion preached on Good Friday, eighteen sermons on the Resurrection preached on Easter Day, fifteen sermons on the Sending of the Holy Spirit preached on Whitsunday, eight Gowrie Day sermons preached on August 5,[31] ten sermons preached on November 5 commemorating the delivery of the nation from the Gunpowder Plot, and eleven sermons preached on other occasions, including one at the annual charity remembrance sermon at Eastertide known as the Spital sermon.[32] One could ring a coin on the conscience of Andrewes, so honest and devout was this holy man, in spite of his role as chief preacher to the king and court. No wonder he found it necessary, according to Buckeridge who preached his funeral sermon, to devote a great part of five hours every day in prayer and devotion to God.

John Donne was the other brilliant star in the Arminian homiletical firmament. Reluctant as he undoubtedly was to give up all hope of secular preferment, he came to love preaching, often recalling the words of St. Paul, "Woe be unto me if I doe not preach the Gospell" (I Corinthians 9:16):

> Who but my selfe can conceive the sweetnesse of that salutation, when the Spirit of God says to me in a morning, Go forth today and preach, and preach consolation, preach peace, preach mercy. And spare my people, spare that people whom I have redeemed with my precious Blood, and be not angry with them for ever; Do not wound them, doe not grinde them, do not astonish them with the bitternesse, with the sharpnesse, with the consternation of my judgements. . . . What a Coronation is our taking of Orders, by which God makes us a Royall Priesthood? And what an inthronization is the comming up into a Pulpit, where God invests his servants with his Ordinance, as with a Cloud, and then presses that Cloud with a *Vae si non*, woe be unto thee, if thou doe not preach, and then enables him to preach peace, mercy, consolation, to the whole Congregation.[33]

Donne knew, however, that the preacher has to proclaim judgment before mercy, to be a Boanerges or son of thunder before he can become a Barnabas or son of consolation. In a Lenten sermon, preached at Whitehall in 1618, he insisted that the preacher must be

> a tuba, a trumpet sounding the alarm, (that is, that awakens us from our security) and that sounds the Battail (that is, that puts us into a colluctation with our selves, with this world, with powers and principalities, yea into a wras-

tling with God himself and his Justice) the same trumpet sounds the Parle too, calls us to hearken to God in his word, and to speak to God in our prayers, and so to come to treaties and capitulations for peace; and the same trumpet sounds a retreat too, that is, a safe reposing of our souls in the merit, and in the wounds of our Saviour Christ Jesus.[34]

The same sermon includes a superb defense of learned eloquence in the pulpit, affirming that while preaching is a grave exercise, it is not sordid, barbarous, or negligent. For this his authority is the Bible itself:

There are not so eloquent books in the world, as the Scriptures: Acept those names of Tropes and Figures, which the Grammarians and Rhetoricians put upon us, and we may be bold to say, that in all their Authors, Greek and Latin, we cannot finde so high, and so lively examples of those Tropes, and those Figures, as we may in the Scriptures: whatsoever hath justly delighted any man in any mans writings is exceeded in the Scriptures. The style of the Scriptures is a diligent, and an artificial style; and a great part thereof in a musical, in a metrical, in a measured composition, in verse.[35]

In a sermon preached on a penitential psalm Donne returned to the same topic, claiming that "the Holy Ghost in penning the Scriptures delights himself, not only with a propriety, but with a delicacy, and harmony, and melody of language; with height of Metaphors, and other figures which may work greater impressions on the Readers, and not with barbarous, or triviall, or market, or homely language."[36] And what a staggering variety of metaphors Donne used, drawn from the law, drama, seafaring, music, commerce, maps, mathematics, human anatomy, zoology, clothing, and patristic analogies.

His most brilliant characteristic, however, was his way of winding into the human heart, his psychological brilliance and empathy, often expressed with all his wit. He knew the variety in his congregation—that he had to supply the ignorant with arguments, the distrustful with encouragement to accept the divine promises, and to recover the relapsed and strengthen the weak.[37] He knew how easy it was to assume that the preacher's barbs were aimed at anyone rather than oneself.[38] But, like God's huntsman, he flushed out the elusive souls that sought the ambush of excuses and struck his prey with the arrows of divine judgment or love. He knew also the danger of complacency and the temptation to flattery in a preacher, and insisted that he should expect assent and not admiration.[39] "How often is that called a Sermon," he observed, "that speakes more of Great men, then of our great God?"[40] The task of the ministers, says Donne, is so to study the Scriptures and live that "the love of Gods truth must shine in our hearts, sincerely there; and in our tongues, assiduously there; and in our hands, evidently there."[41]

Izaak Walton has left us an unforgettable vignette, which he derived in part from Donne's own words, of Donne preaching:

> Preaching the Word so, as shewed his own heart was possest with those very thoughts and joys that he laboured to distill into others. A Preacher in earnest, weeping sometimes for his Auditory, sometimes with them; alwaies preaching to himself like an Angell from a cloud, but in none; carrying some, as St. *Paul* was, to Heaven in holy raptures, and inticing others by a sacred art and Courtship to amend their lives; here picturing a vice so as to make it ugly to those that practised it; and a vertue so, as to make it be loved even by those that lov'd it not; and all this with a most particular grace and an unexpressible addition of comeliness.[42]

Donne had aimed at conversion by his affectionate transmission of the love of the Holy Spirit, for "the Holy Ghost is amorous in his Metaphors."[43] He offered brutish natures "a Metamorphosis, a Transformation, a new Creation in Christ Jesus, and thereby make my Goat, and my Fox, and my Wolfe, and my Lion, to become the *Semen Dei,* The seed of God, and *Filium Dei,*"[44] thus losing their licentious, supplanting, usurious, and ambitious drives.

No other orator of his day could write a peroration like Donne, as in his sermon on Acts 7:60, "And when he had said this, he fell asleep." His superb climax catches the serenity and equanimity of eternity in its perfect balance, as it describes the blessed:

> They shall awake as *Jacob* did, and say as Jacob said, *Surely the Lord is in this place,* and *this is none other but the house of God, and the gate of heaven,* And into that gate they shall enter, and in that house they shall dwell, where there shall be no Cloud nor Sun, no darkenesse nor dazling, but one equall light, no noyse or silence, but one equall musick, no fears nor hopes, but one equall possession, no foes nor friends, but one equall communion and Identity, no ends nor beginnings, but one equall eternity.[45]

The pulpit's profoundest dramatist made his last appearance his most effective. In January 1630 it had been rumored that Donne was dead and at that time he wrote to a friend: "It hath been my desire, and may God be pleased to grant it, that I might dye in the Pulpit. . . ."[46] A year later in Lent he preached "Deaths Duell" on the ending (a pun, *In Fine*) of Psalm 68, verse 20: "And unto God the Lord belong the Issues of Death." Walton sets the scene in the old Gothic St. Paul's:

> and when to the amazement of some beholders he appeared in the pulpit, many thought he presented himself not to preach mortification by his living voice, but mortality by a decayed body and aging face . . . Many that then saw his teares and heard his hollow voice, professing they thought the Text prophetically chosen, and that *Dr.* Donne had preach't his own funerall Sermon.[47]

This was not enough: the lesson must be incised not only on the memory, but also sculpted for the eyes of posterity, so the dean caused his effigy in a winding-sheet to be his final macabre monument in the cathedral. But it is his poems, and more recently his sermons, that later ages will not willingly let die. Their brilliance of thought and passionate intensity, their wit and erudition, their audacious images were worthy of one whom his contemporaries thought of as a second Augustine, but who himself felt a closer affinity with St. Paul, a critic of the Church who had become its defender. It was appropriate that his last sermon should be a "Passion Sermon" antedating the Good Friday of 1631. For Donne (as for Andrewes) the Incarnation was a staggering paradox, but transcended in its generosity by the Passion. Paradox chases paradox in his last sermon:

> That *God*, this *Lord*, the *Lord of life could dye,* is a strange contemplation; That the *red Sea* could bee *drie,* That the *Sun* could *stand still,* That an *Oven* could be *seaven times heat* and *not burne,* That *Lions* could be *hungry* and *not bite,* is strange, *miraculously strange,* but *supermiraculous* that God *could dye;* but that God *would dye* is an *exaltation* of that. But even of that it is a *superexaltation,* that God *shold dye, must dye,* and *non exitus* (said S. *Augustin*) God the *Lord had no issue but by death, oportuit pati* (says *Christ* himself) all this *Christ ought to suffer.* [48]

The sermon ends with another coruscation of paradoxes:

> There we leave you in the *blessed dependancy,* to *hang* upon *him* that *hangs* upon the *Crosse,* there bath in his *teares,* there *suck* at his *woundes,* and *lye down in peace* in his *grave,* till hee vouchsafe you a *resurrection,* and an *ascension* into that *Kingdome,* which hee *hath purchas'd for you,* with the *inestimable price* of his *incorruptible blood.* AMEN. [49]

Thomas Jackson

We now turn for comparison to another Arminian dean, Thomas Jackson. Possibly Andrewes alone could sustain comparison with Donne, but hardly a relatively unknown dean of Peterborough such as Jackson was, although in at least one respect he resembled Donne: he was never elevated to the episcopate. A former president of Corpus Christi College, Oxford, to which Laud had recommended him, on his relinquishing his earlier Calvinism, the Tractarians held him in the highest repute.[50] His chief work was a *Commentary on the Apostles' Creed* in twelve volumes (1613–1648). His sermons, although in the metaphysical manner, show a reluctance to display his considerable classical and patristic lore, and definitely avoid complex divisions. He loves the paradoxes, startlingly phrased, that so delighted the metaphysicals: when speaking of the celibacy of Christ, he says:

> The end and issue of his admirable chastitie, was to institute, that supernaturall and sacred Polygamie, which was (perhaps) by peculiar indulgence of divine dispensation legally foreshadowed in the multitude of *Davids* wives, or in the Polygamie of others, from whom he descended. Howsoever, *as the desolate hath more children than she that hath an husband,* so are the spouses of this chaste and *holy one,* more in number, than the wives and concubines of luxurious *Salomon.* Hee is that everlastinge *bridegroome,* whose Courts no multiplicitie of consorts can pollute: there is no soule, so it bring faith for its dowrie, but may be assuredly espowsed to him.[51]

The sermon has a typically moving close as a prayer: "Accept *This* (good Lord) wee intreat thee for our finall desire, and let it be registred in everlasting Records, as our last will and Testament, *Not as we will, but as thou wilt.* "[52] The echo of Christ's prayer in Gethsemane makes the pathos powerful.

Jackson has other gifts. He can paint a macabre picture of the plague:

But amongst the wofull spectacles, which the calamity of those times presented, none me thinkes more apt to imprint the terrour of Gods iudgements deeper, then to have seen men, otherwise of undaunted spirits, men whom no enemies lookes or braggs could afright, afrayed to hold parley with their native countrey-men that came unto them with words of love and peace, more agast to embrace their dearest friends or nearest kinsfolk, then to graspe an adder or a snake.[53]

Many metaphysical sermons are fascinated by the paradox of God as man in the humility of the Incarnation, but Jackson is one of the very few who extends this to saying that God now has the eyes and ears of men "to entertaine the prayers of men."[54] He is apt at coining maxims, as this of faith: ". . . faith if it be not defective, hath two hands; as well a left hand to apprehend the truth of Gods iudgements threatned, whilst we swarve from the waies of life; as a right hand, to lay hold on the truth of his promises. . . ."[55] He can be wittily pointed in a criticism of some Puritans who seem to conceive that to be the truth is to be as far removed from Roman Catholicism as possible: "*Antarticks* they are, & thinke they can never be farre enough from the *North-pole* untill they runne from it unto the *South-pole*, and pitch their habitation *in terra incognita* in a world and Church unknowne to the ancients, and I feare unto themselves."[56] In this embattled and embittered century he was witty as well as wise in warning that humans should not play the role of Christ in judgment:

To judge of the measures of any mans sinnes by the manner of his punishment here on earth, or to determine of his future estate by his present death or disaster, is to usurpe or trench upon *Christ Iesus* his royall prerogative, which to prejudice by word, or sentence interlocutory, which to preoccupate by any peremptory or censorious thought, is more than a *praemunire*, a branch of high treason, or rebellion against him.[57]

The Jacobean Arminian bishops

Having considered Laud the leader of the Arminians, and Andrewes his mentor, it is appropriate now to provide profiles of the friends, associates, and followers of Laud on the bench of bishops who have left sermons in print. These were John Buckeridge, John Howson, Richard Senhouse, and Theophilus Field. I also include Francis White, who was given preferment and important responsibilities by James I, which were merely confirmed by Buckingham, Laud, and Charles I when he was consecrated in 1626, a year after James's death.

This first group of bishops had all died before the onset of the Civil War, most of them before the political skies were overcast with storm clouds, This is not a period when the bench of bishops, appointed by James I, was distinguished for learning or spirituality. They have been characterized by H. R. Trevor-Roper as "indifferent, negligent, secular."[58] Buckeridge was consecrated in 1611, Lake in 1616, Corbet and Senhouse in 1624, and Francis White in 1626.

They (and their successors—the Caroline Arminian bishops) shared a respect amounting to reverence for their sovereigns, a profound love for the Book of Common Prayer, and for worship expressed in high ceremonial and sacramental devotion. They also had in common a desire to emphasize the continuity between the English Church and the Early Church of the first five centuries. They valued the ecumenical councils before the dichotomy of East and West had taken place, and expressed a consequent admiration for the Fathers of the Church, a respect for human reason, a conviction of the potentiality of universal salvation, and a belief in the freedom of the will to respond to or to reject salvation. Most of them, moreover, had great preaching talents, although they had a sense that the public preferred to listen to sermons rather than to pray for fidelity in serving God (which is the end of sermons). Finally, they had (with certain few exceptions) the conviction that the historic episcopate must be maintained for the sake of the unity, loyalty, and orthodoxy of the Church. In fairness it must be stressed that their conception of the role of a bishop often seemed more pretentious and "Lord Bishoplike" than the view of the Calvinist bishops. Calvinists tended to be primarily Fathers-in-God to their clergy, preachers of the Gospel, Defenders of the Faith, and only a long way afterwards spiritual members of the House of Lords.

It is easy, but inaccurate, to call the Arminian bishops and their followers Erastian. While they affirmed the unity of Church and Nation under royal supremacy, they still believed that the clergy had the right to make ecclesiastical laws under the king. Moreover, as J. W. Allen affirms, "none, or if any, certainly very few of them were believers in royal absolutism."[59] The distinguishing mark of the Arminian was that he believed in discipline as rigidly as did the Presbyterian Puritan, and, in the words of T. M. Parker, "the Laudians substituted for an arbitrary and all powerful God [of Calvinism] the arbitrary and absolute prelate."[60]

John Buckeridge

Dr. John Buckeridge (1562–1631) was first fellow and later president of St. John's College, Oxford, having in the interim been chaplain to Archbishop Whitgift. He was consecrated bishop of Rochester in 1611 and translated to Ely in 1628. A convinced Arminian he had tutored Laud at St. John's College, succeeded Andrewes at St. Giles, Cripplegate, and preached Andrewes' funeral sermon. In addition to this sermon, only two others of his survive.

His wit can be seen (though he is here repeating a gibe of Andrewes) in his calling Puritans who refuse to kneel at the sacrament elephants, thought to have no joints in their knees.[61] He also imitates the staccato style of Andrewes with its Latin tags, but very effectively and wittily, when arguing that it is Christ in the poor man that demands charity, and that our goods are not ours but only lent:

First, *Quis petit?* Who it is, that asks an Almes of thee. Thou takest it to be the poore man, but thou mistakest it: It is *Deus in paupere, & Christus in paupere* . . . Secondly, *Quid petit?* what is it that he doth aske: in short, *Suum non tuum:* He asks not thine, thou hast onely the use, and dispose of it, but he asks his owne, and *what hast thou, that thou hast not received,* even to thy selfe, thy soule; and thy body, all the gifts of Nature, and all the gifts of grace?[62]

He can coin a witty maxim also, with its characteristic Arminian stress on good works as the proof of faith: ". . . true Religion is in no way a *gargalisme* only, to wash the tongue and mouth, to speake good words: it must root in the heart, and then fructifie in the hand; els it will not clense the whole man."[63] He has many references in his sermons to the Fathers, in which he gives the exact source, but summarizes the content. He does not parade his knowledge of the original tongues, and in this lack of ostentation he follows Andrewes, and is the exception among metaphysical preachers.

One favorite theme is the importance of ceremonial as an index of reverence, especially the gestures that express adoration of God, such as prostration and kneeling. Prostration is defended as a "falling downe before him that came downe from Heaven to raise us," and kneeling as "to him that bare our sinnes on the Crosse, and us as lost sheepe on his shoulders."[64] His reasons for stressing the unity of body and soul in ceremonies are: first, that God created and redeemed both body and soul; second, the mutual excitation of the physical and the spiritual; and the third, that both have sinned and both should express contrition.[65] It is curious that he never argued that the soul can only express itself through the body's sign language.

His other favorite theme is the jurisdictional power of kings over persons ecclesiastical. In a sermon on this topic, he insists that kings have four ecclesiastical powers: disciplinary—for the reformation of the Church; summoning councils and synods; legislative—the promulgation of church laws and edicts; and, finally, receiving appeals and making decisions, and the restitution and deprivation of bishops.[66] Both of these themes were of central concern for the Arminian bishops.

Chapter V

John Howson

John Howson (1557?–1632), who was educated at St. Paul's School in London and at Christ Church, Oxford, was successively prebendary of Hereford, Exeter, and Christ Church, and in 1602, when vice-chancellor of Oxford University, attempted to put down Puritanism there. He was chaplain to Queen Elizabeth and to King James. He was consecrated bishop of Oxford in 1619, and translated to Durham in 1628.

A sermon that he preached in St. Mary's, the university church in Oxford, on 17 November 1602, defending the feasts of the Church of England in general, and the commemoration of the Queen's coronation in particular, gave great offense to the Puritans.[67]

Five years earlier as a don at Christ Church he preached a sermon at Paul's Cross, the theme of which was that all buying and selling of spiritual offices is unlawful. His text, Matthew 21:12–13, is an account of Jesus throwing the moneychangers out of the Temple. It shows how vicious the sin of simony is, for which five reasons are provided: it will cause the breaking up of the society and fellowship of mankind, it will turn the two universities into *"desolate and forsaken widowes,"*[68] procure an unsufficient and unlearned Ministerie," prevent the clergy from exercising hospitality, and it may portend great evil to ensue. His wit is seen in his reply to the charge that there are wealthy parsons that this began at "the beginning of her Maiesties reigne, when Benefices went a begging as Ministers doe now."[69] This sermon is larded with references, sixty-six of them to thirty-three authors. But this is exceeded by the second sermon at Paul's Cross that he preached as a continuation of the first, with ninety-four references in all.

This polemical preacher is best left with an ironical and humorous citation, deriding the general lack of charity towards the ministry:

For the allowance which we make unto God to maintaine his family, is thin and bare, *in quantum sitis, atque fames,*

& frigora aposcunt: after the rate of a cup of cold water, and a peece of bread, which shall be rewarded as our Saviour said at the day of iudgement, but to such as are able to give no more: after the rate of a frize coat, or a flannell wastcote, which *Dionysius* thought warme enough for winter, and cold enough for summer; after the rate of *Elias* diet in the desart, or *Daniels* in the Lions denne. And the allowance which we make God in his house in our Churches, is that which *Constituta divalia permiserunt Iudaeis,* that which the constitutions of the Christian Emperours allowed the Iewes in their synagogues: that is, *Tegumen parietibus imponere,* bare walls, and a cover over it to keepe us from rayne.[70]

Richard Senhouse

Dr. Richard Senhouse (died 1626) was educated at Trinity and St. John's Colleges, Cambridge, and was successively chaplain to the earl of Bedford, Prince Charles, and King James. Like Hacket, he became rector of Cheam, then dean of Gloucester in 1621, and bishop of Carlisle late in 1624. He had the honor of preaching the coronation sermon for Charles I. A volume containing four of his court sermons was published posthumously in 1627.

The first sermon is based on the text of Revelation 2:10, "And I will give thee a Crowne of life." The start is flowery and the division is fussy:

> . . . the Text (if you please) might be christened $\beta\alpha\sigma\iota\lambda\iota\kappa\grave{o}\nu$ $\delta\hat{\omega}\rho o\nu$, and accordingly be reduced to three heads: I. The royall excellencie of the gift, *A Crowne of life.* 2. The singular supremacie of the giver, *I; I will give it.* 3. The requisite qualitie of the receiver, *Thee:* Thou that art faithfull unto death, to thee will I give the Crowne of life.[71]

The wit seems strained and over-fanciful, as when he uses the image of the circle of the moon as an isthmus joining eternity and generation in time which expresses the Church triumphant in heaven and militant upon earth.[72] This farfetched trope is used only to illustrate the conjunction "And" in the text. The diction is often rhapsodical, mingling euphuisms with pagan and classical dicta and exempla.[73]

The second sermon uses as text Galatians 4:13, "Am I therefore become your enemie, because I tell you the truth?" Its manner is more straightforward (in keeping with its theme) and the division is simple: the excellency of truth, its harsh reception, and the hearty endurance of that reception.[74] Senhouse wittily reminds his hearers that they should not succumb to a flattering approach, that they should agree with the Protestant martyr Bradford that "the Masse bites not men, nor makes them blush as preaching does." Hence he must ask of his congregation, "cannot ye meddle only with toothlesse truths, as *Balak* did, Neither curse nor blesse at all? serve as in *Iob*, onely the white of an egg without any taste at all?"[75]

Senhouse's third sermon expounds the latter part of Acts of the Apostles 19:28 when the crowd cried out saying, "Great is Diana of the Ephesians." It starts in a lively way, emphasizing that Asia may come nearer England as religion moves to the West, and England could become as materialistic as the silver-smiths of Ephesus. He uses a homely metaphor to illustrate awareness of physical danger, but insensitivity to spiritual danger, "as ducklings stoop and dive at any little stone thrown by a man at them" yet miss the deeper danger to their lives.[76] His final sermon continues the third and uses the same text. Here he accuses the Catholics of having "metamorphosed" the Virgin Mary, "a Heavenly Saint sure," into "a goddess . . . They have often seemed rather to have turned *Maria* to *Minerva.* "[77]

In conclusion, Bishop Senhouse commands considerable rhetorical skill and patristic learning, using assonance, alliteration, antithesis, mottoes, developed tropes, and narrations linking biblical and pagan historical narrations and examples. His introductions are lengthy and occasionally obscure, and his scraps of classical tags, given in the original classical languages, are frequently otiose. Unlike Andrewes, the man is a pedant, and in spite of this he is not even a rigorous exegete. These sermons of his make no use of different interpretations of difficult passages of Scripture, the kind of intellectual interest provided by the sermons of Andrewes, Donne, and Hacket.

Theophilus Field

The most secular and crudely ambitious of all the Arminian bench of bishops was Dr. Theophilus Field (1574–1636). Educated at Pembroke College, Cambridge, where he became a fellow in 1598, after several parochial responsibilities held in plurality, he was appointed both a royal chaplain and chaplain in the service of Bacon, the Lord Chancellor. According to John Chamberlain (letter of 4 June 1619 to Dudley Carleton), he acted as "a sort of broker" in the Chancellor's peculations, and for this he was raked over the coals by Parliament. He was successively bishop of Llandaff, St. David's, and six months before his death reached the apex of his ambition—the wealthy diocese of Hereford. All the while he pestered Buckingham to improve his position either because he had a wife and six children to keep, or because the air of his second diocese was unsalubrious, claiming that "there is not so much as a leech to cure a sick horse" in Llandaff. His printed sermon *A Watch Word, or, the Alarme, or, A Good Take-heed* (London, 1628), preached before King Charles in Whitehall, is marked by wit, patristic citations galore, vivid illustrations, and moralizing. The latter seems to suggest that his motto was: God helps those who help themselves.

Francis White

Bishop Francis White (1564?–1638) was brought up in the Bedfordshire rectory of Eaton Socon, with four brothers all of whom received holy orders in the English Church. Like his brother John (who died at forty-five), he was prominent in the controversy with Rome. He and Laud were required by James I in 1622 to argue with the Jesuit John Fisher in an attempt to resist the Romanist tendencies of Mary, Countess of Buckingham. Preferments followed in quick succession. White was appointed dean of Carlisle in 1622, and was consecrated bishop of Carlisle in 1626 (when Cosin preached the consecration sermon). He was translated to Norwich early in 1628, and thence to Ely late in 1631. Apart from his association with Laud and Cosin, his high churchmanship was evident in his consecration of the splendid college chapel at Peterhouse in 1632, which Crashaw had helped to beautify and in which (a few years earlier) Latin services had been introduced.

Only one sermon of his survives in print, *Londons Warning By Jerusalem,* preached at Paul's Cross in mid-Lent 1619. Its dedication to "his loving friends of the parish of St. Sepulchre's" in the city of London suggests that he was vicar of that parish, and his mention of Lady Mary Hunsden and her son Henry, Lord Hunsden could imply that they were his parishioners or he had been their chaplain.

The division of the text (from Micah 6:9), "The Lords voice cryeth to the Citie, and the man of wisedome shall see thy name: heare ye the rod, and who hath appointed it," is scholastically and unnecessarily complex, with its major and minor parts, and its Latin sub-divisions. There is also much farfetched allegorical interpretation dragged in from Exodus 28:34, on the decoration of Aaron's skirts used as symbols of the Christian ministry, about as relevant as using a Christmas tree for Easter. But there is also brilliant wit, when his imagination plays like a carillon:

Now if ever any Church in the world had in it this ring of golden Bels, it is the Church of *England* at this day. The church of *Rome* hath indeed a ring of Bels, but they be Tinne, they be Lattine Bels, & the Latine, often broken Latine too, which makes the ring so much the worse. For the priests of *Rome* beat so altogether upon Latine, in the services of their Church, that most of them (such is the ignorance of their Masse-Priests) doe often breake it: whereas our ring, it is altogether of golden Bels, sound and sincere preachers of the Gospell.[78]

His primarily ethical irony is vividly employed to ridicule the atheist's hedonism, he whose "drinke-offerings are healths and carowses; the Incense which hee burnes, Indian smoake: his Church, none but a Play-house: the ordinary sermons which he hears, a Comedy: his funerall sermons, a Tragedy: his Morning prayer, God damne mee: His Evening prayer, Devill take body and soule."[79] He can be amusingly colloquial, declaiming against drunkards with beery breath and foul oaths: "And these roaring Boyes, send roaring out of their Pot-guns, in their drunken fits, nothing else but fearefull blasphemies against the God of Heaven."[80]

Finally, White is a psychologist, acutely aware of how evil is cloaked by excuses to disguise its reprehensible character, excuses used by extortionate and corrupt patrons, or by cheating merchants with their scant measures, inaccurate balances, deceitful weights, and lying tongues. "And all we," he declares, "*Adams* sinful posterity, have worn this cloake of excuse even almost thred-bare by long usage of it, in palliating of our sinnes: And we cloake Drunkenness with good fellowship; we cloake Covetousnesse with good thriftinesse; wee cloake Pride with decency and comelinesse."[81] He also clinches the point by illustrating it from the legal experience of Sir Thomas More:

As St. Thomas Moore tels us of a prisoner at the Barre, who being convict of felony, pleads his pardon upon this, how that God had so ordained him to be a Thiefe, and therefore he could no other doe but steale: For who ever resisted the will of God? But the Iudge answered him very well; If God hath ordained thee to bee a Thiefe and to steal, God hath also ordained mee to bee a Iudge, and to hang thee for thy theeverie.[82]

The Caroline Arminian Bishops

It seems most fitting to study first the two eminent liturgiologists, Wren and Cosin, who suffered for their loyalty—imprisonment for Wren and exile for Cosin; then Duppa, who was

Charles I's chaplain and intimate before and during the king's execution; and finally John Gauden, author of the iconic book which preserved the memory of Charles as the martyred champion of the Church of England, the Εικων βασιλικὴ; *the Pourtraicture of His Sacred Majestie in His Solitudes and Sufferings.* Published the day after Charles's execution on 31 January 1649, it ran through forty-seven editions, helped no doubt by being attacked in Milton's *Eikonoclastes.* Wren and Duppa were elevated to the episcopate by Charles I, and Cosin and Duppa by his son Charles II.

Matthew Wren

Wren (1585–1667) was the eldest of the Caroline Arminian bishops and, on the beheading of Laud in January 1644/5, became the leader of the group. More than any others, he and Laud were responsible for the fact that the 1662 revised Book of Common Prayer was not toned down in doctrine and ceremonial to meet the demands of the Presbyterian clergy, who were seeking a compromise liturgy at the Savoy Conference of 1661.[83]

Bishop Matthew Wren (uncle of Sir Christopher Wren and brother of the dean of Windsor) was a protégé of Andrewes. Andrewes was master of Pembroke College, Cambridge, when Wren was admitted as a student, and later elected as a fellow in 1605; and Andrewes made him his chaplain in 1615. In January 1621/2 he was appointed chaplain to Prince Charles and accompanied him on the dangerous and delicate journey to court the Infanta of Spain. (He owed this appointment partly to the fact that King James I recalled his witty skill in academic debate, when Wren advanced the view that the King's dogs "might perform more than others by the prerogative"). Other preferments followed rapidly. He was appointed master of Peterhouse, Cambridge in 1625, dean of the royal peculiar of Windsor in 1628, and he was consecrated bishop of Hereford in 1634. Less than a year later he was translated to Norwich, and in the following March he was appointed dean of the Chapel Royal. The diocese of Norwich was the largest in England, with about two thousand parishes in it. It had been rather neglected during the episcopate of Richard Corbet, and was "shaken with Schism and Faction" when Wren was translated to it "as the fittest man for so difficult a Province."[84] In 1638 he was translated to Ely. It was his disciplining of Puritan clergy in his various dioceses—causing many of them either to look for a more compliant diocesan elsewhere in England or to forsake their native land for Holland—that was to lead to his imprisonment for most of the Commonwealth and the Protectorate, in fact for eighteen years. Clarendon thought him a man of "a severe and sour" nature, but acknowledged him to be "particularly versed in the old liturgies of the Greek and Latin Churches."[85]

The charges made against Wren are significant (and parallel those later made against Laud) for they indicate what it was the Puritans and their supporters found so objectionable in Arminianism. There was the enmity aroused by the disciplinary rigor of bishops such as Wren, in ejecting clergy that disagreed with them: on 15 July 1641 Wren was charged for having in the previous two years and a few months in Norwich banished "fifty godly, learned, and painfull ministers," and also for re-pressing or restraining preaching in various ways. Sir Thomas Widdrington in his speech before the two Houses on 20 July 1641 asserted that Wren had "changed that golden Sentence of (*vae mihi si non predicavero*) into *vae aliis si predicaverint.*"[86] He prevented the saying of prayers before or after the sermon and prohibited afternoon sermons, or sermons preparatory to Holy Communion, unless permission was given by him. He charged church wardens to report their ministers if they preached expositions of holy Scripture not in accordance with the sense of the ancient Fathers. He was further accused of practising superstition, insisting that Communion-tables be placed altar-wise and raised in the chancel, as well as railed in. It was alleged that he celebrated Communion with his back to the people, frequently bowing towards the altar, and highly elevating the consecrated Bread and Wine. Also it was objected that he caused pews and seats so to be constructed that the congregation using them had to kneel facing the East.[87]

Chapter V

The Puritans had long believed that kneeling at Communion implied a belief in transubstantiation, which they considered idolatrous, and crossing they viewed as a superstitious ceremony not authorized by Holy Scripture. Preaching was for them the major ordinance leading to salvation, and so its suppression or limitation, and even the restriction of catechizing only to the questions and answers in the Prayer Book, constituted an affront to their dearest convictions. What hurt most was the rigid imposition of these requirements, and the prohibition of extempore prayers. Readings from the Book of Sports further exacerbated the Puritans, who felt it broke the solemnity of the Sunday, and led to the loss of many conscientious ministers.

Though Wren was a rigorous legalist, who did not understand toleration or the mixture of motives in most normal people, he was as unbending as his opponents. He refused to repudiate or even modify his convictions when offered opportunities for liberation by Cromwell. His private life was as rigid as his public; he was a chaste family man, with certain ascetic convictions; and for almost twenty years he drank no wine, according to Pearson who preached his Latin funeral oration at Cambridge University.[88] At no time did he seek preferment nor offer any bribes; as he might have said himself, *nec prece, nec pretio,* being in this respect so very different from his predecessor, Richard Corbet.

A single sermon of his survives in print, perhaps appropriately for one who preferred liturgy and sacraments to preaching. The sermon was preached before King Charles I at Whitehall in 1627, on a text apt for an Arminian supporter of the divine right of kings. The text was from Proverbs 24:21, "*Time Deum, fili mi, & Regem.* Feare GOD, my Sonne, and the KING." Though the text has only six words, the divisions of the sermon are highly complex: he elaborates on the three great persons and their interrelations, then the duties we owe to each of them, and, finally, the reasons for such duties. The sermon has few patristic references, but many careful and relevant references to both Testaments. It provides etymological analysis and logical development of thought, and the brief citations are in exact Greek. There are satirical references to men showing reverence to superiors and neglecting God, but no images of any vividness. The teaching emphasizes that the firmness of the social order is entirely dependent on the people's duty to God and the king, in that order of priority.

Characteristically, Wren speaks of the necessity of reverence and beauty in worship:

> . . . the *Feare* of the Lord requires the *Worship* of him, and that the due *Worship* of him requires so much Beauty and Reverence, that all our saucy and carelesse demeanour before him, all negligent and perfunctorie performance of our Religion, all slight and unawfull Expressions in it, as in Gods presence, are the foulest Scorn and Abasement that may be; Ungodding him no lesse in true construction, then does rash and unadvised blasphemie.[89]

The sermon ends with an eloquent climax, showing that the godly will also be kings in eternity, as Wren solemnly charges his congregation to show due reverence to both God and the king: "That so approving our selves respectively to God and King, as *Sonnes* to both, ingenuous *Sonnes*, here in the life of Grace; our *Feare* at last may be changed into Ioy, and our Devotion unto Fruition, and we be made not *Sonnes* alone, but *Kings* also with God, in the life of Glorie."[90]

It is unfortunate that Wren's surviving sermon gives no indication of his wit. The waggish Tom Fuller testifies that he possessed it in abundance and refers to a sermon that exhibited it at best in the choice of text. "*One* preached before the Judges," Fuller reports was "on this Text; *And let Judgement run down like waters, and righteousness as a mighty stream*; at what time the *draining of the Fens* was designed, suspected detrimental to the *University.*"[91]

John Cosin

Bishop John Cosin (1594–1671/2) also loved the Anglican liturgy. Through its prayers and sacraments it had formed, together with the English Bible, the spirituality of the English people; it was the link joining the Church of England with the primitive Church through the centuries. Cosin was anxious that the outward ceremonial of the English Church should be an index of the decency, order, and beauty that should characterize worship. When he succeeded Wren as master of Peterhouse in 1634/5, Prynne affirmed that an eyewitness reported "that in *Peter house* Chappell there was a glorious new *Altar* set up; & mounted on steps, to which the Master, Fellowes, Schollers bowed, and were enjoyned to bow by Dr. *Cosins*, the Master who set it up; that there were Basons, Candlestickes, Tapers, standing on it, and a great Crucifix hanging over it."[92] Peter Smart, who had earlier objected to the high liturgical ceremonial introduced by Cosin as a canon to Durham Cathedral, petitioned Parliament to eject Cosin from the headship of Peterhouse because of his "superstititous and popish innova tions." Cosin had further enraged the Parliamentarians by sending the college plate to the Royal Mint in York, so in the March of 1643/4 he was ejected from his post at Peterhouse.

By the order of King Charles I he retired to Paris to become the chaplain to the Protestant members of Queen Henrietta Maria's household. At first he held services in a private home, but as the attendance increased, Sir Richard Brown, the English ambassador to France, had the chapel of the residency equipped so that Cosin was able to celebrate Anglican worship with all the imposing ceremonial that he loved. Thomas Fuller reported that "whilest he remained in France, he was the *Atlas* of the Protestant Religion, supporting the same with his Piety and Learning, confirming the wavering therein, yea, daily adding *Proselytes*, not of the meanest rank."[93]

His liturgical fidelity was rewarded at the Restoration. He was briefly dean of Peterborough in July 1660, where he immediately instituted daily services in the cathedral, according to the Prayer Book order, while others were, according to Pepys, merely "nibbling at the Prayer Book" and waiting to judge in what corner the wind lay. And soon afterwards he was consecrated bishop of Durham. This tall, handsome man of solid character and convictions was well equipped to be the spiritual and temporal leader of the County Palatine in his episcopal castle and palace, and his permanent contribution was the revised Prayer Book of 1662.

His surviving sermons in print date from 1621 to 1659, but we have none from his days as a bishop. His preaching can best be characterized as "liturgical." The texts of his sermons are always taken from the lessons appointed for the day of the Prayer Book Calendar. He begins every festival sermon by providing the reasons for that festival, and often he will cite the collect for the day in his sermon, dilating on the joy suitable to a festival or the sorrow that should accompany a fast. Furthermore, his sermon is so structured as always to begin with the reasons for the service of the day, then to proceed to the Bidding Prayer for the Church and Nation, and to the Lord's Prayer. Then and only then does he announce his text and give its divisions or points. His reason for doing this is to keep Solomon's rule in Proverbs 15:23, namely, *verbum Dei in die suo*, God's Word on God's day.[94] His sermons intend to lead worshippers to gratitude reaching to adoration in spirit, and to practical holiness in life.

The structure of his sermons may be illustrated from a 1621 sermon on the Epiphany preached at St. Edward's Church, Cambridge. His introductory observations begin by repeating the Solomonic dictum of "God's Word on God's day." This is the last day of the Christmas season, he said, when Christ was manifested to the Magi, but it is also important because, according to St. Gregory of Nazianzen, on this same day of the year Christ was baptized, and the miracle of the changing of the water into wine at Cana was performed. Furthermore, St. Augustine, following Origen, says it was the day when Christ fed the four thousand in the wilderness. The importance of the Epiphany or Manifestation, however, is "this day God became the Saviour of the Gentiles."[95] After these observations, he interrupts the sermon with the Bidding Prayers, and there is a typically witty transition at the end of the introduction: "And so I have done with the feast, and from the day I come to the *opus dei,* from the time to the text, though I have not been far from it all the while."[96] He is also witty when he comes to the division of the sermon, articulating its parts and points: "The text would do well to have no division to-day because it is a day of union, wherein they that were divided before were made one under Christ, and therefore I might only call it the Epiphany, one general head, and so away."[97]

Like all the followers of Andrewes, he is driven to his knees by the humility of God as man in the Incarnation. He contemplates four steps in the descent of Deity: God to be born, in unknown Bethlehem, in the manger of an inn, in the cold days of winter, and in the time of the bloody tyrant Herod: "Count we; immortality itself made a mortal man, *natus,* the first step; immortality confined within a cratch, *natus in Bethlem;* the second: eternity measured by time, *in diebus,* the third; power made subject to tyranny, *in diebus Herodis regis,* the fourth."[98] Then he makes the point that the Christian should be humble like his or her Lord:

> The only way to be great is to be little, lowly before God, the only way to be accounted Kings, to be servants to come and worship God; which we acknowledge every day in our Church service, *Cui servire regnare est,* as the old collect goes, "whose service is perfect freedom," that is a Kingdom right.[99]

The end of the sermon also is characteristically witty, excusing his lengthy sermon. He remarks that it has grown late and therefore it is best to stop, otherwise "there be so many steps to be taken in the way, that the night would overtake us ere we should get to the text's end." Therefore, "since we are at Jerusalem, the city of Peace" we might as well "take the peace of God with us and so depart for this time." This leads directly to the *pax* of the blessing: "Now the God of peace, etc."[100]

Cosin is a typically Anglican in his *via media* apologetics. He is capable of anti-Calvinist irony, as well as anti-Roman digs. In a sermon on Christ's Temptation in the wilderness, he criticizes the Puritans who claim to be Pauline, but use short cuts, missing several of the stages on the path to salvation:

> St. Paul tells us that of old there were many degrees in Christianity, preaching, hearing, believing, invocating, all in order and so foreknowing, predestinating, calling, justifying, sanctifying, and at last glorifying, all in order too. Now our new Masters would teach us a shorter cut and make but one degree in all Christianity, as if there were but one step from the ground to the pinnacle. They teach a man to take his raise from predestination, and to give a jump into glorification without any more ado.[101]

Cosin goes on to observe that there is a ladder of Christian practice too: for St. Peter requires the practical pursuit of virtue, knowledge, temperance, patience, piety, and brotherly love.[102] He has a brief but telling anti-Romanist expression in a sermon, preached in Paris on 16 April 1651, on the Octave of the Resurrection. The news of the Resurrection was given to the women, but the apostles (including Peter) were ignorant of this event, which he interprets as undercutting the infallibility of the papacy.[103]

He gives his reasons for the importance of divine worship in a sermon on the fourth commandment, preached in his parish of Brancepath in Northumberland in 1633. These are "God shall have the more honour by it, more by a full congregation than by a few" and because "it makes more for the good of the Church; the prayers are the stronger for it . . . whereas they languish like the congregation itself, when they want half their company to help them."[104] Augustine could have provided Cosin with a more profound rationale: the outgoing love of God finding the response of the household of faith. He is, however, wiser and wittier in expressing the reasons for the sacraments:

> God will have that manifest and real in us which was manifest and true in Him. That whether we celebrate the

feast of His taking our flesh, or the feast of our taking His, they may both tend to the manifest and powerful operation of this piety in the text upon us; to lead to a life that may be somewhat like to His, Whose name we bear, in all godliness and honesty.[105]

Like all metaphysical preachers he abounds in paradoxes and fanciful witticisms, although he rarely invents vivid images. He is fond of citing the Fathers (especially Augustine), and he occasionally uses historical narrations as illustrations of his thought. His sermon divisions are genuinely derived from his texts, but they are rarely terse. Not even a Benedictine monk could have stressed the primacy of worship, as the *opus Dei* in the Christian life, more frequently than he. It is this which is perhaps his finest contribution.

Brian Duppa

Another strong Arminian and defender of the High Church tradition in the Church of England was Bishop Brian Duppa (1588–1662), who was educated at Westminster School and learned Hebrew from Andrewes, then dean of Westminster. Afterwards he was elected a Student or don of Christ Church, and later became a fellow of All Souls College. For a while he was chaplain to the earl of Dorset, and then he succeeded Corbet as dean of Christ Church. Laud recommended him as tutor to the future Charles II during his minority. In 1638 he was consecrated bishop of Chichester (his successor being another old Westminster scholar and a metaphysical poet, Henry King), and in 1641 he was translated to Salisbury. During the Commonwealth he privately ordained priests and deacons, including Thomas Tenison, future archbishop of Canterbury. At the Restoration he was translated to Winchester and appointed Lord Almoner, two offices which the Lancelot Andrewes he so much admired had held under James I. As bishop of Winchester he was the principal consecrator of Sheldon and of four other bishops.

Wood reports that he was a gifted man of great "comeliness

223

of his person and gracefulness of his deportment," adding that his pious conversation had consoled Charles I during his imprisonment on the Isle of Wight. His reputation for holiness recalls Andrewes, especially the anecdote that, when Duppa was on his deathbed in Richmond, he was visited by Charles II who "craved his blessing on his bended knees by his bedside."[106]

He published only two sermons, both in 1648. One was *The Soules Soliloquie: And, A Conference with Conscience* which was preached before Charles I during his imprisonment at Newport. It was on an apt text, Psalm 42:5, "Why art thou cast downe, O my soule, and why art thou disquieted within me?" The second, *Angels Rejoicing for Sinners Repenting*, is on the text Luke 15:10, "Likewise I say unto you, There is joy in the presence of the Angels of God over one sinner that repenteth."

The metaphysical character of these sermons is seen in the startling images and 'farfetched comparisons, the striking openings, the memorable maxims, the historical learning, the ever–present consciousness of death (which seems more Jacobean than Caroline), the expression of charming, easy, and elegant wit, and the sense that God has multiple avenues and approaches to the human soul. Some of these characteristics will be briefly illustrated.

As one striking image, we may note that Duppa thinks of the conscience as God's spy, "For as they whom Statemen employ as Spies, though they mingle with all companies, yet keep themselves concealed: so the Conscience which is Gods *Informer*, sent by him, as a Spie into the Soule, mixeth with all our thoughts, as well as actions; and though we know not what the *Conscience* is, yet what *We* are, our Conscience knowes full well."[107] He advances the analogy further: "Dost thou know withall, that it is a Volume which no *Jesuite* can corrupt, nor no *Index Expurgatorius* strike a Letter out of it; That it is the onely Book of all thy Library that shall goe along with thee into the world to come?"[108] An example of an extreme comparison is one Duppa finds for the heart of man bursting with joy at the divine acceptance of the penitent soul: "But whither am I carried? Sooner shall a Sparrow drink up the Sea, or a

·Moale heave the whole Earth out of the Center, then the heart of man swell to that bigness, as to be able to comprehend his joy."[109]

The start of *Angels Rejoicing for Sinners Repenting* is indeed startling: "Man never yet invented more waies to *damn* himself, then God hath done to *save* him . . . He ransacks the whole Inventory of his Creatures, puts on all shapes to gaine a Soule."[110] Two striking maxims may be cited, "The heart is a kind of Runagate, harder to be fix'd then Quick-silver"[111] and "Sorrow is Sins Eccho."[112] The elegantly sensitive wit of the bishop comes out in *The Soules Soliloquie* when he refers to his text as being possibly discouraging, "But, if there be others that think the Text too melancholy for this Place, that come rather to have their *Eares pleased,* then their *Hearts wounded;* To these, I must alter my Note, and say, as St. *Hierome* did to *Sabinian, Hoc ipsum plango, quod vos non plangitis,* This makes *me* sorry, that nothing can make *you* so."[113] Here we see the iron hand of judgment beneath the velvet glove of courtesy, so necessary in preaching to courtiers.

Finally, there is the marvellous recognition that men cannot be saved like sardines, by the barrel-load, and that God has almost as many approaches as there are souls. Bishop Duppa tells of the variety of divine approaches, exhibiting perhaps the most delightful characteristic of the more liberal Arminians:

To the Traveller he calls, *I am the way;* To the benighted, he shews, *he is the light;* To the Stranger, he opens himself, *I am the dore;* Looke for him among the Plants, you shall find him *a vine;* Search for him in the flock, the Baptist points him out to you, *Behold the Lamb:* or if Metaphors be but *verball* transfigurings, track him in his Parables, which are more reall; if you meet there with a Sower, Christ is that Sower; if you heare of a Bridegroome, he is that Bridegroom; if you see the *man* that brings back his lost sheep in triumph, he is that *man:* or if you find a *woman,* that calls her friends to joy with her, *Rejoice, for I have found the piece which I had lost,* know that that

225

piece is thy Soule, those *friends* are the Angels, he is that *woman* too . . ."[114]

The attraction of this good man is that in his uncensorious way he makes holiness enchanting, not repellent, and is thus able, in the words of a prayer with which he closes a sermon, to "make the Good Conscience Quiet, and the Quiet Conscience Good."[115] He spoke in loud thunder to the seared conscience, and in soft whispers to the wounded conscience.

John Gauden

The fourth member of this group of Arminian bishops was John Gauden (1605–1662), a former Calvinist. Son of a vicar, he was a graduate of St. John's College, Cambridge, and then became chaplain to Robert Rich, the earl of Warwick, sharing his parliamentary sympathies. He preached a sermon before the House of Commons that so charmed his anti-royalist audience that it gained him a silver tankard inscribed, *Donum honorarium populi Anglicani in parliamento congregati Johanni Gauden,* [116] which must have been an embarrassment to him later when he became an Arminian and royalist. However, his difficulties illustrate the problems faced by moderates of a trimming tendency. Although chosen a member of the Westminster Assembly of Divines, he found himself unable in conscience to take the oath of the Solemn League and Covenant, and he published the reasons for this disavowal. Equally, he was unable to continue worshipping according to the Prayer Book. He conformed to the dominant Presbyterianism, while publishing books recommending Anglicanism. Gauden's reward came with the Restoration, when this author of Εικών βασλικὴ, *the Portraicture of His Sacred Maiestie,* was appointed first a royal chaplain, and then bishop of Exeter in November 1660, succeeding Ralph Brownrig. A year later he was translated to Worcester, and died shortly afterwards. Two collections of his sermons were published.

The silver tankard sermon shows due modesty and courtesy, a proper respect for Parliament, and the importance of Truth,

Peace, and Love—the Sacred Trinity, as he calls them from his text taken from Zechariah 8:19. The division is simple and arises naturally from the text. His definitions are clear, and the images are vivid. One of these must have delighted the members of Parliament who heard him, since it argued that it was law that held the State together:

> See then how much *they* deserve *publique hatred*, Who through feare or *flattery*, or base and sinister ends falsifie the minde of the *Law*; at once cutting asunder that great *Cable* which holds the state from shipwrack: turning the *sword of justice* put into their unworthy hands, to cut the *throat* of *lawes* and liberties.[117]

In fact, both his earlier and later sermons show him more at ease with the patristic learning, the historical narrations, the citations for Greek and Latin, the more complex divisions, the paradoxes, the maxims, and above all, the wit characteristic of metaphysical preaching. The ability to charm his auditory is evident in all his sermons, whether preached before the king and court, the judges, Oxford University, or Parliament.

Preaching in the university church, St. Mary's in Oxford, he tells his congregation that he considers himself happy to have the opportunity of recommending a topic, such as the spiritual renewing of the mind, to "so able, so learned, so choice and considerable an Assembly, consisting of Minds and Spirits more elevated, enlarged, and ennobled than ordinary."[118] If this seems obsequious to the modern reader, the soft-soaping is mild compared with the perfumed lather used to flatter a king. His approach in a sermon preached before the judges at Chelmsford is equally courteous. He is pleased that these "Right Honourable and Reverend disdaine not to receive advice from the Pulpit" before going to the bench, that they come to hear God's charge to them, before they give their charge to others.[119]

His maxims have clarity and concision, as the following: "By our bodies we live beasts, by our minds men, by renewed minds Christians, by perfected minds Saints."[120] Holiness he imagines as a ladder, with the lowest rung being humility, and the highest love and devotion, adding that "by this the soule descends to man in charity, and ascends to God in piety."[121] For a difficult paradox, it would be hard to find a more strained example than this: *"Better be holy in hell,* if possible than *unholy in Heaven;* though these two are unseparable; *Holinesse* and *Happinesse;* differing only in degree, not in kinde. For *Holinesse* is the sparke of *Happinesse* and *happinesse* the flame of *holinesse.* "[122]

As for wit, in a sermon before the king he recalls by inference that Moses was placed in a crevice of the rock on Sinai because he could not bear the blaze of God's glory, but he was allowed to see the back parts of the departing Deity. Gauden then speaks of the magistrates as "being *Umbratiles Dij,* the back parts and shadowes of God, they most fully represent in a humane model, the divine perfections."[123] It was a sly, because an ambiguous image.

He seems to belong most fully to the Arminian tradition in his love for learning (his sermon before the judges has thirty-four patristic and classical references in all), his preference for "moderate mirth" rather for "a tedious drooping manner which brings in ill report on Gods wayes,"[124] and in the respect for an appeal to reason.[125]

The minor ministers: controversialists

Peter Heylyn (1600–1662) was the most acrimonious controversialist and an avid partisan of Arminianism. This theologian and historian was elected a demy of Magdalen College, Oxford in 1615, and three years later became a fellow there and celebrated his election by writing a Latin comedy, *Theomachia,* which was acted in the president's lodgings. In 1627 he displayed his theological colors clearly, choosing to defend the visibility and the infallibility of the Church, in direct opposition to the professor of divinity, Prideaux, who, as a Calvinist, maintained the invisibility of the Church (its true members known to God alone) and the infallibility of the Gospel. This brought him to Laud's notice, who saw to it that Heylyn became a royal chaplain in 1630, and a year later a prebendary of Westminster, where he was placed to do battle against the dean of Westminster, Bishop John Williams.

Heylyn was a learned historian and patriot, who wrote *The History of St. George* (1631), the *History of Episcopacie* (1642), the *History of Liturgies* (1642), *Ecclesia Vindicata, or the Church of England justified* (an encomium as much as his *Aerius redivivus, or, the History of the Presbyterians* [1679] is a vilification), *Ecclesia Restaurata, or the History of the Reformation* (1661), and *Cyprianus Anglicus, or the History of the Life and Death of William Laud Arch-Bishop of Canterbury* (1668).

The quarrel between Bishop John Williams, and Heylyn was most bitter from 1631 to 1637. Williams had criticized, as superstitious, Laud's policy of high ceremonialism to inculcate reverence, and in particular the fencing of the communion table with rails to prevent profanity. Heylyn attacked this in an anonymous publication, *A Coale from the Altar.* His biographer defends Heylyn's stand by writing: "in most Country Churches to this day the Table is set at the hither end of the Chancel without any *Traverse* or *Rails* to fence it; Boys fling their Hats upon it, and that which is worse, Dogs piss against it. . . ."[126] In 1637 and 1640 Laud's triumph was complete when Williams was heavily fined by the Star Chamber. In retaliation Williams sat in the decanal pew in Westminster abbey, (one of his several benefices), and loudly interrupted a sermon Heylyn was preaching, ironically, on the need for peace and moderation. Heylyn was deprecating the schisms in the Church of England, and the partisanship of

> some rather putting all into open tumult, than they would conform to a lawful Government, *derived* from *Christ* and his Apostles to these very Times. At the speaking of which words [Williams] sitting in the great Pew . . . knocked aloud with his staff upon the Pulpit, saying, *No more of that point. No more of that point, Peter.* To whom the Doctor readily answered without hesitation, or the least sign of being dashed out of countenance. *I have a little more to say, my Lord, and then I have done.* [127]

As might be expected, Heylyn's sermons are immensely learned and often pedantic, combining citations from the Greek and Latin Fathers, modern commentators, Latin poets and occasionally moralists, and most of all historians, classical and modern.[128] He almost always begins with a sententious citation in Latin, and he always quotes his sources in the original tongues in full. In addition, he affirms the central position of the Church of England, allowing himself to squint neither to Rome nor to Geneva.

In wit as well as learning he is a metaphysical preacher. For example, he scores an amusing point against the Roman Catholics by playing on the meaning of the theme of "rock" as used in both Testaments:

> The holy Ghost hath said of Christ, that he is a Rock, *Petra autem erat Christus*, in St. *Pauls* Epistles; and Christ hath told us of the Confession of his faith, that it is a Rock, *super hanc petram*, in St. *Matthews* Gospel. Now one of the four things that seemeth wonderful and unsearchable in the eyes of *Solomon*, is *via serpentis super petram*, that of a Serpent on a Rock; or, if you like the Application, that of the Devil in subverting the faith of Christ.[129]

He can with equal facility attack Puritans, claiming that they are for the many-headed democracy against monarchy, that they are Stoics believing in predestination and determinism, and even in Judaism, since they wish to impose sabbatarianism on the Church of Christ.[130]

In a more serious vein the controversialist uses church history to point out where he believes the Church of Rome has departed from the Gospel and the primitive Church:

> Tell me what *Caveats* had been entred in the Churches name, by *Gregory* the Great, against the Doctrine of the *Popes* supremacy; by *Berengarius*, against that of the carnall presence; by *Charles* the Great, and all his *Clergy* in the *Synod* of *Frankford*, against the worshipping of Images;

by *Huldrich* B. of Augsburg in defence of the married *Clergy;* by the *Waldenses, Pauperes de Lugdano Clemanges, Petrus de Alliaco, Wiclif, Hus,* and others, (though men that had, I grant, their own personal errors) against the severall corruptions of the Church of *Rome,* both in faith & manners?[131]

He can be most apt in fitting his words to his congregation, as in the following sermon preached at court (which had removed to Oxford). It begins with a citation from Velleius in Latin:

> *Rumpit, interdum moratur proposita hominem Fortuna.* The projects and designes of us mortall men are many times delayed, and sometimes overthrown by a higher Power. Which power, though the Historian being a Courtier (who ascribes all things to good luck) entituled by the name of Fortune; yet the Philosopher, or contemplative man, would have called it Providence.[132]

Like every preacher who wishes to be remembered, he can provide the striking metaphor (as in the case of the insensible growth of heresy like the movement of the shadow on a sundial)[133] or the pithy epigram("successful mischief is oft crowned with the name of virtue . . . The wicked man is not ashamed of doing ill, but of being detected").[134]

Our second controversialist, John White (1570–1615) died before the Calvinist-Arminian polarity became acrimonious. He was one of the five sons of Peter White, vicar of St. Neots, all of whom became clergy. His brother Francis, discussed earlier in this chapter, was also a gifted controversialist but not so gifted a preacher. John White was educated at Gonville and Caius College, Cambridge, and in 1614 was appointed chaplain in ordinary to King James I, presumably as a reward for his Anglican apology, or deterrent to conversion to Roman Catholicism, *The Way to the True Church; Wherein the principal Motives perswading to Romanisme are familiarly disputed and driven to their*

Issues (1608). Its success can be judged from its subsequent reissues in 1610, 1612, 1616, as well as in his collected works brought out by his brother Francis in 1624.

The collected works contain two sermons, both outstanding. The Paul's Cross sermon was preached on 24 March 1615 as a commemoration of the peaceful succession of James I to the throne of Great Britain. It starts by wondering whether the huge congregation is utterly oblivious to the fact that God has saved the nation from shipwreck at the hands of its enemies, "and this day which they prophecied should have been the dismallest that ever rose upon the kingdome, assembled also together in ioy and triumph, men, women, and little children, to celebrate our peace, ringing and singing, and reioycing before the Lord our maker?"[135]

He then turns cynical at the expense of the Elizabethan Jesuit, Parsons, who prophesied that, with no heir born to Elizabeth her death would lead to great danger in England "by the certainty of most bloody civill and forraine wars" (Parsons' words), words disproved by the peaceful succession of King James. White rails at Parsons and mocks his wild imagination: "this *Asses head* sold to the Pope *for* 80. *silverlings,* and his friends rose up in a misty morning when a sheepe seemed to them as big as an oxe"[136] to make their prophecy—such rhodomontade must have been caviare to the general! Next he takes an illustration from "unnatural" natural history to warn against the Jesuits: "They say there is a bird that, when men are at sacrifice, takes fire from the altar, and burnes their houses."[137] The allusion to the Guy Fawkes Conspiracy hatched at a mass would not be lost on the great crowd.

White then reproves England for its sleep. The English are really as well as metaphorically drunkards, and "drinking is now so taken up thorow the whole kingdome, that the Germans I heare, are like to lose their charter." Finally he appeals to the patriotism and devotion of the auditory by telling them of their Protestant king's love of religious observance so that "as much may be said of his Court, as was said of the Court of *Theodosius,* that it was turned into an Oratorie for the daily service of God."[138] The sermon was divided simply, and its learning was evident from the forty references to twenty-seven authors. But, more strikingly, the interest was gained by an intriguing start, and maintained by anti-Catholic philippics, an amusing historical narration about "roaring boies" who were so drunk that they were gulled into thinking they were at sea in a storm, and by some brilliant word-pictures such as the reference to a weakened Samson as "when strength lay asleep on Delilah's knees."[139]

The Spital sermon was preached on Easter Monday, 1613, to the usual gathering of the wealthy mayor and aldermen of the City of London, with some of the nobility, and the desperately poor inmates of orphanages. The text was I Timothy 6:17, a most appropriate charge to the rich to be rich towards God and to the needy poor. He refuses to assume that the rich will not enter heaven, or that the poor are guaranteed eternal life. He cites St. Augustine, wittily observing "that *Lazarus* a poore man, sate in Heaven in Abraham's bosome, that was a rich man."[140] He loves stories, and we can imagine him holding the vast auditory in the palm of his hand as he illustrates the difficulty of dealing with great men by a parable story of fishing and how the larger fish get away and frighten the tiddlers too.[141]

He also attracts attention by using maxims and proverbs, and creates "characters" in the newest mode. He appeals to the fear of the rich with the warming maxim he translates from his favourite Augustine: "Divers devour in this life what afterward they digest in hell."[142] He also reaches out to touch their potential generosity by reminding them of the proverb: "A gift in the bosome prospers which way soever it goes."[143] Finally, he can rivet the attention by drawing a delicate character sketch of Mercy:

Make the picture of this Mercie in a table, and hang it in your houses: let it be a Virgin faire and lovely, her garments green and orient; a Crowne of gold upon her head, the teares of compassion bolting at her eies, pittie and ruth sitting in her face. Let her paths be milke where she sees her foot: let plenty lie in her lap, and multitudes of people draw their breath from her. Let her give sight to the blinde, and feet to the lame, and strength and comfort to the miserable. Let the earth give her all his riches, and the heavens their influence. Let her make the sunne to shine, the day to rise, the clouds to raine, the earth to be fruitfull. At her right hand place the Angels of heaven protecting, at her left hand all Gods mercies attending. Under her feet the devill and covetousnesse. Let pride follow her in bands; let oppression, and envy, and self-love, and unlawfull gaines, flie from her presence: and write upon her breat, in golden letters, *O bona Charitas, alumna coeli, corona soli, haeres vitae, medicina mortis, o bona Charitas.* [144]

The Minor Ministers: Six Cathedral Clergy

The next group of Arminian metaphysical preachers could have been most conveniently summarized as prebendaries, were it not for the fact that William Cartwright, the most celebrated in his day, was only the succentor at Salisbury. Two others, who like Cartwright were educated at Westminster School and Christ Church, Oxford, were Jasper Mayne and John Wall, both canons of Christ Church. The other three include one Cambridge man, Mark Frank, who became a prebendary of St. Paul's, and Robert Willan and Thomas Lushington who were both prebendaries of Salisbury.

William Cartwright and Jasper Mayne

Cartwright (1611–1643) and Mayne (1604–1672) were thought to have the same preaching style. Abraham Wright's *Five Sermons in Five severall Styles* (1656), a fascinating analysis of the dominant styles current in England in the Protectorate, imitated the witty, allegorical, emblematic, and florid style they used in Oxford.[145] They were both playwrights and preachers in great demand. Cartwright's play, *The Royal Slave*, was selected as the climax of the university celebration of the visit of King Charles and his queen to Oxford in 1636. It was so successful that the queen commanded a second performance the following year at Hampton Court. Mayne's domestic comedy, *The City Match* of 1639, was acted before the queen at Whitehall and later at the Blackfriars Theatre. Mayne and Cartwright were firm friends, and on the early death of Cartwright, Jasper Mayne wrote a perceptive tribute to him:

> Thou were a Poet, but thy Sermons do
> Shew thee to be the best of Preachers too; . . .
> What holy Craft did in thy Pulpit move?
> How was the Serpent mingled with the Dove?
> How have I seen thee cast thy Net, and then
> With holy Cosenage catch'd the Souls of Men?[146]

Cartwright's contemporaries had an exaggerated opinion of his preaching, due in part to royal attention, in part to his sonorous voice and handsome presence, and probably also to his early death. Wood claimed that "his preaching also was so graceful and profound withal, that none of his time or age went beyond him." Wood added, "so that if the Wits read his Poems, Divines his Sermons, and Philosophers his Lectures on Aristotles *Metaphysicks*, they would scarce believe that he died a little over thirty years of age."[147] David Lloyd runs out of superlatives in describing him:

> So ravishing by the comelinesse of his presence (for his body was as handsome as his soul) and the beauties of his discourse in his Sermons made up of learned and holy extasies, that . . . he winged up his hearers hearts to the same height with his own. . . .

That may take some swallowing, but the citation continues by asserting that he "expressed strict vertue into the greatest pleasure, strowed the streight way to ease and delight; chained up all thoughts to his, ravishing with a Masculine vigour his hearers, not only by way of perswasion, but command."[148]

It is hardly possible that the single sermon of Cartwright's that survives should be able to illustrate these glories. Its title includes the kind of paradox the metaphysicals loved: *An Off-Spring of Mercy, Issuing out of the Womb of Cruelty*. This Passion sermon was based on the text of Acts 2:23, "Him, being delivered by the determinate counsell and foreknowledge of God, ye have taken, and by wicked hands have crucified and slain." Cartwright proceeds immediately to the division, with Jesus as the suffering person crucified, and the two agents of his death, the supernatural agent in God the Father, and his human agents, the Jews. He then employs the three ways in which Aquinas explained how the Father delivered his Son to death: by preordaining his Passion from His eternal will, by inspiring him with a willingness to suffer, and by not protecting him from his sufferings.

His conclusion is climactic rhetoric, piling paradox upon paradox in the manner of Andrewes. He claims that the Old Testament is swallowed up in the New, the old shadowy sacrifices culminate in the perfect sacrifice of the Cross, and God's goodness shines brilliantly through the evil of man's plotting. The wonder of the Passion is viewed as a series of miracles for which the only possible transcendent language is that of paradox, as he lists the consequences of the Crucifixion:

> A bundle of new miracles as farre beyond the former, as they are opposite to them; A condemnation that absolves us; A curse that blesseth us; A sicknesse that recovers us; a death it self that quickens us; So much was his love stronger then death, who though He were a Son, yet learn'd obedience by the things He suffered; and being made perfect he became the Author of eternall salvation to all that obey him.
>
> Among which number, O Lord, write our names, for his sake who this day suffered to blot out the handwriting that was against us. *Amen.* [149]

What we miss in this sermon are the dazzling images, historical narrations, epigrams and emblems, "unnatural" natural history, and the elegancies of wit that we would expect from so inventive a playwright. At least the paradoxes and the restrained erudition are there, for he has citations or references to Augustine, Leo, Aquinas, Calvin, and Seneca.

From the several surviving sermons of Jasper Mayne, we can get a good idea of not only the preaching of Cartwright, but probably also of what Crashaw's English sermons were like. One would expect a competent poet to produce vivid images and illustrations as a preacher. Mayne does. In his vigorous *A Sermon against False Prophets* he likens deceivers to a squid, "the *Fish* which blacks the *streame* in which it swimmes, and casts an *Inke* from its bowels to hide it selfe from being seen, make *Words,* which were ordained to reveale their *Thoughts,* disguise them."[150] Or he can ironically satirize those Puritans who, faced with an abuse, prefer abolition rather than the right use. For those iconoclasts who find only idolatry in a stained-glass window, he avers this is "to me a *feare* as unreasonable as theirs was, who refused to go to *Sea,* because there was a *Painter* in the City, who limned *Shipwracks.* "[151] He argues that it would be as foolish as to try to banish sun and moon because images have been made of them. He points out that the Muslim false prophets are iconoclasts, and excoriates them as militant troublemakers, arguing that one must not confuse the Qu'ran with the Gospels: "I doe not finde that to come into the *field* with an *armed Gospell,* is the way chosen by Christ to make proselites."[152]

In the same year, 1646, he preached *A Sermon Concerning Unity & Agreement,* at Carfax church, Oxford. His text is the favorite one for this theme, derived from St. Paul's plea for the end of party cries in I Corinthians 1:10. His concern is to refute the recently popular idea that a man may take on the ministry "without the forme of Ordination, or those other slow, tedious, lazie helps of sitting twenty yeares in a College to understand the Bible, may in a few minutes of powerful inspiration spring up an Apostle and go forth a Preacher of the Word of God."[153] He denies those to be true preachers who expound Scripture contrary to its clear meaning, or interpret it to divide a kingdom or confuse a Church, or (worst of all) press a sense distinctive of a party and foment a civil war. His satiric wit is effectively employed against such, when he says: "Tis true indeed the holy Ghost once assumed the shape of cloven Tongues of fire: But that was not from thence to beget Incendiaries of the Church; Teachers whose Doctrine should be cloven too."[154] He deplores the current party divisions, such as Puritans or Roundheads, Papists and Cavaliers, as well as those who boast they are Calvinists, Arminians, or Socinians.[155] He ridicules the self-appointed preachers who followed menial occupations like the Anabaptist leader, John of Leyden, who was reputed to repair old garments for a living. He asks:

> Have we not in our times seen Patriarchs and Prophets as vulgar and mechanicke, as unlearned and base as he? Men who have invaded the Pulpit I will not say from mending old breeches, or cobling old shooes, (pardon the homelinesse of the expression, I beseech you, 'tis but the Historians Latine translated into my English) but from trades so disingenuous, so illiberall, that I should defile your Eares, and the Pulpit to describe them.[156]

The snobbery is mitigated a little by the witty observation that Christ has been worshipped in vile places "which have reduced him the second time to a Stable."[157]

A more serious charge is that the preaching of such illiterates has led to the multiplication of heresies, which are now thought to be double those in the time of St. Augustine. The confusion is now so great that previously uncombined heresies, such as Arianism and Sabellianism, are now lodged together in the same person. For an illustration of this monstrosity he turns to "unnatural" natural history: "Nay, as tis said in *Afrike*, a Lyon will couple with a Tyger, from whence will spring a Libbard; so certaine strange, unheard of, double sex't Heresies are sprung up among us."[158]

Six years later he is equally critical of destroyers of the unity of the Church, in *A Sermon against Schisme: Or, The Separations of These Times*, which he delivered at Watlington in Oxfordshire, "with some interruptions" by the sectarians and schismatics he was trying to refute. It is a very careful analysis of the two major New Testament passages selected by the sectarians to bolster their separations. The point he makes is that the command to separate is from, in the first case, unbelievers who were idolaters, and, in the other, from those whose lives traduce the faith.[159] In neither case, is there any suggestion that Christians should separate from other Christians. Furthermore, he points out that Christ taught a parable that the wheat and the tares were to remain together until harvest, since only God knows which are which; in practising premature separation the schismatic plays God.[160]

Finally, we have the sermon Mayne preached at the consecration of Herbert Croft as bishop of Hereford in 1662, when Mayne had become both a royal chaplain and a canon of Christ Church. His peroration is worth citing fully because it indicates the Arminian defence of bishops and the sense of continuity with the early Church this form of church polity provides:

> And now, *holy Fathers*, if you will heare me draw your Pedigree from the Spring-head downe the *Streame*, your *Order* and the *Christian Church*, with its *Religion* too, had the same divine *Original*, and derives it self from *Heaven*; God sent his *Sonne*, his *Sonne* sent *Apostles*, the *Apostles* made *Bishops*, and those *Bishops* made their *Successors*: And all this by one and the same authentick *Patent*, *As my Father sent me, so send I you*, sayes Christ in the 20. Chapter of Saint *John*, at the 21. Verse. An *Order* which hath stood out all the *Injuries* of Time, *Persecutions* of the Heathens, *Opposition* of Philosophers, *Contradiction* of Hereticks, even all the *Powers* of Hell, which have striven to shake it by their *violence* and *stormes*. An *Order* which hath filled our *Calendars* with Saints, our *Histories* with Fathers, Holy Confessours and Martyrs.[161]

If we compare the printed sermons of Cartwright and Mayne with the imitation of their preaching style by Abraham Wright, we find that Wright notes their defense of unity in both Church and Nation, their love of learning, their wit and their irony,[162] and their fondness for paradoxes. But, in the sermons we have, there is only a hint of typological interpretation in Cartwright, and none in the Mayne sermons we have, and no emblems at all. This only shows how difficult it is to judge a total oeuvre by the fragments which remain.

John Wall

The third product of Westminster and Christ Church is John Wall (1588–1666) who was installed as canon of Christ Church in 1632 and, in Wood's words, a position "which he kept to his dying day, notwithstanding the several revolutions in his time." Wood is also authority for the statement that Archbishop Williams said "that *he was the best read in the Fathers of any he knew.*"[163] Wall was also a canon of Salisbury from 1644. Because he is older than Cartwright and Mayne, his sermons recall the earlier metaphysical preachers, in their euphuistic language, witty divisions, delight in paradoxes, fondness for historical narrations, many learned patristic references, and mixing of classical and Christian lore.

For paradoxical divinity there is the reference to Christ as "such a Lambe as frighteth the Wolfe, scares the Dragon, heales the sting of the Serpent, and makes the Lion to quake and tramble, *Agnus Dei*, and *Agnus Deus*, the Lambe of God and God the Lambe that was slaine from the beginning of the world. . . ."[164] Typically, he wonders at the greatest paradox, God as man: "O the gratious bounty and wonderfull humilitie of so great dispensation. God is become man, the word flesh, the Creator a creature, and (to speake in the language of Saint *Austin*) *Qui regit sidera, lambit ubera.* Hee that governes the influence of the starres, drawes the sweetnesse of his mothers breast, taking that from us whereby hee may save us."[165] His euphuistic tendency is apparent in the following phrases: "we behold with pure eyes the tender bowels of his [God's] unspeakable love, to that Aethiopian Queene, the blacknesse of our nature."[166] His divisions are often complicated, but one brief one is wittily introduced thus: "My whole text is spent in that double contemplation of the Physicks, the one *Motus,* the othe *Quies. Yee that have followed mee,* shewes there is a *Motus. Shall sit upon twelve thrones,* shewes there is a *Quies.*"[167] He also loves a pun: "Should I distinctly prosecute the severall vertues of this seale, you might call for a seale to my lippes."[168] He makes some rather forced references to the Crucifixion: "yet died he like *Seneca* in a bath, not of water, but of blood, and that his owne . . ."[169] or the farfetched comparison of Hannibal crossing the Alps with Christ's cup of vinegar. His meditation on the seven times that blood was spilt in the life of Christ is sensuous in the extremest baroque manner.[170] That was Wall's trouble, he was excessive in his language,[171] his perfervid devotion,[172] his luscious images, [173] and his excessive pedantry, [174] both in historical narrations and patristic citations, often no more than tags.

Thomas Lushington

The fourth member of the cathedral sextet is Dr. Thomas Lushington (1590–1661) who has two claims to fame. He was the tutor at Broadgates Hall (later Pembroke College, Oxford) of Sir Thomas Browne, the author of *Religio Medici;* and he preached what was probably the most scandalous sermon of the century before the University of Oxford in 1624. He was the convivial chaplain and friend of Bishop Corbet of Norwich, who recommended him as chaplain to Charles I. He was presented by Laud to the prebend of Beaminster Secunda in Salisbury cathedral in 1631.

The offending sermon was preached in St. Mary's, the university church, in a Resurrection sermon. It was thought scandalous by those who heard it, and those who heard of it, on two grounds: blasphemy and political meddling. Apparently Lushington preached on the text Matthew 28:13, "His Disciples came by night and stole him away," the excuse of the soldiers guarding Christ's empty sepulchre. It seems that Lushington in dramatic fashion impersonated successively the soldiers, complaining in rough terms that Jesus was a "very Jugler, a neat compiler of Impostures," and his women followers, "gadling *Gossips*" and "night house-wives" and so assumed to be harlots from Galilee. Then by a brilliant turn of wit, Lushington admitted that Christ's body was indeed *stolen:* that is, that the cadaver of a criminal was forfeit to the State, so Christ's repossession of it was a theft! All this can be determined from the revised sermon, which was printed together with the Recantation Sermon Lushington was required by the university authorities to preach on the following Sunday.[175] But the revised sermon does not include any of the offensive political observations. What these were can be gathered from two reports of them by contemporaries. Anthony Wood reports:

> In the year 1624 . . . nothing but War with *Spain* sounding in the ears of the vulgar upon the breaking off of the *Spanish match* with Prince *Charles,* it pleaseth this our Author *Lushington* to utter in his Sermon . . . on Easter Munday these words—*Now the Peasant thinks it comes to his turn under pretence of his priviledge in Parliament, that he should dispose of Kings and Commonwealths, &c.* Afterwards also for this. *Nothing now contents the Commonalty but war and contention, &c.*[176]

A second report is given by the earl of Clarendon who claimed to have heard the sermon, correcting an exaggerated account of it by a Catholic priest, Serenus Cressy. As Clarendon remembered it:

> . . . a *Parliament* being then sitting, the Preacher had unwarily, and very unnecessarily, let fall some Words, which reflected upon their Proceedings; particularly, that now every *Peasant in Parliament,* by the Privilege of his Vote there, cared not how he behaved himself toward the *King,* or the *Church,* or to that Effect.[177]

This is likely to be a reasonably accurate account, in view of the statement by Lushington at the end of the Recantation Sermon: "The last time I had these words. *Now the Peasant thinks, &c.* I had also these words, Nothing contents the Commonalty but war and contention."[178]

What, apart from the charges, is most characteristic of this sermon? It was clearly a daring sermon in its assumption that the rumor spread by the military watch, that Jesus's disciples had stolen his body and that the Resurrection was, as Lushington says in one place, "an Old Wives' Tale," was true. It was also daring because at the outset he had claimed that political views were determinative of religion whether Protestant or Catholic.[179] It was also an exceedingly polemical sermon: in postulating a whole series of possibilities, it sarcastically urged that the resolution can be left to various groups, such as Calvinists, Arminians, Casuists, Nominalists, lawyers, or physicians. It was also clearly a sermon preached to the gallery of undergraduates, who cheered at the close when he refuted the accusations of the soldiers, accusations which affirmed an orthodox Christian interpretation in the decent devotional accents of the disciples. One also has the feeling that he is ridiculing some contemporary trends in preaching by showing how fashionable it is to reconcile contradictions, and by referring to "cursories"—apparently an elegantly casual term for "observations" on his text. Perhaps the importance of the sermon is the proof it supplies of the dangers of a merely witty and ingenious attitude in the pulpit in creating irreverence and disbelief.

Mark Frank

A Cambridge prebendary in our group is the distinguished Mark Frank (1613–1664). Frank is fully in the tradition of Andrewes not only in his preaching but in his academic life. He too became both a fellow and master of Pembroke College (1662), having been appointed the year before as chaplain to Archbishop Juxon, and to Juxon's successor, Sheldon. In 1662 he became prebendary of Islington in St. Paul's Cathedral. In 1641 he had preached a sermon at Paul's Cross on Jeremiah 35:18–19, on the Rechabites as an example of obedience ("never more needful than then"), in which he described the insults then being given to the king, the bishops, and the clergy. Naturally, the king ordered it to be printed because of its anti-democratic sentiments.

His most famous work was published postumously in 1672 in two volumes, entitled, *LI Sermons . . . A Course of Sermons for all the Sundays and Festivals throughout the Year.* This fine series included nine sermons for Christmas Day, three for Epiphany, five for Easter Day, and they resemble Andrewes' in their divisions and subdivisions, their scholarly interest (with fewer citations), their delight in paradoxes, and, above all, in their tender devotion to the person of Christ. W. Fraser Mitchell claims that "from the literary point of view Frank was the best of the Anglo-Catholic preachers."[180] This is a high evaluation (even if the term is unhistorical) and Mitchell rightly stresses the note of reflective gravity in his sermons, though he fails to emphasize the psychological shrewdness and pragmatic relevance they also possess.

A passage on the incarnate infant Christ begins like Andrewes, but ends with direct references to his congregation:

> Will our *Master* be thus dealt with as a Child? thus handled like the *common infant?* And shall *we* hereafter think much the best of us to be used like other men? away with all our nicenesses henceforward, and be content that our *selves* and *ours* should be in all things subject to the common fate of the sons of men.[181]

His analogies are more sustained and subtler than those even of Andrewes, as when, in a Whitsun sermon, he compares the wind and the Spirit:

> For the *Wind* first; They are but general notions we entertain of it. *God brings the winds out of his treasure* says the *Psalmist, cxxxv.* 7. Out of those hidden chambers they come, but where those chambers are we cannot tell. On a suddain they arise, ere we are aware, and away they go; and who can follow them? Who can trace their steps? or track their

way, or over-take them in their lodging at night, or tell us where it is?

Ask Philosophy, and let that answer you. Whence is it that the winds arise? It answers you, From a thin and airy vapour drawn up out of the earth towards the middle Region of the Air, but repercust or beaten back by the grossness of some intervening cloud which drives it down obliquely with that violence we hear and feel. This, or something as obscure, is all the knowledge we can get of it. For, ask now, Where that vapour rose? It cannot tell. Which way it went? It knows it not. In what part of heaven it first became a wind? It cannot point it out. What is become of it, now 'tis gone? It resolves you not. Into what part of the world it is retired when all is still? It cannot answer you.

. . . And yet the ways of the *Spirit* are more unsearchable: we know not anything at all of his eternal Procession, it was before any time we can imagine. We know nothing of his course or motion all that infinite while before the World began. We understand nothing distinctly of it ever since. His motions are so intricate, so various, and so infinite we cannot comprehend them. The dispositions, the gifts, the graces he works daily in us, we do not know how they rise, or how they spread, or how they vanish.[182]

Mark Frank is also capable of wit, but never of that arrogance which claims to know the inner counsels of Almighty God. In a Christmas Day sermon (the sixth) he refers to the 148th Psalm, and imagines nature paying its dues to the Christ child: "But sure when all things else come in throngs to bless him, and even Ice and Snow come hot and eager to this Feast, and willingly melt themselves into his praises, we should not, methinks, come coldly to bless him. . . ."[183] There is a conceit but it is less forced than in the works of the earlier metaphysicals, and his style is far less staccato than that of Andrewes. It shows the metaphysical manner losing its quirkiness, as the new plain style of the Royal Society and the less ecstatic and less florid flights of the Latitudinarians become popular.

Robert Willan

Our sixth prebendary is the almost unknown Robert Willan (?1570–1630), who was a fellow of Corpus Christi College, Cambridge from 1593–1599. Thereafter he was rector of Herringswell, Suffolk from 1599–1614, rector of Cold Norton from 1614, together with the churches of Geslingthorpe and Great Stanway, Essex, until 1630. He was made a prebendary of Lincoln in 1621. Sometime after 1625 he was appointed a chaplain to Charles I.[184]

Only two sermons of his survive. The first was preached at Westminster Abbey before the Judges on 5 November 1622. It was entitled, *Conspiracie against Kings, Heavens Scorne.* Its text is the first three verses of the second Psalm, and is a conventional plea for obedience to the king. The division is interesting because of its typological exegesis: "The Text may be considered three wayes: As a Prophesie, as an Historie, as an Embleme. *David* represents a threefold person. his Saviours, his owne, and ours."[185] His illustrations are vivid and apt, especially for a sermon heard by lawgivers, who would acknowledge that "Lawes are Bandes, for the wilde, to secure them and humble them, for the weake to secure and keepe them: as in vines, they are under-propped and bound up, to make them fruitfull in vessels, they are hooped to contain liquor: so Lawes are bonds to hold the evil in awe, & the good in safety."[186] He is capable of a memorable maxim, as "Earth is but a turfe for man to trample on, heaven is our home."[187] and of wit, again on the subject of heaven: "There is the court of Audience for the Embassadours, which are our teares and prayers." He is learned too, as the thirty-five citations in the sermon show.

Willan's second sermon was at the funeral of Viscount Sudbury on the text I Kings 19:4: "It is now enough, O Lord, take my soule, for I am no better then my Father." It begins in lively fashion:

There are no thoughts more wholsome then those of death, nor any lesse frequently possessing the mindes of men; wee thinke of death as the *Athenians* did treate of peace, never but when we are in blacks: As they which adventure to the *Indies* take not so much into their consideration how many shippes have beene swallowed in the waves, as what some few have gotten by the voyage: So it is with us, we seldom meditate of the Millions dead before us but of the small Remainder surviving with us.[188]

He has a curious illustration from natural history, claiming that as the days are shorter in Norway than in the rest of the world, their birds fly more rapidly to their nests; yet humans are the opposite to these birds.[189] He is witty on the subject of the multiple interpretations scholars have given to this text: "some make it the evaporation of a discontented minde, the weaknesse of a frayle man: others attribute it to the devotion of an holy man. I will strike these severall flints, each of which may afford a sparke to enlighten our text."[190] The wit becomes strained when he declares, apparently unaware that St. Augustine almost certainly had a dark complexion, that "St. *Augustine* wept when he tooke holy Orders, & they were Prognosticating teares fore-running his infinite paynes in washing Blackamores, whose sowles were more tawny then their hides."[191] His phrases can be vivid and apt, as when he writes "preferring the false and fading beauty of recent opinions, before the amiable wrinkles in the face of aged truth,"[192] but they are exaggerated and overblown when he writes of the sword "whose glistring face flashed foorth lightnings of terrour, with blood-shotten eyes wildly staring, his steelie handes offering rough embracements."[193]

Thomas Goffe and Barten Holyday

There was also an unlucky pair that did not obtain appointments as prebendaries[194] though they were of the right ecclesiastical stripe: Thomas Goffe and Barten Holyday. The former died too young (at thirty), and the latter was obdurately opinionated.

Goffe had the right background, having been educated at Westminster School and Christ Church, Oxford. He had even had his tragi-comedy, *The Careless Shepherdess*, performed before the king and queen at Shrewsbury with great success. Barten Holyday became archdeacon of Oxford, but Wood is probably right in observing that he had "a most admirable veine in Poetry and Oratory" and that he "might, had he not acted the vain man, been made a Bishop, or at least a Dean of a rich Church."[195] It is possible that the tedious performance of his play, *Technogamia, or the Marriages of the Arts* (1618) acted before King James and his queen, cost him preferment, for James admired wit if it was quick and sparkling, not slow and flat. As Thomas Fuller said of this king: "His wit was passing sharp and piercing, equally pleased in *making* and taking a *smart* jest. *His Majestie* so much stooping to *His mirth*, that He never *refused* that *coine* which he paid to other folk."[196] The coin of Holyday's wit was leaden and rusty, and as ponderous as his pedantry. Several men, besides these two, deserved preferment and got none. This was certainly the case with Thomas Adams, whose sermons were brilliant. One can only assume that they were so studiously ethical that their Calvinism made them unwelcome to Charles I and his adviser, Archbishop Laud.[197]

Thomas Goffe (1591–1629) must have been considered an outstanding Latin orator by the Oxford University authorities, since he was chosen to deliver the funeral oration for William Goodwin, dean of Christ Church, in the cathedral in 1620, and for Sir Henry Savile in the Theology School in 1622. Both of these orations were published. He fulfilled the literary expectations of many old Westminster scholars in this period by writing three tragedies, which were acted at Christ Church while Goffe was studying there.

There is only a single surviving sermon in English, but it is an important Spital sermon preached on the Wednesday of Easter Week, 1627. Its title is, appropriately, *Deliverance from the Grave*. It was an exposition of the text, Ezekiel 37:3, "And ye shall know that I am the Lord, when I have opened your graves, O my people, and brought you up out of your graves." The division is natural and simple. The metaphysical character of the sermon is found in its wit, paradoxes, Greek and Latin citations, vivid phrasing, and psychological appeal. The sermon also has the kind of visual progression that recalls Donne.

A single citation combines paradox, wit, and patristic borrowing in a reference to the Resurrection: "*Uteri nova forma*, saith a Father, for the Tombe to become a womb to take in a dead man, and bring him forth alive; for the *Grave* to swallow up, not a dead Corps, but Death it selfe."[198] He is not above using a pun either: "The Taylor must *tyre* his wits to *attyre* our Bodies."[199] A subtler series of paradoxes refers to the way of salvation in Christ:

> 'Twas we had forfeited the Bond, and he must be arrested: so a Heard of Tigers came to seize upon the Lamb slaine from the beginning of the world; for whom, he (being God) became Man; they (being men) to him became Devils; they apprehend him with their bloody hands, whom their hearts could never apprehend; all wickedly intending to confound him, who onely intended to preserve them, and thinking one death too little for him, who esteem'd his owne life, and eternitie it selfe a blessing too small for them.[200]

His appeal to the charity of his hearers is as witty as it is moving:

> In your Hospitall lies many a wounded Christian, and in every wound is plac't a tongue, to speake and cry to God him selfe for mercy, continu'd mercy and honour to this Citie. Your *Bethlem* shewes, how he that was borne at *Bethlem*, is borne anew in your hearts, and you againe regenerate and borne in him; for whose sake if a Cup of cold water given shall never goe unrewarded, then surely, *Copiosa erit Merces vestra in Coelis* . . . Thus farre doe the

armes of the Poore lift you their Benefactors and Patrons from your Graves: Thus farre are these livories which attend you, Angels and Messengers to report your Resurrection: Thus high may you stand upon your owne Foundations, those foundations which you have rais'd for them.[201]

This is an erudite sermon, with forty-two references in forty pages to twenty-two different authors, classical, patristic, and indigenous. The three native writers referred to are Bishops Bilson and John King, and the Venerable Richard Hooker.

The visual progression of the sermon is vivid and striking. It moves from the consideration of death (recalled in grim fashion by a recent visitation of the plague) to Christ's Resurrection from the empty tomb, to the Great Assize at the end of history as bodies emerge from their graves in the General Resurrection.

Another former member of Christ Church, Oxford, was Barten Holyday (1593–1661). After taking orders, he became, according to Wood, "a most eloquent and quaint preacher" and "his poetry and sublime fancy were such, that fam'd him second to none in his time at the university."[202] He became chaplain to Sir Francis Steuart, former British ambassador to Spain, in his attendance upon Count Gondomar in the important time when the Spanish Match was being considered. Apparently his "facete and pleasant way" (Wood) put him in Gondomar's good graces. We have suggested that his inordinate vanity and his boring play cost him preferment. One other factor, however, must also be taken into account: his willingness to accept the judgment of Cromwell's Triers in order to obtain the rectory of Chilton in Berkshire. This made him very unpopular with the orthodox royalist clergy. His literary legacy, apart from his three tragedies, comprises translations of Horace's *Odes* and Persius' *Satires*, as well as his sermons.

His sermons show some interesting changes between those of the 1620s and those of the 1650s. The earlier sermons have no patristic citations, though the later ones are full of them. The earlier sermons make little use of etymology, while the later sermons are full of a pedantic Greek and Latin etymology. The early sermons always end with rhapsodical adorations of the crucified or glorified Christ. The later sermons are full of his detailed knowledge of the customs of the Hebrews, the Greeks, and the Romans, told in great detail, whether relevant or not. The sermons, early and late, are very artificial in their eloquence, ever straining to produce paradoxes, quasi-paradoxes, and conceits. He has a voracious curiosity, like Donne, speculating in detail for example on what the Resurrection of Jesus felt like in the sepulchre.

His fondness for paradoxes can be seen in a sermon preached at Paul's Cross on Gowrie Day, 5 August 1623. He refers to David trying to escape from Saul: ". . . but David in the extremitie of wit and banishment disguises himselfe in a false madnesse, making it the best use of his reason to seeme to have lost the use of his reason."[203] Similarly, he jests about Judas's suicide: "It was the wit of justice, hee should lose his bowels, that had lost his compassion."[204] Both examples are rather crude. A subtler one is his advice that a sense of unworthiness should deter no one from receiving Communion: "He that would abstaine from the Sacrament, for Reverence; is, by his Reverence, fit to receive it."[205]

His is a rather cluttered imagination, like an attic, as in the following combination of an historical narration, an example of "unnatural" natural history, and an emblem, all juxtaposed rather than fused:

And if *Sozomen's* Ecclesiastical story be no part *Legend,* we may heare him relate that when *Ioseph* and the Blessed Virgin, who fled into *Aegypt* with our Saviour, were ready to enter the gate of *Hermopolis* (or Thebais) a tree of singular size and beauty sudainly bended it self to the ground, as in Adoration at the presence of the true Lord. This tree was before worshipped by the Heathen *Aegyptians;* the name of which kind of tree was *Persis,* as the historian sayd; adding that this was the constant report of the Christian Inhabitants in his time; as also, that the fruit, or Leaf, or any part of the Bark of it heal'd the sick. We may further take notice that Plutarch long before said that this kind of tree was consecrated to Isis; that also the fruite of it was like a Heart, and the Leaf like a Tongue; which may to us Christians by a devoute Emblem Aptly, though not Articulately, expresse, that the Lord our Saviour should be worshipped and Acknowledged with heart and Tongue.[206]

Similar parts of his sermons read like elementary lectures in comparative religion and one wonders how his congregation could keep from yawning as the result of such pedantry. He is happier commemorating the union of Scotland and England in the coronation of King James. This sermon preached at Paul's Cross on 24 March 1624 was on the apt text, "I will make them one nation" (Ezekiel 37:22). He illustrates the union with the emblems of the two countries:

O happy Britanies united in the same honours, in the same signes of honour; the glorious wreath of our red and white Roses, which was before united with but an Embleme, a knot, being now united surer without a knot, being now defended surer from any irreverent touch by the provision of the Thistle; but ours have the whole Thistle; they had before the sharpnesse of it, but now the company.[207]

Occasionally there are images or phrases that light up his sermons for hearers and readers. Here he is preaching on Paul's image of the Christian striving for an incorruptible crown compared with a corruptible earthly crown: "He that sav'd a Citizen had anciently an Oaken crown; it was a more lasting crown: so shall the Preacher have, that saves a Christian, from the enemy, the devil."[208] An illuminating phrase is provided by going back to the Hebrew original of Proverbs 7:9, usually translated "in the black and dark night." This is better rendered, so he affirms, "as if we should say, *in the apple of the eie of the night.* Yet out of the darkest sorrow, God will at last raise the

252

most cheerful light."[209] Had he tried to be less pedantic and less artificial in expression, his sermons might have been better. The following simple image drawn from the sowing season in spring is effective:

> There is yet one signe more of good ground, and that is, if the crowes and pies doe in greate numbers follow the plow, scraping in the steppes of the plow-man: and it is likewise a signe of a goodly Soul, when the foules of prey, wicked detractours do closely attend the steps and actions of the righteous.[210]

Finally, we should consider his unique imagining of Jesus's experience of the Resurrection, as contrasted with the complete reserve demanded by the saintly Keble in the nineteenth century:[211]

> Doe but imagine, that in the dawning birth of the morning, you saw the revelation of a grave emulating the morning: a coarse [corpse] rising with more comfort and glory then the Sunne: a winding-sheet falling away as an empty cloud: the feet and hands striving which shall first recover motion; the hands helping to raise the body; the feet helping to beare both the body and the hands: the tongue so eloquent, that it can tell you, it can speake againe: the eares so pure, that they can perceive the silence of the grave: the eyes looking forth of their Tombes, as if they were glad to see their own resurrection: Would you not bee as much affrighted, as instructed with this power of a God? Would you not be turned into very coarses, to see this living coarse! Would you not be struck as pale, as the winding-sheet you looked upon? But, when all this shall bee done, as well in mercy, as in majestie . . . How will you not then kisse those hands which before you feared? How will you not then with stedfast eyes examine and adore the resurrection of that body, which is the hope and cause of the resurrection of our bodies?[212]

After the polarization and recrimination between Calvinists and Arminians, and the Civil War between Roundheads and Cavaliers, an impatient man might well cry "a plague o' both your houses." It took a genuine apostle of toleration, like Jasper Mayne, to preach a sermon of reconciliation. It included these healing words:

> They of the more free, and open carriage and behaviour, who call a severe regularity, and strictnesse of life, precise-nesse, and an abridgement of Christian liberty, have called those of a more reserved, and lockt up, and demure conversation, Puritans and Round-heads, and I know not what other names of contumely, and reproach. And they of the more strict behaviour, have equally as faulty, called those of a freer, and lesse composed conversation, Libertines and Papists; the usuall words of infamy made to signifie a Cavallier. These two words, my Brethren, have almost destroyed a flourishing Kingdome betweene them.[213]

NOTES

1. *The Works of the Most Reverend Father in God, William Laud, D. D.*, 9 vols. (Oxford, 1849), 2: xvii.
2. *The Works of . . . Laud*, 2: xiii.
3. Laud's Letter 178 to Joseph Hall, *Works of . . . Laud*, 6: 574.
4. See my *The Worship of the English Puritans* (London, 1948) and my *Worship and Theology in England, From Cranmer to Hooker, 1534–1603* (Princeton, N.J., 1970), 255–324.
5. *The Works of . . . Laud*, 2: xvi.
6. *The Works of . . . Laud*, 3: 408, and 2: 16.
7. *The Works of . . . Laud*, 6: 56f. See also my *Worship and Theology in England, From Andrewes to Baxter and Fox, 1603–1690* (Princeton, N.J., 1975), 289–309. See also A. S. Duncan-Jones, *Archbishop Laud* (London, 1927), 174 and E. C. E. Bourne, *The Anglicanism of William Laud* (London, 1947), chap. 4, on "Laud as Theologian."
8. *The Works of . . . Laud*, 1: 4. A similar example is found in 1: 51: "And *spes* is *quasi pes;* 'hope,' saith Isidore, 'is the foot and the resting place.' "
9. *The Works of . . . Laud*, 1: 39.
10. William Laud, *The Archbishop of Canterbury's Speech: or, His Funerall Sermon, preacht by himself on the Scaffold on Tower-Hill on Friday the 10. of January. 1644.* (London, 1644), 7.
11. Laud, *The Archbishop of Canterbury's Speech*, 13.
12. *The Works of . . . Laud*, 1: 79.
13. *The Works of . . . Laud*, 1: 78.
14. *The Works of . . . Laud*, 1: 83.
15. *The Works of . . . Laud*, 1: 17.
16. *The Works of . . . Laud*, 1: 158.
17. Janel M. Mueller, *Donne's Prebend Sermons* (Cambridge, Mass., 1971), 10.
18. Donne wrote, following St. Augustine, "The art of *salvation*, is but the art of *memory.*" See *The Sermons of John Donne*, ed. G. R. Potter and E. M. Simpson, 10 vols. (Berkeley, 1953–1962), 2: 73.
19. Andrewes, *XCVI Sermons* (London, 1629) which includes as the final item Bishop Buckeridge's funeral sermon for Andrewes. The citation is from 19.

20. John Harington, *A Briefe View of the State of the Church of England . . . to the Yeere, 1608* (London, 1653), 144–145.

21. T. S. Eliot, *For Lancelot Andrewes, Essays on Style and Order* (London, 1928), 20. "About Donne there hangs the shadow of the impure motive, and impure motives lend their aid to a facile success. He is a little of a religious spell-binder, the Reverend Billy Sunday of his time, the flesh-creeper, the sorcerer of emotional energy. We emphasize this aspect to the point of the grotesque." The last sentence invalidates much of the preceding hyperbolical statement, which is oblivious of Donne's honesty and modesty in his Lincoln's Inn sermons, and of his earnest concern in the St. Paul's Cathedral discourses, to commend the faith with every gift of imagination, wit, empathy, and scholarship he could command. It was his very dramatic abilities that enabled Donne to enter the human heart's labyrinthine ways in a manner impossible for Andrewes. His contemporary, Godolphin, commended this in a tributary poem:

Pious dissector: by one houre did treate.
The thousand mazes of the hearts deceipt.
Thou didst pursue our lov'd and subtill sinne,
Through all the foldings we had wrapt it in.
And in thine owne large minde finding the way
By which our selves we from our selves convey,
Didst in us, narrow models, know the same
Angles, though darker, in our meaner frame.

(*Poems by J. D.*, 1635, sigs. Cc6^{v}-Cc7^{v}, cited in David Novarr, *The Making of Walton's Lives*, [Ithaca, N.Y., 1958] 77.)

22. Eliot, *For Lancelot Andrewes*, 30.

23. Andrewes, *XCVI Sermons*, 47–48.

24. Note the *double entendre* in "aspireth" (breathing and ambitious, both).

25. Andrewes, *XCVI Sermons*, 395.

26. Andrewes, *XCVI Sermons*, 402.

27. Andrewes, *XCVI Sermons*, 518.

28. Andrewes, *XCVI Sermons*, 607.

29. Andrewes, *XCVI Sermons*, 420.

30. Andrewes, *XCVI Sermons*, "A Sermon at Saint Maries Hospital, 10 April, 1588," 2.

31. David Mathew, *James I* (University of Alabama, 1968), 89, gives a most reasonable reconstruction of the events behind the so-called "Gowrie Conspiracy."

32. So-called because it was preached in the churchyard of St. Mary Spital [Hospital] where the governors and children of Christ's Hospital and of other hospitals formed part of the vast crowd present.

33. Donne, *Sermons*, 7: 133; see also 4: 195.

34. Donne, *Sermons*, 2: 169–170.

35. Donne, *Sermons*, 2: 170–171.

36. Donne, *Sermons*, 6: 55.

37. See Donne, *Sermons*, 4: 214 where Donne says he preaches *ad ignaros, ad incredulos, ad infirmos,* and *ad relapsos.*

38. Donne, *Sermons*, 3: 363, "We must not be glad, when our sins escape the *Preacher.*"

39. Donne, *Sermons*, 4: 119 and 4: 152.

40. Donne, *Sermons*, 4: 307.

41. Donne, *Sermons*, 4: 112.

42. Isaak Walton, *The Life of John Donne, Dr. in Divinity and Late Dean of Saint Pauls Church* (London, 1658), 47–48. David Novarr, in *The Making of Walton's Lives,* 73, states that the most vivid part of Walton's description of Donne preaching is borrowed in part from Donne's poem "To Mr Tilman after he had taken orders" which includes the lines: ". . . for they [preachers] doe,/ As Angels out of clouds, from Pulpits speake."

43. Donne, *Sermons*, 7: 87.

44. Donne, *Sermons*, 7: 135.

45. Donne, *Sermons*, 8: 191.

46. Quoted in Walton, *The Life of John Donne,* 102.

47. Walton, *The Life of John Donne,* 104–105.

48. Donne, *Sermons*, 10: 243.

49. Donne, *Sermons*, 10: 248.

50. DNB notes that Pusey asserted that Jackson had "one of the best and greatest minds our Church has nurtured" and Jones of Nayland found his works to be "a magazine of theological knowledge."

51. Thomas Jackson, *Nazareth and Bethlehem, or Israels Portion in the Sonne of Jesse, And, Mankinds Comfort from the Weaker Sexe* (Oxford, 1617), 65.

52. Jackson, *Nazareth and Bethlehem,* 75.

53. Thomas Jackson, *Diverse Sermons, with a short Treatise befitting these present times* (Oxford, 1637), 46–47.

54. Jackson, *Diverse Sermons,* 50.

55. Jackson, *Diverse Sermons,* 14.

56. Jackson, *Diverse Sermons,* 66.

57. Jackson, *Diverse Sermons,* 53.

58. H. R. Trevor-Roper, *Historical Essays* (London, 1957), 136.

59. J. W. Allen, *English Political Thought, 1603–1660* (London, 1938), 1: 185.

60. T. M. Parker, "Arminianism and Laudianism in Seventeenth-Century England" in *Studies in Church History,* ed. C. W. Dugmore and Charles Duggan (London, 1964), 1: 34.

61. John Buckeridge, *A Sermon preached before His Maiestie At Whitehall, March 22, 1617.* (London, 1618), 16.

62. John Buckeridge, *A Sermon preached at the Funerall of the R. R. Father in GOD, Lancelot late Lord Bishop of Winchester . . . 1626* (London, 1629), 9.

63. Buckeridge, *A Sermon preached at the Funerall,* 7.

64. Buckeridge, *A Sermon preached before His Maiestie,* 2.

65. Buckeridge, *A Sermon preached before His Maiestie,* 19.

66. John Buckeridge, *A Sermon Preached at Hampton Court before the Kings Maiestie, On Tuesday the 23. of September, Anno 1606.* (London, 1606), 24, 32, 34, 38.

67. John Howson, *A Sermon Preached at St. Maries in Oxford the 17. Day of November, 1602. in defence of the Festivities of the Church of England, and namely that of her Maiesties Coronation* (London, 1603).

68. John Howson, *A Sermon preached at Paules Crosse the 4 of December. 1597.* (London, 1597), 30.

69. Howson, *A Sermon . . . [of] the 4 of December. 1597,* 43.

70. John Howson, *A Second Sermon, preached at Paules Crosse, the 21 of May, 1598 . . .* (London, 1598), 27–28.

71. Richard Senhouse, *Foure Sermons Preached at the Court on severall occasions* (London, 1627), sig. B1.

72. Senhouse, *Foure Sermons,* sig. B2–B2v.

73. Senhouse, *Foure Sermons,* sig. D3–D3v.

74. Senhouse, *Foure Sermons,* sig. E3v.

75. Senhouse, *Foure Sermons,* sig. H4.

76. Senhouse, *Foure Sermons,* sig. L3.

77. Senhouse, *Foure Sermons,* sig. P3.

78. Francis White, *Londons Warning By Jerusalem. A Sermon Preached at Pauls Crosse on Mid-Lent Sunday last.* (London, 1619), 13–14.

79. Francis White, *Londons Warning,* 51.

80. Francis White, *Londons Warning,* 26.

81. Francis White, *Londons Warning,* 36.

82. Francis White, *Londons Warning*, 37.

83. For their contributions to liturgiology, see my *Worship and Theology in England, From Andrewes to Baxter and Fox, 1603–1690* (Princeton, N.J., 1970), 363–393.

84. Christopher Wren, *Parentalia: Or, Memoirs of the Family of the Wrens* (London, 1750), 10.

85. Edward Hyde, first earl of Clarendon, *The History of the Rebellion and the Civil Wars in England*, 3 vols. (London, 1702–1704), 1: 83.

86. *Articles of Impeachment of the Commons . . . against Matthew Wren . . . with Sir Thomas Widdringtons Speech . . .* (London, 1641), 13.

87. A summary of the *Articles of Impeachment*, 1–9.

88. Christopher Wren, *Parentalia*, 43, reports that Pearson said: *ne vini guidem guttulam per viginti pene annos hausit*. Presumably, this was not adhered to at Holy Communion, which Wren valued highly.

89. Matthew Wren, *A Sermon preached before the Kings Maiestie on Sunday the Seventeenth of February last, at White-Hall* (Cambridge, 1627), 33. The same sermon can be found in *Parentalia*, 115–132.

90. Wren, *A Sermon preached . . . at White-Hall*, 42.

91. Thomas Fuller, *The History of the Worthies of England* (London, 1662), section 1: 208.

92. William Prynne, *Canterburies Doome* (London, 1646), 73–74.

93. Fuller, *The History of the Worthies of England*, section 1: 295.

94. *The Works of the Right Reverend Father in God John Cosin, Lord Bishop of Durham*, 5 vols. (Oxford, 1843), 1: 1 and 45. This peculiarity of sermon structure was occasionally used by Andrewes, as also by Basire and Heylyn.

95. Cosin, *Works*, 1: 4.

96. Cosin, *Works*, 1: 8.

97. Cosin, *Works*, 1: 9.

98. Cosin, *Works*, 1: 13.

99. Cosin, *Works*, 1: 18.

100. Cosin, *Works*, 1: 23.

101. Cosin, *Works*, 1: 79. This sermon, since it mentions the plague, was probably delivered in 1625 or shortly thereafter.

102. Cosin, *Works*, 1: 80.

103. Cosin, *Works*, 1: 250. "First, they that are so much for St. Peter above all the Apostles besides, and say that he knew all things and missed nothing after Christ had once given him the keys, every time they read this Gospel they see themselves confuted here by St. John who knew the defects both of St. Peter and himself . . . better

than these men ever knew St. Peter's prerogative above the rest." The text referred to is John 20: 9, "For as yet they knew not the Scriptures, that He must rise from the dead."

104. Cosin, *Works*, 1: 163.

105. Cosin, *Works*, 1: 322.

106. Anthony Wood, *Athenae Oxonieneses*, 2 vols. (London, 1691–1692), 2: 177.

107. Brian Duppa, *The Soules Soliloquie: And, A Conference with Conscience* (London, 1648), 13.

108. Duppa, *The Soules Soliloquie*, 14.

109. Brian Duppa, *Angels Rejoicing for Sinners Repenting* (London, 1648), 8.

110. Duppa, *Angels Rejoicing*, 1.

111. Duppa, *The Soules Soliloquie*, 5.

112. Duppa, *The Soules Soliloquie*, 9.

113. Duppa, *The Soules Soliloquie*, 2.

114. Duppa, *Angels Rejoicing*, 2.

115. Duppa, *The Soules Soliloquie*, 21.

116. DNB.

117. John Gauden, *The Love of Truth and Peace. A Sermon preached before the Honourable House of Commons assembled in Parliament Novemb. 29, 1640,* (London, 1640), 15–16.

118. John Gauden, "A Sermon preached at the University of Oxford in S. Maries, July 11. 1641. Being Act-Sunday," in *Three Sermons preached upon severall occasions* (London, 1642), 126–127.

119. "A Sermon preached before the Iudges at Chelmsford" in Gauden, *Three Sermons*, 39–40.

120. Gauden, *Three Sermons*, 129.

121. Gauden, *Three Sermons*, 19, from "A Sermon preached before His Maiestie."

122. Gauden, *Three Sermons*, 19.

123. Gauden, *Three Sermons*, 22.

124. Gauden, *Three Sermons*, 27.

125. Gauden, *Three Sermons*, 105f. where the appeal is to reason, not to revelation.

126. John Barnard, *Theologo-Historicus, Or, the True Life of the Most Reverend Divine and Excellent Historian Peter Heylyn, D.D., Sub-Dean of Westminster* (London, 1683), 171.

127. Barnard, *Theologo-Historicus*, 192–193.

128. For example, in Peter Heylyn's *The Parable of the Tares Ex-*

pounded & Applied in Ten Sermons Preached before his late Majesty King Charles the First Monarch of Great Britain (London, 1659), Sermon IX, beginning on 237 and continuing for 42 pages, contains forty-nine references to twenty-eight different authors, of whom eleven are historians.

129. Heylyn, *The Parable of the Tares,* 76.

130. Heylyn, *The Parable of the Tares,* in Sermon V, preached at Whitehall, 12 January 1639, 114–116.

131. Heylyn, *The Parable of the Tares,* 77.

132. Heylyn, *The Parable of the Tares,* 276.

133. Heylyn, *The Parable of the Tares,* 75–76.

134. Heylyn, *The Parable of the Tares,* 58.

135. *The Workes of that learned and reverend Divine, John White, Doctor in Divinitie* (London, 1624), 2.

136. *The Workes of . . . John White,* 2.

137. *The Workes of . . . John White,* 13.

138. *The Workes of . . . John White,* 10.

139. *The Workes of . . . John White,* 17.

140. *The Workes of . . . John White,* 4.

141. *The Workes of . . . John White,* 20–21.

142. *The Workes of . . . John White,* 21.

143. *The Workes of . . . John White,* 30.

144. *The Workes of . . . John White,* 31.

145. Wright's third type is "in Dr. Maine's and Mr. Cartwright's Way; before the Universitie at St Maries, Oxford." Wright was a former fellow of St. John's College, Oxford.

146. See the prefatory encomiastic poems to William Cartwright's *Comedies, Tragicomedies, with other Poems* (London, 1651).

147. Wood, *Athenae Oxonienses,* 2: 18.

148. David Lloyd, *Memoires of the Lives, Actions, Sufferings & Deaths of those noble, reverend and excellent Personages that suffered for the Protestant Religion* (London, 1668), 423, which borrows much of the phraseology from the introduction to William Cartwright's *Comedies, Tragicomedies, with other Poems.*

149. William Cartwright, *An Off-Spring of Mercy, Issuing out of the Womb of Cruelty. Or, A Passion Sermon Preached at Christs Church in Oxford* (London, 1652), 30–31.

150. Jasper Mayne, *A Sermon against False Prophets* (London, 1646), 25.

151. Mayne, *A Sermon against False Prophets,* 21.

152. Mayne, *A Sermon against False Prophets*, 17.

153. Mayne, *A Sermon Concerning Unity & Agreement* (London, 1646), 6.

154. Mayne, *A Sermon Concerning Unity & Agreement*, 24.

155. Mayne, *A Sermon Concerning Unity & Agreement*, 30.

156. Mayne, *A Sermon Concerning Unity & Agreement*, 31.

157. Mayne, *A Sermon Concerning Unity & Agreement*, 39.

158. Mayne, *A Sermon Concerning Unity & Agreement*, 51.

159. Jasper Mayne, *A Sermon against Schisme: Or, The Separations of These Times* (London, 1652), 14.

160. Mayne, *A Sermon against Schisme*, 18.

161. Jasper Mayne, *A Sermon Preached at the Consecration of the Right Reverend Father in God, Herbert [Croft], Lord Bishop of Hereford* (London, 1662), 41–42.

162. Abraham Wright gives one amusing example of wit, where he takes the text, "As the Lillie among the thorns; so is my love among the daughters" (*Canticles* 2:2). His commentary on this is "Protect, we beseech thee, thy *Lilly* both in *radice* and *in flore*, from *Rooters* there, and from *Branchers* here . . ." in snide reference to the Root and Branch Bill of the Puritans (*Five Sermons in Five severall Styles*, [London, 1656], 64).

163. Wood, *Athenae Oxonienses*, 2: 259–260.

164. John Wall, *The Lion in the Lambe, Or Strength in Weaknes* (Oxford, 1628), 38.

165. John Wall, *Alae Seraphicae. The Seraphins Wings to raise us unto heaven. Delivered in six Sermons, partly at Saint Peters in Westminster, partly at S. Aldates in Oxford. 1623* (London, 1627), 128.

166. Wall, *Alae Seraphicae*, 4.

167. Wall, *Alae Seraphicae*, 78.

168. Wall, *Alae Seraphicae*, 23.

169. Wall, *Alae Seraphicae*, 56.

170. Wall, *Alae Seraphicae*, 52–53.

171. Wall, *Alae Seraphicae*, see 39, 70.

172. Wall, *Alae Seraphicae*, 55–56, also 9.

173. Wall, *Alae Seraphicae*, 24, especially the overripe paradox on 129.

174. Wall, *Alae Seraphicae*, in the first sermon of the six, there are twenty-two references and historical narrations in twenty-five pages.

175. The original sermon revised and the recantation were first published under a pseudonym, thus: *The Resurrection Rescued from the Soldiers Calumnies, in Two Sermons Preached at St. Maries in Oxon. By*

Robert Jones, D.D. (London, 1659). The terms used of Jesus and his disciples will be found on 8, 10, and 13.

176. Wood, *Athenae Oxonienses*, 2: 172.

177. A reprint appeared with an important preface, entitled *The Resurrection of our Saviour vindicated, and the Soldiers Calumnies against it fully answer'd in a Sermon Preach'd at St. Mary's in Oxford, By Mr. Lushington. Formerly under the feigned Name of Robert Jones, D.D.* (London, 1741), preface, vi. It should be observed that W. Fraser Mitchell, *English Pulpit Oratory from Andrewes to Tillotson* (London, 1932), 356, is incorrect in saying that "The sermon alluded to was never printed."

178. Lushington, *The Resurrection Rescued . . .* , 99.

179. The catchy beginning went thus: "Whats the best News abroad? So we must begin: 'Tis the *Garb* (*les novelles*) the grand salute and common *Preface* to all our talk . . . By their *News* ye may know their *Religion*, and by their *Religion* fore-know their *News*. This week the *Spanish Match* goes forward, and *Bethleem Gabors* Troups are broken; and the next week *Bethleem Gabors* Troups goe forward, and the *Spanish Match* is broken. The *Catholique* is of the *Spanish match*, and the *Protestant* of restoring the *Palatinate*; and each party think that the safety of the *Church* and the success of *religion* depends upon the event of one or the other, and therefore they cross and countertell each others news" (2–3).

Another report of the sermon will be found in *The Diary of John Rous . . . 1625–1642*, ed. Mary Anne Everette Green for the Camden Society (London, 1860), 66: 44. Rous writes: "I asked the drifte of it; he tould me 'witte'. I asked what was remarkable; he said, first the beginning. 'What newes? Every man asks what newes? Every man's religion is knowne by his newes; the Puritan talkes of Bethlehem Gabor, &c.' Besides this, the doctor fell belike to personate the chiefe priests and elders, in a florishing description of our Saviour and his apostles, as impostors, &c. (a wicked witte), and then comes to demande why the soldiers should say it, &c. 'Because,' saith he (yet he mistooke his marke, see verse 14), 'the soldiers were audacious, and durst doe anything. In those times, (said he) the soldiers did depose and chuse emperors, yet the time had beene when the priest did this! But now peasants will doe all, by prerogative of parliament, &c.' "

180. Mitchell, *English Pulpit Oratory, From Andrewes to Tillotson*, 176.

181. Mark Frank, *LI Sermons . . .* (London, 1672), from the second sermon on Christmas Day, 55.

182. Frank, *LI Sermons*, 422–423.

183. Frank, *LI Sermons*, 106.

184. Information from John and J. A. Venn, *Alumni Cantabrigieneses* (Cambridge, 1927), Pt. I (to 1751), 4: 413.

185. Robert Willan, *Conspiracie against Kings* (London, 1622), 3.

186. Willan, *Conspiracie against Kings*, 25–26.

187. Willan, *Conspiracie against Kings*, 34.

188. Robert Willan, *Eliahs Wish: A Prayer for Death* (London, 1630), 1–2.

189. Willan, *Eliahs Wish*, 2.

190. Willan, *Eliahs Wish*, 6. The interpreters are Chrysostom, Eucherius, and Cajetan.

191. Willan, *Eliahs Wish*, 31.

192. Willan, *Eliahs Wish*, 21.

193. Willan, *Conspiracie against Kings*, 12.

194. The number would have been four, if we had included Playfere and Henry Smith, who were considered in our first chapter in the fourth section, "The Three Earliest Metaphysical Divines." It is clear that Playfere's madness prevented further preferment and that Smith's being a lecturer, and therefore incurring suspicions of Puritanism, stopped further recognition.

195. Wood, *Athenae Oxonienses*, 2: 169. Wood knew Holyday well, perhaps too well.

196. Thomas Fuller, *The Church-History of Britain* (London, 1655), Bk. X, 114.

197. Laud mislabelled him a "Puritan", but see the convincing repudiation of the attribute in the 1974 doctoral dissertation of James Laurence Hedges at the University of California, "Thomas Adams and the Ministry of Moderation."

198. Thomas Goffe, *Deliverance from the Grave. A Sermon preached at Saint Maries Spittle in London on Wednesday in Easter weeke last, March 28. 1627.* (London, 1627), 33.

199. Goffe, *Deliverance from the Grave*, 20.

200. Goffe, *Deliverance from the Grave*, 27.

201. Goffe, *Deliverance from the Grave*, 39–40.

202. Wood, *Athenae Oxonienses*, ed. P. Bliss, 4 vols. (London, 1817), 3: 520.

203. Barten Holyday, *A Sermon preached at Pauls Crosse, March the 24, 1624* (London, 1626), 8.

204. Barten Holyday, *Three Sermons upon the Passion, Resurrection, and Ascension of Our Saviour Preached at Oxford* (London, 1626), 24.

205. Barten Holyday, *Of the Bread of Life. A Sermon* (Oxford, 1657), 232. The separate sermons of 1657 were collected and published as *Motives to a Good Life in Ten Sermons* (London, 1657).

206. Barten Holyday, *Of Anathema Maranatha. A Sermon* (Oxford, 1657), 244–245.

207. Holyday, *A Sermon preached at Pauls Crosse, March the 24, 1624*, 40.

208. Holyday, *Motives to a Good Life*, 80.

209. Holyday, *Motives to a Good Life*, 52.

210. Holyday, sermon "Of Gods Husbandry" in *Motives to a Good Life*, 92.

211. See Kebles's lines:
God only and good angels look
Behind the blissful screen,
As when triumphant o'er his foes,
The Son of God at midnight rose
By all but heaven unseen.
This is characteristic of the reserve and chastened joy of the Tractarians. See my *Worship and Theology in England, From Watts and Wesley to Maurice, 1690–1850* (Princeton, N.J., 1961), 264f.

212. Holyday, *Motives to a Good Life*, 55–56.

213. Jasper Mayne, *A Sermon Concerning Unity & Agreement. Preached in Carfax Church in Oxford, Aug. 9, 1646* (London, 1646), 29. Mayne, after his ejection from his parish and his appointment as a don of Christ Church, Oxford, was still able to converse amicably about religion with Hobbes.

Chapter VI

THE USES OF LEARNING AND ELOQUENCE:

DEFENDERS AND CRITICS

A T THE START of chapter two it was maintained that the metaphysical preachers themselves considered the use of recondite learning and wit as their distinguishing characteristics. In most cases this learning included citations from or references to the Fathers of the Church, the schoolmen of the Middle Ages, and the theologians of the Reformation and the Counter-Reformation. In addition, both pagan and Christian poets, historians, philosophers and moralists, natural historians, and the writings of rabbis and cabbalists were consulted and quoted, sometimes in the original languages, but perhaps more often taken from commonplace books or anthologies. Eloquence, whether fancy or plain, was essential to keep the attention of a congregation, and the metaphysical preachers were masters of the art.

In the present chapter learning will be treated in detail for two reasons. The first involves considering the arguments used by the justifiers of learned citations (who were, of course, its practitioners) and the counter-arguments used by their critics.[1] Our second reason is to try to understand the various functions that learning fulfilled in the pulpit oratory of the seventeenth century. Our assumptions are that these considerable resources of learning and scholarship were tapped to provide illumination or illustration for the passages of Scripture expounded, or to provide historical or etymological contexts for the texts selected,

267

or to give the congregations religious or moral examples to follow. It was even used as light relief and distraction in the midst of lengthy and abstract argumentation or controversy. Sometimes it had a higher motive—to elicit wonder at the mighty acts of God, and the miracles of Christ. At other times probably a lower motive dominated—to elicit admiration for the erudition of the preacher who had received a privileged university education available to only a fraction of the congregation.[2] Moreover, it cannot be too frequently stressed that such resources of instruction and delight were essential for captive congregations where non-attendance was penalized by the law.

The defense of learning in the pulpit

It goes without saying that learning and study was recommended by both Arminians and Calvinists, as well as by advocates of the not-so-plain and the plain styles among the Puritans. The real question was: should this learning be paraded *in the pulpit?*

Many defenses were offered to counteract the detractors of obvious erudition. The latter were mainly of two types. One group included the learned Puritan preachers, both Presbyterian and Independent, who were dominant at the Westminster Assembly in the mid-forties: these were the plain preachers who kept close to the advice of such Puritan leaders as Perkins and Sibbes. They had received an education in the classics of Greece and Rome common to grammar school education of the period, and were well versed in the Fathers, the schoolmen, and the Catholic and Protestant theologians and controversialists of the Renaissance, but they felt that such information, however important in the preparation of the sermon in the study, was out of place in the pulpit. It distracted from the Divine Word and drew attention to the preacher rather than to his message. Then there was a second group, as learned as the first, who protested only against the abuse of learning and wit in the pulpit, while still believing that eloquence, citations of heathen poets and moralists, and illustrations drawn from a wide swathe of human experience and culture were valuable. The second group insisted that a modicum of ornament and of recondite learning was appropriate in sermons, but that the main end of preaching was edification, which excessive eloquence, pedantry, and wit diluted or even destroyed. They may be called the "not-so-plain Puritan divines" who, as Lawrence Sasek has demonstrated, were many and erudite.[3]

Both groups would have agreed with George Herbert, poet and clergyman, that translucency was best:

> Lord, how can man preach the eternall Word?
> He is a brittle crazie glasse.
> Yet in thy temple thou dost him afford
> This glorious and transcendent place,
> To be a window through thy grace.[4]

Incidentally, it is intriguing to note that Herbert, in charge of a country parish, recommends the country parson first to know about tillage and pastorage and thus relate biblical knowledge to the callings of his people and lead them from what they know to what they do not know. Instruction in sermons and catechetical classes require him to interpret the Scriptures (aided by a holy life of regular prayer), collated carefully and helped by "commentaries and Fathers who have handled the places controverted."[5] Herbert also recommends the keeping of a commonplace book in which the parson can cull from his reading of the Fathers, the schoolmen, and later authors.[6] As the former Public Orator of Cambridge University, Herbert was acutely aware of the great dangers of learning, rhetoric, and wit, especially in the exposition of Holy Writ, and so he warned that the parson should be "not witty, or learned, or eloquent, but Holy."[7] This statement could as easily have been written by a plain style Puritan as by this gifted metaphysical poet and preacher.

Just as there were two types of detractors of the use of learning and rhetoric in sermons, so there were two kinds of defenders. Most of the metaphysical preachers took the high road, with the view that learning, and rhetoric, as well as wit were auxiliaries of religion to be used gratefully and gladly to the full. Other clergy of the English Church took the lower road: that they were good in their place, modestly and moderately used.[8]

Complicating the issue was the fact that discussants on both sides claimed that there was biblical support for their contradictory views, and they appealed to St. Paul as their sponsor, and with justice.

Thomas Goffe, for instance, cites Scripture to show that Scripture itself authorizes non-biblical knowledge. Asserting that Scripture affords enough light to know God and salvation by, he reminds his hearers in a St. Mary's Hospital sermon in Easter of 1627 that

when St. Paul undertook to make the *Corinthians* know who was the *Lord,* hee profest a wealthy variety of much other knowledge besides the Scripture; and thankes God for it, that he spake with Tongues Πάντων ʿυμων μαλλὸν, more then all they did: and able he was to cite their own poets among the then learned *Athenians,* and to apply a Satyricall Verse out of *Epimenides,* to reprehend the lying, gluttonous and bestiall Manners of the *Cretians* [sic].[9] His powerful language so ravish't the *Lystrians,* in the 14. of the *Acts,* that hee gain'd the report of *Mercury* among them: and questionlesse, the sitting so long at the feet of Gamaliel, made him *vas electionis,* a vessell fit to hold that divine Treasure which the Holy Ghost pour'd into Him.[10]

Henry King, Donne's friend, preaching in St. Paul's Cathedral, criticized (by implication) the view of the stricter Puritans, and possibly also of the sectaries, who think it "a trespasse of high nature to staine their Discourses with a Latin sentence, or authority of Fathers quoted in their own Dialect," or who consider it impermissible to approach God with a set prayer. He advises: "View the Scripture, the Dictate and worke of the Holy Ghost, you shall find, that for the elegance of the phrase and weight of the words, it passes all the weake shallow oratory of Mans tongue. Therefore Saint *Augustine* calls it, *Venerabilem Spiritus Sancti stilem*, the venerable stile of the Holy Ghost." It was a weak argument because easily refutable, since his critics could reply that they relied not on man's tongue, but on the inspiration of the Holy Spirit in prayer as promised in Romans 8:26. More effective is King's final argument: "And in the Gospell the Iewes acknowledged our Saviour for the best Rhetorician that ever was, *He spake as never man spake.*"[11] The same minor metaphysical poet also urged the example of the apostle to the Gentiles: "St. Paul himself . . . makes use of Human Learning, and cites some verses out of *Epimenides*, *Aratus* and *Menander*; which shewed, that he had studied the Greek poets, as *Moses* the learning of the Egyptians, and *Daniel* the wisdom of the Chaldeans . . . supposing Religion to receive much advantage by the study of Human Learning."[12]

It was however King's friend, Donne, who provided the most glowing and persuasive encomium on the eloquence of Scripture, while insisting that it is the Gospel and not the eloquence which is the net that catches souls. The tribute to the eloquence of the Bible is all the more impressive because it was made, as an aside, in his first Prebend sermon:

> And first give me leave by the way, only in passing, by occasion of these words which are here rendred, *Convertentur, & Erubescent,* and which in the Originall, are *Iashabu*, and *Ieboshu*, which have a musicall, and harmonious sound, and agnomination in them, let me note this much, even in that, that the Holy Ghost in penning the Scriptures delights himself, not only with a propriety, but with a delicacy, a harmony, and melody of language; with height of Metaphors, and other figures, which may work greater impressions on the Readers, and not with barbarous, or triviall, or market, or homely language.[13]

He goes on to explain that St. Augustine was put off by the inelegancies of Scripture only because he read the Bible in poor translations. Donne also felt it inappropriate to expound Scripture in irreverent or vulgar language, for which his authority was the modesty of Moses, "O my Lord I am not eloquent, neither heretofore, nor since Thou hast spoken to they servant" (Exodus 4:10). Donne draws this conclusion: "Where we see, there is some degree of eloquence required in the delivery of Gods Messages. There are not so eloquent Bookes in the world as the Scriptures; neither should any man come to any kinde of handling of them with uncircumcised lips, as *Moses* speaks, or with an extemporall and irreverent, or over-homely and vulgar language."[14]

However highly Donne valued rhetoric and eloquence, he insisted that learning in divinity and the humanities was primary for the preacher and rhetoric merely secondary. This he inferred from the rhetorical gifts of David, king and psalmist, for "he had an harmonious, a melodious, a charming, a powerfull way of entring into the soule and working upon the affections of men, but he was *the sweet Psalmist of Israel,* He employed his faculties for the conveying of the God of Israel, into the Israel of God." No divine should be ignorant of "either ornaments of humane, or mysteries of divine knowledge," but some points in both disciplines are unsuitable for preaching.[15] Elsewhere he had insisted that preaching is working on the affections and through the memory, while lecturing on divinity aims primarily at persuading the reason. Also preaching "intends *Exhortation* principally and *Edification* . . . but *Lectures* intend principally *Doctrinall points.* . . ."[16] No one has more exquisitely expressed the biblical profusion of metaphors than Donne, in his famous words, which are themselves a defense of rhetoric: "The Holy Ghost, who is a direct worker upon the soule and conscience of man, but a Metaphoricall, and Figurative expressor of himselfe, . . ."[17] and his contention that the Holy Ghost is "amorous in his metaphors."

Other defenders of learning and rhetoric in sermons referred to the admirable examples set by the Fathers of the Church in their sermons. Dr. Thomas Plume's brief biography of Bishop Hacket is a justification of learning in the pulpit, and itself uses a patristic reference. In it he claims that Hacket was in the front rank of famous London preachers because of "his acute Wit, deep Judgment, flowing Elocution, singular Learning, and great Reading, whereby (as *Porphiry* complained of *Origen*) he made use of all Heathen Learning to adorn the Doctrine of Christianity."[18]

Hacket himself in his seventh sermon on the Incarnation argued, in the fashion of Richard Hooker, that only the very best in music, art, and eloquence was good enough for God, the giver of these talents, and should prevail in worship. He asked why any reasonable man should think it fit to glorify God with scanty provisions, when his Maker has been so generous? Hence, he continued, "no decent Ceremony is superfluous, no rich Ornament too gorgeous, no strain of our wit too eloquent, no Musick too sweet, no Multitude too great to advance his name," for Christians have been raised by the humiliation of God's Son to be able to live with angels in heaven, because of Christ's generosity in being content to lie with beasts in a manger.[19]

Thomas Fuller, too, finds the practice of the Fathers in their preaching good enough authority for learning in the pulpit, and praises their different gifts as exemplified in their sermons. These include Christian philosophy, constant sanctity, orthodox judgment of heresies, manifold learning, valuable biblical commentaries, orthodox judgment of heresies, subtlety in controversy, moral acuity, and humble devotions, which "all contribute to the edification of us, who live in the later Age."[20]

It is interesting to note that two Elizabethan Puritan clergy of the Church of England find it necessary to repudiate the idea that Puritan plainness is mere naive rusticity. Richard Greenham was disturbed that some should assume that plainness was merely rough country preaching in unmeditated homely language. He urged the learning and eloquence of St. Paul and commented on Paul's quotation of three pagan poets, as Henry King did, but went on to observe of Paul that "he made Felix to tremble by his eloquence, was thought Mercury for his eloquence at Lycaonia, by the notable course and vein of his epistles not inferior to the writings of any of the heathen."[21] The same concern motivated Henry Smith to condemn naively rustic preaching then current in the 1580s and 1590s. "There is" he declares "a kind of Preachers risen up but of late, which shrowde and cover everie rusticall and unsauverie, and childish, and absurd Sermon, under the name of the simple kind of teaching." On the contrary, he insists, "to preach simplie, is not to preach rudely, nor unlearnedly, nor confusedly, but to preache plainly and perspicuously, that the simplest man may understand what is taught as if he did heare his name."[22] Arthur Lake, the brother of a secretary of state, and a former learned warden of New College, Oxford, and a bishop, concurred in such sentiments and disapproved strongly of weighting his sermons with exotic, obscure, or arcane learning, or heavy ornamentation.[23]

Puritan plain and not-so-plain styles

Those who mandated plain preaching also appealed to the example of St. Paul. In the first Christian church in Corinth, rife with sectarian divisions, one group had claimed that they were the spiritual sons and daughters of Apollos because that supremely eloquent teacher had been their instructor in the faith. Others claimed to follow St. Peter's example, others again St. Paul's, and yet others with supreme arrogance claimed to be taught by Christ alone. In challenging them to exhibit a supreme allegiance to their Lord, Paul admitted that he "came not with excellency of speech or of wisdom, proclaiming to you the mystery of God," adding that "my speech and my preaching were not in persuasive words of wisdom, but in demonstration of the spirit and of power, that your faith should not stand in the wisdom of men, but in the power of God."[24] These words were interpreted by the dominating Puritan clergyman of Elizabethan days, William Perkins, as a command to observe "an admirable plainness and an admirable powerfulness."[25]

The marks of the Puritan style were defined with greater clarity by two later Puritan clergy of the English Church who were men of great influence, Sibbes and Reynolds. Richard Sibbes stressed three dominant features of style: "brevity" (as contrasted with divagating prolixity), "perspicuity" (as contrasted with the obscurity of recondite and often irrelevant arcane scholarship and even pedantry), and "spirituality" (as contrasted with human wisdom manifested in intellectual pride and ostentatious eloquence).[26]

The other distinguished Puritan clergyman, who was both an important member of the Westminster Assembly and who accepted a bishopric at the Restoration, was Edward Reynolds. He defined the essence of the Puritan style in greater detail, both positively and negatively. He discussed rhetorical virtues and vices, the virtues being "choice, purity, brevity, perspicuity, moderate acrimony, and vehemency." The vices comprise "sordidness, tediousness, obscurity, flatness of conceit, arguteness and 'minutiae,' gaudiness, wordiness, and empty ostentation."[27] Thus, in summary, we may note that the ideal of the Puritan plain style was to be plain but not crude, eloquent but not self-advertising, and that different practitioners of it interpreted these terms with considerable flexibility, depending on education, experience, occasion, and audience.[28]

Once again it must be observed that the not-so-plain Puritan clergy, while rejecting the blandishments of the theatre and the suggestive vulgarity of ballads and romances, yet accepted much of the Renaissance rediscovery of the Greek and Roman classics. The wisdom of the pagan and pre-Christian writers was "baptized" for Christian use. After all, these were the staple of the language-training in the English grammar schools. Here the pupils were familiarized with Greek and Latin prose and poetry, which they were required to translate, and then to retranslate back into the original languages. Thomas Gataker, an erudite Puritan, adverted to the value of reading pagan writers for establishing standards of politeness. "What difference will there be," he asked, "between a Christian and an heathen, a Christian schoolmaster, and an heathen, if the parent or schoolmaster teach his children and scholars matters of civility and human learning alone?"[29]

The objections to pagan writers were occasionally to the immorality they encouraged, occasionally to the displacement of Christian writers, and chiefly to the errors of their religion. The latter charge was muted in the cases of those pagan writers whose works contained adumbrations of that Christian revelation which both fulfilled and corrected it. The two pagan writers most often cited by the Puritan clergy were the moralists, Seneca and Plutarch, because they were exponents of the four cardinal virtues: prudence, temperance, fortitude, and justice. This was a classification ultimately derived from Plato and Aristotle, which had been partly expounded by St. Ambrose and St. Augustine, but more fully and systematically by St. Thomas Aquinas, the great Dominican theologian.[30] To this foundation the medieval Church added the three theological virtues—faith, hope, and charity.

Lawrence Sasek points out that the gap between Christian and pagan writers which was theoretically unbridgeable (because of the supremacy of Christian revelation over human wisdom) was overcome in practice.[31] For this there were two reasons. In the first place, the preachers could point to the ethical purity of the teaching and practice of "the ethnicks." Secondly, knowledge of the Church Fathers seemed particularly apposite when, in controversy, they could be appealed to for many interpretations of cruxes in Scripture, or to maintain or challenge the antiquity of certain doctrines and liturgical practices and ceremonial customs.

The hierarchy of authorities, in tabular form, for all the clergy of the Church of England (whether metaphysicals or high or low Calvinists) can be represented as follows in descending order of authority:

1. The Bible
2. The Church Fathers (for Arminian Anglicans)
3. Modern Reformed theologians (2 and 3 would be interchanged for Calvinists and Puritan Anglicans)
4. Scholastic theologians
5. Heathen moralists

6. Heathen historians and English historians (e.g. Foxe, Camden, and Bacon)
7. Pagan poets (a) epic
               (b) satirical
               (c) lyrical.[32]

The rather mixed picture of the Puritan plain and not-so-plain styles in the central decades of the century is fairly described by Lawrence Sasek:

> Gataker's words reveal a more intense interest and a more profound response to classics of the humanistic tradition than do those of his fellow London preachers, such as Gouge. Hieron's almost naive enjoyment of verse, Perkins's cautiously worded approval of poetry, Walwyn's enthusiasm for Montaigne, Taylor's distrustful glances at belles-lettres, Reynolds's eagerness to employ literature in the service of religion, Bolton's strangely inconsistent use of Catullus—all these seem highly personal phenomena, affected by education, experience, and temperament, undoubtedly, but not determined by political or religious affiliations.[33]

All we need to add is that the style changed as certain preachers (for example, Featley, Gauden, and Reynolds) changed their allegiance from the Parliamentary to the Royalist side, and as the occasion and social context also changed.

The uses of learning in sermons

It was obvious that Protestant clergy of whatever stripe or party had to be able to expound Scripture faithfully and whenever possible to be able to translate from the original languages—Hebrew for the Old Testament and Greek for the New Testament. A knowledge of Latin as well was invaluable as the learned language of the Renaissance world, as well as providing a key to the Latin Fathers (chiefly Ambrose, Augustine, Jerome, and the later Montanist, Tertullian, not therefore classified as a Church Father). Latin also made familiarity with the medieval schoolmen possible, and with the controversialists of the Reformation and the Counter-Reformation. Greek, it might be added, opened the way to study of the Cappadocian Fathers (Basil of Caesarea, Gregory of Nyssa, and Gregory of Nazianzen) and the much-quoted Chrysostom, preacher to the Byzantine court.

Thomas Playfere, in a funeral sermon for Edward Lively who had taught Hebrew at Cambridge for thirty years,[34] pointed out the advantage of knowing the older sacred tongue, and Bishop Hacket boasted that the Protestant clergy had mastered the biblical languages to the consternation and discomfiture of their Roman Catholic critics. "I confess," said Hacket, "it is the wisdom of *God* which teacheth learned men their exact insight into the Sacred Tongues, and the Lord hath furnish'd many Heroes of the *Reformed Churches* with such exquisite skill far beyond our Adversaries, that out of their overflowing envy they have called us *Pedants* and Grammarians."[35]

The primary value of learning was for the illumination of obscure and difficult parts of Scripture. There is, for example, the much disputed reference by St. Paul to "the messenger of Satan" (II Corinthians 12:7). In a sermon preached on the penitential Psalm 6:4–5, Donne cites the guesses at its meaning offerred by Patristic, Reformed, and Roman expositors: Augustine confesses his ignorance of its import, while Theophylact suggests it is a headache; St. Thomas Aquinas calls it *ad Morbum iliacum*, while Gregory of Nazianzen and Basil think it is gout or stomach pains; other Fathers believe it to be concupiscence; Oecumenius considers it a reference to heretical adversaries; and Cardinal Cajetan interprets it as devil-sent temptations.[36] Donne does not clear up the difficulty or decide which interpretation is most probable in this case, but his learning does at least indicate the complexity of biblical interpretation even with Patristic aids, and provides his congregation with a salutary reminder that even the renowned apostle to the Gentiles had to struggle to attain holiness with the aid of Divine grace. Donne himself enjoys the various suggestions since they stimulate his avid curiosity and, presumably, served to intrigue the congregation.

Andrewes, on the other hand, in dealing with a crux, briefly adduces the readings of the Fathers, but makes a decision from among the alternatives. For example, an Easter sermon on the text I Peter 1:3–4 contains the words "Blessed be God, and the Father of our Lord Jesus Christ, which according to his abundant mercie, hath begotten us againe unto a lively hope by the resurrection of Jesus Christ from the dead." The crux is "from the dead," which Andrewes translates "from the heart of the earth." He then gives the polysemous Patristic interpretations and his own decision: *"The heart of the earth* (with *Iustine Martyr, Chrysostome, Augustine*), I take for the *grave:* though (I know) *Origen, Nyssen, Theodoret* take it for *hell,* for the place where the *Spirits* are (as, in the bodie, that is the place of them)."*[37]*

Andrewes could, however, by his independent knowledge of the biblical tongues make felicitous interpretations. One in particular is most illuminating. He points out that נשר (the Hebrew word only appears in the margin of the printed sermon) also means good news, a singularly apt *aide-memoire* for a sermon on the Incarnation where the eternal Son of God in the flesh *is* the Gospel:

> It will not be amisse to tell you; the *word* which is *Hebrew* for *flesh,* the same is also *Hebrew,* for *good tydings,* (as we call it, the *Gospell;*) Sure, not without the Holy Ghost so dispensing it. There could be no other meaning; but that, some *Incarnation,* or *Making flesh,* should be generally *good newes* for the whole world.[38]

Similarly, Bishop Joseph Hall's knowledge of Hebrew enables him to inform his congregation that the Hebrew word "דֶּבֶר which signifieth 'the plague', is derived from מִדְבָּר which signifieth 'a desert:' certainly the plague turns the most populous city into a desert."[39]

While Donne respects [40] and consults the Church Fathers

usually in the original Latin, he frequently disagrees with them, thus showing not only his erudition but also his independence of mind. The same is true of Thomas Adams. Donne, for example, points out that when Jesus, in an exemplary act of humility, washed the feet of the disciples (John 13:4–5), the Fathers disagreed as to whose feet Jesus washed first. Augustine and Bernard opt for Peter, Origen and Chrysostom for Judas, while Donne is sure it is the feet of the beloved disciple, John.[41] In a similar manner Adams disagrees with Ambrose, Augustine, and Jerome in maintaining that the struggle in the womb of the mother of Esau and Jacob was warlike, not playful.[42]

Patristic learning, as Donne showed, was able to protect the congregation from becoming the prey to ancient heresies which were once more rearing their ugly heads. This was exhibited in a sermon preached on Whitsunday, probably in 1624, according to the editors of Donne's sermons, Potter and Simpson.[43] It included a summary of the views of six heretics. These were Cerinthus and Ebion, who both denied the divinity of Christ, Apelles who claimed Jesus created his own body, Cerdon and Marcion who as Docetists claimed that the body of Jesus was a mere phantom, and Basilides who denied that Jesus suffered on the Cross, and asserted that Simon of Cyrene was his substitute.[44]

Donne's learning in Scripture was probably never shown to better advantage than in two sets of sermons he delivered while preacher at Lincoln's Inn. One set was aimed at overcoming the difficulties caused by texts that were in appearance totally contradictory, as for example John 5:22, affirming "The Father judgeth no man, but hath committed all judgement to the Sonne," and John 8:15, in which Jesus says, "I judge no man." These sermons were to be preached in the mornings during the legal terms, and in the evenings he preached a different set of sermons, on texts that he believed the Roman Catholics misinterpreted or (in his own word) "detorted." Both sets of sermons occupied him for a whole year.[45]

Patristic learning was also valuable as a resource in controversy with both Puritans and Roman Catholics. If, in Andrewes' opinion, the Puritans made sermons the be-all and end-all of worship, he can point out that in the Early Church the service proper only began when the preparatory sermon, to be heard by all non-members, was ended:

It is well knowne, that, all the time of the Primitive Church, the Sermon was ever done, before the *Service* began. And that to the Sermon, Heathen men, Infidels, and Iewes, Hereticks, Schismatikes, *Energumeni* [possessed persons], *Catechumeni, Poenitentes, Competentes* [those finishing preparation for Baptism], *Audientes* [beginners in the Catechumentate], all these, all sorts of people were admitted: But when they went to service, when the *Liturgie* began, all these were voyded; not one of them suffered to stay. It were strange, that, that should be the onely, or the chiefe Service of God, whereat, they which held no servants of God, no part of the Church, might and did remaine no lesse freely, then they which were.[46]

The erudite Peter Heylyn, in preaching an extensive series of ten sermons on the parable of the tares, included in one of them a denunciation of the weeds (symbols of unscriptural traditions) which the Roman Catholic Church introduced into God's wheatfield.[47] These, in his view, included the primacy of Peter as monarch of the Church, the celibacy of the priesthood, the ascription of adoration to the Virgin as Queen of Heaven, the invocation of saints, and indulgences for past sins and sins to come. He backed his charges by a plethora of references to the Church Fathers and the schoolmen, citing Minutius Felix three times and the following once each: Ambrose, Tertullian, Cyprian, Jerome, Lactantius, Gregory of Nazianzen, Cyril of Jerusalem, Anselm, Bernard of Sens, Biel, Peter Damien, and Paschasius, as well as Homer, Aristotle, Juvenal, and Virgil. He also cited the Catholic Bellarmine four times, solely for the purpose of refuting him. Thus in a single sermon of thirty pages in print, he had references to eighteen authors, eight of them Church Fathers and five of them schoolmen. He was not untypical.

Patristic learning can be used to back up a particular interpretation of Christ's presence in Holy Communion. This Barten Holyday does in a sermon entitled "Of the Bread of Life," on the text John 6:34, "Lord, evermore give us this bread." The sermon cites seventeen different Fathers (Ambrose thrice; Cyprian, Jerome, and Chrysostom twice) and the Reformation divines, Calvin, Beza, and Peter Martyr. He wishes to confute the literalism inherent in transubstantiation in favour of virtualism—a spiritual manducation, not a corporal one. He argues thus:

> They say, this bread of life in the sacrament is so verily Christ, that it is not bread: thus whiles they feare that they be not Devout; they do not feare to be Idolatrous. Which seems not to agree with the old preface to this Sacrament; *sursum corda*; Lift up your hearts; which rather excites to a spirituall food, by Faith; than to a corporall food by sense.

He continues by asserting that "indeed to eate Sacramentally, Mystically, and Spiritually, are termes not opposite, but most consistent and congruous."[48]

A further use of learning was etymological. Its function was the clarification of Scripture. This was used moderately and modestly or pedantically and ostentatiously. Lancelot Andrewes is an excellent example of the good use, Bishop John King and Barten Holiday of the overuse of this linguistic erudition.

Andrewes, for example, makes the attitude of hypocrisy, as a pretense, come alive for his congregation by explaining that "hypocrite" is the Greek term for stage players or professional actors, who may in one play be a sultan and in another a slave. Then he follows this by giving biblical examples: "Will you see *Almes* playd? Out comes *Judas* sagely, with a sentence in his mouth, *ut quid perditio haec?*"[49] Similarly, he enables the king and court to appreciate the significance of sincerity thus: "Sinceritie (that is) *cleannesse of life:* (a word thought to be taken from *honie,* which is then *mel sincerum,* when it is *sine cera,* unmingled, without wax, or any baggage in it."[50] The etymological lessons of Andrewes are apt to be brief and practical.

Bishop John King is prolix in comparison. In a sermon commemorating the marriage of Elizabeth, daughter of King James, to the Elector of the Palatinate, he is commending the married estate, as "complementarity" of male and female qualities, oddly old-fashioned in our day. But his illustration, from a rabbinical source, is illuminating if long-winded:

> It is a device of the Rabbins, but the moral is good, that in the names of ISH and ISHA, is included IAH the name of God; and that if you take out י and ה *god* and *He,* whereof the name consisteth, there remaineth nothing but אש אש *ignis, ignis,* the fire of dissention and brawle, which burneth and consumeth to the fire of hell. The meaning is that God must be present at the ioyning of man and woman. . . .[51]

Another value of learning, especially of the more arcane type, was the fascination it elicited in the listener. Could anyone, for example, remain disinterested when John Donne was illustrating his sermons from the Qu'ran, the Cabbala, or from traveller's tales? In a sermon at the marriage of Sir Francis Nethersole, Donne took as his text Genesis 2:18, "And the Lord God said, It is not good that man should be alone: I will make him a helpe, meet for him." In recommending marital unity of spirit and recognizing the wonderful individuality of the bride and groom, he tells his hearers: "It was the poor way: that *Mahomet* found out in his Alchoran, that in the next life all women should have eies of one bignesse, and a stature of one size; he could finde no means to avoid contention, but to make them all alike: But that is thy complexion, that is thy proportion which God hath given thee."[52]

Donne never ceased to be enchanted by the mystic meanings

of the names of God, ultimately deriving from the Cabalists.[53] He is fascinated, for instance, by the phrase "Therefore in the shadow of thy wings will I rejoice," (Psalm 63:7), and asks what the Holy Ghost intends by this metaphor of wings? For him the *sub umbra alarum* means "a Refreshing, a Respiration, a Conservation, a Consolation in all afflictions," and he adds that this is also a metaphor of power, for "in this metaphor of *wings*, doth the Holy Ghost expresse the *Maritime* power of some Nations at Sea, in Navies, (*woe to the land shadowing with wings;*) that is, that hover over the world, and intimidates it with her sailes and ships."[54]

Another intriguing source of illustrative material for sermons lay in travel stories. These caught the attention of the Elizabethan and early Stuart public, whether they were accounts of the "derring-do" of Sir Francis Drake, Sir Walter Raleigh, or of Hawkins, or the descriptions (exaggerated or sober) of travelling in exotic countries by Purchas, and Coryate, and the three travelling brothers Shirley. Well-documented was the delight in seeing Princess Pocahontas in London and reading of the American Indians in the English plantations and colonies overseas.[55] Donne himself had travelled widely to Spain, the Azores, France, and the Low Countries, and the predominance of sea imagery in his sermons is striking.[56] It was particularly appropriate for one who in London overlooked the great masts of the island nation "set in a silver sea."

Donne caught the attention of the congregation at St. Paul's Cathedral by referring to the asperities of travel and the hope of arrival in life's pilgrimage: "And he [God] hath not discovered, but made that Northerne passage by the frozen sea of calamity, and tribulation to Paradise, to the heavenly Jerusalem. There are fruits that ripen not but by frost."[57] On another occasion, he spoke of catching whales in an extended image which was an illustration of the way to catch the conscience. The vividness of the analogy suggests that this is clearly an eyewitness account:

The rebuke of sin, is like the fishing of *Whales*; the Marke is great enough; or can scarce misse hitting; but if there be not sea room and line enough, and a dexterity in letting out that line, he that fixed his harping Iron, in the Whale, endangers himselfe, and his boate; God hath made us *fishers of Men*; and when we have struck a *Whale*, touch'd the conscience of any person, which thought himselfe above rebuke, and increpation, it struggles and strives and as much as it can endevours to draw fishers, and boate, the Man and his fortune into contempt and danger. But if God tye a *sicknesse* or any other calamity to the end of the line, that will winde up this Whale againe to the boate, bring back this revellious sinner better advised . . . onely calamity makes way for a rebuke to enter.[58]

Donne was evidently intrigued by the huge mammal. In a sermon preached in St. Paul's on the evening of the day of St. Paul's conversion in 1628/9, his text was Acts 28:6, "They changed their mind and said, that he was God." In the course of it, he hit upon a brilliant image to describe the ultimately isolated state of anyone relying on the bubble of popularity and on fairweather friends, "for they will change, and at such an ebbe, the popular man will lye, as a whale upon the sands deserted by the tide."[59]

Donne also provides a different example of travellers' tales. He is arguing that Genesis 1:2, "And the Spirit of God moved upon the Face of the Waters," cannot be any wind because God was before creation. He continues: "In Lapland, the witches are said to sell winds to all passengers; but that is but to turne those windes that Nature does produce, which way they will; but in our case, the Jews, and they that follow them, dreame winds, before any winds, or cause of winds was created; The Spirit of God here cannot be the Wind."[60]

Andrewes, too, knew of his countrymen's interest in travel and refers to the foundations of Christian hope in a court sermon at Easter 1616, on I Peter 1:3–4. He gives his third basis of assurance in travel terms, thus: "Heer, then is a *third Cape of Good Hope:* that though one had been downe as deep in the entrailes of the spirituall Great *Leviathan,* as ever was *Ionas* in the sea whales, yet, even there also, not to despaire."[61]

If a metaphysical preacher lacked Donne's wide experience of travel, there were other sources to draw upon to intrigue and charm his congregation. The wonders evoked in Pliny's *Natural History* enabled one to live "several lives" by walking in the shoes of other men and women of other times; and the "unnatural" history of Pliny and his dependents stretched the imagination.

Four metaphysical preachers who were particularly fond of historical allusions were John King, bishop of London, Dr. Peter Heylyn who used eleven historical references in a single sermon,[62] Archdeacon Barten Holyday of Oxford who became enamored of and knowledgeable about the customs of everyday life in Greece and Rome, and Dean Thomas Jackson whose fascination was with modern history as well as ancient. Of course, many other preachers of the same group, including Andrewes and Donne, used occasional historical examples.

Bishop John King preached a Paul's Cross sermon on 11 April 1619 at a public thanksgiving for the recovery of James I from a serious illness. His text was Isaiah 38:17. He drew a witty parallel between Jacob fighting with the angel at the ford of Jabbok and Jacobus (the Latin for James), which he introduced by a historical narration:

> Ariston was a good King, but wanted issue: and the people desirous to have one of his race to govern after him begged him Issue of their gods. That Sonne so obtained they named *Demeratus* because the people had gained him by their prayers. I doubt not that our King was another *Demeratus,* begged by his people at the hands of God; or rather (according to his own name) that our *Iacob* was another *Israel* and that he & his people wrestled with God [Genesis 32] by their earnest supplications, to gaine a blessing of health from him: and although as to *Israel,* a sinew of his thigh be shrunke, that is, the ability and strength of his body somewhat abated; we trust that in time God will also restore that.[63]

Barten Holyday in a sermon on spiritual sorrow needs a historical illustration which will parallel the Christian experience of repentance and also wittily show that epilepsy can be an analogy of falling down into sin. Here is how he meets his double requirement:

> Euripides, being troubled with the falling evill, when he travail'd into *Aegypt*, was by the appointment of the *Aegyptian* Priests dipt in sea-water; and so was cured: such washing in the salt-waters of spirituall sorrow is the best remedy again the spirituall epilepsie, the falling into sin.[64]

Dean Jackson prepared a treatise on God's forewarnings, as he tried to read the signs of the times. This was a summary of some sermons he published in 1637.[65] The first sermon was on Luke 13:5, "I tell you nay; but except yee repent, ye shall all likewise perish." He argues that God forewarns each nation before plaguing its people, and this gives them the opportunity for repentance. Then he shows that in heathen as well as in biblical historiography it is believed that there are portents to herald threatened destruction. His sermon is remarkable for its references to modern as well as ancient historians and writers. The sermon includes two references to Herodotus, three to Machiavelli (all the more effective because this atheist cannot be fairly accused of superstition), and one each to the following: Philip de Commines, an unnamed historian (using Sir David Lindsey's testimony), Martin Fumée (a French historian of Hungary), Silius Atticus, and Valerius Maximus (a Roman historian). The list shows exceptionally wide historical reading.

Our consideration of historical exempla may well conclude with an instance used by Bishop Lake to induce the congregation to be charitable to ministers:

> In the life of *Charlemaine* it is reported, That warring against the *Sarazins* in *Spaine*, he so farre pressed them, that their King was content to become a Christian, so that Peace might be granted them. During the Treatie, *Charle-*

maine feasted *Aigoland,* the *Sarazin* King. As they sat at meat, the *Sarazin* perceived a companie of men in the same Roome meanely attended, and thinly dieted; and asked *Charlemaine,* what they were? *Charlemaine* and his Nobles answered; Oh, these be the Ministers of God: The *Sarazin* replyed: In sooth, yours is a pettie God, that hath such miserable and contemptible servants: And thereupon, as the Storie addes, brake off the Treatie, and would not become a Christian.[66]

The appetite for wonders in the way of comets and monsters and storms was strong in the Elizabethan age, and abated little, except that it was turned more to travels in the Jacobean age. It was satisfied in part by the preachers turning to "unnatural" natural history. There are many such in the sermons of Play- fere, only one I think in Andrewes' sermons, few in Donne's sermons, and they have almost entirely disappeared in the Res- toration period. It would seem that they fell entirely out of fashion because of the growing scientific spirit of the age.

Robert Willan, one of the chaplains of Charles I, wished to remind mourners of the swiftness of life's passing—that old theme of human mutability—and drew a moral from the sup- posed superior speed of Norwegian birds:

They report that the birds of *Norway* flye faster than the fowles of any other Countrey, not because Nature hath given them more nimblenesse or agility to their wings, but by an instinct they know the dayes in that Climat to bee very short, not above three houres long, and therefore they make more haste unto their nests: Strange that birds should make such use of observation, and we practically knowing the shortnesse of our lives, yet make no haste to our home the house appointed for all living![67]

An even more improbable example of this genre is provided by Donne's lithospermus, "which being no firmer than a bull- rush or a reed, produces and beares for the fruit thereof no other but an intire and very hard stone."[68] From this he draws as conclusion that temporal affliction produces spiritual stoniness which, though unnatural, is yet a common result.

An even more unlikely example of "unnatural" natural history comes in Playfere's amusing belief that panthers have four claws on their hind feet compared with five on their front feet to symbolize the fact that "though they be weake world-ward, yet they are strong to God-ward."[69] This is as likely as the existence of the Egyptian Nabis, described by Bishop Barlow, preaching on the Essex rebellion. This revolt, he claims, is a compound of many rebellions "just as the *Nabis* in *Egypt* is a beast shaped of many beasts."[70]

There were four other sources of learning with which the metaphysical preachers held the attention of their listeners: maxims, proverbs, riddles, and fables. Sententiousness was cultivated by the divines, partly because it suited the gravity of their calling, and partly because it left a summary lesson in the minds of their hearers. Peter Heylyn, for example, seemed to think a sermon defective if he did not begin it with a weighty maxim, and often one borrowed from one of the ancients. For example, his first sermon in the series, *The Parable of the Tares* (1659), begins with a citation from St. Augustine to the effect that God gave us as much knowledge as is necessary in the Scriptures, and these provide wisdom for the simple, and enlarge the minds of the most thoughtful clergy. The third sermon has a quotation from Seneca, "*Prosperum ac felix scelus virtus vocatur.* Successful mischief is oft crowned with the name of virtue." Successive sermons begin with an anonymous epigram, *Latet anguis in herba* (the snake lies in the grass), followed by those of Cyprian, Minutius Felix, Velleius Paterculus (twice), Lactantius, and Velleius again.

Other maxims are less tributes to scholarship than shrewd insights, such as Brownrig's "Popery is a religion for the eye, ours for the ear."[71] One of Donne's is a variation on this theme: "The organ that God hath given the naturall man is the eye; he sees God in the creature. The organ that God hath given the Christian is the ear."[72] Playfere can teach two Bible lessons concisely in a single maxim: "That we be not too distrustfull, we are sent to the lillie: and yet that we be not too negligent, we are sent to the ant."[73] Some of them are elaborate, particularly those of Bishop Gauden. One example that only just stops short of pomposity goes thus: "One faire and spotlesse Lilly of preserved Peace is a greater ornament to a Princes Diadem, than to have it beset with many Red Roses of bloudy triumphs."[74] The maxims of several of our preachers strike both conscience and imagination, arrows in their direction and drive. Such is Henry Smith's reminder: "Sinnes and excuses are twinnes, borne at a birth, & one followeth another."[75] A similar piercing thought, though gently spoken, is Donne's opening to a sermon: ". . . Christ who read *Hearts* better than we doe *faces*, and heard *Thoughts* clearer than we doe words. . . ."[76]

Just as maxims were an indication of learning if obtained from classical sources, or of ingenuity if they expressed shrewd insights into human behavior, so were proverbs, but with one difference. They would be well-known, so that preachers could captivate a wide audience of simple as well as intelligent folk. Such a preacher was the ever popular Thomas Adams, who offered five reasons for his extensive use of proverbs. Briefly these were for their "antiquitie, brevity, significancie, experience and truth."[77]

Adams did use proverbs in a different and more complex manner. Using a Latin example he declared:

> You have often heard that old verse:
>   Daemon languebat, monachus tunc esse volebat.
>   Daemon convaluit, daemon ut ante fuit.
> And as wittily Englished:
>   The Devill was sicke, the devill a Monke would be,
>   The Devill was well, the devill of Monke was he.

This illustrated that God had better take what devotion he can when we are in misery.[78] Another of Adams' proverbs came from France. Here he claimed that the loss of a nail led to the loss of an army, which he explains thus: "The want of a nayle looseth the shooe, the losse of a shooe troubles the horse, the horse indangereth the rider, the rider breaking his ranke molests the company, so far as to hinder the whole Army."[79] The moral is that careless beginnings can lead to destructive endings.

Others of Adams' proverbs were meant to act as goads to the consciences of some members of the professions in his congregation in London. Of lawyers he said: "The *Italiens* have a shrewd proverbe against them: The Devill makes his Christmas-pyes of Lawyers tongues, and Clerkes fingers."[80] Other proverbs he used are just sound common sense, such as "the emptiest Barrel makes the loudest sound."[81]

Lancelot Andrewes also made good use of proverbs. One he ingeniously adapted to the Passion of Christ: "Spots will out with water; some will not with anything, but with *blood.*"[82] Another criticized political magnates: "It is an old *Simile* . . . that *The Lawes* are like *Cobwebs:* that they hold fast the seely flies, but the great *Hornetts* break through them as oft as they list."[83]

Others of our preachers also used proverbs as minatory moral reminders. Bishop Hall cautioned overfond parents: ". . . thus many a son may, according to the apologue, bite his mother's ear while he is climbing up to the gallows."[84] It is less effective for having been borrowed from a classical source. It was with similar intent that Thomas Fuller declared: "The out-landish Proverbe saith, That the Glutton digs his grave with his own teeth, hastens his death by his intemperance."[85]

Bishop Morley advised modesty, using two proverbs, urging that ". . . our *English* Proverb, that *the Greatest Clerks, are not always the wisest men;* or, as it is more sharply express'd in the *Scotch* Dialect, *an ounce of Mother Wit is worth a pound of Clergy.*" Donne used the simple proverb, that all eggs that the hen sits upon are not hatched, to show that not even Christ was able to get all potential souls converted.[86]

More unexpected, perhaps, is the quotation of a popular proverb only to refute it, because the preachers think it woefully misleading. Adams does this on two occasions.[87] And Archbishop Ussher argues that a proverb urged by a worldling is valueless to a Christian, when he imagines a worldly wiseman saying, "Must I let go all my pleasures in this life for hopes only [in the next]? Shall I forego a bird in the hand for one in the bush? I will not."[88]

Fables also, like historical anecdotes, were a delightful addition to metaphysical sermons. The use of such appears to have been fashionable in Elizabethan days but generally outmoded by the time of the early Stuarts. We find them used in the sermons of Latimer and the Elizabethan preacher Bridges;[89] and Thomas Playfere, who uses them the most, was to all intents and purposes an Elizabethan since he ceased to preach after 1606.[90] But it is noticeable that when Donne comes to use a fable he is careful to call it a parable.[91]

Playfere's fables are plainly derived from Aesop. One used the tale of the ass disguised as a lion as an analogy for death, who "stands now like a Silly Asse, having his Lyon skinne pulled over his eares, and is so far from terrifying any that it benefits all true Christians. . . ."[92] Another of Playfere's illustrated how a leopard tricked an ape by pretending to be dead, and so did Christ trick the devil by his three days in the grave between the Crucifixion and the Resurrection.[93] This illustration, however striking, can nevertheless be charged with Docetism.

Adams usually employed fables satirically. For example, one fable was used to discourage cursing. It concerned three sons whose father left the patrimony to his true, not illegitimate son. However, since it was not known who he was, the judge set up the father's corpse and told the sons to shoot at his heart. The two eldest hit the mark, but the youngest "utterly refused to shoote: good nature would not let him wound that man dead, that bred and fed him living. Therefore the Iudge gave all to this sonne, reputing the former bastards."[94] God, Adams concludes, will not give his patrimony to those who wound his son by swearing.

Bishop Hacket used two noteworthy fables. One illustrated the trivial reasons people have for wishing to die, and how many petitionary prayers "are but avaritious craving, or unchristian presumption, unless we say, *Lord* let it be according to thy word."[95] The second fable Hacket derived from Theocritus to induce his hearers to trust the Providence of God. To illustrate this he chose the story of a devout shepherd, imprisoned in a hollow tree by his hard master, who was fed honey by bees.[96]

A final device for arousing curiosity was the riddle. Its purpose is at once to intrigue, delight, and instruct. It has the further advantage that it is as attractive to the wise as to the simple, to old as well as young, whereas the paradox, a parallel, seems designed to appeal only to the intelligent.[97] The single disadvantage of the riddle is that when the answer is disclosed, it often seems no more than verbal legerdemain.

This may be the reason why there are relatively few examples in the sermons of the metaphysical preachers, despite the metaphysical nature of the most famous riddle in the Bible, that which Samson posed to the Philistines. It may be recalled that he had killed a lion and a swarm of bees fed on its carcase making honey. He demanded of the Philistines the meaning of the cryptic saying, "out of the eater came forth meat, and out of the strong came forth sweetness." The Philistines threatened Delilah, Samson's wife and a Philistine, and she wheedled the answer from Samson. Hence the Philistines were able to reply, "What is sweeter than honey? and what is stronger than a Lion?"[98] Brownrig recalls Samson's riddle when he is demonstrating the change that conversion causes, the change from ferocity to gentleness in the case of Paul's gaoler who "before his Conversion, he was a Tyger and Vulture, now Grace makes him a Lamb and a Dove."[99] Fuller also made a reference to this riddle: "Today therefor part of *Samsons* Riddel shall be fulfilled in your ears: *Out of the Devourer came meat: Gluttony*, that vice which consumeth and devoureth food."[100] Fuller also asserted that Christ posed a riddle in the logion reported in Matthew 11:11, "Among them that are borne of women there hath not risen a greater than *John* the Baptist: Notwithstanding, he that is least in the Kingdome of Heaven is greater than he." This biblical knot is untied as follows:

293

> *John* Baptist was the greatest among the Children of Women, because other Prophets foresaw Christ, He saw him; others spake of Christ, He spake to him, and had the high honour to baptize him with water, by whose Spirit he himselfe was baptised; Yet was he the least in the Kingdome of Heaven (which properly began with Christs Ascention), because though perchance acquainted with the generals thereof, the particulars of the time, place, meanes and manner were as much conceal'd from him as cleerly revealed to us.[101]

This complex answer would hardly have been listened to if Fuller had not put it in the form of a conundrum, the unveiling of which kept the curiosity of the congregation alert.

Hacket's sermons also have two examples of riddles. One recounts how Philip of Macedon at a feast of thoughtful men propounded this riddle: What was the greatest thing in Nature? Several answers were given, including Philip himself, Olympus, the oceans, and the sun. All were judged inadequate, and finally Philip answered, "*Sed cor quod res maximas despiceret,* the greatest of all things was an heart that despised the greatest things which are in this world beneath."[102] The second riddle he is found in the text he selected for his second sermon on the Passion of Christ. It is from Matthew 27:24, and is spoken by Pontius Pilate, "I am innocent of the bloud of this just Person, see you to it." Hacket aroused interest by saying: "Here is as very a Riddle as the old *Sphinx,* made of three divers forms . . . in the fore-part a *Lyar,* in the next a *true one,* in the third a *Prophet;* and all three in my Text."[103] One has the suspicion, however, that Hackett uses the term "riddle" for an apparent contradiction, or a paradox.

To Playfere, on the other hand, a riddle means a conundrum to keep his congregation on its toes. One of his riddles illustrates what a Christian "newter" is, that is, one who progresses only to regress in the spiritual life. So he begins:

> *Panarches* riddle was this, how a man and no man, can with a stone and no stone, kill a bird and no bird, sitting

upon a tree and no tree? *Athenaeus* makes the answer, That an eunuch, is the man, and a Pumeise is the stone, A Batte is the bird and fennell is the tree.

The moral is:

After the same sort a *Newter* is a very hard riddle. You cannot tell what to make of him. For going forward and backward, he is a Christian and no Christian.[104]

Playfere could have easily eliminated the conundrum and merely used the metaphor of the eunuch, but this would have been far less memorable.

In conclusion, learning proved an invaluable ally for the metaphysical preachers. Their sermons give evidence of their study of the biblical languages and etymology, of patrology, the schoolmen, the classical authors, controversial divines of the Reformation and Counter-Reformation, and their use of historical narrations, natural history, travel literature, epigrams, proverbs, fables, and riddles. All this enabled them to admonish or encourage, to fascinate, delight, and instruct their congregations, as well as to fasten on their memories the spiritual lessons of their sermons.

NOTES

1. The serious critics were often plain style Calvinists. The arguments or tirades of the radical sectarians of Commonwealth days are neglected, since on this issue they appear to be only simplistic versions of the arguments of the Puritan clergy. Both, to a greater or lesser extent, thought self-advertising obscurity unwarrantable in sermons.

2. See Lawrence Stone, *The University in Society*, 2 vols. (Princeton, N.J., 1974), *passim*.

3. See Lawrence A. Sasek, *The Literary Temper of the English Puritans* (Baton Rouge, Louisiana, 1961), chap. 5.

4. "The Windows," lines 1–5, from *The Temple* (first published 1633), *The Works of George Herbert*, ed. F. E. Hutchinson (Oxford, 1941), 67.

5. *A Priest to the Temple* (written 1632, published 1652), *Works of George Herbert*, ed. Hutchinson, 228–229.

6. Herbert, *A Priest to the Temple*, chap. 5, "The Parsons Accessory Knowledge."

7. Herbert, *A Priest to the Temple*, chap. 7, "The Parson Preaching." Yet Herbert commends earnestness, stories in moderation to elicit interest, illustrations, and applications of the doctrine to particular groups, as, for example the young and old, the rich and poor.

8. Oliver Ormerod's *The Picture of a Puritan* (London, 1605), 64 gives the stricter Puritan view in this citation: "My heart (saith one of them in a certain schismatical Booke that is very rife among our Puritans) waxeth colde, and my flesh trembleth to heare you say, that a Preacher should confirme his matter out of the Fathers and humaine writers; doth preaching consist in quoting of Doctors, and alleadging of Poets and Philosophers? In what part of his commission hath a Minister warrant to do so?" The moderate Calvinist view was admirably expressed by Daniel Featley: ". . . sharpness of wit, and true eloquence are gifts of *God*, and therefore best of all to bee employed in holy things . . ." (*Ancilla Pietatis, Or, the Handmaid to Private Devotion* [London, 1626], 23). Earlier (21), in the same much reprinted volume, Featley had argued against overmuch ornamentation and ostentatious eloquence, which he termed "puf-past."

9. I Titus 1:12 reads: "One of themselves, a prophet of their own, said, Cretans are always liars, evil beasts, idle gluttons."

10. Thomas Goffe, *Deliverance from the Grave* (London, 1627), 6–7.

11. Henry King, *An Exposition Upon the Lords Prayer* (London, 1628), 48–49. Yet King is critical of pedantry and prefers the "naked" to the overly "clothed" style. See his *A Sermon preached at Lewes in the Diocese of Chichester* (London, 1663), 18. Jasper Mayne in *A Sermon Concerning Unity and Agreement* (London, 1646), 16–17, insisted how educated in secular as well as sacred lore St. Paul was, "which are helps to the Ministery."

12. Henry King, *An Exposition Upon the Lords Prayer*, 25–26.

13. *The Sermons of John Donne*, ed. G. R. Potter and E. M. Simpson, 10 vols. (Berkeley, 1953–1962), 6:57. See also 10: 147, where he warns against the excessive use of ornament in sermons.

14. Donne, *Sermons*, 6: 55.

15. Donne, *Sermons*, 9: 252–253.

16. Donne, *Sermons*, 8: 95.

17. Donne, *Sermons*, 9: 328.

18. Prefatory biography to John Hacket's *A Century of Sermons* (London, 1675), xiii.

19. Hacket, *A Century of Sermons*, 64.

20. Thomas Fuller, *A Sermon of Reformation. Preached at the Church of the Savoy, last Fast day, July 27, 1643*, contained in Fuller's *Collected Sermons*, J. E. Bailey and W. E. A. Axon, eds., 2 vols. (London, 1891), 1: 311.

21. This citation is owed to Lawrence Sasek's *Literary Temper . . .* , 48.

22. *The Sermons of Maister Henrie Smith* . . . (London, 1593), 311–312. The sermon is titled, "The True Triall of the Spirites" and is on the text, I Thessalonians 5:19–22, "Quench not the Spirit, despise not prophesying: Trie all things, and keep that which is good. Abstaine from all appearance of evill."

23. The brief prefatory biography to Arthur Lake's *Sermons with some Religious and Divine Meditations* (London, 1629) says that his sermon style avoided the fashion "wherein ornaments of speech, varietie of illustrations, allegations, allusions, and the like, are affected and used even to an excesse. . . ." All these were, in fact, used by Bishop Lake, but from memory.

24. I Corinthians 2:1–4. I disagree with Sasek's comment (*Literary Temper . . .* , 41) that these are "relatively ambiguous words" for they plainly denounce self-advertising eloquence and prideful human scholarship.

25. William Perkins, *Of the Calling of the Ministerie* (London, 1618),

430. In his famous *Arte of Prophesying* (*Works* [London, 1631], 2: 673), Perkins insists that "humane wisdom" should be concealed because the preacher is declaring a divine not a human message, yet adamantly denies that this is to be interpeted as barbarism, and warns that the reader "must understand that the Minister may, yea and privately use at his libertie the arts, Philosophy, and variety of reading, whilest he is in framing his sermon: but he ought in publike to conceale all these from the people, and not to make the least ostentation." For accounts of the development of the Puritan plain style, see William Haller, *The Rise of Puritanism, 1570–1643* (New York, 1938), 129–134, and Perry Miller, *The New England Mind: From Colony to Province* (Boston, 1960), 331–362.

26. Sibbes, *Certain Sermons*, 16. This and the following quotation are owed to Lawrence A. Sasek's careful and original study, *Literary Temper . . .* , 48.

27. *The Whole Works of the Right Rev. Edward Reynolds*, ed. Alexander Chalmers, 6 vols. (London, 1826), 6: 309–313. Reynolds, dean of Christ Church, Oxford (1648–1650 and 1659) was consecrated bishop of Norwich in 1661. He had attempted a reconciliation between the Presbyterians and the Episcopalians at the Savoy Conference which had vainly tried to produce a liturgy acceptable to both groups. See my *Worship and Theology in England* (Princeton, N.J., 1975), 2: 636–672, which includes references to Reynolds' contributions.

28. Chapter nine of this book is devoted to the impact of audiences on the style and content of sermons, in city or country, court or Inns of Court, cathedral or parish church, with a university trained or relatively illiterate congregation. The particular occasion and the setting also had an impact on the subject and style of pulpit discourses.

29. This citation is quoted in Sasek, *The Literary Temper . . .* , 77.

30. See his *Summa Theologica*, Qu. 61 ("De Virtutibus Cardinalibus").

31. Sasek, *The Literary Temper . . .* , 87f.

32. Sasek, *The Literary Temper . . .* , 87, modified and expanded to fit both Calvinist and Arminian clergy.

33. Sasek, *The Literary Temper . . .* , 122–123.

34. *Nine sermons Preached by that eloquent divine of famous memorie TH. PLAYFERE Doctor in Divinitie* (London, 1621), 218–219. Playfere stresses the importance of Hebrew.

35. John Hacket, *A Century of Sermons*, 670. From the third Whitsunday sermon on Acts 2:3, "and there appeared unto them cloven tongues

as of fire, and it sat upon each of them." The charge of pedantry was exemplified in Barten Holyday, *Motives to Good Life in Ten Sermons* (Oxford, 1657). They are excessively pedantic, although those of the 1620s (*Three Sermons on the Passion, Resurrection and Ascension of our Saviour* of 1626) are not so. The charge of pedantry might well apply to Andrewes and his imitators with their etymological word-crumbling and word-by-word analysis: for example, Immanuel, in the Ninth Nativity Sermon, *XCVI Sermons,* (London, 1629), 77, and elsewhere.

36. Donne, *Sermons,* 5: 374. Peter Heylyn also points out disagreements in the Fathers, for example, in *The Parable of the Tares Expounded in Ten Sermons* (London, 1659), 37–38.

37. Andrewes, *XCVI Sermons,* 513. From "A Sermon Preached before the Kings Maiestie at White-Hall, 31 March 1616," the eleventh sermon on the Resurrection.

38. Andrewes, *XCVI Sermons,* 46. From "A Sermon Preached before the Kings Maiestie at White-Hall on 25 Dec. 1611."

39. *The Works of . . . Joseph Hall,* ed. P. Wynter, 10 vols. (Oxford, 1863) 5: 149. From a sermon preached at Whitehall on 29 January 1625/6 at a "Public thanksgiving for the wonderful Mitigation of the Late Mortality." The text is Psalm 68:19–20.

40. Donne, *Sermons,* 1: 256. Here Donne says "For we [ministers] steal our preferment if we bring no labour, nor learning to the service; and we steale our Learning if we forsake the Fountaines, and the Fathers, and the Schooles, and deal upon Rhapsoders, and Commonplaces, and Methodmongers."

41. Donne, *Sermons,* 5: 179. From a sermon preached at the churching of Frances Edgerton, Countess of Bridgewater, on the text Canticles 5:3, "I have washed my feet, how shall I defile them?"

42. *The Workes of Tho: Adams* (London, 1629), 123. From a sermon entitled, "Plain-Dealing A Precedent of Honestie," on the text Genesis 25:27, *"Iacob* was a plaine man, dwelling in tents."

43. Donne, *Sermons,* 7: 114. The text is I Corinthians 12:3, "Also no man can say that Jesus is the Lord, but by the Holy Ghost."

44. Donne, *Sermons,* 6: 123f.

45. Donne, *Sermons,* 2: 325.

46. Andrewes, *XCVI Sermons,* 992. From the ninth Gunpowder sermon, preached before King James at Whitehall on 5 November 1617 on the text, Luke 1:25, the seventh and eighth verses of the Benedictus.

47. Peter Heylyn's Sermon IV is on Matthew 13:26, "Then ap-

peared the tares also." It was preached at Whitehall on 7 January 1638. The series was entitled *The Parable of the Tares Expounded & Applied in Ten Sermons.*

48. Holyday, *Motives to a Good Life in Ten Sermons,* 217–218. Similarly, in a sermon "Of Baptisme," 197–198, he counters the Roman Catholic assertion that unbaptized adults go to hell and infants to limbo, and that grace is annexed to the outward sacrament of baptism, by providing a summary history of the sacraments, and its accompanying ceremonial. Also, arguing on biblical grounds, he maintains that the thief on the Cross went to heaven though unbaptized, and that Simon Magus, though baptized, received no grace (citing Acts 8:13, 21). Compare the mildness of the criticism of Andrewes who, in passing, says in an Ash Wednesday sermon of 1622, "Not like them, that make it an *opus operatum:* so it be done, it skills not *how* with them" (*XCVI Sermons,* 231). The Roman Catholics are not even mentioned but merely to be inferred.

49. Andrewes, *XCVI Sermons,* 232.

50. Andrewes, *XCVI Sermons,* 455. From his sixth Easter Sermon preached in 1612 on the text, I Corinthians, 5:7–8.

51. John King, *Vitis Palatina* (London, 1614), 13. The text is Psalm 28:3, "Thy wife shall be as the fruitful vine by the side of thine house." The linguistic pedantry of Holyday is too boring to quote but examples can be found in *Motives to a Good Life in Ten Sermons,* 34, 97, 103.

52. Donne, *Sermons,* 2: 343.

53. See J. S. Chamberlin, *Increase and Multiply. Art-of-Discourse Procedure in the Preaching of Donne* (Chapel Hill, North Carolina, 1976), 106f, where the devices of the *Notarikon* and *Gematriya* are referred to as these subtle anatomizations and reconstitutions of Divine words which were transmitted from Judaism to the Renaissance by Pico in the *De Arte Cabalistica* and by Reuchlin, the Hebrew scholar of Protestantism, thence to Donne in *Sermons* 9: No. 2 on Genesis 1:26, and 7: No. 1 on Psalm 63:7.

54. Donne, *Sermons,* 7: 67.

55. See the perceptive analysis of Donne's travelling metaphors and their religious implications in Gale H. Carrithers, Jr., *Donne at Sermons. A Christian Existentialist World* (Albany, N.Y., 1972), 91, 95. Donne also told the story (*Sermons,* 9: 207) of a West Indian king who, being instructed in the Apostles' Creed, "When he came to that, *He was crucified, dead, and buried,* and had no longer patience,

but said, If your God be dead and buried, leave me to my old god, the Sunne, for the Sunne will not dye," (from an Easter Day sermon of 1630 preached in St. Paul's Cathedral).

Some lively examples of travel literature are *Coryats crudities* (London, 1611), *Purchas his pilgrimage* (London, 1613), the travels of the Shirley brothers as recounted by Anthony Nixon in *The Three English Brothers* (London, 1607), and Edward Pellham's account of five men marooned in Greenland, *Gods power and providence* (London, 1631).

56. See William R. Mueller, *John Donne: Preacher* (Princeton, N.J., 1962), 139–146. Of Donne's predominating water imagery, Mueller writes, "Donne makes even more frequent and manifold use of *water* as a symbol than of *light* . . . It is both the *sine qua non* of life and the harbinger of death, the element of life-giving baptism and of the life-destroying flood" (139). See also, on the marine tropes, Winfried Schleiner, *The Imagery of John Donne's Sermons* (Providence, Rhode Island, 1970), 87f.

57. Donne, *Sermons* 6: 212–213. From a "Sermon preached at Pauls the Sunday after the conversion of St. Paul" (1624/5).

58. Donne, *Sermons,* 5: 199–200. From the revised or second version of a sermon preached at the churching (after childbirth) of the countess of Bridgewater on the text Micah 2:10, "Arise and depart, for this is not your rest."

59. Donne, *Sermons,* 8: 234.

60. Donne, *Sermons,* 9: 96. Donne may be theologically correct in his comment but he is etymologically in the wrong, for the Hebrew word *ruach* means both "spirit" and "wind."

61. Andrewes, *XCVI Sermons,* 515.

62. Preached in Christ Church Oxford, 5 January 1644. The ninth sermon of the ten sermons on *The Parable of the Tares.*

63. John King, *A Sermon of Publike Thanks-giving for the happy recovery of his Maiesty from his last dangerous illnesse. Preached at Pauls-Crosse the 11 of Aprill, 1619* (London, 1619), 45.

64. Holyday, *Motives to a Good Life in Ten Sermons,* 39. The second sermon is on the text Jeremiah 9:1, "Oh that my head were waters, and mine eyes a fountain of tears that I might weep day and night for the slain of the daughter of my people!"

65. Thomas Jackson, *A Treatise Concerning the Signes of the Times, Or Gods Forewarnings. Containing the Summe of some few Sermons delivered partly before the Kings Majesty, partly in the Town of New-Castle upon Tine* (Oxford, 1637), the first sermon.

66. Lake, *Sermons,* 11. See also Brownrig's more prosaic use of the same story in indirect speech in *Sixty Five Sermons* (London, 1674), 224.

67. Robert Willan, *Eliah's Wish: A Prayer for Death. A Sermon preached at the Funeral of the Honourable Viscount Sudbury, Lord Bayning* (London, 1630), 2. The text is I Kings 19:4, "It is now enough, O Lord, take my soule, for I am no better then my Father."

68. Donne, *Sermons,* 7: 55. The second Prebend sermon preached at St. Paul's on 29 January 1625, on the text Psalm 3:67.

69. Playfere, "The Pathway to Perfection," the St. Mary's Hospital sermon for 1593 (bound in the 1616 edition of his sermons entitled *The Meane in Mourning,* 162).

70. William Barlow, *A Sermon preached at Paules Crosse, on the first Sunday in Lent, Martij. I, 1600* (London, 1601), sig. D5.

71. Ralph Brownrig, *Sixty Five Sermons,* 83.

72. Donne, *Sermons,* 2: 114.

73. Playfere, *Nine Sermons . . . ,* 25.

74. John Gauden, *Three Sermons Preached upon Three Publike Occasions* (London, 1642), 10.

75. *Sermons of Maister Henrie Smith,* 899.

76. Donne, *Sermons,* 9: 109. A Paul's Cross sermon preached on 22 November 1629, on the text, "And blessed is he whosover shall not be offended in me" (Matthew 11:6).

77. This citation and the following expansions of the terms from Adams' *Commentary or Exposition upon the Divine Second Epistle Generall written by the Blessed Apostle St. Peter* (London, 1633) I owe to the Ph.D. dissertation of Dr. James L. Hedges, "Thomas Adams and the Ministry of Moderation" (University of California at Riverside, 1974), brought to my attention by Professor Stanley Russell. Adams says proverbs are "the extracts of experience" and an assurance of traditional wisdom, along with the Scriptures and the Fathers (*Commentary,* 1431) and their pointed speech is "no lesse familiar then profound: as intellegible as succint," and further "they are concise and compendious, and so more portable for the memorie" (*Commentary,* 1080).

78. *The Workes of Tho: Adams* (London, 1629), 634–635. From the sermon, "Gods House: Or the Place of Prayses," using Psalm 66:12 as text. For another translated Latin proverb see *The Workes,* 733.

79. *The Workes of Tho: Adams,* 714. From the sermon, "The Bad Leaven: Or the Contagion of sinne," on the text Galatians 5:9.

80. *The Workes of Tho: Adams,* 1059. From the sermon, "The Forrest of Thornes," on the text Hebrews 6:8.

81. *The Workes of Tho: Adams,* 62.

82. Andrewes, *XCVI Sermons,* 59. From a court sermon preached on 25 December 1612, on the text Hebrews 1:1–3.

83. Andrewes offers unusually straight from the shoulder speaking in this Spital sermon delivered in 1588 on the Wednesday of Easter Week (*XCVI Sermons,* 1–2). Its text, frequently used by others on this occasion, was I Timothy 5:17–19.

84. Hall, *Works,* 5: 659.

85. Fuller, *Collected Sermons,* 1: 200. The sermon is "A Glasse for Gluttons" and is on the text, Romans 13:13, "Not in Gluttony."

86. Morley, *A Sermon preached at the magnificent Coronation of the Most High and mighty King Charles the II . . . 23rd April 1661* (London, 1661), 40. The Donne reference is *Sermons,* 9: 148.

87. *The Workes of Tho: Adams,* 484, 498. This however had an English precedent in Latimer; see J. W. Blench, *Preaching in England in the late Fifteenth and Sixteenth Centuries: A Study of English Sermons 1450-c.1600* (Oxford, 1964), 144.

88. Ussher, *The Whole Works* (Dublin and London, 1847–1864), 13: 461. Ussher has already insisted (445) "Now our hope to us is a most sure anchor, if (as the apostle to the Hebrews speaketh) we pit it upwards within the veil, into the holy of holies."

89. See Blench, *Preaching in England,* 180. Of course, medieval preachers had also made considerable use of Aesop's fables for illustrations.

90. Playfere died in 1609, but had lost his reason in 1606.

91. Donne, *Sermons,* 7: no. 14, preached probably on 11 February 1626/7 where Donne introduces it thus: "We need not call that a *Fable,* but a *Parable,* where we heare . . ."

92. Thomas Playfere, *The Meane in Mourning,* 28 (London, 1616 edn.), originally preached as a St. Mary's Hospital sermon in 1595.

93. Playfere, *The Meane in Mourning,* 31. There is marginal reference to "Erasmus's *Proverbes: Pardi mortem adsimulat,*" from which it was obtained at second hand.

94. *The Workes of Tho: Adams,* 154. From the sermon on James 3:8, entitled "The Taming of the Tongue." Adams uses open satirical fables in *The Workes,* 968, where he terms it "a smart invention" when he imagines the Pope and the Emperor reconciled; and in *The Workes,* 794, where he borrows an anti-Roman Catholic fable from a book, *Poenitentiarius Asini, The Asses Confessor.*

95. Hacket, *A Century of Sermons,* 96. The fable is: ". . . like the woman in the Fable that was miserably poor, and gathering sticks

for her fire, and herbs for her sustenance, being vexed with extreme want, she bursts out into this forwardness, O that death would come to me, says the Fable, death did come to her to know what she would have, Help me with my bundle of sticks, says she, I have nothing else to say to you." Adams, it is worth mentioning, has a remarkable compassion for the poor whereas Hacket in repeating the fable is less than his compassionate self.

96. Hacket, *A Century of Sermons,* from the ninth sermon on Christ's Temptation.

97. Paradoxes were considered previously in chapter two, section 9.

98. Judges 14:4–18.

99. Brownrig, *Sixty Five Sermons,* 279, 281.

100. Fuller, *Collected Sermons,* 1: 198.

101. Fuller, *Collected Sermons,* 1: 300.

102. Hacket, *A Century of Sermons,* 448. From the fourth sermon on the Transfiguration.

103. Hacket, *A Century of Sermons,* 484.

104. Playfere, *The Meane in Mourning* (1616 edn.), 175. From the Spital sermon preached on Wednesday in Easter Week, 1593.

Chapter VII

INNOVATIVE THEMES

SINCE THE MAJOR DIFFERENCE between the Calvinist and Arminian preachers concerned the number of the saved (the chosen few who were elect, or the potential all who might be redeemed), and the degree to which individuals had the freedom and the rationality to respond to the offer of salvation (little of both on the part of the Calvinists who took the blindness of human reason and the crookedness and feebleness of the will for granted as the result of original sin, as contrasted with the Arminians who evaluated both the reason and the will more highly), one might assume that these issues would dominate the preaching of the metaphysicals. In fact, while these matters are part and parcel of their preaching, the interest in them is far from being dominant. This was partly because up to about 1620 Calvinism was the accepted orthodox majority opinion[1] in England and Arminianism the heterodox view of the minority, and partly because discussion in the pulpit of politics and "the deep points of predestination" was forbidden by James in 1622.[2]

From the outset it must be understood that English Arminianism differed considerably from Dutch Arminianism. While the latter was the cause of dissension within the Dutch Reformed Church, the English Church at the Reformation had retained both a liturgy, partly derived from the Catholic past and partly from Lutheran church orders, and also an episcopacy. The primary channel for the mediation of divine grace within the European Reformed tradition was, of course, the Word of God, heard in preaching and sealed by the Holy Spirit; but for English Arminians the sacraments were the main channels of grace, received in Baptism and the Eucharist. The consequence of this high evaluation of the sacraments was threefold. First, the clergyman was less a minister of the Word of God than a priest. Secondly, the communion table became an altar: it was Archbishop Laud who had said that the altar was "the greatest place of God's residence upon earth" and even "greater than the pulpit; for there it is *Hoc est Corpus meum*, 'This is my Body'; but in the pulpit it is at most but *Hoc est verbum meum*, 'This is my Word.' "[3] The third consequence was a more profound reverence in the gestures and in the splendor of the accoutrements of worship. Echoes of these controversies will be heard resonating through the sermons. We shall also see, in the following chapter, a considerable interest in the traditional doctrines of the Holy Trinity, the Incarnation, the Atonement, and the hope of life everlasting, which have been constants in Christian preaching through the centuries.

We shall also find considerable interest in epistemology as this applies to soteriology. The main interest however, in this chapter, will be ecclesiology, the doctrine of the Church and its sacraments in England. This became distinctive among the Arminian preachers and their Calvinist critics, because the sovereign was the official head of the Church of England, as had been the case since the time of Henry VIII. This was the inevitable result of Henry VIII's attempt to preserve the hereditary succession to the throne with a male heir. After his failure to get a divorce from the pope he set himself up as the "Supreme Head" of the Church in England.

Other reasons for the preachers' fascination with the doctrine of the Church were the apologetic need to steer a middle course between Papalism and Puritanism (which had been the case from Hooker's time onwards), and the disputes about worship, the beauty of holiness and the holiness of beauty, and the relative roles of preaching and the sacraments. All these became more acute after the majority consensus had been broken by the official support of Arminianism by Charles I. In this Charles had the support of William Laud, who became bishop of London two years after the king's accession, and Laud's policy was indeed "thorough."

The Church Militant and Triumphant

Calvinists and Arminians both treat the Church as the Christian community militant upon earth and triumphant in heaven, a terrestrial mixture of wheat and tares, but a winnowed celestial harvest. Henry Smith describes the state of Christians as a perpetual fight to maintain faith: "This is the state of the church militant: she is like the Arke floating upon the waters, like a Lilly growing among thornes, like the bush which burned with fire, and was not consumed, so the citie of God is always besieged, but never ruined. Christians and persecutions close together, like Christ and his Crosse."[4] Donne gives a deeply personal impression of what it is to be attached to the Church: ". . . let thy Spirit beare witnesse with my spirit, that I am of the number of thine elect, because I love the beauty of thy house, because I captivate mine understanding to thine Ordinances, because I subdue my will to obey thine, because I find thy Son Jesus Christ made mine, in the preaching of thy word, and my selfe made his in the administration of his Sacraments."[5] It is an Augustinian and Reformed definition of the role of the Church.

Bishop Brownrig insists that the Church was always a mixed community, never a perfect community of saints: "In this Field of the Church, there grows Wheat and Tares, *Matth.* 13:38. In this Floor of the Church, there is good Corn and Chaff, *Matth.* 3." The upshot is that at the divine Judgment Day there will be a separation of the sheep from the goats, and that anyone who would be free from the association with the wicked "must go out of the Church, and out of the World too."[6]

It is rare for any preacher to do more than mention the Christian hope of life everlasting, as one of the two Protestant eschatological destinies. Bishop Hacket is one exception but this only in a single sermon; Donne on the other hand makes the topic his continuing delight. In a sermon on the text of Revelation 6:9, "I saw under the Altar the Souls of them that were slain for the Word of God, and for the Testimony which they held," Hacket claims that Christ has opened the curtains of heaven to let us see what the blessed saints do. But it requires such a sustained imagination to do justice to the theme that he falters at the prospect. "It is one of the most difficult tasks in Divinity to understand the several quarterings, and Mansion-places of heaven. I confess I have no skill in *Ouranography.*"[7] The preacher who was the ouranographical expert was Donne, as God's trumpeter in St. Paul's and as a court preacher. It is doubtful if Donne the poet ever evoked the life in heaven better than in the rhythmical cadences of his great sermon at Whitehall on the first Friday of Lent on 29 February 1627/8. His text was Acts 7:60, "And when he had said this, he fell asleep." The sermon climaxed as Donne described Jacob's experience at Peniel, when, after fighting to the point of exhaustion with the angel, he fell asleep and dreamt of the angels moving up and down the ladder linking heaven and earth, then woke to say solemnly, "Surely the Lord is in this place." Donne takes this as a foreshadowing and anticipation of Christians waking in heaven. His expression of this is arranged antiphonally to emphasize its music:

> They shall awake as *Jacob* did,
>   and say as *Jacob* said,
> *Surely the Lord is in this place,*
>   *and this is none other but the house of God,*
>   *and the gate of heaven,*
> And into that gate they shall enter,
>   and in that house they shall dwell,
> Where there shall be no Cloud nor Sun,
>   no darkenesse nor dazling,
>   but one equall light,
> no noyse nor silence,
>   but one equall musick,
> no fears nor hopes,

        but one equall possession,
    no foes nor friends,
        but one equall communion and Identity,
    no ends nor beginnings,
        but one equall eternity.[8]

Donne also has related sermons on the beatific vision:[9] the ascent of the soul heavenward, with a memorable image;[10] the unity of body and soul at the Resurrection;[11] the communion and community of saints and Christ as the everlasting husband of the soul;[12] Christ's Resurrection as the basis of our four resurrections from persecutions, from sin, from temptations, and from death;[13] the consolation that the righteous are in God's hands and will rise again;[14] and the disintegration at death and the reintegration at the General Resurrection.[15] Donne has sometimes been criticized for his morbid obsession with death and its disintegration, but this concern is almost always matched with a positive emphasis on the reintegration at the general Resurrection in an atmosphere of joyful celebration[16] in the company of the saints of all the ages.

The Church of England as the *via media*

All the metaphysical preachers, whether Calvinist or Arminian, rejoiced that the Church of England stood midway between Rome and Geneva in polity, liturgy, and ceremonial. George Herbert celebrated its median position in terms of ceremonial and vestments:

        A fine aspect in fit aray,
        Neither too mean, nor yet too gay,
        Shows who is best.[17]

Donne was for a time deeply concerned by the intermediate role of the English Church, because it seemed a compromise of relatively recent and nationalist growth, in contrast to the internationalism and long tradition of Roman Catholicism with which his family had distinguished historic and contemporary ties. His concern is anguished in the sonnet which begins

Show me deare Christ, thy spouse, so bright and cleare.
What, is it she, which on the other shore
Goes richly painted? or which rob'd and tore
Laments and mournes in Germany and here?

And, in the third Satire, Donne depicted Mirreus seeking true religion at Rome, "because hee doth know/ That shee was there a thousand yeares agoe,/ He loves her ragges so." These rags are the unhappy additions to Rome's pristine purity. In reaction Crantz rushed in the opposite direction, following what "at Geneva is call'd/ Religion, plaine, simple, sullen, yong,/ Contemptuous, yet unhansome." The troubling question was this: Was the Church of England (to use Belloc's biting book title) "The English Accident"—an insular compromise created by and maintained by cynical sovereigns, without the historic foundation of Rome or the reforming zeal of new men of God? Not everyone was convinced either by Foxe's martyrology,[18] or by Hooker's insistence upon the legality of the Church of England (as reflecting the laws of the universe), and by the judiciousness of its amiable and reasonable defender.

Donne came finally to accept the *via media* as part of the Church of Christ and he accorded the same status to the Roman Catholic and the Eastern Orthodox Churches, acknowledging "The Church, *Roman* and *Reformed,* and all other distinctions of place, Discipline, or Person, but one Church, journeying to one *Hierusalem,* and directed by one guide, Christ Jesus."[19] His sermons celebrated the Church of England for its basis in Scripture, which he believed the Roman Catholic Church had departed from, and he also admired its corporate unity and patristic fidelity. This ecumenical attitude is reflected in his funeral sermon for Magdalen Herbert, Lady Danvers, whom he commends because "Shee never diverted towards the *Papist* in undervaluing the *Scripture;* nor towards the *Separatist,* in undervaluing the *Church.*"[20] In a sermon preached in St. Paul's on Whitsunday, 1628, he answers Roman Catholic charges and affirms the modest wisdom of the Church of England in its stand upon Scripture:

When the Romaine Church charges us, not that all is not truth, which we teach, but that we do not teach all the truth, And we charge them, not that they do not teach all the truth, but that all is not truth that they teach, so that they charge us with a defective, we them with a superfluous religion, our case is the safer, because all that we affirm, is by the confession of parts true, but that which they have added, requires proof and the proofe lies on their side; and it rests yet unproved.[21]

The Church of England was reformed because it gave primacy of authority to the Scriptures, not equating their authority with tradition as Roman Catholics had done at the Council of Trent. On the other hand, Anglicans were glad to use such traditions of the Primitive Church as were affirmed by the earliest Fathers and ecumenical Councils, for these were witnesses nearer to the time of the formation of the New Testament canon. Far from this being the particular concern of the Arminians, it was equally affirmed by two Calvinist prelates in the Church of England. The long-lived Thomas Morton (1564–1659), in a sermon preached before King Charles in the cathedral church of Durham, made this moving reference to the Primitive Church: "The ancient *Catholike Church*, and *Mother* of all Churches Christian, ought also to be acknowledged our blessed Nurse, from whom we may suck the most pure and *wholsome milke*, which the multitude of *Martyrs, Confessors*, and *Professors* did; who, notwithstanding the 300 yeeres persecution for Religion, never used, or professed any *forcible defence*."[21]

Another unyielding Calvinist, Archbishop Ussher, judges that the forefathers of the Church of England who lived in communion with the Church of Rome, will be included in the mercy of God, because the foundation of the Church is "that common faith . . . in the unity whereof all Christians do generally accord."[22] The high-priest of Arminianism, Archbishop Laud, however, is never compliant to Roman Catholic claims. In an early sermon, on the psalmist's text, "Pray for the peace of Jerusalem . . ." (Psalm 122:6–7), he criticizes both the Puritans and the Catholics, observing of the latter, "The Church of Rome challengeth us for breach of this peace in our separation from them; but we say, and justly, the breach was theirs, by their separation not only from disputable, but from evident truth. Nor are we fallers out of the Church, but they fallers off from verity. Let them return unto primitive truth, and our quarrel is ended."[23]

Anti-Romanist propaganda in sermons

One consequence of the *via media* ecclesiology was the necessity to defend the Church of England from Roman Catholic criticisms. These were very effectively presented by the master controversialist Cardinal Bellarmine, and by English exiled Jesuits, whose criticisms of the Church of England supported the faith of the English Catholics suffering suspicion, isolation, and the penalties of heavy fines for their recusancy.

A single anecdote will illustrate the bitterness of anti-Catholic feeling in England. It is particularly significant because it concerns the attitude of the highly intelligent headmaster of Westminster School, Dr. Richard Busby, to another intelligent man of high principles, the Jesuit Father Petre, or Peters. Their encounter is reported by Abraham Pryme in his diary, at second-hand. While it may be apocryphal, even as a rumor it is significant as an index of the virulence of anti-Roman Catholic attitudes.

As the doc[tor] was walking out one evening in K[ing] James reign, to take the air, he met by chance with Father Peters, who had formerly been his scholar. Peters saluted him. "How," says the doc[tor] "are you that Peters that was our scholler?" "Yes" says he again. "Well, but how came you to have this garb on?" (he being a Jesuit); to whom he reply'd, "I had not had it on, honourable master, but that the Lord Jesus had need of me." "Need of thee?" (says the doct.) "I never heard that our Lord and Saviour had need of anything, but an ass.[24]

Chapter VII

If such was the attitude to a Jesuit father, it is no surprise to find that preachers involved with the controversy with Rome forget the dignity that should characterize pulpit utterances, and all too often become scurrilous.

The anti-Roman feeling had been exacerbated by the Gunpowder Plot of 5 November 1605, by the countrywide anxiety about the future of Protestantism engendered by the prolonged negotiations over the proposed marriage of Prince Charles to the Infanta of Spain, and by the presence of the Catholic Queen Henrietta Maria and her confessors in their canonical habits in the palace of Whitehall.

A single preacher, William Barlow, can speak for the fears of almost all Englishmen, as he reconstructs the Popish Plot and the immediate reaction to it in a sermon preached five days after the event at Paul's Cross. The preface states that Barlow himself could easily have been one of the members of the House of Lords to have been blown up if the plot had succeeded. His task of preparing this sermon at short notice was assisted by the speeches of King James and the Lord Chancellor in Parliament the previous day, and also by information given him by the King's principal secretary, the earl of Salisbury. In its analysis the sermon stresses the terrifying heinousness of the plot: "a *cruell execution, an inhumane crueltie, a brutish immanitie, a divelish brutishnes*, an *Hyperbolicall*, yea an *hyperdiabolicall divelishnes.*"[25] Clearly, no words are sufficiently polysyllabic to describe the horror of the event. Details make the bishop's charges concrete and moving. The cruelty intended would be seen "in the multitude of the slaine . . . his provision was so large, that if fire had beene given . . . the *Hall of Iudgement, the Courtes of Records*, the *Collegiate Church* [Westminster Abbey], *the Cittie of Westminster*, yea, *White-Hall*, the Kinges House, had been trushed and overthrowne. . . ."[26] The brutish inhumanity was in the manner of the death, "*not man-like to kill*, but beastlike to discorpe, and teare parcell meale the bodies of such personages."[27] Moreover, this "Divell of the Vault" (Guy Fawkes) had aimed at "the second death of the soule" of his victims, who would die with their minds unprepared and their sins unrepented.[28] Other preachers at the annual commemoration of the Gunpowder Treason or Plot (both titles were used for the event) would add a further horror—that the Roman Catholics who had hatched the plot took their murderous oaths at a Mass, thus turning the "Sacrament of Charity, the strongest tie of love that ever God made," into "an Oath to unite the malice of Satan."[29] Small wonder then that the intended Gunpowder conflagration joined with memories of Mary's persecuting fires in Smithfield to keep the national Protestant imagination of England white–hot for centuries to come.

The criticisms of the Roman Church offered by the preachers were of three kinds. First, there was strong objection to the political interference by the papacy in the affairs of sovereigns and of independent nations. There were also strong objections to the departures of Roman Catholic doctrines and practices from the norm of the Scriptures and the primitive Church. Finally, there was the complaint that Roman Catholicism encouraged both ignorance and superstition on the part of its parish priests and its laity.

The first charge—of Papal interference in the affairs of independent nations—is heard in many, many sermons. Bishop Buckeridge, contrary to papal claims, asserts in a sermon of 1606 delivered before King James, that kings have jurisdictional powers over persons ecclesiastical, that they have the right to summon councils and synods, that they have the duty to promulgate church laws and edicts, and that one of their responsibilities is to hear appeals and give decisions involving the restitution or deprivation of bishops, and other punishments.[30] He cites two Old Testament kings, Josiah and Hezekiah, as well as several Latin and Greek Fathers, as precedents or authorities.

John Donne claims that in the Roman Church "It is not the *Divine* that is the Minister of Salvation, but the Canonist."[31] He claims that Rome encourages treasonable "whisperers" who will strangle with a stiletto of gold, and smother with the down of phoenixes, that this leads to betrayals, and by implication makes a man unfaithful to his king.

Bishop Brownrig denies the primacy of Peter among the

apostles. "We find not any act of forwardness in *Peter*," he claims, "but it is made by the Papists an Argument of Precedency." He continues ironically, "Bellarmine reckons up twenty Arguments of his Prerogative. If *Christ* do but enter *Peter's* Boat, it is to invest him in a Supremacy. Whereas, not Supremacy, but Fervency, and sometimes Infirmity, often makes him, outstrip his fellow-Apostles."[32] Bishop Howson concurs with Brownrig in the view that Peter had no monarchical power over the rest of the bishops, and publishes four sermons with that sole aim in view.[33]

Henry King hits the target of political interference in the dead center, with this outburst:

> Had the consideration of States never entered the Conclave of Cardinals, and had the Iesuites not entred into the secrets of Kingdomes; but like Regular men lived within their Cloister, many Princes had gone downe to their Graves, *Sicca morte*, with white winding sheets, not stained or discoloured with their owne bloud.[34]

Bishop Morton, preaching on Romans 13:1, "Let every soul be subject to the higher Powers," says that the pope refuses this command: "*Every soul subject?* Not I, saith the *Pope*, and so all Popes of after-times, for we have power over all *Powers*, be they *Emperours* themselves, to kick off their Crowns with our feet; to depose their persons, and to dispose of their Kingdoms."[35] According to Morton, Jesus in his "render to Caesar" response to the Pharisees affirmed the duty of subjection to the temporal powers that be.[36]

Our preachers affirm with great unanimity that it is the duty of subjects to be obedient to the king, even if they feel themselves wronged. This is the uncompromising view of Brownrig, Prideaux, and Wren, and crosses the division of Calvinists and Arminians. Brownrig provides several biblical examples of wronged personages who did not rebel, and concludes: "but Magistrates, armed with Authority, if they prove heavy and injurious; they must be proofs of our patience, not provocations of our Revenge."[37] Prideaux preached a sermon at court, which was published in 1636, whose title was: "Reverence to Rulers."[38] Matthew Wren, in a sermon before King Charles I on the 7th of February, 1627, chose as his text Proverbs 24:21, which reads, "Feare GOD, my sonne, and the KING." The sermon ends with a charge to the consciences of his hearers that they show a due fear and respect to "God and the King, both together; and shew a due *feare* of them Both, but yet both in that Order."[39] We may take leave of this political aspect of anti-Roman Catholic sentiment with the objection of Donne that the papacy has become legalistic, that it uses force where persuasion is more appropriate, especially on the part of leaders of a religion supposedly dedicated to reconciliation. And he goes further, to maintain that the pope has imprisoned even the Holy Spirit:

> And since they could not make him [the Holy Spirit] King over Christ himselfe, they have made him a Prisoner, and a slave to Christs Vicar, and shut him up there, *In scrinio pectoris*, (as they call it) in that close imprisonment, in the breast and bosome of one man that Bishop: and so, the Holy Ghost is no longer a dove, a Dove in the Ark, a Dove with an Olive-branch, a Messenger of peace, but now the Holy Ghost is in a Bull.[40]

Donne descends to crude if amusing scurrility when he adds that the Holy Spirit was sent "from Rome in a Cloak-bagge, and upon a Post-horse" and hence is no longer omniscient but "as a Sea-Captaine receives a ticket" so the Holy Ghost waits to learn the truth from the papal legate.

To turn from the first criticism, of political interference, to the second, our Protestant divines are critical of Roman Catholicism's departure from the scriptural norm in both doctrine and practices. Donne, for example, claims that this makes them dive into a bottomless sea because they have no Scripture to anchor on,[41] and he insists that Scripture is enough and needs no bolstering by tradition:

Have we seen that face of Christ Jesus here upon earth, which Angels desired to see, and would we see a better face? Traditions perfecter than the Word? Have we read the four *Evangelists,* and would we have a better Library? Traditions fuller then the Word? *Cum credimus, nihil desideramus ultra credere;* when I beleeve God in Christ, dead, and risen againe according to the Scriptures, I have nothing else to beleeve.[42]

Traditions in the Roman Catholic Church are treated as malignant growths to be attacked with the scalpel of Scripture. This allows the metaphysical preachers to criticize various Roman Catholic doctrines: that of transubstantiation which lies behind the conception of the propitiatory sacrifice of the Mass; works-righteousness and the giving of communion in one kind; the belief in Purgatory as the intermediate state between Heaven and Hell and the indulgences that reduce the stay in Purgatory; and such practices as invoking the intercession of the saints (among whom the Virgin Mary is preeminent), and the adoration or at least veneration of relics and images.

Donne preached two sermons which he acknowledges as "meerly polemicall" on the text of I Corinthians 15:29, "Else what shall they doe which are baptized for the dead? If the dead rise not at all, why are they then baptized for the dead?" This was chosen simply because Catholics had made this text their justification for prayers for the dead, purgatory, and indulgences, beliefs which Donne sets out to refute point by point.[43] The particular objection was to purgatory, an imaginary place, rather than believing that those who had died should be commended to the care of God, though here it was the later Arminians rather than the Calvinists who would stress the value of such commendatory prayers in their intercessions at the Eucharist.[44]

Thomas Adams can speak for all Protestants in his contention that the Roman Catholics hunt desperately for scriptural texts to bolster their presumed invention of Purgatory. When he is exegeting Psalm 66:12, "We went through fire and through water: but thou broughtest us out into a wealthy place," he claims that the Catholics regard these words as "direct proofs of Purgatory," "with as good reason, as *Sedulus,* on that dreame of *Pharaoh's* Officer, Gen. 40:10. *A vine was before me; and in the vine were three branches:* sayes that the *Vine* signifies St. *Francis;* and the *three branches* the three Orders derived from him."[45] The whole structure of working out one's salvation by gaining indulgences to reduce the pains and years in Purgatory was, of course, the main thrust of Luther's criticisms of Roman Catholicism and a prime cause of the Reformation. As we can see, it continued to be a leading criticism of Roman Catholicism by later generations of Protestants.

Henry Smith claims that "as the Romanes then did crucifie Christ upon a Crosse, so they crucifie him now upon their Alter . . . ,"[46] while Adams sarcastically says that Catholic priests "have such almighty power that they can make their Maker."[47] Bishop Hacket, preaching on Christ's response to Satan (Matthew 4:10), "Thou shalt worship the Lord thy God, and him only shalt thou serve," decries all worship of the Blessed Virgin Mary and the other saints and angels as idolatry, the worship of creatures not of the Creator, to whom alone worship is due.[48] Bishop Senhouse accuses the Catholics of making the Virgin Mary another Diana of the Ephesians, of having turned "Maria to Minerva."[49] Donne takes a more pragmatic line, arguing that there is no point in bothering the saints for the very mercies God himself can give. He insists that if Christ had intended us to pray to the saints "he would have taught us to say, *Frater noster qui es in Coelis,* and not only *Pater noster.* . . ."[50]

The Church of England's distrust of relics was admirably expressed by Bishop Joseph Hall, like Donne a man of letters before he became a clergyman and a wit, who emphasized that the saints are honored and even imitated,

> But to dig up their holy bones, that I may borrow Luther's word, out of their quiet graves and to fall down before these worm-eaten monuments of the Saints, to expect from

them a divine power, whether of cure or of sanctification, equally to respect Francis's cowl, Anna's comb, Joseph's breeches, Thomas's shoe, as Erasmus complains, with the Sone of God Himself, can seem no better to us than a horrible impiety.[51]

Bishop Hacket's "Twentieth Sermon upon our Saviours Tentation" confutes the notion that either the relics of the saints, or the consecrated elements in Holy Communion, or images of Christ and his saints are to be adored.[52]

A final double charge against the Roman Catholic Church was its supposed encouragement of both ignorance and superstition. The charge of encouraging ignorance was based partly on the refusal to translate the Mass into the vernacular. It was also based upon the deliberate cultivation of mystery and miracle in that climactic service of the Mass, with its insistence upon the almost magical *ex opere operato* action in the sacrament, independent of any response of faith on the part of the recipients. There was also the imputation that the mass-priests in England were ignorant, though no sensible person could make the same charge against the Jesuits or the Benedictines. The second part of the charge was critical of the penchant of Catholicism for multiplying miracles beyond all reason and experience, and thus encouraging a superstition that builds on credulity. Like Latimer, Adams ridicules the childishness of empty ritual and sums up the charges in his inimitably racy way:

Come you into their Temples and behold their Pageants, and histrionicall gestures, bowings, mowings, windings and turnings; together with their service in an unknown language, and (like a deaf man, that sees men dancing when he heares no musicke) you would iudge them madde. Behold the masse-Priest with his baked god, towzing, toffing, and dandling, upward and downward, backward and forward, till at last, the iest turning into earnest, he chops it in his mouth at one bitte; whiles all stand gaping with admiration.[53]

Brownrig bluntly refers to "the gross error of the corporal presence of Christ's body in the Sacrament."[54] This Calvinist bishop would defend his statement, it might be supposed, by insisting that the risen body of Christ was located "at the right hand of God the Father" (as the Apostles' Creed has it), and he would also presumably argue for the spiritual presence of Christ in the Lord's Supper exactly as in the preaching of the Word, both of these beliefs confirmed by the internal testimony of the Holy Spirit. Further, following Calvin and Beza, he would almost certainly consider the "gross error" to be the confusion of the symbols (bread and wine) with the reality they signify (the Body and Blood of Christ).[55]

Bishop Francis White makes a passing injurious reference to the ignorance of the Roman priesthood: "For the priests of *Rome* beat so altogether upon Latine in the services of their Church, that most of them (such is the ignorance of their Masse-Priests) doe often breake it."[56] Donne is even more scathing in his denunciation of the miracle-mongering of the Catholic Church "where miracles for every natural disease may be had at some shrine, or miracle-shop, better cheap than a Medicine, a Drugge, a Simple at an apothecary's."[57]

The anti-Romanism of the Protestant pulpit in England was no more virulent than the anti-Protestantism of the Counter-Reformation pulpits. Calvinists and Arminians were equally critical, though the Calvinists were probably more strident because of their insistence upon an exclusively biblical theology. Even Laud, so often wrongly accused of pro-Catholic sentiments, while affirming the real presence in Holy Communion denied a corporal presence in the elements, and required faith for the reception of grace.[58] "Instrumental symbolism" or "dynamic receptionism" are terms which most fairly describe the seventeenth-century understanding of Christ's presence in the English Church's communion services. This view affirms both the objective reality of divine grace in the sacrament and subjective apprehension and reception of it by the believers in faith. According to this view the sacraments are seals of grace, communicating what they symbolize. To this interpretation the

Arminians would add a carefully guarded sense of sacrifice, avoiding any suggestion of the Church renewing the sacrifice of Calvary but insisting that the Church commemorates the eternal self-offering of Christ to the Father, in which the Church participates as Christ's Body on earth.

Anti-Puritan controversy

The Church of England maintained its "middle way" by criticizing Puritans together with Papists. In this case the Arminians were more critical than the Calvinists, since the latter regarded Geneva as, at least in part, their spiritual home.

What were the commonest charges of the metaphysical preachers against Puritans? They claimed that Puritans stressed the dominance of sermons to the neglect of prayers and sacraments, as well as condemning the preference, on the part of some Puritans, for extemporary prayer rather than the set forms of the Book of Common Prayer. They also maintained that Puritan anti-ceremonialism left the Church naked at worship, and led to casualness and even irreverence. They also deprecated the denial of the Christian Year with its special festivals, and the exaggerated concern for a narrow justification by faith which could lead to a total neglect of good works. Furthermore, the metaphysical preachers deplored the fissiparous tendencies within the Puritan ranks. The Arminians among the preachers also decried the limited atonement consequent upon the insistence on double predestination, and the assertion of the irresistibility of grace with its resulting depreciation of human reason and freedom in the response to grace. These criticisms we shall find expressed in vivid passages of the sermons.

Bishop Lancelot Andrewes complains that there was much criticism of auricular confession, "but now all is turned to Auricular Profession" for "all *godlinesse* with some, what is it, but *hearing a sermon.*"[59] Donne insists that God's house is a house of prayer, not of preaching,[60] and Bishop Buckeridge pillories those who "turne Oratories into Auditories, and Temples into scholes, and all adoration and worship into hearing of a Sermon: As if all, soule and body, were turned into an eare. . . ."[61]

321

John Cosin in a Consecration sermon in 1626, while not wishing to decry preaching, thinks it is thought too much the exclusive duty of the clergy, "as if we had nothing else to do, and an office independent too, as if we were all bishops when we preach."[62]

From the days of Elizabeth the Puritans had mounted a campaign against vestments, such as surplices and copes, that were reminiscent of the older Roman sacerdotalism—Milton would later call them "rags from old Aaron's wardrobe." They also attacked the "noxious ceremonies," signing with the cross at baptism, kneeling at the reception of Holy Communion, and the ring in marriage. All of these were thought of as retaining ceremonial for which there was no scriptural authority and therefore relics of Romanism.[63] Since these ceremonies had been abolished in other Reformed Churches, the Puritans wanted them removed from the English Reformed Church. They were told that these were things indifferent, neither commanded nor refused—*adiaphora*. The Puritans' reply was that, whatever was the case in theory, the Prayer Book and ecclesiastical canons *demanded* that they be used and that those who did not use them were disciplined. The counter reply, justifying their use, was that these were decent and becoming customs approved by the primitive Church. Moderate Puritans accepted them as a condition of remaining in the Church of England until there was further opportunity to have them abolished. Ministers who scrupled them, like Henry Smith, had to be satisfied with remaining as lecturers, supplementing parochial worship with weekday sermons. Finally, many Puritans unable to bear the yoke of persecuting Arminian bishops (who were equally convinced of the rightness of their ceremonies) sought refuge in Holland or in the New World.

This issue of ceremonies smoldered throughout the seventeenth century and was inevitably reflected in the sermons. In this matter the Calvinist bishops were less rigorous in enforcing ecclesiastical law than the Arminians, though they had no alternative but to be defenders of the ceremonial. Both Calvinists and Arminians were united in deploring the Separatists as schismatics. Defenders of ceremonies asserted that they were suited to the mixed spiritual–sensuous nature of human beings, were apt reminders of the homage due to the King of Kings, as well as incentives to religious adoration and confession, and as ways of encouraging the common people to respect the hierarchy in Church and State. As the contention between the royalist and parliamentarian parties became more acute, the Puritans began to feel the iron hand in the soft sleeves of the Laudian prelacy. They started to equate ceremonialism with absolutism, pomposity, and pretentiousness, and saw ceremonies as empty formalities, and, as a result, tended to equate simplicity with sincerity. Arminians, however, equated ceremonialism with reverence to God and respect to the king who ruled by divine right.[64]

Andrewes does not mention the Puritans but clearly has them in mind when speaking thus ironically: "A plausible theame, not to burthen the Church with ceremonies: the Church to be free: which hath almost freed the Church of all decencie."[65] Donne at St. Paul's Cathedral obviously had difficulties with those occasionally unceremonious and irreverent Puritans, who had status in the City Guilds where they were numerous and influential. He may have had one in mind, but several were being rebuked in the name of one, for his refusal to bow his knees in prayer. Presumably the Puritan critic thought this was idolatry or conformity with Catholic ceremonial, and at the Communion service might be interpreted as favoring transubstantiation. Donne's application of his text was a pointed as his indignation:

> *Deus stetit,* saies *David, God standeth in the Congregation;* [Psalm 82:1] does God stand there and wilt thou sit, sir, and never kneele? I would speake so, as the congregation should not know whom I meane; but so, as that they whom it concernes, might know I meane them; I would speake: for, I must say, that there come some persons to this Church, and persons of example to many that come with them, of whom (excepting some few, who must therefore

have their praise from us, as no doubt they have their thanks and blessings from God) I never saw Master nor servant kneele, at his comming into this Church, or at any part of divine service . . . And, if humility in the service of God here, be madnesse, I would more of us were out of our wits, then we are; I would all our Churches were, to that purpose, Bedlams.[66]

Another Puritan objection to the Prayer Book was its provision of festivals and fasts marking special days in the Christian Year. The Puritans themselves kept the weekly Sabbath or Lord's Day as the single red-letter day, with occasional and irregular days of thanksgiving and humiliation to mark divine providences in national, local, family, or individual life. The Sabbath was important to Puritans because on it the Creator rested from his works, and it symbolized the eschatological rest of heaven. Further, it was a day to be devoted to developing the spiritual life: attendance at worship; preaching of the Word; catechism, prepared for and followed by private and family prayers at home; the requirement that sermons should be rehearsed by the children and servants in the presence of the head of the family. It was an intense and serious regimen.[67]

With Puritan dissenters in mind, Dr. John Howson, a future bishop but at the time Vice-Chancellor of Oxford University, preached a sermon "in defence of the Festivities of the Church of England" on 17 November 1602, which was republished in 1603. He claims that festival days are to mark the extraordinary blessings of God in the Christian saga, and gives as his authority the Law of Moses which states that days should be set aside to signalize great occasions for gratitude to God. Other reasons Howson adduces are that this has been the practice and authority of Christ's Church since its foundation according to Christ's promise given in Matthew 18:4, and the injunction of Paul the Apostle that "Everything must be done decently and in order" (I Corinthians 14:40). His argument is supported by patristic references to Ambrose, Gregory the Great, Origen, Eusebius, Augustine twice, and Bernard of Clairvaux.[68]

John Cosin cannot hide his impatience at Puritans who decry the special days of the Church Year, and excoriates them thus:

> I'd warrant you every tradesman will tell you (specially if he has got a twang in his head) that all these observations of times are but popish customs, they will not celebrate ye a day longer, nay, not so long neither, but for the law; the day of the Gentiles' calling, [Epiphany] what is that to them? They have a tribe and a calling by themselves that was marked out for heaven sure long before either Jews or Gentiles were stirring.[69]

In fairness to the Church of England, however, the Prayer Book did not reproduce the Roman Catholic Calendar indiscriminately, for, with the exception of the New Testament saints, it retained the Christological and rejected the sanctoral Calendar.

Puritans also often preferred spontaneous, extemporary prayers to what they considered to be the dulling routine of set prayers which resulted in the atrophy of ministerial gifts of prayer. They claimed Romans 8:26–27 was the charter for their preference, where Paul affirms that "in like manner the Spirit also helpeth our infirmity: for we know not how to pray as we ought; but the Spirit himself maketh intercession for us with groanings which cannot be uttered; And he that searcheth the hearts knoweth what is the mind of the Spirit, because he maketh intercession for the saints, according to the will of God." The Independents (and the Separatists before them) refused even to use the Lord's Prayer because they thought it was a model for individual prayers rather than one to be repeated.

Donne has little patience for the abolition of the Lord's Prayer, and considers this attitude no better than that of the Cathari who left out the petition for forgiveness in the Lord's prayer since they thought they needed none, but "our new men leave out the whole Prayer, because the same Spirit that spake in Christ, speaks in their extemporall prayers, and they can pray as well as Christ can teach them."[70] Donne had equal impatience with extemporary preaching. The penitent thief on the Cross made a brief extemporary sermon: although he had premeditated nothing, says Donne, "he is no more a precedent for extemporal preaching, then he is for stealing. He was a Thief before, and he was an extemporal preacher at last: But he teaches no body else to be either."[71]

The other major criticisms of Puritanism are of its theology: in particular what was considered to be its over-emphasis on faith to the derogation of good works; the limited nature of its salvation, presupposed by asserting the doctrine of predestination; and the low evaluation of human reason and of the will implied by the doctrine of the irresistibility of grace.

Cosin insists that Puritans do not even follow out their own order of salvation in the Pauline manner, but abbreviate it in a jump from predestination and election to glorification,[72] eliminating the intervening stages of the *ordo salutis*.

Donne faults the Calvinist and Puritan reduction of the potential number of the saved in the doctrine of double predestination. His marginal reference to the Cathari indicates that he has the Puritans in mind (even if he is too shrewd to mention them by name), who "will abridge and contract the large mercies of God in Christ, and elude and frustrate, in a great part, the generall promises of God." They are unwilling "that God should speak so loud as to say He would have all men saved, and loth that Christ should spread his armes or shed his bloud in such compasse, as might fall upon *all*. Men that think that no sinne can hurt them because they are *elect*, and that every sin makes every other man a *Reprobate*."[73]

William Barlow exposes the danger of an exclusive emphasis on *sola fide* (by faith alone) and claims that it is hypocrisy "which in the *invisibilitie* of *sole-faith* (from hence misunderstood) may freely *cousen* and *dissemble*; hence *stupid security*" which "causes reason and conscience to stay dead asleep." He adds that, while it was once a matter of hard work to be a Christian, now it is merely a matter of "*dispute & talking*, now of *doctrin* only."[74] If the one danger was resting in faith without good works, the other was in too much prying into God's will and the anxious introspection that the doctrine of predestination provoked. This was the view of the future Bishop John Bowle, who thought the remedy was to link each stage of the order of salvation to Christ. He advised:

> Looke into every linck of the chaine of Heaven: How are we predestinated to the adoption of children? By Jesus Christ . . . How are we called to glory? By Jesus Christ . . . How are we justified? By Jesus Christ?[75]

Donne was particularly worried by the futile attempts to wrest secrets from God—the *Arcana Imperii.*[76]

In another sermon the charity and warmth of the great dean is exhibited in his unwillingness to anticipate the Final Judgment and, without scriptural warrant, reduce the number who will be saved. He urges: "Let us embrace the way which God hath given us, which is, the knowledge of his Sonne, Christ Jesus: what other way God may take with others, how he wrought upon *Iob* and *Naaman*, and such others as were not in the *Covenant*, let us not inquire too closely, too curiously, determine too peremptorily, pronounce too uncharitably." He goes on to argue that the 144,000 of the saved named in the Apocalypse is only a term for a vast multitude. If the term be restricted to the Jews, then Genesis 22:17 must be recalled, where Abraham's seed is likened to the stars of heaven and the dust of the earth, and "there are an infinite number of stars more than we can distinguish, and so, by God's grace, there may be an infinite number of soules saved, more than those, of whose salvation, we discerne the *wayes*, and the *meanes.* "[77]

There was an inevitable struggle between the Presbyterian conviction of the parity of ministers, and the Church of England's commitment to the hierarchical conception of the ministry of bishops, priests, and deacons. Archbishop Laud felt that there should be hierarchy in Church and State, in parallel form. Moreover, he was of the opinion that the other Reformed

Churches with their elders and deacons were giving too much power to the laity, who would always demand more, and that this was destructive of good order. His answer to the Presbyterian system of church government was to insist, "Well, first, this 'parity' was never left to the Church but Christ. He left Apostles, and disciples under them. No 'parity.' " He continued: "It was never in use with the Church since Christ; no Church ever, anywhere, till this last age, without a Bishop." Then he made a prophesy in 1625, which echoed James I's Hampton Court prophesy, "No bishop, no king." These were words which foresaw his own downfall twenty years later, and that of his king four years after that:

> And one thing more I will be bold to speak out of a like duty to the Church of England, and the "house of David." They, whoever they be, that would overthrow *sedes Ecclesiae*, the "seats of ecclesiastical government," will not spare, if ever they get power, to have a pluck at the "throne of David." And there is not a man that is for "parity,"—all fellows in the Church—but he is not for monarchy in the State.[78]

Finally, as an extension of the previous criticism, the leaders of the Church of England were convinced that there was a fissiparous principle in Puritanism which was bound to lead to schism after schism, and possibly to heresy as well. That long-lived Calvinist, Bishop Morton of Durham, is scathing in his criticisms of the sectaries, using the Pauline metaphor of the Church as Christ's Body and He its directing Head:

> But in these times the hand and foot both mutine because they are not eyes and except our Coblers and Weavers bee allowed for Ministers, they will acknowledge no head nor member; how these should receive so much tolleration anywhere within this Church I know not, except men thought themselves worthy to bee led with blind guides: when as there might be as true Doctrin some time expected

from Bedlam, whereof some examples might be given, if such Doctrines were not fitter for a Stage then a Pulpit.[79]

He adds that such enthusiasts, who always inveigh against the papacy, are popish themselves because they are supreme and infallible judges of doctrine!

Thomas Jackson says their major principle is to be as far as possible from the Roman Catholics in everything: "*Antarticks* they are, & thinke they can never be farre enough from the *North-pole* untill they runne from it unto the *South-pole*, and pitch their habitation in *terrâ incognitâ* in a world and Church unknowne to the ancients, and I feare unto themselves."[80]

Relation to the Primitive Church

The primary authority of the Church of England for its doctrine and customs in worship and government was Scripture. Where, however, the Bible was silent or ambiguous, secondary and tertiary authorities were employed. The secondary authority was the tradition of the Primitive Undivided Church of the first four General Councils.[81] In the creeds and canons of such Councils, and in their interpretations by the Church Fathers, the standards for doctrine, liturgy, and church polity were laid down. The tertiary authority, human reason, a reflection of the Divine intelligence, was used only when Scripture and primitive tradition were not decisive, and when it did not contradict either the Bible or tradition.

It is the use of these secondary and tertiary authorities which distinguished the Church of England from the Roman Catholic Church, other Reformed Churches, and the Puritans of the extreme left wing. Roman Catholicism was viewed as having departed from Scripture in some doctrines and customs, especially after the split between the Western and the Eastern Churches, and of having developed its own traditions. Puritans insisted upon an almost exclusive reliance on the biblical criteria of doctrine, customs, ceremonial, and polity. It was these distinctive customs, neither Roman nor Reformed, that required the controversialists of the Church of England to familiarize themselves with biblical hermeneutics, patrology, and ancient and modern controversial writings. John Jewel's *First Apology*[82] had concentrated its fire and learning against the Roman Catholics in the interest of the Reformed Church of England, while Richard Hooker's *Of the Laws of Ecclesiastical Polity*[83] was a defense primarily prepared against the Puritans. The citation of the Fathers became a distinctive mark of the sermons of the metaphysical preachers in both controverted and uncontroverted matters throughout the seventeenth century. This lore was as characteristic as their wit.

From the days of the Elizabethan Settlement, the Church of England was deeply attached to the primitive Church. Why was this so? It was a normative ideal because it was solidly founded on the Scriptures, and its doctrine, polity, and worship were defended and expounded in the writings of the early Church Fathers and the decrees of the first four General Councils in the first five centuries of the history of the Christian Church.

The affection of the metaphysical preachers for the early Church Fathers is proved by the frequency with which they were quoted or referred to in their sermons. This holds good for both Calvinists and Arminians, which we shall see by analyzing the sermons of the Arminians John White and John Donne first, and then those of three Calvinist prelates, Prideaux, Henry King, and Ussher.

John White's Paul's Cross sermon, delivered on 24 March 1615, cites twenty-seven authors in forty references, including three references each to Ambrose, Augustine, and Chrysostom; two each to Gregory of Nazianzen, Tertullian, and Epiphanius; and one each to Justin Martyr, Cyprian, and Jerome.[84]

Potter and Simpson, the editors of the modern critical edition of *The Sermons of John Donne*, estimate that Dean Donne cites Augustine seven hundred times in his one hundred and sixty sermons, as compared to approximately seven thousand biblical references.[85] In the completed analysis of three of the ten volumes of the same edition, while there is a total of 226 references to Augustine, there are seventy-six references to Jerome, fifty-eight to Chrysostom, and fifty to Tertullian.[86]

John Prideaux preached a sermon at court in 1636, entitled

The Patronage of Angels. He cites twenty-one authors and has a total of twenty-five references. Most are to authors of commentaries on the Bible, and most are Roman Catholic, but there are also two references each to Augustine, Jerome, Gregory the Great, and John of Damascus; and one each to Hilary, Basil, and the great Dominican, Aquinas.[87]

Henry King's twelve sermons, offering *An Exposition Upon the Lords Prayer* (1628), were delivered in St. Paul's Cathedral. Extending to 365 pages in print, they contain fifty-eight references to Augustine, fifteen to Ambrose, twelve to Chrysostom, nine to Cyprian, eight each to Jerome and Tertullian, six to Bernard, four each to Popes Leo and Gregory the Great and Minutius Felix, and two each to Origen, Gregory of Nazianzen, Eusebius, and John of Damascus. There are also many references to classical authors, Catholic controversialists, and Reformed divines.[88]

James Ussher in a sermon in St. Margaret's, Westminster preached before the House of Commons on 18 February 1620, includes thirty-one references in forty pages, many of them to Roman Catholic expositors, but also he has the following patristic references: six to Augustine, and one each to Jerome, Cyril of Jerusalem, Lactantius, and Sozomen, the ecclesiastical historian.[89]

These five preachers are fairly typical in that they regularly employ citations and references from the Fathers in their sermons. They were, of course, more likely to do so on special occasions and in special contexts, as for example if preaching at court before a king who, like James I, admired learning, or before the nobility and gentry at Paul's Cross, or before the gentry in cathedrals and the chapels of the colleges of the universities or at Inns of Court, rather than in country parishes. Even in the context of ordinary sermons some found it difficult to break the habit, and it would seem that even some rustics felt cheated if they were not bombarded with citations.[90]

The polity of the Church of England

The polity of the Church of England came under fire from opposing ends. The Roman Catholics insisted that only the successor of Peter, the pope, had the right and authority to govern the Church. In this he was assisted by his advisers the cardinals, and the threefold ministry of bishops, priests, and deacons. The defenders of the Church of England denied that Peter ever had a primacy over other bishops, except insofar as there were several patriarchs in the early Church, all more or less equal. Thus the primacy of Rome was seen as an usurpation, undoubtedly stimulated by two facts: Rome was the burial place of the two earliest great leaders of the Church after the earthly life of the Incarnate Lord was over, namely, Peter and Paul; in addition, it was the capital of the greatest empire the world had known until the Christian era and for centuries afterwards. When the empire disintegrated under the attacks of the Goths, Huns, and Vandals, it was the steadfastness of the popes that held what remained of it together. The "Rock" of Peter was interpreted by Protestant exegetes as the confession of the divinity of Jesus Christ which the Holy Spirit enabled Peter to make, not Peter as a person. As we have seen, the temporal power asserted by the pope to interfere in the life of earthly kingdoms was much resented by earthly rulers. The Church of England preachers, accused of Erastianism and of being totally under the thumb of the territorial ruler, delighted in pointing out that the most important General Councils, from Nicaea in 325 A.D. onwards, were called to define Christian orthodoxy and to reject heresy (Arianism in the first case), and were summoned to meet by emperors. Constantine, the first Christian Roman emperor who convened the Council of Nicaea, was happy to be called "the thirteenth apostle." Few clergy in the Church of England, except the impatient Puritans of the Independent and Presbyterian groups, were disturbed that its polity resembled Lutheranism rather than that of the Reformed Churches in Scotland, Germany, and France. And the temporary dominance of Presbyterianism was the price paid by English Puritanism for the assistance of the Scots in the Solemn League and Covenant of 1643.

It was only when the king, Charles I, ruled without Parliament as an absolutist, that the patience of some of the Calvinists in the Church grew thin, and even a prelate like Ussher proposed the establishment of an apocopated apostolic order of reduced bishops. Otherwise all bishops, whether Arminian or Calvinist, believed alike that the only possible relation of all three orders (bishops, priests, and deacons) to their ecclesiastical superior was obedience. Even Donne, who flattered the king far less than most royal chaplains, was heard in a sermon preached at Whitehall on the 30 April 1620 to urge the congregation to gratitude because they were born in a "Christian Church, a Reformed Church, in a Monarchy, in a Monarchy composed of Monarchies, and in the time of such a Monarch, as is a Peace-maker, and a peace-preserver, both at home and abroad. . . ."[91] Bishop Brownrig, in his first Gunpowder treason sermon, observed that *"No wrong or injury can exempt or discharge our persons from our lawful Soveraign"* and illustrates this from the patience of the Hebrews under Pharaoh, the refusal of David when pursued by Saul to rebel, as also Jeremiah when pursued by Zedekiah. Yet Brownrig insists that magistrates must not wield their powers recklessly, and "they must be proofs of our patience, not provocations of our Revenge."[92] Prideaux's title for a sermon preached at court tells its own story, *Reverence to Rulers,*[93] as does the text that Bishop Matthew Wren chose for his discourse, taken from Proverbs 24:21: "Feare GOD, my sonne, and the KING."[94] The sermon ends with the charge that both God and the king be served, but with the priority going to God.

Several preachers also referred to the ecclesiastical rights and privileges of kings. Lancelot Andrewes, in a sermon preached before James I in Hampton Court on Sunday, 28 September 1606, after ransacking the Bible for precedents, finds the power to summon assemblies was never in the priests' hands but always in the king's, even for religious and ecclesiastical purposes;[95] and he notes that the first seven ecumenical councils were summoned by emperors;[96] and that, on the breakdown of the Roman empire, kings exercised the same authority.[97] As we have seen earlier in this chapter, Buckeridge and Laud acknowledge the king's considerable disciplinary powers over the episcopate, and insist that hierarchy in State and Church, maintained by obedience of the lower orders to the higher, supports the fabric of the nation which otherwise would be torn to shreds.

It was when this seemed likely to happen that the pulpit sounded the summons to unity and the closing of the ranks. The preachers are largely one in their appeals for unity against the divisions caused by separatists. But they also combine to revolt against the assertion of absolutism in Church and State, although the preachers among the metaphysicals seemed largely unaware of the last. In fact royal absolutism had been encouraged by their obsequious and servile flattery of royalty, and their failure to forewarn Charles of its dangers, as the prophet Nathan had warned David.

In any case the metaphysical pulpits in the late 1620s and (too late) in the 1630s and early 1640s rang with the appeals of Morton, Senhouse, Ussher, Mayne, and others for toleration and charity. Ussher, the archbishop of Armagh and a Calvinist, and Jasper Mayne, Student of Christ Church and an Arminian, echo each other's sentiments in their appeals to stop name-calling in the Church. Ussher, preaching before the king at Greenwich on 25 June 1627, used Paul's First Letter to the Corinthians (14:33) as his text: "For God is not the author of confusion, but of peace, as in all churches of the saints." He urged, "I advise that all opprobrious names be suppressed. I see that those that will not yield to that new doctrine which hath disturbed the low countries [Arminianism], there is an odious name cast upon them, and they are accounted puritans, which is a thing tending to dissension."[98] He continued by saying in the most solemn way that even if he maintained the five points of Arminianism, since "the greatest number of prophets blow their horns another way, I hold, I were bound in conscience to hold my peace, and keep my knowledge to myself, rather than by unseasonable uttering of it to disturb the peace of the Church."[99]

Jasper Mayne also criticised name-calling in a sermon preached in Carfax Church, Oxford, on 9 August 1646, using

I Corinthians 1:10 as his text: "Now I beseech you, Brethren, that ye all speak the same thing, and that there be no Divisions among you: but that ye be perfectly joyned together in the same minde, and in the same judgement." Having pointed out how seriously Roundheads and Cavaliers misjudged each other, he added, "But we for some late yeares have chosen to our selves names more moderne, and fallible to divide our selves by; whilst some have said, 'We are of Calvin,' others, 'We are of Arminius,' others, 'We are of Socinus.' These, to the blemish and reproach of the Christian Religion, have beene made names of strife, and faction."[100] Alas, too few preachers stressed the theme of unity and were too late to prevent the tearing apart of the English Church in the civil war. It is a division which has still not been mended three hundred and twenty-five years later.

Worship: the liturgy and sacraments

If the polity of the Church was irregular in combining Catholic elements with Protestantism, so was the worship, and for the same reason. This was felt to require explanation because of the deviations from both Roman Catholic and Reformed norms.

Having a liturgy in itself was not abnormal since all Lutheran and Reformed Churches had a liturgy, including the Church of Geneva with its *forme et manière des prières, selon la coûtume de l'église ancienne.* At the outset, the Puritans did not object to the idea of a liturgy, but only to some particulars in the rubrics, the ceremonies, and the wording of the Book of Common Prayer. These included the three "noxious ceremonies," the requisite use of the surplice, the wording in the services of Thanksgiving after childbirth (commonly called "the churching of women"), and in the burial office with its declaration that all were buried "in sure and certain hope of resurrection" to life everlasting.

It was only with the growth of the Independents (proto-Congregationalists) with their demand for free prayers, and with the compromise made between them and the Presbyterians at the Westminster Assembly of 1644, that the Book of Common Prayer was rejected by the nation. In its stead was produced a *Directory for the Publick Worship of God*. In it topics and rubrics were provided, but the actual wording of the prayers were left to the discretion of the ministers presiding in worship. The Book of Common Prayer was now regarded by the dominant Puritans and Roundheads as an Arminian engine of despotism. They saw it as the means of displacing conscientious ministers, and its high ceremonial of crossings and bowings as idolatrous compliance with Rome, this resulting in the disuse of ministerial gifts of prayer.[101]

For their part, the Roman Catholics saw in the vernacular English liturgy a diminution of mystery and the falling into disuse of Latin, the international language of scholars and religion that had united western Europe since the fall of the Roman Empire. Communion in both kinds seemed to them unnecessary since the wafer symbolized the entire body of Christ, which included the blood. They saw the rejection of the miracle of transubstantiation for its inconsistent substitute explanations, varying from virtualism to memorialism, as the intrusion of rationalism and reductionism. Furthermore, they viewed the inclusion of medieval collects and high ceremonial as an attempt to suggest a continuity in religion where discontinuity reigned, as a deception that would only fool the simpleminded.[102]

Clearly, it was important to defend the Elizabethan Settlement and the Stuart "Compromise" with the best available skill at Paul's Cross and in the other leading pulpits in the cathedrals, Inns of Court, university chapels, and in the larger parish churches, as well as at court. This the metaphysical preachers did with great loyalty, learning, and shrewdness.

John Donne, having Puritan criticisms in mind, offers a pragmatic defense of the Book of Common Prayer. He insists that public prayers require public authorization; just as the law of the land is one's own law, so the prayers of the Church are our own prayers, because as sons we have some interest in them. Hence

Baptisme is mine, and my Absolution is mine because the Church has given them to me, and so are her prayers mine. You could scarce thank a man for an extemporal Elegy or Epigram or an Panergerique in your praise, if it coust the Poet or the Orator no paines.[103]

Moreover, there were higher grounds on which to defend the Prayer Book. It was, as all Protestants familiar with Foxe's *Book of Martyrs* remembered, sealed with the blood of Cranmer and the other Marian Protestant Martyrs burnt at the stake. It was therefore a holy book, second only in importance to the Bible itself.

Donne himself had insisted in an Easter sermon, preached in St. Paul's cathedral in 1624, that the value of preaching the Word and celebrating the sacraments was not to be reduced to pragmatic considerations. Rather it was to be based upon the highest theological authority: they were ordinances instituted by Christ to be used by his Church. In typically imaginative language he declares:

Christs first tongue was a tongue that might be heard; He spoke to the shepheards by angels; His second tongue was a Star, a tongue which might be seene; He spoke to the Wisemen of the East by that. Hearken after him in the two wayes: As he speakes to thine eare, (and to thy soul, by it), in the preaching of his Word, as he speakes to thine eye, (and so to thy soule by that), in the exhibition of his Sacraments: and thou shalt have thy part in this first Resurrection.[104]

Sometimes, because the controversy between Calvinists and Arminians was so bitter on the issue of ceremonies, one might imagine that this was all that mattered, for this is so stressed in the sermons of Andrewes,[105] Donne,[106] Howson,[107] and Laud.[108] Even Fuller finds it necessary to protest against the profanation and defilement of those who "turne the Church into a Counting-house, there to rate their neighbours both to value their estates, and too often revile their persons. Others make it a Market-place there to bargaine in; yea, some turne it into a Kennell for their dogs, and a mew for their Hawkes, which they bring with them."[109] Yet despite the attention irreverence receives, and the correlative emphasis on ceremonial as good manners towards God as in Buckeridge's sermons,[110] the Church of England was more concerned through its preachers to emphasize the celebration of the sacraments as channels of Divine grace.

No one has preached more passionately or at greater length on the importance of the two Dominical sacraments of Baptism and Holy Communion than John Donne. His dependence upon Calvin's doctrine of the sacraments is clear from his calling them "seals," for Calvin defined them as *sigilla Verbi*, seals or confirmations of God's promises in Christ, the Word made flesh. In a sermon preached before the King in Whitehall on 24 February 1625/6, he attests, "God hath given thee *Seales* of his *Mercie* in both his *Sacraments*; Seales in *White*, and Seales in *Redde Waxe*; Seales in the participation of the candor and innocencie of his *Sonne*, in thy *Baptisme*, and Seales in the participation of his *Body* and *Bloud*, in the other."[111] He did not affirm, with the Roman Catholics, that the sacraments worked *ex opere operato*, that is independently of the virtue of the officiant or of the faith of the recipients. Nor did he restrict the value of Communion to a recalling of the redemptive act of Christ in the Upper Room and on Calvary, as Zwingli was thought to have done, turning the Lord's Supper into a badge of church membership.[112] He described the seals as "marks and testimonies of thine inseparable presence with me, in thy Baptisme, and other Ordinances."[113] As Winfried Schleiner[114] has pointed out, the images of sealing and stamping are important in Donne's general theology as well as in reference to the sacraments. The saga of salvation can be designated in terms of sealing or stamping by three successive steps. First, the Divine Logos (or Reason of God) in the Creation impressed a seal upon man that reflects the Divine image. This image was then defaced in the Fall, and needed to be restamped. The Incarnation of the Logos made possible the restamping of the Divine image, and thus the renewing of the *imago Dei*. This, in fact, is what Donne asserts[115] with the assumption that the Divine image is renewed in Holy Communion thus eliminating actual sins. A parallel case is Baptism with its removal of the effects of original sin. Sealing was, in the incarnation, a legal confirmation or ratification for Donne of the inheritance of forgiveness for the Christian, and of the promise of eternal life, a guarantee of God's continuing mercies.

Brownrig's sermon on Acts 2:38 ("Then Peter said unto them, Repent, and be baptized every one of you in the Name of Jesus Christ, for the remission of sins, and ye shall receive the gift of the Holy Ghost,") claims that four qualities of water make it an apt conveying symbol for Baptism. It drowns all things, including the penitent's sins so that "when he enters into this Red-Sea, all his iniquities are drowned and abolished." (We may observe that the Red Sea signifies the blood of Christ shed on the Cross to attain reconciliation and atonement; and the Red Sea from Egypt to the opposite coast was typologically considered as good a liberation for Jews as Christ's *transitus* from the Cross to the Resurrection and Ascension was for the benefit of the Christians moving from earth to heaven). Secondly, as water quenches thirst, so also Baptism helps to quench concupiscence. Thirdly, water is a cleansing element and it washes away filthiness as does Baptism. Fourthly, it is fructifying element, so this "Sacrament of Divine institution and benediction is a Fountain of living Water, a Font, and Laver of Regeneration."[116] Brownrig concludes his sermon by declaring that the Holy Spirit conveys three gifts: a sanctifying and enabling grace, a seal confirming our assurance, and the *osculum* or kiss of comfort and consolation for us.[117] Once again the Augustinian-Calvinist tradition of the sacraments as communicating and conveying, not merely commemorating, seals is evident in Brownrig's explanation. Donne defends the ceremonies and other appurtenances of the worship of the middle way in a characteristically vivid fashion:

. . . we stript not the Church into a nakedness, nor into rags; we divested her not of her possessions, nor of her Ceremonies, but received such a Reformation at home, by their hands whom God enlightened, as left her neither in a Dropsie, nor in a consumption; neither in a superfluous and cumbersome fatness, nor in an uncomely and faint leanness and attenuation . . . We need not clime up seven hills, nor wash ourselves seven times in a Lake for it.[118]

The carnival outfit of Rome and the funereal black of Geneva were both avoided, as well as the caperings of the former and the sepulchral gloom of the Genevan gown of the latter.

Fuller explanations can, of course, be found in catechisms and treatises, but it is interesting that so much doctrinal and devotional information can be provided by the way in sermons.

This chapter has attempted to show that metaphysical preachers, whether Calvinist or Arminian, loyally defended the uniquely middle way ecclesiology of the Church of England, despite the growing tensions that became more divisive in the late thirties and early forties of the century. One might also hazard some generalizations about some slight differences in which these distinctive themes of the Church, the Prayer Book and its ceremonial, and the sacraments, were handled respectively by Calvinists and Arminians.

While both party representatives were equally critical of Roman Catholicism, the Calvinists seemed to view it as a greater threat than the Arminians because it had departed from Scripture, whereas at the outset the Arminians were readier to grant a more subordinate role to the tradition of the Early Church than the Calvinists. The Calvinist bishops, reluctant as they might first seem to be, ultimately had no option but to appeal to this tradition for the defense of their position in the hierarchy, and because they had to discipline the more rigorous Calvinist separatists. The Arminians were closer to the Roman Catholics than the Calvinists in the higher role they gave to both reason and human freedom, and also to high ceremonial. But the Calvinists took the deleterious effects of original sin as a consequence of the Fall more seriously than the Arminians. In their understanding of Holy Communion, their doctrine (however different the ceremonial, vestments, and architectural setting desired by the Arminians) was very close indeed. But it was the Calvinists who gave a high evaluation to preaching, while the Arminians (outstanding preachers as several were) thought the end of preaching was prayer, and the end of the sacraments the adoration of God. Some of the Arminians also practised celibacy, fewer of the Calvinists did so, though they were faithful enough in their marriages. One might suppose that the Calvinists initially would favor the lonely red-letter day of their Calendar, the Sabbath, rather than the Church Year with its great feasts at Christmas, Easter, and Whitsuntide, and its fasting in Lent. This would certainly seem to be the case for Henry Smith and Thomas Adams, but Calvinist bishops such as Brownrig and Hacket, produced impressive festival sermons with great regularity, vying with Andrewes, Donne, and Cosin in this respect. Indeed, both Hacket and Brownrig treat us to no fewer than seven sermons each on the Transfiguration, and Hacket has a total of seventy sermons on the Christian Year, as compared with sixty-seven for Andrewes and fifty-five for Donne.

It is their basic unity rather than their party differences that is the striking factor, though it was far from being apparent to most of their contemporaries and, in many cases, to themselves. It is, however, only too easy to judge a past and divisive era with the benefit of two centuries' hindsight and so Cowley's reminder is in order: "A warlike, various, and a tragical age is best to write of, but worst to write in."[119] The very same applies to our own century.

Nonetheless, one can still wish that the metaphysical preachers (as well as the plainer Puritan pulpiteers) could have written with the abounding charity of a Donne. He who had been racked by anxiety over where the true Church was to be found, and was driven by deep religious divisions in his own family, whose brother was a martyred Catholic priest and whose mother remained Catholic to the end, penned these words to

Sir H. R. in which he refused to fetter or imprison religion, "without immuring it in a *Rome*, or a *Wittenberg*, or a *Geneva*; they are all virtual beames of one Sun . . . Religion is Christianity."[120] Donne was one of the earliest ecumenists.

NOTES

1. This interpretation is ably set forth in the essay of Nicholas Tyacke, "Puritanism, Arminianism and Counter-Revolution" in *The Origins of the English Civil War*, ed. Conrad Russell (London, 1973), 119–143, especially 120 and 130. See also Dewey D. Wallace, Jr., *Puritans and Predestination. Grace in English Protestant Theology, 1529–1695* (Chapel Hill, North Carolina, 1982), 220, fn. 2, for the author's independent arrival at the same conviction as Tyacke. Both however do exaggerate the Laudian leaning towards Rome, for neither Laud nor the Anglican Arminians accepted transubstantiation though affirming the "real presence" in Holy Communion, nor did they accept purgatory, relics, invocation of the saints, etc. Furthermore, they were critical of the political interference of the popes and they remained Protestants with a deep respect for the undivided early Church and the ecumenical councils of the first six centuries. This can be seen, for example, in part of John Cosin's letter to the Countess of Peterborough in Cosin's *Works*, 5 vols. (Library of Anglo-Catholic Theology, Oxford, 1843–1855), 4: 332–336, also to be found in P. E. More and F. L. Cross, *Anglicanism* (London, 1957), 53–56.

2. See Donne's Paul's Cross sermon of 15 September 1622, explaining King James's action in banning sermons on controversial political or theological issues. (*Sermons of John Donne*, eds. G. R. Potter and E. M. Simpson, 10 vols. [Berkeley, 1953–1962], 4: No. 6.)

3. *The Works of . . . William Laud*, 9 vols. (Library of Anglo-Catholic Theology, Oxford, 1847–1860), 6: Pt. I, 56f.

4. *The Sermons of Maister Henrie Smith* (London, 1593), 491–494, from the sermon, "The Triall of the Righteous."

5. Donne, *Sermons*, 8: No. 13, 311. Adams cheerfully stresses the conjunction of the inhabitants of heaven and earth: "They sing *Hosanna's* for us, and we *Halleluia's* for them: They pray to God for us; we praise God for them . . ." (*The Workes of Tho: Adams* [London, 1629], 739). Donne also stresses the unity of the Church triumphant and militant in *Sermons*, 7:255.

6. Ralph Brownrig, *Sixty Five Sermons* (London, 1674), 239.

7. John Hacket, *A Century of Sermons* (London, 1675), 1000.

8. Donne, *Sermons*, 8:191.

9. Donne, *Sermons*, 8: No. 9.

10. Donne, *Sermons,* 2: No. 9, especially 210–211: ". . . and like a Lily in Paradise, out of red earth, I shall see my soule rise out of his blade, in a candor, and in an innocence, contracted there, acceptable in the sight of his Father." The ascent with a different image is also used in *Sermons,* 7: No. 9, 254–255.

11. Donne, *Sermons,* 3: No. 3, especially 110 and 113.

12. Donne, *Sermons,* 3: No. 11, as the conclusion to a marriage sermon preached at St. Clement Dane's, 30 May 1621.

13. Donne, *Sermons,* 6: No. 3, sermon preached at St. Paul's on Easter Day evening, 1624.

14. Donne, *Sermons,* 7: No. 15, 384–385; Easter sermon delivered at St. Paul's, 1627.

15. Donne, *Sermons,* 8: No. 3, especially 88–89; from a sermon on Matthew 22:30: "For in the Resurrection they neither marry nor are given in marriage, but are as the angels of God in heaven."

16. The same criticism might more readily be laid at the doors of such Jacobean tragedians as Webster and Tourneur. Moreover, there was much in the reign of James I to countenance such a melancholy cast of mind: after the glorious days of Elizabeth and the victory over the Armada in 1588, Jacobean days seemed unheroic and anticlimactic, with even the future of religion uncertain during the shilly-shallying over the Spanish marriage, and the devastating plague of 1625. (For the latter see Donne's *Sermons,* 6: No. 18). The plague visitation marked the very beginning of Charles I's reign.

17. "The British Church," *The Works of George Herbert,* ed. F. E. Hutchinson (Oxford, 1961), 109.

18. For the great impact of the book and its role in maintaining a sense of the costliness of the introduction of Protestantism into England, comparable to the blood of the martyrs that became the seed of Christianity in early days of persecution, see William Haller, *Foxe's Book of Martyrs and the Elect Nation* (London, 1963).

19. *John Donne, Essays in Divinity,* ed. E. M. Simpson (London, 1952), 51. For accounts of the unwillingness of Church of England theologians of the seventeenth century to unchurch other Christian Communions, Roman, Reformed or Orthodox, or even to imply that sacraments administered by those who had not received episcopal ordination were invalid, see Leonard Hodgson, *The Doctrine of the Church as Held and Taught in the Church of England* (Oxford, 1948), and Norman Sykes, *The Church of England and Non-Episcopal Churches in*

the Sixteenth and Seventeenth Centuries (London, 1949); also Helen Gardner, *Donne's Divine Poems* (Oxford, 1952), Appendix C.

20. Donne, *Sermons,* 8: No. 2, 90; also in Logan Pearsall Smith, *Donne's Sermons: Selected Passages with an Essay* (Oxford, 1919), 44.

21. John Donne, *A Sermon preached before the Kings Most Excellent Majestie, in the Cathedrall Church of Durham. Upon Sunday, being the fifth day of May. 1639.* (London, 1639), 35.

22. *The Whole Works of the Most Rev. James Ussher . . . ,* 17 vols. (Dublin and London, 1847–1864), 2:490.

23. Ussher, *Works,* 1:13.

24. Abraham Pryme, *Ephemeris Vitae Abraham Pryme, or, A Diary of my own life* (Surtees Society, Durham, London, and Edinburgh, 1780, No. 54), 60. Father Petre became chaplain to King James II.

25. William Barlow, *The Sermon Preached at Paules Crosse, the tenth day of November, being the next Sunday after the Discoverie of this late Horrible Treason* (London, 1606), sig. C2v.

26. Barlow, *The Sermon Preached at Paules Crosse . . . ,* sig. C3.

27. Barlow, *The Sermon Preached at Paules Crosse . . . ,* sig. C3.

28. Barlow, *The Sermon Preached at Paules Crosse . . . ,* sig. C3v.

29. For example, Bishop John Hacket in his first sermon on the fifth of November said: "And now, I pray you, call to mind the bloody conjuration of this day, to whose secresie those desperate Pseudo Catholics swore even at the *Table* of the *Lord.* Was not Religion turned topsie turvy, when those sulphurous traitors, and their Father *Jesuits,* turned the Communion of our Saviour to a non-communion to link and combine themselves into eternal silence? That Sacrament of Charity, the strongest tie of love that ever God made, became an Oath to unite the malice of Satan," (*A Century of Sermons,* 745).

30. John Buckeridge, *A Sermon preached at Hampton Court before the Kings Maiestie, On Tuesday the 23. of September, Anno 1606.* The four points were made on 24, 32, 34, and 38.

31. Donne, *Sermons,* 7: No. 16, 402. From a sermon preached before King Charles I on 1 April 1627.

32. Brownrig, *Sixty Five Sermons,* 68. From the fifth sermon on the Transfiguration.

33. John Howson, *Certaine Sermons made in Oxford, Anno. Dom. 1616, Wherein is proved, that Saint Peter had no Monarchicall Power over the rest of the Apostles against Bellarmine, Sanders, Stapleton, and the rest of that Companie* (second edition, London, 1622). The four sermons total

164 pages and are aimed at a scholarly audience, thus constituting a treatise.

34. Henry King, *An Exposition Upon the Lords Prayer. Delivered in Certaine Sermons, in the Cathedrall Church of S. Paul* (London, 1628), 100. A marginal reference says that *sicca morte* in the citation comes from Juvenal.

35. Thomas Morton, *A Sermon Preached before the Kings Most Excellent Maiestie in the Cathedrall Church of Durham, Upon Sunday, being the fifth day of May, 1639* (London, 1639), 3.

36. Morton, *A Sermon Preached before the Kings Most Excellent Maiestrie,* 11.

37. Brownrig, *Sixty Five Sermons,* 37. From Brownrig's first sermon on the Gunpowder Treason.

38. John Prideaux, *Reverence to Rulers. A Sermon preached at the Court* (Oxford, 1636).

39. Matthew Wren, *A Sermon Preached before the Kings Maiestie on Sunday, the seventeenth of February last, at White-hall* (Cambridge, 1627), 42.

40. Donne, *Sermons,* 8:265.

41. Donne, *Sermons,* 7:296.

42. Donne, *Sermons,* 10:151.

43. Donne, *Sermons,* 7: No. 6. This sermon was preached in St. Paul's on 21 May 1626. *Sermons,* 7: No. 7, also used the same text for the same purposes.

44. See, for example, Herbert Thorndike, *Just Weights and Measures* . . . (London, 1662), accessible in *Theological Works of Thorndike* (Library of Anglo-Catholic Theology) 6 vols. (Oxford, 1844–1846), 5:186f., where the author approves of prayers commending the dead to God, but denying purgatory, for him an illusory place.

45. *Workes of Tho: Adams,* 614. See also 1049, where Adams calls purgatory "a larder to the Pope's Kitchin."

46. *Sermons of Maister Henrie Smith,* 888.

47. *Workes of Tho: Adams,* 509.

48. Hacket, *A Century of Sermons:* "The Nineteenth Sermon upon Our Saviours Tentation."

49. Richard Senhouse, *Foure Sermons preached at the Court upon severall occasions* (London, 1627), sig. P3.

50. Donne, *Sermons,* 9:321.

51. *Sacred Polemics, Part the First. No Peace with Rome,* chap. 3, section

iii, in *The Works of Joseph Hall,* 12 vols. (Oxford, 1837–1839), 11:368, 370 (Latin text opposite).

52. Contained in Hacket's *A Century of Sermons.*

53. *The Workes of Tho: Adams,* 508. From "Mysticall Bedlam: Or, The World of Mad-men."

54. Brownrig, *Sixty Five Sermons,* 214. From the fifth Easter sermon.

55. For the various theories current in the seventeenth century on the presence of Christ in the Eucharist, see H. Davies, *Worship and Theology in England, From Andrewes to Baxter and Fox, 1603–1690* (Princeton, N.J., 1975), chap. VIII, 286–325.

56. Francis White, *London's Warning by Jerusalem* (London, 1619), 14. From a sermon preached at Paul's Cross in mid-Lent 1619.

57. Donne, *Sermons,* 8:366. Bishop Hall also ridicules the blind obedience and superstition of Roman Catholics: "Blind obedience is their best guide. Are they bidden to adore a God which they know the baker made? they fall down upon their knees and thump their breasts, as beating the heart that will not enough believe in that pastry deity. Are they bidden to go on pilgrimage to a chapel, that is a greater pilgrim than themselves, that hath four several times removed itself, [the Santa Casa at Loretto], as Turselline confidently? they must go and adore those wandering walls," (*Works,* 5:265–566). Hall's prejudice is, at least, laced with wit.

58. The Canons proposed in 1640, which Parliament refused to pass in 1641 (E. Cardwell, *Synodalia* [Oxford, 1842] 1:404f.), make it plain that Laud rejected all of "the gross superstition of Popery" in the "idolatry of the Mass." Respect for the Holy Table "doth not imply that it is, or ought to be esteemed a true and proper Altar, whereon Christ is again really sacrificed."

59. Lancelot Andrewes, *XCVI Sermons* (London, 1629), 240. From a sermon preached before King James on Ash Wednesday, 1623.

60. Donne, *Sermons,* 4:310. From a Christmas Day sermon at St. Paul's, 1622. John Howson makes the same point in *A Second Sermon preached at Paules Crosse, the 21 of May, 1598* (London, 1598), 44.

61. John Buckeridge, *A Sermon preached before His Maiestie at Whitehall, March 22, 1617, being Passion-Sunday* (London, 1618), 10.

62. *The Works of . . . Cosin,* Volume 1: *Sermons* (Oxford, 1843), 96. The sermon was preached at the consecration of Dr. Francis White as bishop of Carlisle on the first Sunday in Advent, 3 December 1626.

63. See Horton Davies, *The Worship of the English Puritans* (London, 1948), chap. 6, for a full account of the objections of sixteenth–century Puritans to the "noxious" ceremonies.

64. For the Arminian and Puritan view of ceremonies in the seventeenth century, see Horton Davies, *Worship and Theology in England* (5 vols., 1961–1975, Princeton, N.J.), 2: chap. 5, "Styles in Worship: Prestigious or Plain?", 187–214.

65. Andrewes, *XCVI Sermons*, 519. From a sermon preached before King James at Whitehall on Easter Day, 5 April 1618.

66. Donne, *Sermons*, 9:152.

67. For the different calendars in England in the seventeenth century of the Roman Catholics, Church of England, and the Puritans, see Horton Davies, *Worship and Theology in England*, 3: chap. 6, "Calendar Conflict: Holy Days or Holidays?", 215–252; and Howard Happ, "Calendary Conflicts in Renaissance England," Ph.D. dissertation at Princeton University, 1974.

68. John Howson, *A Sermon preached at St. Maries in Oxford the 17. Day of November, 1602 in defence of the Festivities of the Church of England, and namely that of her Maiesties Coronation* (second impression, Oxford, 1603).

69. *Works of . . . Cosin*, 1:4. This sermon was delivered in St. Edward's church, Cambridge on 6 January 1621 and at Coton on the second Sunday after Epiphany.

70. Donne, *Sermons*, 7:264.

71. Donne, *Sermons*, 1:260.

72. *Works of . . . Cosin*, 1:79. A sermon preached probably in 1625 because of its reference to the plague.

73. Donne, *Sermons*, 9:119. From a sermon preached on Whitsunday 1629 in St. Paul's.

74. William Barlow, *Christian Liberty described in a Sermon preached in the Collegiate Church at Westminster, by a Minister of Suffoke* (London, 1606), sig. D1.

75. John Bowle, *A Sermon preached at Mapple-Durham in Oxfordshire* (London, 1616), 24.

76. Donne: *Sermons*, 5:298. From a sermon preached on the penitential psalms.

77. Donne: *Sermons*, 6:161.

78. Laud, *Works*, 1:82. A sermon preached on Monday, 6 February 1625, at the opening of Parliament.

79. Thomas Morton, *The Presentment of a Schismaticke. A Sermon preached at the Cathedrall Church of Saint Pauls the 19 June 1642* (London, 1642), 23–24.

80. Thomas Jackson, *A Treatise concerning the signes of the times Or God's forewarnings* (Oxford, 1637), 66. A series of sermons preached before the king at Newcastle-upon-Tyne.

81. See Richard Field, *Of the Church,* Bk. 5 (London, 1606), as excerpted in *Anglicanism,* eds. P. E. More and F. L. Cross (London, 1957), 144–145.

82. See John E. Booty, *John Jewel as Apologist of the Church of England* (London, 1963) and his edition of *The Apology of the Church of England* (Folger Shakespeare Library and Cornell University Press, Ithaca, N.Y., 1963).

83. See the critical edition of the *Works* of Richard Hooker now being published by the Harvard University Press under the general editorship of W. Speed Hill. See also the impressive two volume Sorbonne dissertation of Olivier Loyer, *L' Anglicanisme de Richard Hooker* (Libraire Honoré Champion, Paris, 1979).

84. *The Works of that learned and reverend Divine, John White, Doctor in Divinitie* (London, 1624), including the first of two sermons.

85. Donne, *Sermons,* 10:295, 346.

86. Donne, *Sermons,* 10:347.

87. John Prideaux, *The Patronage of Angels. A Sermon Preached at Court* (Oxford, 1636).

88. Henry King, *An Exposition Upon the Lords Prayer* (London, 1628).

89. Ussher, *The Whole Works . . . ,* vol. 2, which includes *A Sermon preached before the Commons House of Parliament in St. Margaret's Church at Westminster, the 18th of February* (1621).

90. A learned orientalist, Dr. Edward Pocock (according to Twells's biography published in 1816, 1:92–95) decided to preach simply to his country congregation, omitting all words borrowed from foreign languages, only to be scolded by them for not including Greek, Latin, and Hebrew in his sermons. This information is derived from W. Fraser Mitchell, *English Pulpit Oratory From Andrewes to Tillotson, A Story of its Literary Aspects* (London, 1932), 106.

91. Donne, *Sermons,* 3:80.

92. Brownrig, *Sixty Five Sermons,* 37.

93. This sermon was on the text Acts 23:5: ". . . thou shalt not speak evill of the Ruler of thy People."

94. Matthew Wren, *A Sermon preached before the Kings Maiestie on Sunday the Seventeenth of Februarie last, at White-Hall* (Cambridge, 1627), ending at p. 42.

95. Andrewes, *XCVI Sermons,* 107.

96. Andrewes, *XCVI Sermons,* 109.

97. Andrewes, *XCVI Sermons,* 110.

98. Ussher, *Works,* 13:348.

99. Ussher, *Works,* 13:350.

100. Jasper Mayne, *A Sermon concerning Unity & Agreement* (London, 1646), 30. It is a sustained appeal for charity among ecclesiastical parties within the English Church.

101. For the history of the Puritan objections to the Book of Common Prayer, see Horton Davies, *The Worship of the English Puritans.* John Gauden, the presumed author of the anonymously printed *Eikon Basilike* (London, 1648), paragraph 16, has a telling criticism of the Puritan *Directory of Publicke Worship of 1644:* "That these men (I say) should so suddenly change the Liturgy into a Directory, as if the Spirit needed help for invention, though not for expressions; or as if matter prescribed did not as much stint and obstruct the Spirit as if it were clothed in and confined to, fit words,—so slight and easy is that legerdemain which will serve to delude the vulgar."

102. For a modern account of seventeenth-century Roman Catholic criticisms of the Church of England, its doctrine, polity, and worship, see George Tavard, *The Seventeenth-Century Tradition: A Study in Recusant Thought* (Leiden, 1978). Parsons and Stapleton were the chief English Jesuit critics of the Church of England for its dilutions of, or deviations from, Roman Catholicism, and Cardinal Bellarmine was their Hector.

103. Donne, *Sermons,* 9:219. From a Lenten sermon preached before King Charles I on 20 April 1630.

104. Donne, *Sermons,* 6:79.

105. See Andrewes, *XCVI Sermons,* 475–476 and the first two sermons on the Second Commandment, preached at St. Giles, Cripplegate in 1592, reprinted in *XCVI Sermons* at the end.

106. See Donne, *Sermons,* 9:52, cited earlier in this chapter.

107. John Howson, *A Second Sermon, preached at Paules Crosse, the 21 of May, 1598* . . . (London, 1598).

108. Laud had said in a speech before the Star Chamber on 4 June 1637, at the censure of Bastwick, Burton, and Prynne: "But this is the misery, it is superstition nowadays for any man to come with

more reverence into a Church, than a tinker and his bitch into an ale-house. The comparison is too homely, but my just indignation at the profaneness of the times makes me speak it," (*Works,* 6: Pt. 1, 564).

109. *The Collected Sermons of Thomas Fuller,* ed. J. E. Bailey, 2 vols. (London, 1891), 1:130.

110. John Buckeridge, *A Sermon preached before His Maiestie At Whitehall, March 22, 1617. being Passion-Sunday, Touching Prostration and Kneeling in the worship of GOD* (London, 1619). Buckeridge provides a full and thoughtful defense of the use of reverent ceremonies in worship. He gives three reasons for the uniting of body and soul in ceremonies: (1) the debt or duty of the whole man to God for creation, redemption, and resurrection in Christ and sanctification through the Holy Spirit; (2) mutual excitation; and (3) as soul and body share in offending God, they must concur in the "pacification of God" (19).

111. Donne, *Sermons,* 7:90.

112. Donne, *Sermons,* 5:263.

113. Donne, *Sermons,* 5:74; 2:578.

114. Winfried Schleiner, *The Imagery of John Donne's Sermons* (Providence, R.I., 1970), 295f.

115. Donne, *Sermons,* 4:124.

116. Brownrig, *Sixty Five Sermons,* 268–269. This is the third sermon for Whitsunday.

117. Brownrig, *Sixty Five Sermons,* 272.

118. Donne, *Sermons,* 4:106–107.

119. Abraham Cowley, *Poems,* ed. A. R. Waller (Cambridge, 1905), 7, cited from the preface to his *Works* (1669).

120. *The Life and Letters of John Donne,* ed. Edmund Gosse, 2 vols. (London, 1899), 1:29. See also 2:78, where he writes in a letter to Sir Henry Goodyer that the Roman Catholic Church and the Church of England are "sister teats of His [God's] graces."

Chapter VIII

TRADITIONAL THEMES

I N THE LAST CHAPTER the concentration was on the ecclesiology, worship, and sacraments of the Church of England as reflected in the sermons of the metaphysical preachers. This was often controversial theology, making clear the distinctive standpoint of the middle way between the Roman Catholics and the Puritans and Separatists. In the present chapter I hope to demonstrate that the metaphysical preachers were lively expositors of the great age-old traditional themes that have been the staple of the pulpit from the earliest centuries, but that they often approached these themes with a new slant, or at least with the freshness of rediscovery. Not all of these topics will be seen to be treated with "calm of mind, all passion spent," for the issue of religious epistemology still divided Calvinists and Arminians to a considerable extent. On the whole, however, on the central and orthodox doctrines of the Holy Trinity, the Incarnation, the Atonement, the Resurrection and Descent of the Holy Spirit, and eschatology (the doctrine of the four last things—death, judgment, heaven, and hell), there is a remarkable unity among the preachers, even if sometimes one gets the impression that the Calvinists seem to be more familiar with the dark contours and torrid temperature of hell, and the Arminians with the light, glory, rest, and the community of the saints in heaven.[1]

Epistemology: the roles of faith and reason

Unity rather than difference characterizes the proclamations of the preachers on the communication of divine revelation

353

to humanity, except that the earlier Calvinists like Henry Smith and Thomas Adams emphasize the impairment of the human heart through original and actual sin, while the Arminians are more optimistic about the responsive powers of the individual, despite what Augustine called the *damnosa haereditas*. All seem to agree that there are vestiges of reason in fallen man.

Donne, for example, sees the image of God in man defaced by the Fall but restamped by the Divine Logos in the flesh (the Incarnate Christ), and channeled through the sacraments.[2] Brownrig believes that there are a few faint vestiges of reason in humanity. For him the unredeemed soul is like a plundered palace, "the plate and the hangings, and all the rich furniture all carried away; but yet some of the Fabrick is left standing still." These "glimmerings of truth" which shine like a few dim stars in a pitch black night, are like the sense of justice which, when rejected, strike us with horror as an abomination, and "even an unregenerate conscience, it will give back at some gross impieties." Yet "Virtues without grace are no better than Vices, little indeed for spiritual purposes."[3] So the reason needs strengthening by faith, otherwise it will stumble blindly in the dark. This gloomy assessment of the role of reason *in religion* is typically Calvinist, though Calvin himself thought highly of reason in areas such as law and architecture.

Cosin is typically Arminian in his higher evaluation of reason. He argues that the world with its harmony and the subordination of its parts requires an artificer, that such an artificer would want to take care of his work, and God the Artificer deserves service and worship from his creation. The need of worship must be made known, and also the permanent manifestation of the divine will is necessary, and this is what Scripture provides.[4] Cosin also insists, in another sermon, that while revelation goes beyond reason, it never contradicts it. He expresses his view with characteristic clarity:

In the meanwhile we preach no mysteries against reason when we say they go beyond it, for in this case religion and reason are not opposite, but subordinate; and where they be otherwise . . . there we must have leave to suspect them, and avoid them, and oppose them too; but where we bring the word and authority of God for them, there is no more to be said, for then we have all the reason in the world to receive them.[5]

His conviction was that what is not grounded upon reason ought not to be called faith, and that the strongest reason is grounded on the Scripture, the fullest expression of God's mind to mankind.

Donne too, believes that reason leads to faith, as a stick supports a vine.[6] Knowledge cannot save us, he insists, but we cannot be saved without knowledge. This was the theme of his first sermon as dean of St. Paul's, in which he affirmed that Christ is the light of nature, of reason, of grace, and of glory.[7] So far he and Cosin agree, but Donne is closer to Brownrig in affirming that reason gives only a glimmering of light, but that "the meridionall noone is in faith."[8]

An intriguing emphasis in the sermons of the metaphysicals is their conviction that God attracts individual souls through their interests, a view shared by Calvinist Adams and Arminians Donne and Duppa. Adams believes that our joys are the filings which the magnet of God attracts to himself. He pleads: "Welbeloved, since this is Gods mercy, to allure us to him by our owne delights, let us yeeld our selves to be caught." Then he continues in charming fashion:

Love you hunting? learne here to hunt *the Foxes, the little* Cubbes those crafty sinnes sculking in your bosomes. Would you dance? let your hearts keepe the measures of Christian joy; and leape, like *Iohn* the Baptist in *Elizabeths* wombe, at the salvation of *Iesus.* Delight you in running? *Paul* sets you a race. *So runne that yee may obtaine* . . . Love you musick? Here are the Bels of Aaron still ringing; the treble of Mercy, and the tenor of *Iudgement; Levis* Lute, and *Davids* Harpe. There are no such songs as the songs of *Sion.* . . . Lovest thou dainty cheare? here be the best

cates, the body and blood of thy Saviour, the bread of
life: no hunger after it. . . . Are you ambitious? there is
no preferment like that is to be had here, in the Court
of the King of Kings. . . . Desire you stately buildings?
Alas, the whole world is but a Cottage, a poore transient
Tabernacle, to the *Mansions* promised by Christ. Lastly,
are you covetous? Yet I neede not aske that question, but
take it as granted. Why then here is *gold*; more precious
then that of *Arabia*, or of *Havilah*: rust or theefe may dis-
tresse that; this is a treasure can never be lost. . . . Which
way soever your desire stands, God doth allure you.[9]

This is a theme to be found in Augustine's *Confessions*, with
the recognition that our hearts are restless until they rest in
God, an effect which C. S. Lewis terms *sehnsucht*, a longing
to be fulfilled only by God.[10]

Bishop Brian Duppa emphasizes the variety of avenues along
which God calls to the soul, in much the same way as Adams
did, less colloquially but with elegant antithetical balance, and
even greater dramatic power. God, he claims, "ransacks the
whole Inventory of his Creatures, and puts on all shapes to
gaine a Soule." God, in fact, invented more ways of saving
man, than man ever invented to damn himself. Here is Duppa's
application of his theme:

To the Traveller he calls, *I am the way*; To the benighted,
he shews, *he is the light*; To the Stranger, he opens himself,
I am the dore: Looke for him among the Plants, you shall
find him *a vine*; Search for him in the flock, the Baptist
points him out to you, *Behold the Lamb!* or if Metaphors
be but *verball* transfigurings, track him in his Parables,
which are more reall; if you meet there with a Sower,
Christ is that Sower; if you heare of a Bridegroome, he
is that Bridegroome; if you see the *man* that brings back
his lost sheep in triumph, he is that *man*: or if you find
a *woman*, that calls her friends to joy with her, *Rejoice,
for I have found the piece which I had lost*, know that that

piece is thy *Soule*, those *friends* are the Angels, he is that
woman too. . . .[11]

Donne also believes that God addresses souls according to
their interests, and will make us listen to him whether by attraction or repulsion. On the one hand, "If I be *covetous*, God wil
tell me that heaven is a pearle, a treasure. If cheerfull and affected with mirth, that heaven is all *Joy*. If ambitious and hungry for preferment, that it is all *Glory*. If sociable, and conversa-
ble, that it is a *communion of Saints.*" On the other hand God's
disfavors and our sins also speak the divine message too. "God
will make make a *Fever* speake to me, and tell me his minde,
that there is no health but in *him*; . . . God will make a *storme*
at Sea, or a *fire* by land, speake to me nay, God will make
my *sinne* speake to me, and tell me his minde; even my sinne
shall bee a Sermon, and a Catechisme to me." His conclusion
is God speaks to humanity through acclamations, hosannas,
or through the condemnations of the world, so that "The whole
yeare, is, to his Saints, a continuall *Epiphany*, one day of
manifestation."[12]

While our preachers may think highly of the world of creatures as God's book in nature, and of our reason as the mode
of reading it, especially when the book of Scripture is brought
in for further confirmation to be read with the eyes of faith,
they also advise their congregations to beware of too much
curiosity, too much attempting to pry into the mind of God.
The pride of the intellect must be watched or it will presume
to know the inner workings of the transcendent Deity, who
has only unveiled as much as we need to know in the Incarnation. Donne, for example, uses the very suggestive image that
God gives audience, but not in the bedchamber; the ordinances
of preaching and the sacraments are his outer chambers, but
He is not to be pressed on his unrevealed purposes.[13] In another
sermon Donne warns, in his paradoxical mode, against trying
to break into God's privacy: "So, though God be our businesse,
we may be too busie with God; and though God be infinite,
we may go beyond God, when we conceive, or speak otherwise
of God, then God hath revealed unto us."[14]

Henry Smith concurs, believing that "it is good to leave off learning, where God hath left off teaching," and he advises against asking unnecessary questions.[15] Bishop Lake agrees, and advises against wading too far into the mind of the Triune God, for "he that pries too neare into this glorious Majesty, shall find to his ruine that it is an incomprehensible mystery."[16] One is reminded of the definition of God provided by Henry Vaughan, the mystical metaphysical poet:

> There is in God—some say—
> A deep, but dazzling darkness; as men here
> Say it is late and dusky, because they
> See not all clear.[17]

Yet Lake also sees the value of a persistent faith. In an interesting sermon preached at St. Cross, Winchester, where he was warden for a while, he retells the story of the woman of Canaan whose daughter had an evil spirit whom the disciples besought to send away (Matthew 15:21–22). The importunate woman's faith led to the recovery of her daughter, Christ's commendation of her, and the lesson "Christ shewes, that what He deferres He doth not deny, but then yeelds when it is most fit, both for Him, and also for us."[18]

However strong faith, reason, and the freedom of the will appear to be or not to be, there is no denying the fact of the universal propensity towards sin, both hereditary and actual. If this were not so, there would be no need for redemption, a position which is theologically unthinkable. Hence three of our preachers speak vividly about original sin. Donne thinks of it in the traditional way, with echoes of Augustine:

> Miserable man! a Toad is a bag of Poyson, and a Spider is a blister of Poyson, and yet a Toad and a Spider cannot poyson themselves: Man hath a dram of poyson, originall-Sin, in an invisible corner, we know not where, and he cannot choose but poyson himselfe and all his actions with that; we are so far from being able to begin without Grace,

as then where we have the first Grace, we cannot proceed to the use of that, without more.[19]

He expressed it even more wittily in reference to the unredeemed: "The coare of Adam's apple is still in their throat . . . Adams disobedience works in them still, and therefore Gods Physick, the affliction, cannot work."[20]

Bishop Francis White, seizing on the excuses offered by Adam and Eve in Eden for their disobedience to God (Adam blaming it on Eve, and Eve on the serpent that beguiled her), finds rationalizations of this kind the essence of original sin. He claims that "all we, *Adams* sinfull posterity, have worne this cloake of excuse almost thred-bare by long usage of it, in palliating of our sinnes: And we cloake Drunkenness with good fellowship; wee cloake Covetousnesse with good thriftinesse; wee cloake Pride with decency and comelinesse. . . ."[21]

Adams can argue metaphysically about sin as *amissio boni*, the absence of the positive principle of goodness or virtue, in which he asserts that sin is a privation, or a bastard that came in at the back door when man forsook grace, and was brought in by stealth. Yet he shows how small sins spread like a contagious disease.[22] Bishop Barlow like Adams sees sin starting as a small fire, that overreaching itself through pride becomes a mighty conflagration which rushes out of control. This he applies to the inordinate pride of the earl of Essex and his rebellion against Queen Elizabeth.[23]

It is clear that where there is sin, it must be attributed to blindness—incapacity to see the right way of virtue or obedience to God, or to weakness of the will—inability to follow the right way. If both can be overcome by our own will, then we have Pelagianism, and moralism is substituted for a religion of grace. This necessarily involves our preachers in the anatomizing of sin and particular sins.

Vices and virtues

The traditional seven deadly sins are pride, covetousness, lust, envy, gluttony, anger, and sloth, and of the seven traditional virtues three are theological (faith, hope, and charity) and four are cardinal (justice, prudence, temperance, and fortitude). How far are these virtues and vices central to seventeenth–century Protestant pulpit thought in England?

The cardinal virtues, which were themselves a summary of pagan morality, were held to be valid in the political world, but hardly the business of preachers,[24] but the three theological virtues were, understandably, given thorough consideration in sermons, as will be seen. Among the vices pride was inevitably given first place because Genesis traced the origin of sin, in Milton's words, to "Man's first disobedience and the fruit of that forbidden tree." Covetousness was also flayed by some of the preachers, in the forms of usury—common among the merchants of the City of London, and among churchgoers reluctant to pay tithes to their clergymen,[25] and simony.[26] The opposing virtue, charity, was, following St. Paul's evaluation,[27] given the highest ranking among the virtues, both because Christ's self-emptying (*kenosis*) in the Incarnation and the Crucifixion was its paradigm, and because love of God and love of the neighbor were Christ's own summary of the Mosaic Law.[28]

Turning now to pride (and its antidote and opposite, the grace of humility) Donne castigates its forms, as exhibited in the congregation in two ways. He notes the worldly respect that brought the well-to-do to show off at divine worship in their finery, and then points out that they seek to rule after their deaths in the sumptuous monuments erected to their memory. These men are often those whom, when living, gave nothing to the poor.[29] Donne knew that the desire for precedence began in the cradle and, apart from grace, could only be suffocated in a shroud. Adams discerns the same desperate desire for preferment in a man who was "out of square with being a Squire, and shoots at knighthood . . . This is not enough, the world must count him a *Count*, or hee is not satisfied." Its cure is repentant humility.[30] Adams wittily describes humility as represented by Zaccheus who came down from the sycamore tree to entertain Jesus:

Whosoever will entertaine *Iesus,* must come downe. The haughty *Nebuchadnezzar,* that thinkes with his head to knock out the starres of heaven, must stoop at this *gate,* or he cannot enter. Be you never so lofty, you must bend. Gods honour must be preferred before your honours. It is no credit to your Worships to worship God.[31]

More simply, Ussher reminds his hearers that the Gospel itself leads to humility, bidding them to strike sail and pull down their proud hearts to stoop to Jesus Christ.[32]

Vanity, another form of pride, is castigated in thoroughly medieval fashion by Henry Smith, who accuses some husbands of laying their pride on their wives, not caring how slovenly they themselves look as long as their wives parade like peacocks. Such women, forgetting that it was as a rebuke that Eve's nakedness was once covered with leaves in Eden, "but now they cover themselves with pride . . . ruffe upon ruffe, lace upon lace, cut upon cut, four & twentie orders, until the woman be not so precious as her apparell." A man with such a wife, emulating dancing Herodias whose "too many ornaments, frisled locks, naked brests, painting, perfume, & especially a rolling eye are forerunners of adulterie," is wedded to a plague.[33]

The most vivid account of pride comes from a remarkable sermon of Adams in which he introduces a whole series of "characters" in the way made popular by Bishop Joseph Hall, Sir Thomas Overbury, and Earle. Here Pride comes strutting out of his sermon:

Pride, you know must be foremost; and that comes out like a Spanyard, with daring looke, and a tongue thundering out braves: mounted on a spiritely Iennet named *Insolence.* His Plumes and Perfumes amaze the beholders eyes and nosthrils. Hee runnes as if he would overthrow Gyants and Dragon: . . . and with his lance burst open heaven gates. But his Iennet stumbles, and downe comes Pride.

You know how wise a King hath read his destinie; *Pride will have a fall.* [34]

The sin most commonly flayed was that of covetousness; and its cure, the grace of *caritas*, was held forth for admiration. Henry Smith has two sermons excoriating usury. He begins by saying there are three sins which are not counted as such: bribery, pluralist clergy who do not reside in their parishes, and usury. Because they are gainful they are thought to be legitimate occupations. His chief condemnation is kept for the usurer as a legal thief, because he tells the borrower how much more he will steal and "this word *more*, comes in like a sixt finger, which makes a monster, because it is more then should bee." [35] The conclusion of his second sermon is that "I would have no man paie interest unto Usurers but for necessitie, even as a travailer giveth his purse unto a theefe, because he cannot chuse." [36]

It is Adams, Donne, and Andrewes whose sermons show a genuine concern for the poor. Adams is particularly sensitive to the needs of the disinherited in the countryside, many of them forced to beg for bread or to become vagrants. He sounds like a latterday Amos in his indigation commingled with compassion:

> Heare this ye oppressors! Be mercifull: you will one day be glad of mercy. The yellings of of the poore in the Countrey, are as loud as your roarings in the City. The Cups you drinke, are full of those teares that drop from affamished eyes, though you perceive it not. You laugh, when they lament; you feast, when they fast; you devoure them, that doe you service. God will one day *set these things in order before you.* [37]

In a later sermon Adams deplores the splendor of some churches and the poverty of some members of the Body of Christ, complaining that this is an ancient defect still unreformed. He concludes: "Deny not due cost to the dead walls; but first satisfie the living bowles; that Christ may say, *Come ye blessed.*" [38]

Donne, too, castigates the uncaring rich, warning them that if they prove insensible to the cry or curses of the poor, they will experience the howlings and gnashing of teeth in the world to come.[39] He is equally scathing of those who believe that they are generous to the poor, but are in fact not so:

> To give old cloathes, past wearing to the poore, is not so good a worke as to make new for them. To give a little of your superfluities, not so acceptable as the widows gift, that gave all. To give a poore soule a farthing at that doore where you give a Player a shilling, is not equall dealing; for this is to give God *quisquilias frumenti, The refuse of the wheat.*[40]

By his life and his teaching Bishop Andrewes was an apostle of charity. As a bishop, required by the New Testament to practice hospitality, Andrewes gladly invited several poor men to his table every time he sat down to dinner. His friend and admirer, Bishop Buckeridge, caught his spirit perfectly when, in the funeral sermon he preached for Andrewes, he pointed out that it is not the poor man who seeks alms, it is God begging through the pauper, and Christ calling through the beggar, and what he asks for belongs finally to God: "in short, *Suum non tuum:* He asks not thine, thou hast onely the use, and dispose of it, but he asks his owne, and *what hast thou, that thou hast not received,* even to thy selfe, thy soule; and thy body, all the gifts of Nature, and all the gifts of grace?"[41]

Andrewes has a fine analysis of the various meanings of the term love, as applied to the woman who ran early on Easter Day to the empty tomb of Christ. He sees this divine love in response to the love of Christ having four characteristics: "*Amor, a morte,* when it surviveth *death:* When it buyeth dearely, it is *Charitas;* When it sheweth all *diligence,* it is *Dilectio:* When it goeth *per Saxa,* when *stones* cannot stay it, it is *Zelus,* which is especially seene in *encountering difficulties.*"[42] This is as fine a demonstration of the meaning of *agape* or *caritas* as we can find in all the sermon literature of the golden age of the English pulpit.

Adams is the preacher who provides in his "character" sketches the fullest gallery of vices. In a single sermon, "Loves Copie," the following vices mounted on a variety of elegant steeds or sorry nags enter the horse race: Pride, Prodigality, Envy, Covetousness, Hypocrisy, and Lust. One example will convey the liveliness of the imagination of the preacher:

> *Envie* will be next, a lean meager thing, full of malicious mettle, but hath almost no flesh. The horse he rides on is *Malcontent.* He would in his iourney first cut some thousand throates, or powder a whole kingdome, blow up a State; and then set on to heaven. But the hangman sets up a Galowse in his way, whereat he runnes full butt and breakes his necke.[43]

The pointed reference to the Gunpowder Plot would not be missed by the congregation at St. Gregory's under St. Paul's Cathedral. It is worth noting that Adams retains four of the traditional seven deadly sins: pride, envy, covetousness, and lust, and misses out gluttony, anger, and sloth. The Protestant work-ethic made sloth an improbable sin on any large scale, and the humility encouraged along with meekness in the Beatitudes may have made anger seem less likely. Gluttony, however, was chauvinistically regarded as a German sin, along with drunkenness. Both were recognized as complementary vices and England was now beginning to rival Germany in their frequency of occurrence.[44]

Of greater importance is the recognition of the role of hypocrisy, a sin excoriated by Jesus in the Gospels, which Adams dissects thoroughly in his sermon "The White Devil, Or the Hypocrite Uncased." This sermon also deals with those virtues which are seen as the fruits of the Holy Spirit, such as joy, peace, patience, and hope, not forgetting the other two theological virtues previously considered, faith and love. Adams has an impressive sermon on the theological virtues, "The Three Divine Sisters."

Donne is the great laureate of joy, but Gauden, Hacket, Playfere, and Adams (whom we have already mentioned as saying that God allures humanity through its delights), are not far behind him. In a sermon preached to the earl of Exeter and his company on 13 June 1624 from Revelation 7:9, Donne contemplates the joys of heaven. He emphasizes the community who share those joys in striking terms that unite the images of God's people in the Old and New Testaments: "Religion is not a *melancholy;* the spirit of God is not a *dampe;* the Church is not a *grave:* it is a *fold,* it is an *Arke,* it is a *net,* it is a *city,* it is a *kingdome,* not onely a house, but a house that hath *many mansions* in it. . . ."[45] The repeated emphasis on joy and the reference to the many mansions must have caught the attention of the company of the earl of Exeter, who were the seventeenth-century equivalent of the jet-setters and who were gathered in the mansion of the earl. From these earthly symbols, he could by analogy rise to the higher joy of blessedness and to the Johannine promise of Christ, "In my Father's house are many mansions; if it were not so, I would have told you; for I go to prepare a place for you."[46]

The ultimate joy for Donne is what Itrat Husein calls "the holy joy of the illumined soul"[47]—a joy far superior to the joyful pleasures of youth. It is more accurately the blessedness of the Beatitudes. Donne compares the two kinds and ages of joy: "And as the Sunne may say to the Starres at Noone, How frivolous and impertinent is your light now? So this joy shall say *unto laughter* [juvenile laughter] *Thou art mad,* and *unto mirth, what dost thou?*"[48] The future Bishop Gauden, as a Calvinist refusing to accept the Solemn League and Covenant and preaching before the king in 1642, also expressed his sense of the joy in holiness, declaring that "no man hath more right to moderate *mirth* (which is the onely true) than he which is in the way of Holinesse" as contrasted with "a tedious drooping and dejected manner which brings an ill report on Gods wayes."[49]

The sense of joy radiated the life of Bishop Hacket of Lichfield and Coventry, according to his biographer Dr. Thomas Plume. He was cheerful at table, his wit was never bitter and biting, he avoided all sarcasm since he said that "*mirth* was too good a creature to be abused with any affrontive jeasts, scurrility, or bawdry," and he insisted with admirable common sense and proportion that "*God Almighty* never forbad lawful pleasures, and *they* are not more religious and spiritual who are more *austere* and *morose* than others." He reminded his company that Jesus condemned the sullenness of the Pharisees, and held that "*melancholy* of all humours . . . was fit to make a *Bath* for the *Devil.*"[50]

In an early sermon entitled "Hearts Delight," preached at Paul's Cross in 1593, Thomas Playfere took as his text Psalm 27:4, "Delight thy selfe in the Lord & he shall give thee the desires of the heart." Playfere contrasts worldly delight with Christian joy, arguing that it has an important place in the Christian life as delight. He cites Bernard of Clairvaux's unusual metaphor, supposedly derived from Egyptian hieroglyphics, depicting meat in the teeth for taste and meat in the throat for better taste, and cites the Canticles for the sweet taste in the throat Christ gives the soul. He says that Christ eats supper with us when we entertain him, with either contrition or integrity, "as *Marie* did with the salt teares of repentance and griefe, and as *Lot* with the sweet bread of syncerity and truth."[51] For our part, we must welcome him with music, with "Psalms, hymns, and spiritual songs, making melody in our hearts to God."[52]

In addition to joy, other Christian virtues such as peace and patience were praised and encouraged. Lancelot Andrewes, in his eighth Resurrection sermon, stresses the universal longing for inner peace, or *sehnsucht*: "We seeke rest: Specially, they are that tossed in a tempest, how doe they desire a good *haven, a harbor of rest!* . . . None but, sometime, hath sense of the *verse* in the *Psalme:* Oh but I had wings like a Dove! Then *would I flye and be at rest.*"[53] One reflects that this was the inner peace promised in the blessing at the end of every service.

Patience is demanded by both Henry Smith and Thomas Adams. For Smith patience is required for undergoing the crosses which God sends to test his servants, crosses which should be expected since their Master underwent the same experiences.[54] Adams claims that patience is accompanied by an armed soldier, called Christian fortitude, to help her encounter the three animals that are enemies of the soul, meaning the lion who is the devil, the leopard who is the spotted world, and the fox who is concupiscence.[55]

Finally in our consideration of virtues and vices we must quote two outstanding sermons, one by Adams and the other by Donne. Adams' great sermon is entitled "Faiths Encouragement," in which he shows that a true faith is best displayed in adverse circumstances and is neither cloistered nor fugitive:

> To bee good in good company is little wonder: for Angels to bee good in heaven, *Adam* in Paradise, *Iudas* in Christs Colledge, had beene no admirable matter: to apostate in these places so full of goodnesse was intollerable weaknesse. But for *Abraham* to be good in *Chalde*; *Noah* in the old world, *Lot* in *Sodome*: for a man to bee humble in Spaine, continent in France, chaste in Venice, sober in Germany, temperate in England, this is the commendation. Such a one is a Lilly in a forest of thornes, a handfull of wheate in a field of cockle.[56]

Donne's sermon on hope was preached as a commemoration of the Lady Danvers, his great and godly friend, and the mother of George Herbert. Donne had celebrated her when alive in the memorable lines:

> No Spring, nor Summer beauty hath such grace,
> As I have seen in one Autumnal face.[57]

The dean defined man as possessed with a future hope, compared with inferior creatures who live only in the present; and God as a future God, in view of his promises to mankind.

And the greatest of these promises is that of eternal life, which generates hope for the Christian who can confidently face the day of Judgment at the end of history:

> And, therefore, let *Schoole-boys* looke after *holy-dayes*, and worldly men after *rent-days*, and *Travellers* after *Faire-dayes*, and *Chap-men* after *Market-dayes*, *Neverthelesse*, *We* that have laid hold upon *God*, and laid hold of him by the right *handle*, *According to his promises*, *Expectamus*, We *looke* for this day of the *Lord*, and *Properamus*, We are glad it is so neere, and we desire the further hasting of it.[58]

One of the glories of seventeenth-century religious thought in and out of the pulpit is its dominating concern with ethics, whether this be in the form of casuistry and the various moral "Directories" published during this period, or in the virtues and vices vividly represented as characters, or the insistence of the correlation of faith with good works. Bishop H. R. McAdoo, himself an Anglican ethicist and historian, comments on how widespread the phenomenon was: "What strikes the moral theologian with fresh force the further he penetrates, is the universal interest of the seventeenth century in 'practical divinity' and the importance accorded to it, officially and parochially throughout the period. Have we here a clue to the great power of Caroline preaching which concerned itself with basic issues?"[59]

The other striking characteristic of seventeenth-century preaching in the Church of England is its devotional character. No matter how much the mind may be stretched in considering alternative interpretations of Scripture, or by cases of conscience, or even by controversy, and no matter how much the imagination may be expanded by witty conceits and exotic figures, the ultimate end is to lead to adoration of the living God. This is abundantly clear, of course, in the great festival sermons of Christmas, Easter, and Whitsuntide, and in the entire correlation of the lections and collects of the Book of Common Prayer with the Christian Year. This is, of course, dominant in the preaching of Lancelot Andrewes, John Donne, John Cosin, John Hacket, Ralph Brownrig, and Mark Frank, all of them properly "liturgical preachers." It is also true of almost all of the preachers who were instructing their congregations in the imitation of Christ.

The Imitation of Christ through the liturgical year

The great traditional themes that led to the adoration and imitation of Christ as Lord were associated with the three greatest festivals, but there also other occasions besides his Birth, his Passion and Resurrection, and his sending of the Holy Spirit, when the earthly life of the Incarnate Lord was gratefully remembered. These were chiefly the correlations of Christ's first coming with his second Advent, his temptations during the Lenten season, his Transfiguration, and his Ascension and rule at God's right hand.

The Nativity of Christ staggered our preachers by its inherent paradoxes: God's Logos or Word in the flesh yet an unspeaking one (literally "infant"), his birth of a maiden Mother, in a stable not a palace, in unimportant Bethlehem, and the surprising homage of simple shepherds and distant sages alike. The Incarnation was cause for adoring wonder and gratitude at the Divine humility and generosity. Andrewes is, of course, the great preacher on this theme, stressing each paradox in order that every knee should bow. The humility is one outstanding feature which strikes Andrewes:

> For Him to condescend to be *borne*, as *Children* are borne; to become a *Child*; great humilitie: Great, *ut Verbum, infans* . . . that the word not to be able to *speake a word*; He, that *thundereth* in heaven, *cry* in a *cradle*; He that is *so great and so high*, should become so *little* as a *Child*, and so low as a *manger*. *Not to abhorre the Virgins wombe*, not to abhorr the *beasts manger*, not to disdaine to be *fedd with butter and* honey; All, great humilitie.[60]

A royal Christmas sermon led naturally to an invitation to share in the Eucharist: "With this Act then of mutuall *taking,*

taking of his flesh, as He hath taken ours, let us seale our dutie to Him this day."[61] The Word is preached in the Sacrament of the Word made flesh.

Hacket, too, thinks the Incarnation the greatest miracle that ever was brought to light, borrows some of the paradoxes of Andrewes, and adds his own: "He that decketh himself with light as with a garment to be wrapt in swadling clouts, he that opens his hand, and filleth all things with plenteousness to suck a few drops of milk at a womans breasts, we are able to answer nothing to this, but with the *Angel* to cry out, *Rev.* v. 12. *Dominion and power unto the Lord, and to him that sitteth on the throne for evermore.*"[62] His ninth sermon on the Incarnation begins most seasonably, talking of God keeping the best house at Christmas, with liturgical joy:

> would you wish a more delicious banquet then such Confessions, such Collects, such Litanies, such heavenly Prayers, as our Church hath appointed . . . what delicacies are contained in the holy Scriptures both read and preacht unto you? what edifying Doctrine in the *Homilies* which are read on the *Saints days,* together with the *Divine Service?* and above all, what *Nectar,* what *Manna?* what restoring Cordials are received in the Blessed *Sacrament?*

Nor is the ethical divorced from the devotional, for the sermon ends:

> This is the house which God keeps, who also allows you to be chearful at home at this season, and commends it to you to feed the hungry; but especially show your thankful heart in frequenting his Church of Saints, that you may hear his word gladly, and obey it dutifully, and reign with him eternally. *Amen.* [63]

Cosin and Adams are both impressed by the humility of God become man. Cosin defines it as a ladder with four steps,[64] while Adams sees the contrasts in the omnipotent Creator becoming an impotent creature, God "in *whose presence is fulnesse of ioy*, becomes *a man full of sorrowes*" and "Eternal rest betakes himselfe to unrest: having whilst he lived *passive action*, and when he died *active passion.*"[65] While most of the preachers find the Incarnation and its paradoxes occasions for wonder, Adams also sees that the very lowliness of the outward accoutrements of Christ's nativity is an occasion for exercising faith. The meaning is that

> God doth often strangely and strongly exercise the Faith of his; that their perswasion may not be guided (*Oculis,* but *Oraculis*) by their Sight, but his Word. The eye of true Faith is so quicke sighted, that it can see through all the Mistes, and Fogges of difficulties.

The Magi must believe that this humble child is the King of Kings, though uncrowned; and human faith must, believing in the promises of God, trust "that in prison there is libertie, in trouble peace, in affliction, comfort, in Death life, in the Crosse a Crowne, and in a Manger the Lord *Iesus.*"[66]

It was Dean Jackson who saw—or rather, divined—what the Incarnation might mean to the life of God, and therefore what its profoundest consequence was: "God has now eyes and ears of men."[67] Hence the Son of God has become humanity's High Priest and prays for his people at the right hand of God the Father. Hence God became man, that humanity might be made Godlike.

The liturgical year in the Book of Common Prayer meant that the members of the Church of England were able to follow the earthly life of their Lord, from the Nativity and Epiphany, to his Baptism, and the period of Temptation when he considered in the forty days of fasting in the wilderness the nature of the appeal he would make as Messiah.

The two preachers with the largest number of published Lenten sermons were Andrewes with fourteen, and Hacket with twenty-one (not counting six on the Baptism of Christ). Hacket was a scholar of Westminster School whom Andrewes, then dean of Westminster, noted and "constantly cherished both at School and University to his death," according to Hacket's biographer Thomas Plume, who added that "our young Scholar ever rever'd this great Person *in loco Parentum*, often retired to him for advice in his studies. . . ."[68] If imitation is the sincerest form of flattery, this would account for the many Lenten sermons of both Andrewes and his protégé Hacket.

Andrewes makes repentance his central Lenten theme, as his various texts make clear. In a sermon before Elizabeth he is fanciful and allegorical. He argues that the voice of the turtle is mournful, that the Hebrew name for a stork suggests its nature, mercy, and the fact that the swallow's nest is near God's altar in Psalm 84, together with the vigilance and abstinence of the crane, are all emblematic examples for Christians to mourn their sins, to accept the divine mercy, to worship God frequently, and to fast at this holy season.[69] His 1619 sermon before King James deals with the different terms used in the Bible for repentance: "Of *renewing*, as from a *decay* (*Heb.* 6.6.) Of *refining*, as from *drosse* (*Ierem.* 6.29.) Of *recovering*, as from a *maladie* (*Dan.* 4.24.) Of *cleansing*, as from soile, Of *rising*, as from a *fall* (Ierem. 8.4). In no one, either for sense more full; or for use more often, then in this of *turning*."[70] Other sermons speak of fasting, correlate fasting and repentance, and insist that repentance must be more than momentary.[71]

Hacket, as we have indicated, was unusual in having frequently (at least six times) preached on the Baptism of Jesus, as well as on Lenten themes. These sermons treat the Baptism of Jesus as a covenantal parallel to the rainbow sign given to Noah in the Old Covenant. They offer comfort to those who died desiring Baptism but did not receive it, and to parents whose children suffered the same mishap. They also stress the paradox of John the Baptist baptizing God, see God as His own orator at the Baptism, and contrast the thunder of the Law at Sinai with the gentleness of the dove seen hovering above Christ at his Baptism.[72]

Hacket's twenty-one sermons "Upon the Tentation of our Saviour" are founded on the conviction that divines are guilty of a great omission if they allow poets to write endlessly about the wars of Troy, without "setting down the most terrible battel that ever was fought between *Christ* and *Satan,* the trustiest Champion, and the deadliest Enemy of mans Salvation against one another."[73] This central theme of Ignatian spirituality was taken up by the Protestant Hacket to fill a yawning chasm, as he saw it. He shows considerable psychological penetration in the understanding of temptation's power, in describing what he calls both deadly bullets of the Devil and "the two tables of the *Devils* Law." These are that "whosoever is in distress, let him think himself to be none of *Gods* children. The second on this wise, whosoever is in want let him raise his own fortune by hook or by crook, and as it were in despite of *God* let him care for himself."[74] Hacket is incisive in exposition, witty and solemn by turns in manner, and—in this differing from Andrewes—directly minatory about obsequious courtiers. He challenges Machiavelli's opinion (later to be Nietzsche's), that Christian humility depresses the spirits and weakens courage, with this retort: "I cross his opinion utterly, and say, that the truly humble Christian hath the most generous and lofty stomach of all others, which defies Flattery and fawning, and *Court-crowching,* and stands upon resolute terms to be beholding to none but *God* and integrity for exaltation."[75] Moreover, Hacket was never afraid to take the unpopular side, as befitted the preacher of heroic faith, who saw Christ as a victorious champion over all the sleights and subtleties and malice of the evil one.

Brownrig and Hacket are the two preachers who have the most printed sermons on the Transfiguration of Jesus, four each. Brownrig's sermons on this anticipatory glorification of Christ before His Passion and Crucifixion are occasionally marred by anti-Roman Catholic gibes,[76] and usually lacking in subtlety and devoid of a wit which might otherwise have been lenitives. But Brownrig did at least see the importance of the Mount of Transfiguration experience, with Christ acknowledged by Moses and Elijah, and the ensuing descent to the Valley of Humiliation to demonstrate the Messiah's healing and preaching. Hacket sees the implications of the Transfiguration thus: "Light of grace in this world: Light of glory in the next: And the light of mercy and comfort in them both."[77]

It is rare that sermons on the Crucifixion deal adequately with their high theme, but Donne's last sermon, *Deaths Duell*, is probably the greatest Passion sermon in English during the seventeenth century. Among other outstanding sermons on this topic are those by Adams, Ussher, and Joseph Hall. Adams with his "Majestie in Miserie, or, The Power of Christ even Dying," and his "A Crucifixe, Or, A Sermon upon the Passion," emphasizes the fact that Christ's was a life-long Passion, suffered "at all times, in all places, in all senses [all five of them], in all members."[78] It succeeds fully in its aim "to present to the eye of the conscience, the grievous Passion and gracious compassion" of Christ's total oblation.

Archbishop Ussher, the learned Calvinist, has one very impressive sermon on the text, Philippians 2:8, "And being found in fashion as a man, he humbled himself, and became obedient unto death, even the death of the cross." Its three main points are the Crucifixion's accursedness, its shame, and above all its pain.[79] It could almost be a commentary on the Eisenheim altarpiece of the gangrenous Christ, for its poignance without a trace of sentimentality. A twentieth–century analogy would be the Christ in agony at the base of the great tapestry in Coventry Cathedral designed in blacks and blues by Graham Sutherland.

Another man of brilliance, learning, and dedication, was the Calvinist bishop Joseph Hall who preached "The Passion Sermon," (so titled) at Paul's Cross on Good Friday, 14 April 1609, on the text John 19:30, "When Jesus therefore had received the vinegar, he said, It is finished: and gave up the Ghost." Its theme is the bitter and victorious Passion. It offers a meditation on the Lord's sufferings, tender but not sentimental, and is unflinching in its recognition of brutal cruelty:

That head, which is adored and trembled at by the angelical spirits, is all raked and harrowed with thorns; that face of whom it is said, *Thou art fairer than the children of men*, is all besmeared with filthy spittle . . . , and furrowed with his tears; those eyes, clearer than the sun, are darkened with the shadow of death; those ears, that hear the heavenly concerts of angels, now are filled with the cursed speakings and scoffs of wretched men; those lips, that *spake as never man spake*, that command the spirits both of light and darkness, are scornfully wet with vinegar and gall; those feet, that trample on all the powers of hell, (*His enemies are made his footstool,*) are now nailed to the footstool of the cross; those hands, that freely sway the sceptre of the heavens, now carry the reed of reproach, and are nailed to the tree of reproach; that whole body, which was conceived by the Holy Ghost, was all scourged, wounded, mangled: this is the outside of his sufferings.[80]

Hall continues by analyzing "the passions of his Passion" and deals most movingly with the Cry of Dereliction. The moralist in Hall goes on to show the heinousness of human sins, which means that Christ is crucified afresh in them. The last words on the Cross, "It is finished," are therefore only partially true. Hall's last plea is that his hearers may also give up their spirits to God, as Christ did, for God does not love an unwilling guest, but a glad guest God will receive "with that glory and happiness which can never be conceived and shall never be ended.

> *Even so, Lord Jesus, come quickly.*
> *Gloria in excelsis Deo.* "[81]

Although Donne preached many Good Friday sermons, the theme was so demanding of adoration and ecstasy,[82] rather than of brilliant verbal display, that he left only one printed sermon on the central paradox of the Christian faith, that the holy God should die for unholy humanity, and that was "Death's Duell." His last words ever preached were full of faith and hope in the Resurrection:

There *bath* in his *teares*, there *suck* at his *woundes*, and *lye downe in peace* in his *grave*, till he vouchsafe you a *resurrection*, and an *ascension* into that *Kingdome*, which hee *bath purchas'd for you*, with the *inestimable price* of his *incorruptible blood.* [83]

This felicitous literary transition can be ours in treating the sermons of our preachers on the Resurrection and Ascension of Christ.

Of the eighteen printed Resurrection sermons of Andrewes, it is difficult to select a single one for exemplification. The fifteenth is chosen because it is a court sermon, employs an unusual text, is divided in complex fashion, cites the different opinions of three Fathers of the Church, uses wit and paradox, and ends with an application for the hearers. All of these elements are characteristic of Andrewes. The text is the words of the risen Christ to Mary Magdalene, John 20:17, and is given in the Vulgate Latin and King James versions: "*Noli me tangere.* IESUS saith unto her, Touch me not." The division is as follows:

We may divide it (as the Iewes do the Law) into *Do not* and *Do;* somewhat *forbidden* there is, and somewhat *bidden. Forbidden,* doe not, *not touch me; Bidden,* but doe, *Goe your wayes, and tell.* The *forbidding* part stands of two points: a *Restraining;* and a Reason . . . The *Bidding* part of three. 1. a Mission, or *Commission,* to goe doe a message, *Vade & dic.* 2. The Parties to whom: to my *Brethren,* that is, to his *Disciples.* 3. The Message it selfe; I ascend to my Father, &c.[84]

The wit was in the very first paragraph, at the end of which he comments on the text: "Make the best of it, a repulse it is: but a cold salutation for an *Easter-day* morning."[85] It is also in the wordplay of "bidden" and "forbidden." The three Fathers whose opinions differ are Chrysostom, Gregory the Great, and Augustine. The first, says Andrewes, thought the cause of the rebuke was because the Magdalen was being too forward; the second thought "her touch no Easter-day touch; her *tangere* had a *tang* in it (as we say)"; and the third thought it a device to get her to rush with the news to the other disciples so they should know he was risen.[86] Augustine, says Andrewes, believed that Christ meant "to wean her from sensual touching, but by the spiritual touch of faith."[87] This was the moral for the congregation, but it was also a paradox, a reason beyond reason.

Donne's many fine sermons on the Resurrection make several different attempts to divine its meaning. One stresses that it is a final victory over death;[88] another that it will be the union of body and soul for members of his congregation, not divided and distracted as they are in church;[89] while a third[90] shows that it was, for Donne, the central enthralling fact about Christianity, a preacher always so concerned about vermiculation. This third sermon was preached on Easter Day, 1627 at St. Paul's, and it had special meaning for Donne himself after the recent death of his daughter Lucy. Its theme is that the dead are not lost, and its text is Hebrews 11:35, "Women received their dead raised to life againe: and others were tortured, not accepting a deliverance, that they might obtaine a better Resurrection." His fine opening aphorism is "Mercy is God's right hand, with that God gives all; Faith is man's right hand, with that man takes all."[91] He asks himself, seeing that the heathen feasted when their sons died,

> If I had fixt a Son in Court, or married a daughter into a plentifull Fortune, I were satisfied for that son and that daughter. Shall I not be so, when the King of Heaven hath taken that son to himselfe, and maried himselfe to that daughter, for ever? I spend none of my Faith, I exercise none of my Hope, in this, that I shall have my dead raised to life againe.

He continues with a *credo* that is heart-deep: "This is the faith that sustains me, when I lose by the death of others, or when I suffer by living in misery my selfe, That the dead, and we,

377

are now all in one Church, and at the resurrection, shall be all in one Quire."[92]

For all the preachers of the English Church, Easter Day was the climax of the Christian Year and the most joyful feast. They celebrated it biblically as God the Father's vindication of his eternal Son by raising him from the dead,[93] as the ultimate death of death,[94] and as the sure hope of everlasting life for Christians living in faith and loyalty to Christ and charity to their neighbor. They rejoiced in the consolation that "if we endure, we shall also reign with him,"[95] and celebrated the joy of companionship with Christ here and hereafter in the Communion of Saints—though exiles on earth their citizenship is in heaven.[96]

Even so our preachers did not forget that the reality of the Resurrection had been disputed in the first century,[97] initially by the disciples themselves[98] as well as by other skeptics.[99] The sermon of Dr. Thomas Lushington in St. Mary's, Oxford caused scandal largely by his dealing dramatically and at length, with the criticism that the disciples stole Christ's body, whereas he repudiated it only briefly. In contrast Andrewes shrewdly meets the criticism by arguing that there was much doubt at the time of the Resurrection in order that there should be none later.[100]

The Ascension was also celebrated but, since this took place on a weekday not a Sunday, it was not as popular a feast as Easter. Its implications for Christ were more significant than for the believer, and so very few sermons for this occasion were printed. Nor are they remarkable. It was seen as the glorification of Jesus in the return to the Father, who, as at his Baptism and at the Transfiguration, declared "This is my beloved Son, in whom I am well pleased." It was the completion for Jesus of the great parabola of Humiliation, going "from God to God" via the Incarnation, the Passion, the Crucifixion, Death, Resurrection, and Ascension.

Now all that remained of the Christological cycle was the fulfilment[101] of Christ's promised Holy Spirit[102] at Pentecost or, as the English termed it, Whitsunday. This was, as it were, the birthday of the Church, and the return of Christ at the end of history as Judge of the Great Assize and determiner of destiny.

All this is admirably summarized in Bishop Hall's claim that the Church's Calendar is a theological instructor for the plain man. He started a sermon before King Charles I in 1640 with these illuminating words:

If we mark it, your very calendar so as the wisdom of the church hath contrived it, is a notable catechism. And surely if the plain man would but ply his almanack well, that alone would teach him gospel enough to show him the history of his Saviour.[103]

Sermons for Whitsunday are many and impressive. The Holy Spirit was variously and abstractly conceived as the *vinculum caritatis,* or bond of love, uniting God the Father and God the Son, and as the bridge of unity across which the Divine love came to God's people. The Holy Spirit was also the source of illumination, inspiration, and regeneration.

For Andrewes the Holy Spirit was the Advocate or Paraclete, the defender of the faithful Christian in all difficulties. He was also "Love it selfe, the essential *love* and *love-knot* of the two persons of the God-head, *Father* and *Sonne.*"[104] Also, because of his multifarious activities, the Holy Spirit was variously imaged in Scripture: "*Water* sometimes, sometime *fire:* One while *winde,* one while *ointment:* and according to our severall wants, we are to send to him for *fire* to *warme;* for *winde,* to *coole;* for *water* to *clense us;* for *oil* to *supple* us."[105] Equally, of course, fire and water could be interpreted as symbols of purification, ointment for healing, and wind as symbol of the invisible power of God.

Hacket's five varied and imaginative sermons "upon the descent of the Holy Ghost" will serve to represent those of all the metaphysical preachers. The first compares and evaluates six different authorities attempting to decide in which house the disciples were at Pentecost. It also stresses the unity of the disciples, "like grapes they hung together in one cluster."[106]

The second sermon is more fanciful and suggests that if we had been asked to guess what the sound of Pentecost was like we might have thought of the humming of bees, or the purling of soft streams, or "the voice of harpers playing on their harps" as in Revelation 14:2; in fact it was described "as a rushing mighty wind," which he insists was the *fragor* of the wind.[107] He goes on to refer to the theological insight of "that great *Scholar Bishop Andrewes*," that the Spirit is not universally diffused but it is only at God's pleasure and at the place where Christ has his Church"—a curious limitation of the *Creator Spiritus*. The sermon ends practically: "The purpose of giving the *Holy Ghost* is to make the Seed of the Word fruitful in our hearts, that we may believe the *Gospel*, that we may live holily according to the profession of our Faith, and that through Faith, which must work by love if it be true faith, we may be saved."[108] The third sermon deals with "the cloven tongues of fire" at Pentecost, which symbolize the apostles' ability to preach to many—a duty which some bishops neglect to perform—while they were "cloven" like flames to symbolize the gospel is to be preached in many tongues, thus rectifying the chaos of Babel by the ordered unity of Pentecost.[109] The fourth Pentecostal sermon praises God for the wisdom "which teacheth learned men their exact insight into the Sacred Tongues, and the Lord hath furnish'd many Heroes of the *Reformed Churches* with such exquisite skill in their kind. . . ."[110] Hacket's fifth and final sermon deals with the varied reception of the Holy Ghost by the world, "First, a great Miracle, for it wrought these three things; first amazement . . .; secondly, doubt . . .; thirdly, earnest Search and Inquisition . . . yet divers turned to Mockery."[111] His logic and his wit find ample opportunity to exhibit themselves in the interpretation of the charge of intoxication laid against the apostles. The logician in Hacket claims it was impossible to be overtaken with new wine "for there is no such liquor to be had in *May*, not till *September* at the soonest"[112] (true in England but not necessarily so in the Middle East). Spiritual drunkenness, he ingeniously argues, has four effects: it enables the disciples to forget the ceremonial; the person giddy with wine makes no distinction of persons, nor must the apostles for the sake of the Gospel; wine gives an edge to valor and so the Spirit of God is undaunted; and, as a drunken man reveals secrets, "so the *Holy Ghost* coming down this day did open the fountain which was sealed up before; the Mysteries of *Gods* eternal counsel, brought to pass in time by the Incarnation of his Son, were made manifest to all the world."[113] Hacket's wit does not fail him when he reminds the congregation that they will be receiving the cup or chalice at the communion table as the climax of the service of the festal day: "This cup is that which ravisheth our Souls, and carries up our Spirit to *Heaven* to partake of the body and bloud of Christ when we come to his holy Table; this is *Sobria ebritas, non madens vino, sed ardens Deo;* This is a sober drunkenness, an inflammation, not with wine, but with the love of the *Lord Jesus.*"[114]

Whitsuntide (followed by Trinity Sunday) completes the Christological cycle of the Calendar. While Trinity Sunday is doctrinally important since it proclaims the essential mystery of the Triune God (which to explain is to explain away), and distinguishes Christianity from its mother Judaism and its son Islam, yet it is not a festival of the Calendar, but rather a liturgical summary. Our preachers have left relatively few printed sermons for Trinity Sunday largely because they deal with the Holy Trinity at Pentecost. The exceptions are Donne with seven, and Adams and Lake with one each.[115] The topic will be dealt with more briefly than it deserves.

Adams has a fine title for his Trinity Sunday sermon, "The Spiritual Navigator bound for the Holy Land," which he derives from the text, Revelation 4:6, "Before the Throne" there was "a Sea of Glass like unto Chrystall." He then offers seven different glosses on this sea, ranging from the fullness of grace which the Church derives from Christ, to the Gospel with its crystalline clarity, and to Baptism. He has a fine passage commenting on St. Paul's "the fashion of the world perisheth"—

a most vivid entropy in which "the starres doe but twinckle; as if they were dimme, and look'd upon the earth with spectacles" while the sun is drowsy and the moon sick with age.[116] It concludes with an ascription of praise to the eternal Triune Unity.

Donne's sermons for Trinity Sunday do not measure up to his festival sermons at Christmas and Easter, and fall below even his Whitsun sermons. One, preached in 1621, does however include a deeply moving meditation on the Crucifixion, beginning "I see those hands stretched out, that stretched out the heavens, and those feet racked, to which they that racked them are foot-stooles; I heare him, from whom his nearest friends fled, pray for his enemies, and him, whom his Father forsooke, not forsake his brethren."[117] A second sermon, preached at St. Dunstan's on Trinity Sunday, 1624, employs a text related to Christ's Baptism by John the Baptist, recording the acknowledgment of God the Father, "And lo, a Voyce came from heaven, saying, This is my beloved Sonne in whom I am well pleased" (Matthew 3:17). This leads Donne to say that Christians born blind (through original sin) are given the eye-salve, *collyrium*, in Baptism so they can see by faith. But faith itself is approached by reason as a flower is upheld by a stake. He finishes with a fine flourish, borrowing an image from Augustine, and typically paradoxical, "If the Dove [symbol of the gentleness of the Holy Spirit] bite, it bites with kissing, if the Holy Ghost rebukes, he rebukes with comforting."[118] A third sermon on the four living creatures full of eyes in the Apocalypse (on the text, Revelation 4:8) interprets them traditionally as the four evangelists. This gives Donne a chance to inform the congregation of the qualities needed in ministers: ". . . every Minister of God is to have all, that all foure had; the courage of a *Lion*, the labouriousnesse of an *Oxe*, the perspicuity and clearesight of the *Eagle*, and the humanity, the discourse, the reason, the affability, the appliableness of a *Man*."[119] One is impressed by the ingenuity rather than by the profundity or theological instruction in the doctrine of the Holy Trinity in these sermons.

Chapter VIII

Eschatology

Eschatology, or the study of the four last things—death, judgment, hell, and heaven—inevitably and appropriately occupy the last section of this chapter, and, since the Resurrection has already been considered, little need be said of heaven.

Donne was obsessed with the thought of death, as were many poets and dramatists of the Jacobean age, such as Shirley, Webster, Tourneur, and, supremely, Shakespeare. For Donne it seemed to be the thought of vermiculation and disintegration in the grave that most worried him, as throughout "Death's Duell" until the conclusion:

> . . . this whole *world* is but an universall church-yard, but our *common grave*; and the life and motion that the greatest persons have in it, but as the shaking of buried bodies in their graves by an *earth-quake*. That which we call life, is but *Hebdomeda mortium, a week of deaths*, seaven dayes, seaven periods of our life spent in dying, *a dying seaven times over*; and there is an end . . . Our *youth* is *hungry and thirsty*, after those *sinnes*, which *infancy knew not*; And our *age* is *sorry* and *angry*, that it *cannot pursue* those *sinnes* which our *youth* did. And besides, al the way, so many deaths, that is, so many deadly calamities accompany every condition, and every period of this life, as that death it selfe would bee an ease to them that suffer them.[120]

This was, of course, the utterance of a sick and dying man, and it has more of the *taedium vitae*, of sheer weariness of life, than is common with the dean of St. Paul's, although the product of an earlier serious illness of 1623, *Devotions upon Emergent Occasions* published in 1624, shows how thoroughly his introspective mind had meditated on death. Thoughts of death were also present in a sermon preached before the Prince and Princess Palatine, on their way to Germany. In this he suggests that as the dying man's eyes close in darkness "thou shalt see, that though in the eyes of men thou lye upon that bed, as a

Statue on a Tomb, yet in the eyes of God, thou standest as a *Colossus*, one foot in one, another in another land; one foot in the grave, but the other in heaven; one hand in the womb of the earth, and the other in *Abrahams* bosome: And then *vere prope*, Salvation is truly neer thee, and neerer then when thou believedst, which is our last word."[121] At another time, he thought of "Death the Leveller"—to use the title and lines from Shirley's poem, with its recognition that "sceptre and crown/ Must tumble down/And in the dust be equal made/With the poor crooked scythe and spade,"—ending: "and when a whirel-winde hath blowne the dust of the Church-yard into the Church, and the man sweeps out the dust of the Church into the Church-yard, who will undertake to sift those dusts again, and to announce, This is the Patrician, this is the noble flowre, and this the yeomanly, this the Plebeian bran."[122] He was also concerned how the disintegrated bodies of the world would be reintegrated for the Last Judgment.[123] But death is also for Donne an occasion of great hope because the Day of Death is, for the Christian, the Day of Resurrection: "We die in the light, in the sight of Gods presence, and we rise in the light, in the sight of his very Essence."[124]

What is more to be feared than death is the Great Assize at the end of history, when Christ as Judge will decide who are the obedient sheep and who the wayward goats. This will be ushered in by the Second Coming of Christ. Brownrig insisted that

> Death, in its own nature, is God's Serjeant and Officer; the appearance such as one to a debtor or malefactor, is fearful, and they run from him; but to a friend or acquaintance, he is a messenger of love, and we willingly admit of him. This Officer comes to a Christian, not to arrest, or attach him, but lovingly to invite him.[125]

Hacket says that no annual consideration of Judgment Day is kept because it would be presumptuous and "prescribe God to an appointed time, who must not be prescribed."[126] Lake asks his congregation to think of the images, all of uncertainty, which are used to describe this day: it comes as upon a woman in labour, like a thief in the night, or like a hunter.[127] Adams, after insisting on the parity of humans at death, observes that this is followed at Judgment by imparity again, but of a different character, "for then, the least in the worlds estimation shall sit downe, with the blessed Kings and Patriarches in Heaven, when Kings and Patriarchs without grace shall be excluded. If you desire your names to be registred with the pen of Eternity, write them yourselves with the pen of Charity."[128]

The real horror of the Judgment Day is that human souls will be utterly undisguised and naked before the presence of the holy Christ. This is Ussher's warning, that the experience is like a knight's degrading, when he is divested of his sword and his golden spurs, "and then go Sir Knave." So is the soul stripped of its moral virtues and then "see what an ugly soul he hath; he had hope before, now he is without hope: he had some patience in the world, but he made no good use of it; and now his patience is taken from him: and when thou shalt come to a place of torment, and thy hope and patience taken away from thee, what case wilt thou be in?"[129] Donne also bids his hearers think of that terrible day, when their sins will be recalled, the hypocrisy in their apparently good deeds revealed, and the sins they enticed others to commit laid open. He ends citing St. Bernard: "*Quis non cogitans haec in desperationis rotetur abyssum?* Who can once thinke of this and not be tumbled into desperation?"[130]

Adams, too, dilates on the theme in a sermon titled, "Presumption Running into Despaire" which is based on Revelation 6:16, "They said to the mountaines and rockes, Fall on us, and hide us from the face of him that sitteth on the Throne, and from the wrath of the Lambe." Christ the Judge is both omniscient and omnipotent, and therefore a source of fear for evil-doers. Adams threatens the terrors of hell, and insists upon the contrast between Christ's first and second comings:

Then in humilitie, now in glory: then with poore shepheards, now with mighty Angels; then the contempt of nations, now with the terrour of the world: then crowned

385

with thornes, now with maiestie: then iudged by one man, now iudging all men: then in a cratch, now in a *Throne.*

He ends with the reassurance that the godly shall find the Judge "a Lambe indeed; as will now to save them, as before to suffer for them."[131]

One of the most interesting eschatological sermons is a particularly vivid one preached as a Spital sermon by Thomas Goffe, entitled "Deliverance from the Grave." The text selected was Ezekiel 37:13, "And ye shall know that I am the Lord, when I have opened your graves, O my people, and brought you up out of your graves." The sermon was delivered on 28 March, the Wednesday in Easter Week, 1627. The sermon progresses, in a powerfully visualized manner, from the consideration of death (recently all too deeply etched on the memories of the congregation by a visitation of the plague), to the Resurrection from the grave of Christ, to the General Assize at the end of history as bodies emerge from their graves at the General Resurrection. Goffe ends with a renewed plea for charity, praising the donors that "Your *Bethlem* [Hospital] shewes, how he that was borne at *Bethlem,* is borne anew in your hearts, and you again and regenerate and borne in him; for whose sake if a cup of cold water given shall never goe unrewarded, then surely, *Copiosa erit Merces vestra in Coelis . . .* Thus farre doe the armes of the Poore lift you their Benefactors and Patrons from your Graves. . . ."[132]

Goffe promised Heaven to the generous for Christ's sake; other preachers, notably the Calvinists Ussher, Smith, and Adams, dangled their hearers over the pit or threatened them with the undying flames of hell, or the undying worm in their entrails. Smith describes the terrifying descent into hell from the Sessions of Judgment:

and he which hath made his pleasure of sinne, so soone as he heares this doome, *Depart from me yee wicked* shall goe down by a black waie with many a sigh and sob, from God, from the Angels, from the Saints, from ioie, from glory, from blisse, with the fiends of hell, to sup in the Pallace of darkenes with the Princes of horror at the table of vengeance, in the chaire of calamitie, with *the crowne of death upon his head:* & he which tempted him to sinne, shall plague him for sinning, until he crie like Cain, *My punishment is greater than I can beare.* [133]

Adams, however, excels him in Dantesque descriptions, and has been well described as "hell's local colorist."[134] Consider the unending fate of sensualists who scorn religion:

from snakes they shall turne upon Adders, from both to Scorpions, from all to unquenched flames, where they spend not hours but ages, nay, that eternitie of time, in waylings and howlings, grones and torments; when for every ounce of vanity, they shall receive (downe weight) a whole pound of sorrow: smoake, blackenesse, boyling Cauldrons, fiery burnings of Brimstone and Sulphure, kindled and continued by the breath of an offended God.[135]

In another sermon he shows how all the five senses are assailed by torments in which each is worse than the last:

The sight is afflicted with darkness and ugly devils: the hearing with shrikes and horrible cries: the smelling with noysome stenches: the taste with ravenous hunger & bitter gall: the feeling with intolerable, yet unquencheable fire.[136]

He adds that his listeners must imagine "a gloomy, hideous and deep lake, full of pestilent dampes and rotten vapours, as thick as clouds of pitch, more palpable then the fogs of Egypt; that the eye of the Sun is too dull to pierce them, and his heate too weake to dissolve them." Finally to add misery to misery, he concludes this description of the landscape of hell: "Adde hereunto a fire flashing in the reprobate face; which shall yeeld no more light then with a glimpse to shew him the torments of others, and others, the torments of himselfe;

yet withall, of so violent a burning that should it glow on mountaines of steele, it would melt them like hils of snow."[137]

On two other occasions at least Adams threatens like a Boanerges, a veritable son of thunder.[138] He will not allow his
large congregation to sleep in their sins, and if he cannot woo
them he will win them with wrath. The ending of one sermon
sums up his Calvinist faith: "God hath *sowne*, and hee will
reape; *sowne* his Word, and will *reape* his Glory. His glory either
in your instruction or destruction, conversion or conviction,
life or death . . . turne not that to your desolation which God
sends for your consolation."[139] To modern eyes this may seem
abominably lipsmackingly vengeful of God and his interpreter,
even barbarously sadistic. To which Adams would reply that
our sentimentality has prevented us from heeding the minatory
Word of God in both Testaments, that we gloss over the parable
of the poor man Lazarus in heaven and the miserly sick man
in torment in Hades, and that we should not forget some of
Jesus' trenchant eschatological sayings.[140]

The coolest analysis of the torrid temperatures of hell is Archbishop Ussher's, third member of our trio of Calvinists. His
text is fearsome, Revelation 21:8 "But the fearful and unbelieving, and the abominable and murderers, and whoremongers
and sorcerers and idolaters, and all liars, shall have their part
in the lake which burneth with fire and brimstone, which is
the second death." Ussher does justice to the text. The penalties
imposed by God are partly of loss, and partly of physical torment. "Now darkness is a privation of all light, so is hell of
all comfort." A greater loss is to be banished from God's presence in heaven, which is the greatest good. To make it doubly
worse, this banishment shall be in sight of heaven and for
ever.[141] Further, hell is a prison, where the miserable compan-
ions are devils and damned howling ghosts, "and a place of
torment, where the tormentors are the Devil, one's self, and
God almighty."[142]

Donne, too, can bring home the horrors of hell with equal
force.[143] It is significant that he contrasts the darkness, isolation,
misery, ignorance, and chaos of hell with the incandescent light,

the blessed community of the Holy Trinity and the saints, the unending joys, the vision of God seen face to face, and the serenity and order of those celestial citizens. Adams too speaks of heaven's joys, but concisely, as a banquet: "Where these four things concurre, that makes a perfect feast: *Dies lectus, locus electus, coetus bene collectus, apparatus non neglectus.* A good time, eternitie. A good place, Heaven. A good Companie, the Saints. Good cheere, Glory."[144]

It needed Donne's powerful imagination to transport the earthbound worldlings in his congregations to heaven, but this was Donne's supreme poetic gift in the pulpit. First he was able to make his hearers feel how trivial in eternity the concerns of time must seem:

> Heires of the joy, and heires of the glory of heaven; where if they look down and see Kings fighting for Crownes, thou canst look off as easily, as from boyes at stool, balls for points here; and from Kings triumphing after victories, as easily as a Philosopher from a Pageant of children, here.[145]

On another occasion Donne discourses etymologically on the "Mansions" in heaven (Christ's promise to his disciples), because the term "signifies a *Remaining,* and denotes the perpetuity, the everlastingness of the state." Then he explains the paradox of the endless day of eternity, which is only a single day, because it will never be followed by night. Yet it is a day longer than a thousand million million years. As usual, he manages to be vivid on the most abstract concept:

> *Methusalem,* with all his hundreds of yeares, was but a Mushrome of a nights growth, to this day, And all the foure Monarchies with all their thousands of yeares, And all the powerfull Kings, and all the beautifull Queenes of this world, were but as a bed of flowers, some gathered at six, some at seaven, some at eight.[146]

On a third occasion Donne thinks of the brilliant radiance that illumines heaven, and of the beatific vision of God, and compares these with the faint light of natural reason and the slightly brighter light of faith. A comparison makes the point clearer to his congregation: "To this light of glory, the light of honour is but a glow-worm; and majesty it self but a twilight; The Cherubims and Seraphims are but Candles; and that Gospel it self, which the Apostle calls the glorious Gospel, but a star of the least magnitude."[147]

All this superbly imagined splendor then, on yet another occasion, fuels the hope of the Christian—that is the practical bent of all sermons on the Resurrection and heaven—for "Man is a future Creature. In a holy and usefull sense, Wee may say that *God is a future God;* to man especially hee is so; Mans consideration of God is especially for the future."[148]

The metaphysical preachers had other topics, of course. For example, blasphemy and cursing were sins that worried several preachers including Donne and Adams.[149] The same pair of outstanding preachers was also deeply concerned to awaken compassion for the poor,[150] as were the annual preachers at St. Mary of Bethlehem's Hospital (the Bedlam Spital). Both Andrewes and Donne, we may recall, were delighted to exalt the role of women, and celebrated the friends of Jesus who, in bringing the first news of Christ's Resurrection to the disciples, were apostles to the apostles. The marks of a good marriage and its purposes were the concern in sermons preached by many, including Smith, Donne, and Cosin.[151] Smith's two expanded sermons constitute a 73-page treatise on the topic.

The glory of the seventeenth–century English pulpit was to be seen alike in the development of both innovative and traditional themes. In this chapter, however, we have looked at the close correlation of theology (as instruction in doctrine, worship, and behavior) with the Bible. This in turn was linked to the Book of Common Prayer and its Christological calendar, and it is this aspect that gave it its considerable distinction and relevance. Thus preaching led to the understanding of God's will—to the adoration of his holiness and mercy as well as to a charitable concern for the unfortunate.

NOTES

1. Even this contrast may be overstated. Certainly Henry Smith and Thomas Adams convey the idea of hell in a powerful manner, though Donne can also describe it effectively, and no one can equal Donne in suggesting the glory, brilliant light, rest, and the communion of saints in heaven.

2. See Winfried Schleiner, *The Imagery of John Donne's Sermons* (Providence, Rhode Island, 1970), 109–118, for a thorough consideration of the role of the image of God and its sealing in Donne's sermons. Donne believes that the sacraments renew the image of God in the soul.

3. Ralph Brownrig, *Sixty Five Sermons* (London, 1674), 238. From the first Whitsunday sermon, which is a characteristically dim evaluation of natural religion.

4. This is a summary of Sermon 20 of 1651 (New Style), "On the Feast of Christ's Nativity," in *The Works of . . . Cosin*, Volume 1: *Sermons* (Oxford, 1843), 285–286.

5. *Works of . . . Cosin*, 1:310. From Sermon 22, a Christmas sermon of 1655 preached in Paris before Duke James (the future King James II, *coram Iacobo*).

6. *The Sermons of John Donne*, eds. G. R. Potter and E. M. Simpson, 10 vols. (Berkeley, 1953–1962), 6:143. From the sermon for Trinity Sunday, 1624.

7. Donne, *Sermons*, 3:37–38. See also 3:359: "So the common light of reason illumines us all; but one imployed this light upon the searching of impertinent vanities, another by a better use of the same light, finds out the Mysteries of Religion."

8. Donne, *Sermons*, 6:143.

9. *The Workes . . . of Tho: Adams* (London, 1629), 844–845.

10. C. S. Lewis in his *Surprised by Joy*, as in his earlier *Pilgrim's Regress*, draws attention to *sehnsucht*, which is adumbrated in Augustine's *Confessions* where he says that our hearts are restless until they rest in God: *cor nostrum inquietum donec requiescat in Te.*

11. Brian Duppa, *Angels Rejoicing for Sinners Repenting* (London, 1648), 1–2. The text is Luke 15:10, "Likewise I say unto you, There is joy in the presence of the Angels of God over one Sinner that repenteth."

12. Donne, *Sermons,* 10:111, from a sermon on Philippians 3:2, "Beware of the Concision," preached at St. Paul's Cathedral.

13. Donne, *Sermons,* 5:298, a sermon on Psalm 51.7, one of the Penitential Psalms.

14. Donne, *Sermons,* 5:58, a Whitsunday sermon, circa 1622, possibly preached at St. Paul's.

15. *The Sermons of Maister Henrie Smith* (London, 1593), 998.

16. Arthur Lake, *Sermons (with some Religious and Divine Meditations)* (London, 1629). From a sermon preached at Paul's Cross on Trinity Sunday on the text of Jude 5:20–21.

17. Henry Vaughan, *Silex Scintillans,* "The Night," ll. 44-47.

18. Lake, *Sermons,* 50.

19. Donne, *Sermons,* 1:292. From a sermon preached at Whitehall, 19 April 1618, on the autobiographical text, I Timothy 1:15, "This is a faithful saying and worthy of all acceptation, that Christ Jesus came into the world to save sinners, of whom I am the chiefest."

20. Donne, *Sermons,* 9:396.

21. Francis White, *London's Warning by Jerusalem. A Sermon Preached at Pauls Crosse on Mid-Lent last* (London, 1619), 36. This an example of psychological insights, not uncommon in the metaphysical preachers.

22. *Workes of Tho: Adams* 694–695, 714. From the sermon, "The Bad Leaven: Or The Contagion of Sinne" expounding Genesis 5:9, "A little Leaven leaveneth the whole lumpe."

23. William Barlow, *A Sermon preached at Paules Crosse, on the first Sunday in Lent, Martij. I, 1600* (London, 1601), sig. Ciii.

24. There is, however, an important exception. Much reference was made by the seventeenth-century preachers, Arminian and Calvinist, to the classical pagan moralists and the cardinal virtues as exemplified by non-Christians for the purpose of chiding the Christians. See the fascinating fifth chapter, "As the Heathen man sayeth," in Lawrence A. Sasek, *The Literary Temper of the English Puritans* (Baton Rouge, Louisiana, 1961), 77–91.

25. Donne preached a Spital (St. Mary's Hospital) sermon in 1622 criticizing the evasion of London tithes, a topic often also referred to in Paul's Cross sermons. He moves rapidly from brief indignation to extended sympathy. Only the abrupt start is quoted here: "I may be bold to say, that this City hath the ablest preaching Clergy of any City in Christendom; must I be fain to say that the Clergy of this City hath the poorest intertainment of any City that can come

into comparison with it? it is so" (*Sermons,* 4:113). See also William Gifford, "Time and place in Donne's sermons," *PMLA,* 82 (1966):388–398. Adams (*Workes,* 864) criticizes the impropriation of tithes with indignation, as does Hacket, *A Century of Sermons* (London, 1675), 727.

26. Bishop John Howson preached a sermon at Paul's Cross in December 1597 which offered five reasons for the evil of simony, that is buying and selling of spiritual promotions. They are the fracture of society, the production of an inefficient and unlearned ministry, the reduction of ministerial hospitality to their congregation, the reduction of theological students for the two universities, and a general disintegration. From *A Sermon Preached at Paules Crosse the 4 of December, 1597* (London, 1597).

27. I Corinthians 13:13.

28. Luke 10:27.

29. Donne, *Sermons,* 10:3. Donne also says (*Sermons,* 3:236) that "for spirituall things, the things of the next world, we have no roome; for temporall things, the things of this world, we have no bounds."

30. *Workes of Tho: Adams,* 461. The sermon is entitled, "The Soules Sicknesse: A Discourse. Divine, Morall, and Physicall."

31. *Workes of Tho: Adams,* 655. The sermon "Heaven-Gate; Or the Passage to Paradise" is based on Revelation 22:14 *in fine,* "And may enter in through the Gates into the Citie." The reference to these "honours" and "worships" suggests the presence of the Lord Mayors (past and present) and the aldermen of the city of London. It might therefore have been a Spital sermon.

32. *The Whole Works of . . . Ussher,* 17 vols. (Dublin and London, 1847–1864), 13:529. From "A Sermon Preached before the King at Greenwich, Sunday June 25, 1627.", on 1 Corinthians 4:33.

33. *Sermons of Maister Henrie Smith,* 57. From a sermon which is virtually a treatise entitled "A Preparative to Marriage." The quotation might suggest Henry Smith is a male chauvinist, but he speaks of the joys of marriage and reminds husbands to be tender to their wives. More typical is the following passage in the same sermon, 7–8:

> Lastlie, in all Nations the day of mariage was reputed the joyfullest day in all their life and is reputed so still of all, as though the sunne of happinesse began that day to shine upon us, when a good wife is brought unto us. Therefore one saith: that mariage signifieth merrie-age, because a play-fellow is come to make our age merrie, as Isaac and Rebecca sported together.

Smith, too, criticizes men who "put a pedlars shop upon theyr backs, and colour their faces, and prick their ruffes, and frisle theyre hayre," (*Sermons*, 434–435).

34. *Workes of Tho: Adams*, 815, from the sermon "Loves Copie."

35. *Sermons of Maister Henrie Smith*, 162–163.

36. *Sermons of Maister Henrie Smith*, 168.

37. *Workes of Tho: Adams*, 404.

38. *Workes of Tho: Adams*, 590.

39. Donne, *Sermons*, 8:280. From a sermon preached at St. Paul's on 23 November 1628.

40. Donne, *Sermons*, 10:95. From a Candlemas Day sermon on Matthew 5:16, "Let your light so shine before men that they see your good works and glorifie your Father which is in heaven." "The refuse of the wheat" is a quotation from Amos 6:8.

41. John Buckeridge, *A Sermon Preached at the Funerall of the R. R. Father in GOD LANCELOT late Lord Bishop of Winchester. In the parish church of St. Saviours in Southwarke On Saturday the xi. of November A.D. MDCXXVI* (London, 1629), 9. It is also included in the *XCVI Sermons* of Andrewes (London, 1629).

42. Andrewes, *XCVI Sermons* (London, 1629), 405. From the third sermon on the Resurrection, preached before the king at Whitehall on the 26 March 1608, on the narrative passage in Mark 16:1–7.

43. *Workes of Tho: Adams*, 815. The same theme is treated at 448. Anger (447) and sloth (449) are also considered. From the sermon "The Soules Sicknesse."

44. Adams (*Workes*, 349–350) insists that gluttony leads to drunkenness and lust: "As the myst and waterish groundes bring forth nothing but frogs and toades, so the belly and watrie stomache that is stuffed like a tunne, bringeth forth nothing but a drousie minde, foggie thoughts, filthie speeches, and corrupt affections: therefore the Phisitian saith, nothing better for the bodie then abstinence, the Divine saith, nothing better for the soule then abstinence, the Lawyer saith, nothing better for the wits then abstinence." Adams seems to be only preacher who keeps to the medieval seven deadly sins, although he adds hypocrisy as a sin. See also Henry Smith's two sermons on "A Looking-Glasse for Drunkards" (*Sermons*, 595ff.) which deal with the deformity of drunkenness, men turned into drivelling, flaming-faced, reeling-footed, and trembling caricatures of themselves, mere beasts.

45. Donne, *Sermons*, 6:152.

46. John 14:2.

47. Itrat Husein, *The Dogmatic and Mystical Theology of John Donne* (London, 1938). This interesting early study of Donne's theology is almost certainly erroneous in describing Donne's theology as mystical. It is indeed Christian orthodoxy, but a historical, rational, and psychological theology rather than mystically interpreted. Donne longs for rather than expresses the *unio mystica* that inflames the devotion of St. Ignatius Loyola, or supremely that of St. John of the Cross and St. Teresa of Avila. See Louis Martz, *The Poetry of Meditation: A Study in English Religious Literature of the Seventeenth Century* (New Haven, 1954), a fascinating work which claims, on slender historical grounds, that Donne's education by Jesuits led to his Ignatian spirituality. Robert C. Bald, *John Donne, a Life* (New York, 1970), 39, says this was impossible as Jesuits were engaged fulltime on a mission to reconvert England. Barbara Lewalski, in chapter 5 of *Protestant Poetics and the Seventeenth Century Religious Lyric* (Princeton, N.J., 1979), corrects in part and complements Martz by showing that there was a powerful and pervasive Protestant tradition of meditation from which the metaphysicals could and did borrow.

48. Donne, *LXXX Sermons* (London, 1640), 79.

49. John Gauden, *Three Sermons Preached upon Severall Publike Occasions* (London, 1642), 27.

50. Hacket, *A Century of Sermons*, xlvi, from the life by Plume.

51. Thomas Playfere, *Hearts Delight* (Cambridge, 1617), 45. From a sermon preached in the Easter term, 1593.

52. Ephesians 5:19.

53. Andrewes, *XCVI Sermons*, 465. From a sermon on the text, Colossians 3:1–2, preached before the king at Easter, 18 April 1613.

54. *Sermons of Maister Henrie Smith*, 480. From "The Triall of the Righteous," a sermon based on Psalm 34:19, "Many are the troubles of the righteous, but the Lord delivered him out of all."

55. *Workes of Tho: Adams*, 655. The marginal references indicate I Peter 5:8 for the lion, and Canticles for the foxes that spoil the grapes. None is given for the leopard, but its spottedness is an obvious allegorical symbol for its worldliness.

56. *Workes of Tho: Adams*, 717. The text is Luke 17:19, "And hee [Jesus] said unto him, Arise, thy faith hath made thee whole."

57. *Elegies*, no. 9, "The Autumnal."

58. Donne, *Sermons*, 8:78–79. This sermon was preached at Chilsey, where Magdalene [Herbert], Lady Danvers, was buried. The text was I Peter 3:13, "Nevertheless, we, according to his promises, looke for new heavens and a new earth wherein dwelleth righteousnesse."

59. H. R. McAdoo, *The Structure of Caroline Moral Theology* (London, 1949), preface, xi. McAdoo is also the author of *The Spirit of Anglicanism* (London, 1965), an analytical and historical study of the Church of England in the seventeenth century.

60. Andrewes, *XCVI Sermons,* from "A Sermon preached before the Kings Maiestie at Whitehall," Christmas Day 1606, on the text, Isaiah 9:6, "For unto us a Child is borne, and unto us a Sonne is given . . . ," 16.

61. Andrewes, *XCVI Sermons,* Christmas sermon, 1605, 9.

62. Hacket, *A Century of Sermons,* 55. From the sixth sermon on the Incarnation, using Luke 2:11 as text, "For unto you is born this day in the City of David, a Saviour, which is Christ the Lord."

63. Hacket, *A Century of Sermons,* 87.

64. *The Works of . . . Cosin,* 1:13. An Epiphany sermon of 1621 on the text Matthew 2:1–2. This passage has already been quoted in full. The four steps of humility are: immortality made mortal by birth, confined in a cradle, in Bethlehem, eternity subjected to time and subject to the tyrannical Herod. The fact that Jesus was not a victim of the Massacre of the Innocents is an argument against Christianity in Camus' *The Fall.*

65. *Workes of Tho: Adams,* 879. From the sermon "The Lost are found," using Luke 19:10 as text, "For the Sonne of man is come to seeke and to save that which was lost."

66. *Workes of Tho: Adams,* 160. The sermon "Christ His Starre: Or, The Wise Mens Oblation," an Epiphanytide sermon on Matthew 2:11.

67. Thomas Jackson, *Diverse Sermons, with a Short Treatise befitting these present times* (Oxford, 1637), 50. From the second sermon preached on II Chronicles 6:39–40.

68. Biographical memoir prefatory to *A Century of Sermons,* v.

69. Andrewes, *XCVI Sermons,* 200. The sermon was preached on 17 February 1602.

70. Andrewes, *XCVI Sermons,* 205.

71. It is worth noting that, while Andrewes preached twice before Queen Elizabeth on Ash Wednesdays (1599 and 1602), he also preached Lenten sermons before her in 1589, 1590, 1593, and 1596. He regularly preached Christmas, Ash Wednesday, Easter, and Whitsun sermons before King James as well. No other court preacher rivaled him in popularity, biblical fidelity, scholarship, and, alas, servility.

72. These "Six Sermons on the Baptism of Our Savior" are found in Hacket's *A Century of Sermons,* 147–201.

73. Hacket, *A Century of Sermons*, 214. The second paragraph of the second sermon on Christ's Temptations, on the text Matthew 4:1.

74. Hacket, *A Century of Sermons*, 264. From the seventh sermon on Christ's Temptations.

75. Hacket, *A Century of Sermons*, 365. From the seventeenth sermon on Christ's Temptations.

76. Brownrig, *Sixty Five Sermons*, 68, 83.

77. Hacket, *A Century of Sermons*, 424. From the second sermon on the Transfiguration.

78. *Workes of Tho: Adams*, 816. The "Maiestie in Miserie" sermon will be found on p. 761.

79. Ussher, *Works*, vol. 13, the tenth sermon; see 151 for the plan, and 153–154 for the pain of the Cross.

80. *The Works of the Right Reverend Joseph Hall, D.D., Bishop of Exeter and afterwards of Norwich*, ed. Philip Wynter, 10 vols. (Oxford, 1863), 5:35–36.

81. *The Works of . . . Hall*, 5:54. These excerpts do less than justice to the range, profundity, and learning of this sermon.

82. Donne, *Sermons*, 2:132.

83. Donne, *Sermons*, 10:229 begins "Deaths Duell."

84. Andrewes, *XCVI Sermons*, 544. The Easter sermon was preached before the king at Whitehall on 1 April 1620.

85. Andrewes, *XCVI Sermons*, 543.

86. Andrewes, *XCVI Sermons*, 550.

87. Andrewes, *XCVI Sermons*, 551.

88. Donne, *Sermons*, 4: No. 1, preached at Whitehall during Lent on I Corinthians 15:26, "The last enemie that shall be destroyed is death."

89. Donne, *Sermons*, 3: No. 3, preached at Lincoln's Inn on Job 19:26, "And though, after my skin, wormes destroy this body, yet in my flesh I shall see God."

90. Donne, *Sermons*, 7: No. 15.

91. Donne, *Sermons*, 7:385.

92. Donne, *Sermons*, 7:385ff. The thought of the Resurrection and heaven inspired Donne's finest perorations. These are on the ascent of the soul to heaven in *Sermons*, 7:71 and 7:254–255, 272; and finest of all, the experience of eternity, 8:191, previously quoted. It begins: "They shall awake as Jacob did."

93. Acts 2:22.

94. I Corinthians 15:26.

95. II Timothy 2:12.

96. Philippians 3:20.

97. Matthew 28:13.

98. Mark 16:11, 13.

99. I Corinthians 15:35.

100. Andrewes, *XCVI Sermons,* 385.

101. Acts 2:14.

102. Luke 24:49, Acts 1:4–5.

103. *The Works of . . . Hall,* 5:485. From a sermon on 1 John 1:5, "God is light," entitled "Divine Light and Reflections."

104. Andrewes, *XCVI Sermons,* 619.

105. Andrewes, *XCVI Sermons,* 636.

106. Hacket, *A Century of Sermons,* 643, 642.

107. Hacket, *A Century of Sermons,* 648.

108. Hacket, *A Century of Sermons,* 653.

109. Hacket, *A Century of Sermons,* 658f.

110. Hacket, *A Century of Sermons,* 670.

111. Hacket, *A Century of Sermons,* 673.

112. Hacket, *A Century of Sermons,* 677.

113. Hacket, *A Century of Sermons,* 678–679.

114. Hacket, *A Century of Sermons,* 678.

115. Arthur Lake's sermon on Trinity Sunday is an uninspired Paul's Cross sermon. It merely asserts the unwisdom of trying to fathom mystery and the need to continue in faith, and concludes that Christians have "great wages for so little worke; for doeing our duty, eternall felicitie." It is the second sermon preached on Jude 5:20–21, and it begins on p. 35 of *Ten Sermons upon Severall Occasions, Preached at Saint Pauls Crosse and Elsewhere* (London, 1640). The citation comes from p. 45.

116. *Workes of Tho: Adams,* 406. The sermon starts on p. 393.

117. Donne, *Sermons,* 3: No. 14, 308. The text is I Corinthians 16:22.

118. Donne, *Sermons,* 6:149.

119. Donne, *Sermons,* 8:41. It was preached in St. Dunstan's Church on Trinity Sunday, 1627.

120. Donne, *Sermons,* 10:233–234.

121. Donne, *Sermons,* 2:267. The text of the sermon was Romans 13:11, "For now is our salvation nearer."

122. Donne, *Sermons,* 4:53. The sermon was preached at Whitehall, 8 March 1621, on the text from I Corinthians 15:26, "The last enemie

that shall be destroyed is death." See also 4:272–273. Death the Leveller is also the theme of Adams, *Workes*, 2.

123. Donne, *Sermons*, 3:96, one reference among several. Barten Holyday wonders if folk eaten by cannibals can finally regain their own bodies, in *Three Sermons upon the Passion, Resurrection and Ascension of our Saviour* (London, 1626), 64–65.

124. Donne, *Sermons*, 7:272. From a funeral sermon for Sir William Cokayne, alderman of London, 12 December 1626, on John 11:21 "Lord, if thou hadst been here, my brother had not died."

125. Brownrig, *Sixty Five Sermons*, 313. A funeral sermon preached on I Kings 19:4, "It is enough, now, O Lord, take away my life; for I am no better than my Fathers."

126. Hacket, *A Century of Sermons*, 849.

127. Arthur Lake, *Ten Sermons upon Severall Occasions* (London, 1640). From the tenth sermon, preached at Saint Crosse, near Winchester, on Matthew 24:37, "But as the dayes of Noah were, so shall the comming of the sonne of man be."

128. *Workes of Tho: Adams*, 2. From the sermon, "The Gallants Burden," on Isaiah 21:11–12.

129. Ussher, *Works*, 13: Sermon 7, 105. The text is Romans 6:23, "The wages of sin is death."

130. Donne, *Sermons*, 7:235.

131. *Workes of Tho: Adams*, 760. Joseph Hall also contrasts the first and second advents of Christ, the first of his sojourn, the second of his return to ransom us and to judge the world. See Sermon III, part 1, "The Impress of God," in *The Works of . . . Hall*, 5:55.

132. Thomas Goffe, *Deliverance from the Grave* (London, 1627), 39–40. Goffe had said a little earlier, 39, most felicitously: "In your Hospitall lies many a wounded Christian, and in every wound is plac't a tongue to speake and cry to God himselfe for mercy, continu'd mercy and honour to this Citie!"

133. *Sermons of Maister Henrie Smith*, 847.

134. William Mulder, "Style and the Man: Thomas Adams, Prose Shakespeare of Puritan Divines," *Harvard Theological Review*, 48 (1955): 148.

135. *Workes of Tho: Adams*, 15. From "The Gallants Burden" on the text Isaiah 21:11–12, "The burden of Dumah. He calls unto me out of Seir, Watchman, what was in the night? The Watchman said: The morning commeth, and also the night. If ye will aske, enquire: returne, and come."

136. *Workes of Tho: Adams,* 242.

137. *Workes of Tho: Adams,* 242.

138. *Workes of Tho: Adams,* 591f.,648.

139. *Workes of Tho: Adams,* 650.

140. See Luke 16:19–31 for the parable, and among the logia of Jesus, Matthew 8:12, "But the sons of the kingdom shall be cast forth into outer darkness: there shall be the weeping and gnashing of teeth" and Mark 9:47, "And if thine eye cause thee to stumble, cast it out: it is good for thee to enter the kingdom of God with one eye, rather than having two eyes to be cast into Hell, where their worm dieth not, and the fire is not quenched." These two citations are obviously the bases for the preachers' descriptions of hell.

141. Ussher, *Works,* 13: Sermon 8, 115–119.

142. Ussher, *Works,* 13: Sermon 8, 120–124.

143. Donne, *Sermons,* 5:267. From a sermon preached to the earl of Carlisle and his company, from the blunt text "He that beleeveth not shall be damned" (Mark 16:16). The date is probably 1622, according to Potter and Simpson.

144. *Workes of Tho: Adams,* 244.

145. Donne, *Sermons,* 5:75. From a Whitsunday sermon, possibly preached at St. Paul's in 1622. The text is Romans 8:16, "The Spirit it selfe beareth witnesse with our spirit, that we are the children of God."

146. Donne, *Sermons,* 7:138. Preached on 18 April 1626 before Charles I, on the text "In my Fathers House are many Mansions; if it were not so, I would have told you" (John 14:2).

147. Donne, *Sermons,* 8:233. From a sermon preached at St. Paul's on Easter Day, 1628, on the text: "For now we see things darkly, but then face to face; now I know in part, but then I shall know, as even I am known" (I Corinthians 13:12).

148. Donne, *Sermons,* 8:75.

149. Donne, *Sermons,* 5: No. 3, on the text Matthew 12:31; and Adams, "The Fatal Banket, The Second Service" which includes profanity as the fifth vial of stolen waters, in *The Workes,* 186f.

150. See Donne's *Sermons,* 8:280 and 10:95; and *Workes of Tho: Adams,* 590.

151. See *Sermons of Maister Henrie Smith,* 1–73; Donne, *Sermons,* 3: No. 8; and *Works of . . . Cosin,* 1: Sermon 3.

Chapter IX

AUDIENCES

APREACHER'S REQUIREMENTS were determined in part by the audiences to which he preached. These could vary from a homely country congregation to preaching at Whitehall before the king and court, with intermediate sermons at universities, in cathedrals and fashionable London churches and at the Inns of Court, or before the City and Guilds and the Parliament. Each required a slightly different style and aimed at different intellectual and social levels and interests.

A successful metaphysical preacher might be required to preach to a fashionable city congregation in a famous church like St. Giles, Cripplegate (where Lancelot Andrewes held the living) or St. Andrew's, Holborn (where John Hacket held the living) or at St. Dunstan's (which was Donne's living). He might also expect to preach to congregations in Great St. Mary's in Cambridge, or St. Mary's, Oxford, or in Christ Church Cathedral, where the temptation to display the liveliness of his learning was greatest. The proof of his reliability and popularity would come with his appointment as a royal chaplain, and the opportunity to preach before the king, the royal family, and the peerage and nobility of England. Here the temptation would be to show off his wit and intelligence among the worldly-wise, the shrewd, the ambitious, and the utterly indifferent. Special professional insight would be required by those appointed chaplains to one of the Inns of Court, as John Donne was at Lincoln's Inn. Interestingly enough his preaching, as dean of St. Paul's Cathedral, lost much of its complexity in plan and hermeneutics, though none of its fidelity and application, presumably because the congregation did not contain as many intellectuals as at Lincoln's Inn.

Court sermons

The greatest honor was to be appointed a royal chaplain and to be required, at regular intervals on major feast days, to preach at Whitehall before the king and courtiers. This privilege was afforded most conspicuously to Bishop Lancelot Andrewes who preached with unfailing regularity on Christmas Day, Easter Day, and on Whitsunday as well as on Ash Wednesday, not to mention on Gowrie Day and on Gunpowder Day. Two other very popular court preachers were Donne and Hacket.

Donne's popularity may have been partly due to the fact that he was a *succès de scandale*—that "Jack" had become "Dean John Donne"—and partly to his contacts among aristocrats and in the diplomatic world—he had been chaplain in an embassy to the Palatinate. It was also undoubtedly due to the brilliance of his conversation, and perhaps most of all to his breadth of experience and his insatiable love of knowledge in all its varieties. Donne had been a courtier and, but for his clandestine marriage when a brilliant private secretary to a secretary of state, he might have reached the pinnacle of favor.

On the other hand, Hacket's popularity as court preacher seems to outstrip even that of Andrewes, for he was a regular preacher at the courts of James I, Charles I, and Charles II. The dedication to Charles II in his posthumously published *A Century of Sermons* (London, 1675) makes the staggering statement that Hacket "in his ordinary attendance upon your Majesty, your Royal Father, and Grandfather, had the Honour to preach more than Eighty times at Court."[1]

It is worth examining some of the court sermons of the three most popular preachers to determine what kept them in royal favor.

A primary concern was that they should be reliable in two

respects. They would be expected to toe the line in Church and State matters: that is, they must be unambiguously against both Roman Catholicism and Puritanism as defenders of the English *via media*. Equally they must approve the English monarch as the head of the English Church. Regular doses of flattery of the monarch would also be expected—as we shall see this occasionally descended from obsequiousness to sheer grovelling servility, and on one occasion even to the canonization of the king.

We can observe Donne, for instance, in his earliest court sermons proving his reliability. Sermon four is characterized by thorough scholastic reasoning, with references to Hebrew etymology, to reassure both the pedantic King James and the courtiers of Donne's learning. Sermon six assures them even further of Donne's sense of pulpit responsibility by its many patristic citations and the evenhanded criticisms of Rome and Geneva. There was nothing here to rock the royal galleon in doctrine or application.[2]

Andrewes' sermons gave great assurance because they exalted the *via media*. Andrewes first came to attention because of his success in persuading recusants to join the Church of England, and his sermons were eminently reasonable as well as highly learned in linguistics and patristics. These qualities together with their undoubted wit delighted King James as they had Queen Elizabeth. His sermons made orthodoxy's paradoxes enchanting.

Andrewes in his sermons is less openly critical of Rome and Geneva than Donne or Hacket, but where his barbs are aimed is clear. In his thirteenth Easter sermon, for example, he praises reverent gestures in good ceremonial and refers to the nakedness advocated by the Puritans ironically, yet without naming them: "A plausible theame, not to burthen the Church with ceremonies: the Church to be free: which hath almost freed the Church of all decencie."[3]

Equally Andrewes' great learning in historical theology puts all concern about his orthodoxy at rest. Whether he is condemning Manicheanism in asserting the reality of Christ's flesh in the Incarnation ("Made it was, against the *Manicheans* holding that he had noe true body; as if *factam* had been *fictam*, or *making* were *mocking*")[4], or criticizing Donatism's view that "one that is not himselfe inwardly *holy*, cannot be the meanes of *holinesse* to another,"[5] in every case he maintains an adamantine patristic orthodoxy in doctrine. Nothing could be more reassuring to King James I who fancied himself as a theologian and a *fidei defensor* in reality as well as in name.

Bishop Hacket, as a Calvinist, was more severe on the Catholics than the Puritans in his court sermons, though the latter, if contumacious, were not spared his sarcasms. This anti-Roman rigor might have been expected from a man who defended the following theses for the degree of bachelor of divinity at Cambridge: *Vota Monastica perfectionis (quae dicitur) sunt illicita,* and *Judicio Romanae Ecclesiae in Sanctis canonizandis non est standum.*[6]

Hacket had been encouraged by Andrewes when at Westminster School. He was as reliable as Andrewes in his numerous sermons on the paradoxes of orthodox Christian doctrine, affirmed in the Incarnation and the Resurrection of Christ, and in the detailed references in his court sermons to the doctrines taught by the Fathers of the Church. His anti-Roman references refute the idea that saints or their relics or images are to be adored,[7] condemn the Gunpowder conspirators, who swore their evil oath of secrecy at a Mass so that "the Sacrament of Charity, the strongest tie of love that ever *God* made, became an Oath to unite the malice of *Satan.*"[8]

The Puritans are castigated in a Lenten sermon at Whitehall for attempting to change the liturgy of the Book of Common Prayer,[9] and are criticized clearly in Hacket's stout defense of festival days in a Coronation sermon in which he avers ". . . we ought to do some religious service on *His Day,* who is the *Defender of our Religion.* Next under the Providence of *God* who but the *King* doth maintain the Truth among us? . . . We have no *Romish Superstition,* no *Anabaptistical* or *Presbyterian Anarchy* to make this holy place irksom unto us."[10] Hacket thereby expresses his loyalty to the *via media,* by hitting Rome, Geneva, and the radical Reformation as equally hostile targets.

Chapter IX

It was, of course, not enough that the court preachers should be reliable in the orthodoxy of their theology. They must also be the defenders of the divine rights of kings, especially as the English sovereign was the governor of the English Church. Their encomia of the monarch could hardly avoid flattery.

Andrewes, for instance, had learned as early as 1594 in Hampton Court that Queen Elizabeth expected a royal compliment when present at a sermon. Andrewes had chosen to deliver a minatory sermon on Lot's wife, who, for disobedience to God and backsliding, was turned into a pillar of salt. "Blessed be God and the Father of our Lord Jesus Christ," said Andrewes, "that we stand in the presence of such a *Prince:* who has ever accompted *Perseverance*, not onely as *Regina virtutum*, the Queen of vertues; but as *virtus Reginarum*, the vertue of a Queen."[11]

Donne, who owed his deanery to King James, provided a touching reference to the dead king when preaching in Denmark House, the residence of the queen, where the royal corpse was lying in state:

> How dead things must you necessarily think *Titles and Possessions* and *Favours*, and all when you see that Hand, which was the *hand of destinie*, of *Christian Destinie*, of the *Almightie God*, lie dead? It was not so *hard a hand*, when we touched it last, nor so *cold* a hand when we kissed it last: That hand, which was wont *to wipe all teares from our eyes*, doth now but presse and squeaze us as so many spunges, filled one with one, another with another cause of teares.[12]

In a sermon at court preached in April 1620, Donne had provided a gracious tribute to his king and country:

> . . . all we owe to God an acknowledgement of blessed-nesse, that we are borne in a Christian Church, in a Reformed Church, in a Monarchy, in a Monarchy composed of Monarchies, and in the time of such a Monarch, as is a Peace-maker and a peace-preserver, both at home and abroad.[13]

Hacket, too, found it necessary to include expressions of sincere loyalty in his court sermons, but always insisted that the king was head of the Church *under God*. We may note this emphasis repeated twice in a single sentence of homage to King James I as "our David," who is "under Christ not only the supreme Head, but under Christ the most careful watchman of our Churches."[14]

In an earlier sermon Hacket had warned against the dangers of court flattery in a splendid retort to Machiavelli's charge that Christian humility dejects the spirits. On the contrary, he claims, "the truly humble Christian hath the most generous and lofty stomach of all others, which defies Flattery, and fawning, and *Court-crowching*, and stands upon resolute terms to be beholding to none but God and integrity for exaltation."[15]

Donne, too, was equally aware of the danger in sermons preached at court of being the king's man, and not the ambassador of the King of Kings. Donne refers to Amaziah, the royal priest at the court of Bethel, who rejected God's prophet Amos, and reflects that every man preaching at court brings his own Amaziah with him "in his owne bosome, a little whisperer in his owne heart, that tels him, *This is the Kings Chappell, and it is the Kings Court*, and these woes and judgements, and the denouncers and proclaimers of them are not so acceptable here."[16] He insists that the court preacher must also have his own Amos with him to give him courage.

This was a fear that had occurred to him earlier in a sermon preached at Lincoln's Inn, when he had asked rhetorically: "Is there no being a *Silver-smith* but he needs make shrines for *Diana of the Ephesians?* No being a *Lawyer*, without serving the passion of the client? No being a *Divine*, without sewing pillows under great men's elbows?"[17] This last phrase is one that Andrewes had employed in a sermon, indicating that he too was aware of the peril of compromise in a royal pulpit.

The leading metaphysical preachers refused to grovel before the king, but lesser metaphysicals were obsequious in the extreme. This was particularly the case with Archdeacon Barten Holyday. In a Gowrie Day sermon preached at Paul's Cross

in 1623, Holyday claimed that "Maiestie is a deputy-divinity;
and to deny Royalty is civill atheism. . . ."[18] That was pushing
loyalty far, but he fell overboard in canonizing the recently
deceased James I in a sermon in the cathedral at Oxford,
preached on Ascension Day 1625, when he remarked, "and now
without going to Spaine, wee can find a Saint James, Saint
James of Britaine, Defender of the Faith and the cleargie!"[19]

Many preachers could combine dutiful respect to the king,
and keep within the confines of the Stuart Church, preaching
orthodox doctrine, yet were never appointed as court preachers.
What other gifts did they require?

The sermons of the more famous metaphysical preachers indicate that besides royal and ecclesial loyalty, they also needed
to be witty without irreverence, and learned without pedantic
prolixity. They had also to possess an easy and elegant affability
of manner, be without presumption, have a psychological empathy with the life of the courtier, and above all the rhetorical
gift to startle and surprise the bored or indifferent, to find
appropriate images and analogies to make their messages seem
relevant.

A previous chapter has already demonstrated the wit of the
metaphysical preachers,[20] and another their scholarly eloquence,[21] so that these characteristics in court do not need to
be illustrated further. However, the elegant, easy, and affable
manner, the psychological insights, and the tricks of rhetoric
warrant exemplification.

For ease and elegance one can cite Donne, a master of the
art. In a sermon preached in Denmark House, where the newly
widowed Queen Anne was residing, Donne refers to her piety
without flattery by comparing her to the Anna who awaited
the Messiah's coming in the temple at Jerusalem. His incidental
compliment ran: "It was a great part of *Annae's prayse*, that
she departed not from the Temple, day nor night."[22]

Preaching in the chapel of Holyrood House before James I
in his native Edinburgh, on Whitsunday 1617, Andrewes
suavely congratulates the king on attaining his fiftieth year, a
jubilee and an occasion of joy, "and so referre it to the late

great *Joy* and *Jubilee,* at your *Maiesties* receiving hither to your *Nazareth.* . . ."[23] This, despite its near approach to blasphemy, would please King James who believed that, like Christ, he was anointed by God.

Bishop Duppa was a Caroline divine who had a captivating and charming manner. He was courtly in the best sense of the term. Consider the grave courtesy with which he reproaches those who think his sermon before King Charles at Newport in the Isle of Wight is too melancholy. His sermon was preached on 25 October 1648, when the king's fortunes were at a low ebb, and his text was Psalm 42:5, "Why art thou cast downe, O my soule, and why art thou disquieted within me?" He defends the choice: "But if there be others that think the Text too melancholy for this Place, that come rather to have their *Eares pleased,* then their *Hearts wounded;* to these I must alter my Note, and say, as St. *Hierome* did to *Sabinian, Hoc ipsum plango, quod vos non plangitis.* This makes *me* sorry, that nothing can make *you* so."[24]

Hacket too can compliment the king delicately and aptly, by referring to him as "our David" and "A *King* who is an uniter of kingdoms as *David* was of *Judah* and *Israel,* none more zealous, no not *David* himself for the prosperity of *Jerusalem* and the magnificence of the holy temple." He adds that the bishops "have not found the smallest place in the love of our gracious sovereign."[25] Crude servility and fawning obsequiousness were not part of Hacket's style, as they were in the compliments of lesser and more gauche preachers.

The psychological empathy of the court preachers with the courtiers can easily be documented. Though not in a court sermon, yet one addressed to the nobility—preached to the earl of Exeter and his company—Donne indicated that he knew the uncertainties of a courtier's life: "Here in the *militant Church,* you stand," he declared, "but you stand in the *porch,* there in the *triumphant,* you shall in *Sancto sanctorum,* in the *Quire* and the *Altar.* Here you stand, but you stand upon ice, perchance in high and therefore *slippery places.*"[26]

Bishop Theophilus Field, as was perhaps natural in such a

timeserver, understood the humblest courtier's disappointment
and offered him comfort in a sermon preached before King
Charles I in 1628:

> What though the unprefer'd and unprovided for *courtier*
> be compared to a *Blackamore, In ortu solis positus, habet colorem
> noctis,* He lives where the sunne riseth every day in his
> eies, and yet his face looks like night. Disconsolate man
> who ever thou be, if thou waitest upon *God,* know that
> his eyes are upon thee *for good,* and that a *roab* and a
> *crowne* is laid up for thee.[27]

Cosin preached an Epiphanytide sermon on humility. He
made the point of how important this virtue was for the personages of this world, using the example of the Magi. It is the
duty of great men to honor Christ "wherever they can find
him, though it be in His great humility, in His cratch or on
His cross, the cratch of His contempt, or the Cross of His
persecutions . . . there to come and acknowledge Him, and
with all their greatness and all their train. . . ."[28] A similar
lesson on the mutability of worldly greatness is preached by
Bishop Joseph Hall, at Whitehall on 29 January 1625. The
bishop reminds the congregation that, in spite of their worldly
importance, they are still little in God's sight, and their life
and honor is only transient:

> We honour as we ought your conspicuous greatness, o
> ye eminent potentates of the earth: but alas, what is this
> to the great Lord of heaven? When we look up thither,
> we must crave leave to pity the breath of your nostrils,
> the rust of your coronets, the dust of your graves, the
> sting of your felicities, and if you take not good heed,
> the blots of your memories.[29]

It was however the sermon title and theme of Bishop Prideaux that penetrated the courtier's psychology most shrewdly.
His text was I Peter 5:6, "Humble yourselves therefore under

the mighty hand of God, that he may exalt you in due time." His title caught the whole interest of the courtier perfectly, "A Plot for Preferment." He offered the courtiers "a *plain course* laid downe for *honest men* to take; that may save them *great travell,* more *trouble,* heavy *expences,* and yet neverthelesse be still *effectuall.* "[30] The sermon's witty conclusion deserves citation: "Let us rest therefore faithfully in him, [God] and that will bring us at length to the *highest preferment,* his eternall rest, through his *deare sonne,* the highest master of Requests. . . ."[31]

It is time to illustrate the rhetorical devices by which the metaphysical preachers captivated a potentially indifferent audience. One method was to provide surprising openings to a sermon.

Andrewes begins a Whitsun sermon thus: "This day holde we holy to the Holy Ghost, by whom all *holy dayes, persons,* and *things* are made holy." Immediately he contradicts by implication the Roman Catholic Church's presumption of canonization: "And with good reason hold we it: He that maketh all *holy dayes,* it is meet should be allowed one, himselfe. And if we yeeld this honour, to this and that *Saint;* much more to the *Saint-maker;* to *Him,* that is the onely true Canonizer of all the *Saints* in the Calendar."[32] It was an opening both profound and striking.

Donne had even greater dramatic skills than Andrewes. A Lenten sermon of 1620 begins thus: "The Kingdom of heaven is a feast: to get you a stomach to that we have preached abstinence."[33] Another surprise was Donne's selection of an Easter text for Lent, with the following ingenious explanation: "This is a text of the Resurrection, and it is not Easter Eve; all Lent is but the Vigill, the Eve of Easter: to so long a festivall as shall never end, the Resurrection, wee may well begin the Eve betimes."[34]

Another way of sustaining the attention of courtiers in sermons was to use courtly analogies or illustrations. Bishop Barlow preached before Queen Elizabeth a Lenten sermon in 1601 entitled "The Eagle and the Body" on the text from Luke 17:37,

"He said unto them, wheresoever the Body is, there will the Eagles be gathered together." Deciding where the eagles might get the choicest meat, he first mentions the court and continues:

. . . a full *Bodie,* in fatnesse and marrow whereof hath fetched many *Eagles* from all corners, in so much that *Proverb* hath begotten *Proverb, No fishing to the Sea, No Service to the Court:* because no booty so gainfulle, no gaine so easie, no office so affected, as those of *this Place.* [35]

Bishop Joseph Hall gained the attention of courtiers by going into the history of heraldry and referring to the mottoes of royalty, as in the following passage:

So the word of the faithful King is *Dominus mihi adjutor;* or when he would thankfully ascribe his peace to God, *Exurgat Deus, dissipentur inimici:* So of a good prince either, "I serve" to express his officious care, or, "One of your own," to signify his respective love: so the good stateman's should be given him by Solomon, *Non est consilium contra Dominum, No policy against the Lord:* a good courtier's by Samuel, *Honorantes me honorabo. . . .* [36]

Heylyn and Jackson intrigued the court by speaking much of historical figures in their sermons. Heylyn, for example, began a sermon with an apt citation from Velleius showing that man's plans can be delayed or overturned by a higher power, following it with the shrewd and apt observation: "which power, though the historian being a Courtier, (who ascribes all things to good luck) entituled by the name of Fortune: yet the Philosopher, or contemplative man, who had studied in the government of human affairs, would have called it Providence."[37] Dean Jackson, in a sermon before King Charles in Newcastle in 1637, refers to seven different historians in nineteen instances, believing that the past can provide guidance through the darkling present to a brighter future.[38]

Donne employs a devastatingly appropriate image in a Whitehall sermon for courtiers on 29 February 1627/8. It is that of a statue, bearing no subscription—that is, a man who has achieved nothing worthy of remembrance: "He that stands in a place and does not the duty of that place, is but a statue in that place and but a statue without an inscription; Posterity shall not know him nor read who he was."[39] If any image was likely to penetrate the skull of a man who was out for fame and found none, Donne here hit upon an image that would sink deep into the conscience of a courtier, and force him to rethink the purpose of his life.

Perhaps the most convincing way of demonstrating what was expected in a royal court sermon can be illustrated from the change of style visible in the sermons of the witty Thomas Fuller, when he switched from the Parliamentary and Puritan side to the Royalist and Cavalier. Prior to this change, his sermons had concentrated on the interpretation of extensive passages of Scripture, according to the Puritan structure of doctrine, reason, and use. In his first court sermons of 1644, by contrast, there are found gracious references to James I's book on the Lord's Prayer, and an appreciation of King Charles' decision to keep Tuesdays religiously as Fast days. There is also a proliferation of patristic citations and references, where previously these were kept few and brief. Furthermore, he (who rarely used such hitherto) now included two historical narrations. One referred to Constantine the Christian Emperor carrying twelve baskets of soil on his own shoulders toward the foundation of a church; the other to a Captain Terentius who begged the Emperor Valens that one church might be given to the orthodox as a reward for honored service. But both types of sermons were notable for their unfailing humor. Thus wit, knowledge of the Fathers, historical lore, and loyalty to the king and Church were the acknowledged essentials of court sermons.[40]

Thus court sermons, in sum, asserted the preachers' loyalty to Church and king, affirmed their doctrinal orthodoxy and their patristic learning, seasoned their instruction with wit and elegant affability, and demonstrated both their shrewd psychological understanding of the perilous and unstable role of the courtier, while at the same time offering spiritual consolation. Finally, they jolted him awake with striking starts or maxims, and kept him alert with lively and apposite analogies and images. It was a singular achievement never again repeated in the history of English preaching.

Paul's Cross sermons

The next highest honor to being a royal chaplain, invited to preach regularly on the festival days of the Church calendar before the court, was that of preaching as an offical exponent of royal and ecclesiastical policies at the famous open-air pulpit of St. Paul's Cross under the shadow of the cathedral.[41] There the selected preacher faced the powerful of the land, seated before him in hierarchical order, and, in the lee of the transept, the royal balcony where the king (rarely present) sat with members of the royal family. Only the most celebrated and reliable divines were invited at critical times to expound and justify or rationalize official policy. In general, the plain style was preferred on these occasions.

In Elizabeth's days Playfere, Henry Smith, William Barlow, and Arthur Lake preached at Paul's Cross. Bishop William Barlow had the delicate task of explaining the execution of the earl of Essex in the spring of 1600, and why it had been necessary to punish the popular leader of the rebellion.[42]

Thomas Adams was invited on five occasions, an indication of his great popularity. John Donne appeared there first on 24 March 1617 preaching an accession sermon, and subsequently five times. Probably his weightiest assignment was on 15 September 1622, when he was required to defend James I's orders preventing preachers' including such speculative doctrines as predestination in the pulpit—a direct hit at the Puritans—and meddling with politics. He had a second problem—to assure the populace, after the long drawn-out marriage negotiations between Prince Charles and the Infanta of Spain, that the king remained a loyal Protestant.[43] Chamberlain reported that on the second issue, Donne gave little satisfaction, and did not even appear to have convinced himself.[44] Donne's sermons regularly defended the Anglican *via media* position, whether, as in 6 May 1622, he defended the Erastian position of the ecclesiastical state dependent on the civil state, or, on 22 November 1629, when he defended the Protestant doctrine of good works as consequences of justification by faith against the Catholic doctrine.

Henry King, the poet-bishop, was pushed by his father, the bishop of London, to preach at St. Paul's Cross when he was only twenty-three years of age. His sermon preached on 5 November 1617 was unimpressive in content and manner. He also preached there on three subsequent occasions. Once, on 25 November 1621, his delicate task was to contradict the *Protestants Plea,* in which a Catholic propagandist claimed that Bishop John King, his father, had converted to Roman Catholicism on his deathbed.[45]

Thomas Adams alone almost equalled Donne's popularity as a preacher at Paul's Cross, for between 29 March 1612 and 5 August 1624 he preached five times at the Cross. His indictments were largely apolitical. His first sermon criticized atheists, epicures, and profane persons. His second, the famous "White Devil," was a condemnation of contemporary thievery, and especially of usury where a "Paternoster is a pawn."[46] His third sermon was a warning, after several calamities had befallen the nation such as plagues and the Gunpowder Plot, to cease to treat Christ scurvily. The last sermon criticized those who attended church only because they idolized the preacher, and it also attacked the idols of vain honor, vain pleasure, and riches.[47] His sermons were profoundly ethical and superbly illustrated.

By contrast Archbishop Laud, preaching the Accession sermon on 27 March 1631, defended Charles I as a godly king, criticized those who criticized him, and threatened that the king might have to pull out the stings of such waspish persons.[48]

Spital sermons

It was almost as impressive and important to be invited to preach a Spital sermon as a Paul's Cross sermon. It was so–

called because a series of such sermons was delivered annually on the Monday, Tuesday, and Wednesday of Easter Week in the churchyard of St. Mary of Bethlehem Hospital (abbreviated to "Spital") before a vast congregation. These included the Lord Mayor of London, who issued the invitation, the aldermen or senior councillors of the city, and the governors and children of Christ's Hospital and of the other hospitals. These were charity sermons, encouraging the wealthy to donate generously to the poor, the orphans, the infirm, and the insane, who were supported by the affluent. William Gifford, in an important article, pointed out that this was not a merely ceremonial gathering, but an important opportunity for raising charitable funds. When Bishop John King of London tried to wrest from the civic authorities the right to appoint the preachers, the reply came:

> Such a course would be displeasing to the citizens, and hinder their wonted charity to the poor. And the Masters and Governors of the several Hospitals of the City would be discouraged, both in their daily care and pains, and in the observation of that decent order used at those times when they and all the children and poor people of each Hospital resorted to those sermons, where they had built a place to sit and show themselves to their benefactors and of the comforts they received, and thus to stir up imitation in others.[49]

Collections were also made for special causes at the Spital sermons: as, for example, for Englishmen incarcerated in Turkish prisons, or for impoverished Protestant foreigners who were refugees in England.

Apart from the main topic of inducing the wealthy to give to the poor and thus gain treasures in heaven, a frequent theme of sermons was the poverty faced by many ministers as a consequence of the non-payment of the tithes due to them. It was a subject for frequent lament at Paul's Cross.[50]

The size of the audience, the competition among the several preachers delivering sermons on three successive days, and the two-hour length of the sermons, made the occasion a trial of endurance for both preachers and their auditors. Donne, who preached here on Easter Monday in 1622, observed that he had entered his second "glass," and near the end complained that his voice was enfeebled through sheer weariness.[51] Even the usually indefatigable Playfere in 1595 had to admit to being "almost quite spent with speaking so long."[52]

It was a very colorful scene, with the Lord Mayor dressed in furs, the golden chain of office about his neck, the aldermen in scarlet on Mondays and Tuesdays and in violet gowns on Wednesdays, while the boys of Christ's Hospital appeared in bright blue cassocks.

Those invited to this preaching marathon were all popular and respected preachers. Who then were these popular preachers? Their number included the following metaphysical preachers: Thomas Playfere, Lancelot Andrewes, John Donne, Joseph Hall, John White, Thomas Adams, John Hacket, and Thomas Goffe. Two exceptions, both with strong Puritan inclinations, were Henry Smith the "silver-tongued" preacher, and George Downame, popular Puritan theologian, who preached a Spital sermon in 1602.

It is Donne and Goffe whose sermons seem to be most clearly directed to the members of their congregations. Donne, preaching in 1622, is acutely aware of the contrast between rich and poor seated on opposite sides of the triangle at whose apex is the pulpit. It is his sympathetic understanding that enables the very orphan children to think that, in the Divine providence, there may be a distinguished future for some of them:

Make thou also the same interpretation of this *Idem Deus*, in all the Vicissitudes and Changes of this World. Hath God brought thee from an Expositious Child laid out in the streets, of uncertain name, of unknown Parents, to become the first foundation-stone of a great family, and to enable a posterity? Hath God brought thee from a Carriers Pack, upon which thou camest up, to thy change of Foot-Cloathes, and Coaches? Hath God brought thee from one of these Blew-Coats, to one of those Scarlet Gowns? Attribute not this to thine own Industry, nor to thine own Frugality; (for, Industry is but Fortunes right hand, and Frugality her left;) but come to *Davids* Acclamation, *Dominus Fecit, It is the Lords doing.*

Finally, Donne insists that God is the same "In the Hills and in the Vallies too, in spiritual as well as in temporal prosperity and adversity too," ending with the admonition that the Christian child, like the adolescent Jesus himself, must grow in wisdom and in stature.[53]

Goffe, preaching on the same occasion five years later, gave a very enticing picture of the merchants as venturers and even as potential missionaries:

Let me beseech you, who-ever you are, that dedicate your-selves to treade the untrackt paths of the sea, and negotiate with remote Kingdomes, either for the Gold of *Ophir*, or the Spices of *Arabia*, to carry with you, along for exchange . . . this Merchandize, sold at so low a rate now with us, The *knowledge* of this Lord. Let every one of you be a Taper to the darkned understandings of the Heathen, by which they may at least see that you *know* the Lord.[54]

Goffe in the same sermon painted a noble picture of London's generosity through its charities:

In your Hospitall lies many a wounded Christian, and in every wound is plac't a tongue, to speake and cry to God himselfe for mercy, continu'd mercy and honour to this Citie. Your *Bethlem* shewes, how he that was borne at *Bethlem* is borne anew in your hearts, and you againe regenerate and borne in him, for whose sake a Cup of cold water given shall never goe unrewarded, then surely *Copiosa erit Merces vestra in Coelis* . . . Thus farre does the armes of the Poore lift you their Benefactors and Patrons from your Graves: Thus farre are these Livories which attend you, Angels and Messengers to report your Resurrection: Thus high may you stand upon your owne Foundations, these foundations which you have rais'd for them. . . .[55]

This was as moving an appeal to compassion on Christian grounds as one was ever likely to hear, and it perfectly explained the purpose behind the Spital sermons.

University sermons

Sermons preached before the universities of Oxford and Cambridge were not strikingly different from those preached at court or at St. Paul's Cross, for it was essentially the same clergy that preached in all three locations.

However, there were occasions, such as when "preaching the Act"—that is, after being examined and approved for the degree of Doctor of Divinity—when the neophyte doctors were expected to display their learning and their intelligence. On other university occasions the university preacher was expected to be both wise and witty.

A most interesting pair of sermons on the Act, on 10 July 1625, were preached by the two sons of the Bishop of London, Henry and John King at St. Mary's, the university church in Oxford. The themes of the sermons complemented each other. Henry King, royal chaplain and poet, took as his morning topic, "Davids Enlargement" and preached on the text Psalm 32:5, "I said I will confesse my sinnes (or transgressions) unto the Lord. And thou forgavest the iniquitie of my sinne." John King, prebendary of Christ Church, took as his theme for the afternoon sermon, "Davids Strait." His text was II Samuel 24:14, "And David said unto God, I am in a great strait: Let us fall now into the hand of the Lord (for his mercies are great) and let me not fall into the hand of man."

Henry King's sermon is almost an anthology of patristic citations, including eighteen from Augustine, three each from Ambrose and Jerome, and ten other Latin writers, including Bernard, Bonaventure, and Richard of St. Victor. He also cites seven Greek authors including Origen and Chrysostom. There is a total of forty-two references; citations from Catholic commentators like Lombard and Biel are also included, not forgetting the Reformed theologian Bullinger. His facility in Greek and Latin is also demonstrated. In addition, he supplies allegorical images of man as a theatre and a commonwealth, maxims with a tendency to pomposity, wit ("Thus you may perceive there are no Arrerages left in Gods Audit; he forgives both the *Guilt* of the sin, & the *punishment;* both the suit & the damages"),[56] and an appropriately devout conclusion. The sermon even included a criticism of auricular confession as used in the Roman Catholic Church, while commending the form of Confession in the Book of Common Prayer. In short, this was a proper sermon for an ambitious young clergyman of the Church of England—safe, but pious, learned, and moderately witty.

John King's sermon proved that he was familiar with Greek, Latin, and Hebrew. It began wittily, and while it had fewer patristic and classical citations than the morning's sermon, it made up for it with biblical citations and exempla.

The other university sermons to which we will refer, were delivered by more mature preachers but wisdom, learning, and wit were always expected on these occasions. Perhaps the distinctive characteristic of university sermons was the customary direct appeals to the undergraduate and the practicality of the ethical applications. Certainly this was true of the university sermon preached at Oxford by Dean Jackson, and the Cambridge University Commencement sermon preached by Hacket, both utterances being definitely *ad homines.*

Jackson's concluding peroration is a moving appeal for loyalty to Christ and the English Church to "these noble stemmes, or other hopefull plants here seated in this famous nurserie of arts." He wishes them to know much of the lore of other nations, but pleads that they "returne at length to these your cities of *Israel,* and visite *Nazareth* wherein the Lord hath wrought his wonders, . . . and let Jesus of *Nazareth . . .* be alwaies Load-starre of your thought."[57]

Bishop Hacket's Commencement sermon in Cambridge fulfills the requirement of learning more thoroughly than most of his other sermons, for it contains fifty-one references to twenty authors, nine of them theologians and eight of them to classical writers. Its conclusion is most pointed for it warns the new graduates going out into the world against lust, and its consequence, syphilis.[58]

If the undergraduates of either university had been asked what element in a sermon made it most exciting for them, some might have said wit, and others iconoclasm. The latter is what Thomas Lushington provided in abundance in his daring sermon delivered in Christ Church, Oxford's cathedral. This sermon, which we have previously discussed, alarmed the authorities so much that Lushington was reprimanded by the vice-chancellor, Dr. Piers, and he was forced to preach a recantation sermon on the following Sunday.

The sermon was iconoclastic in several ways. It was casually conversational in its opening, in which it assumed that religious choice was determined by political considerations as Catholics and Protestants watched the ebb and flow of the Hundred Years War on the continent. It also gave offense by a scathing reference to the low origins of some members of the House of Commons. The chief offense given was, however, religious. Lushington so convincingly mimicked the accent, vocabulary, and manner of the soldiers who were supposed to guard the sepulchre in which Christ was buried when they insisted that Christ's disciples had stolen the body, that one could easily believe that the Resurrection was an illusion and an imposture.[59] Eventually he brought the sermon to the orthodox Christian conclusion, but only after a lengthy suspense. Naturally, the undergraduates applauded loudly.

The immediate insistence upon the retraction of the sermon indicates how difficult it was for unorthodoxy to get a hearing in the Stuart pulpit. During the Commonwealth and Protectorate, however, the floodgates of heterodoxy were opened with sermons by Levellers, Diggers, Fifth Monarchists, Ranters and Familists, and others in profusion.[60]

Chapter IX

University sermons, we may conclude, were like court sermons. They aimed at elegance and wit, but they also required more learning, and a direct approach to undergraduates to encourage them in their faith and to warn them against infidelity and immorality.

Cathedral sermons

The demands made of preaching cathedral sermons were not significantly different from those required in any famous London parish church, except that canons residentiary and prebendaries shared the burden in a cathedral, while the rector or vicar of a parish was almost the sole occupant of the pulpit every Sunday.

The deans of cathedrals, like John Donne, were responsible for preaching on the great festivals—Christmas, Easter, and Whitsun. While the cathedral preachers were expected to be as learned as university preachers, they also had to deal with a wider range of persons than dons and undergraduates. Their large congregations were a mixed multitude, women as well as men, middle-aged as well as old and young. Furthermore, there were not only representatives of the professions but also tradesmen, and the affluent as well as the poor. Because of social and educational differences in the congregation of the cathedral, the preaching had to be more popular, the teaching had to be simpler and more easily remembered, and the illustrations had to be drawn from a wider range of experiences and observations of life.

In this connection, it is worth noting the changes in Donne's sermons from those he delivered as a chaplain at Lincoln's Inn to those he delivered in St. Paul's Cathedral. The sermons delivered to his legal congregation were much more intellectual—they tended to use careful and precise definitions in considering various possible interpretations of *cruces*, and in explaining and co-ordinating apparently contradictory texts—than those preached in St. Paul's, and his illustrations are less restricted to the profession of the law.[61] At the same time, an ex-lawyer himself, Donne never ceased to utilize the orderly arrangement and precise statements on controversial issues which he had learned in his legal training at Thavies Inn and Lincoln's Inn.

Joan Webber argues that Donne's sermon style varies with the change in his audiences. Thus, she says, "he is an orator at St. Paul's, a wit at Lincoln's Inn, a scholar at Whitehall, and a parson at St. Dunstan's."[62] (One assumes that by "parson" she means a pastor with spiritual concern.) This is a fair generalization as long as it is recognized that Donne did not cease to be scholarly, witty, pastoral, and an orator at St. Paul's, as well as with his other audiences.

But Donne as dean of St. Paul's is no longer as tentative and apologetic as he was as chaplain of Lincoln's Inn: he is the surer spokesman for the Church of England. He is also less paradoxical and complicated in his expression, making sure that even the simplest minds in the congregation will understand him.[63]

Above all at St. Paul's Donne exhibits "a development in human sympathy and an imaginative grasp of the problems of his audience as men and women."[64] Not only this, but Donne himself realizes that plain preaching can effectively reach the conscience—"God can pierce as far into a conscience, by a plain, as by an exquisite speaker."[65]

His psychological insight and empathy are noticeably deeper in the St. Paul's sermons. One example alone must suffice. It concerns our ability to think that others rather than ourselves are intended in warnings from the pulpit, because we suffer from a fatty degeneration of conscience:

When this inordinate love of riches begins in us, we have some tenderness of conscience; and we consult with Gods Ministers: after we admit the reprehensions of Gods Ministers when they speak to our Consciences; but, at last, the habit of our sin hath seared us up, and we find that it is we, that the Preachers mean; we find that he touches others, but not us. Our wit and malice is awake but our conscience is asleep; we can make a sermon libel against others, and cannot find a Sermon in a Sermon to ourselves. It is a sickness, and an evil sickness.[66]

Chapter IX

One cannot but notice the immense expansion in the fields of images that Donne uses as dean of St. Paul's. Londoners would be delighted by the appositeness of marine images, as inhabitants of Britain's greatest port,[67] and by the sheer simplicity of the images. Could one indicate to a Londoner more clearly and simply, the ease of access a Protestant has to the heavenly Father than in the following analogy? Christ, said Donne,

> might well say, *Father, forgive them,* which is the first room of this glorious Palace. And in this contemplation, O my unworthy soule, thou art presently in the presence. No passing of guards, no ushers. No examination of thy degree or habit. The Prince is not asleep, nor private, nor weary of giving, nor refers to others. He puts thee not to prevaile by Angels or Archangels. But lest anything might hinder thee from coming into his presence, his presence comes to thee. And lest Majesty should dazell thee, thou art to speake but to thy Father.[68]

We can see the same development from complexity and intellectuality to simplicity in the sermons of Donne's friend, Henry King, when he preached as a resident canon in St. Paul's Cathedral. His sermon plans here have fewer divisions, his illustrations are simple, vivid, and apt. For example, he points out the folly of the disuse of prayer.

> 'Tis a dangerous opinion for any to think he hath no need of God. And 'tis high time God should grow weary of doing good to that man who growes weary of serving him. An intermittent pulse is one of the fore-runners of death, and a cessation from Prayer, which is the soules pulse, shewing all her sicke distemper, wants and grievances, is the argument of a desparat forlorne condition.[69]

While he has numerous citations from the classics and the Fathers, they are brief, and instead of lengthy citations in Latin and Greek we are given only tags. Here is a striking difference between university and court sermons, on the one hand, and cathedral or parish church sermons on the other.

It may well be that the greatest metaphysical sermons were not preached in the limelight of the court, but at the great festival gatherings in the cathedrals or large parish churches where there was wit, learning, and vivid illustrations, all illuminated by the love of the pastor for the people he cherished as the family spiritual physician. There was less tendency to show off and a more direct concern to edify and encourage rather than to stupefy with paradoxes and esoteric learning in unfamiliar tongues. Donne and his contemporaries may have been more brilliant at court or at St. Paul's Cross or in the competition of the Spital: they were more domesticated in their cathedral or church, and could say of Christ as John the Baptist did: "I must decrease and He must increase."

NOTES

1. Sig. A2v.
2. References to sermons four and six are to volume 1 of the Potter and Simpson critical edition, *The Sermons of John Donne*, (Berkeley, 1953).
3. Lancelot Andrewes, *XCVI Sermons* (London, 1629), 519.
4. Andrewes, *XCVI Sermons*, 46.
5. Andrewes, *XCVI Sermons*, 696, from a Whitsunday sermon of 1616.
6. See Thomas Plume's prefatory life in *A Century of Sermons . . . by John Hacket* (London, 1675), vii.
7. In the twentieth sermon on Christ's Temptations in Hacket's *A Century of Sermons*. In the nineteenth sermon on the same topic Hacket had decried worship of the Virgin Mary, saints, and angels.
8. Hacket, *A Century of Sermons*, 745. From the first sermon on the Gunpowder Plot.
9. Hacket, *A Century of Sermons*, 819.
10. Hacket, *A Century of Sermons*, 691.
11. Andrewes, *XCVI Sermons*, 308.
12. Donne, *Sermons*, 6:290. Sermon of 26 April 1625.
13. Donne, *Sermons*, 3:80.
14. Hacket, *A Century of Sermons*, 737.
15. Hacket, *A Century of Sermons*, 365. From the seventeenth sermon on Christ's Temptations.
16. Donne, *Sermons*, 2:348–349. Sermon preached at Whitehall on 3 March 1619/20.
17. Donne, *Sermons*, 2:105.
18. Barten Holyday, *A Sermon preached at Pauls Crosse, August the 5, 1623* (London, 1626), 4.
19. Barten Holyday, *Three Sermons upon the Passion, Resurrection and Ascension of our Saviour, preached at Oxford* (London, 1626), 92.
20. Chapter III.
21. Chapter VI.
22. Donne, *Sermons*, 6:290.
23. Andrewes, *XCVI Sermons*, 699.
24. Brian Duppa, *The Soules Soliloquie: And, A Conference with Conscience . . .* (London, 1648), 2.

25. Hacket, *A Century of Sermons*, 740.

26. Donne, *Sermons*, 6:165. Preached on 13 June 1624.

27. Theophilus Field, *A Watch-word, Or, the Alarme, Or, A Good Take Heed. A Sermon preached at White-Hall in the open Preaching place last Lent before King Charles* (London, 1628), 42–43.

28. *The Works of . . . John Cosin*, Volume I: *Sermons* (Oxford, 1843), 299. This sermon was preached before Queen Henrietta Maria's Protestant courtiers on 5 January 1653 (New Style).

29. *The Works of . . . Joseph Hall*, Volume V: *Sermons*, ed. Philip Wynter, (Oxford, 1863), 249.

30. John Prideaux, *A Plot for Preferment. A Sermon Preached at Court* (Oxford, 1636), 1.

31. Prideaux, *A Plot for Preferment*, 27.

32. Andrewes, *XCVI Sermons*, 608. A sermon preached before the king at Greenwich, 24 May 1608.

33. Donne, *Sermons*, 2:47.

34. Donne, *Sermons*, 4:45. A sermon preached at Whitehall, 8 March 1621. The text is I Corinthians 15:26, "The last enemie that shall be destroyed is death." Another arresting text and opening of a court sermon is found in *Sermons*, 7: No. 14, 349. Another Lenten sermon used the fascinating text, "And when he had said this, he fell asleep" (Acts 7:60) and began with the striking maxim, "He that will dy with Christ upon Good Friday, must hear his own bell toll all Lent" (*Sermons*, 8:174).

35. William Barlow, *The Eagle and the Body; described in the Sermon Preached before Queene Elizabeth of precious memorie, in Lent, Anno 1601* (London, 1609), sig. B1v-B2.

36. *The Works of . . . Joseph Hall*, 5:58–59.

37. Peter Heylyn, *The Parable of the Tares Expounded and Applied in Ten Sermons Preached before his late Majesty King Charles The Second Monarch of Great Britain* (London, 1659), 276.

38. Thomas Jackson, *A Treatise Concerning the Signes of the Time, Or Gods Forewarnings* (Oxford, 1637). The first sermon is on the text Luke 13:5, "I tell you nay, but except yee repent, ye shall all likewise perish."

39. Donne, *Sermons*, 8:178. Donne often fitted his figures to his audience. He was especially fond of the analogy of God and the king, as Winfried Schleiner points out in *The Imagery of John Donne's Sermons* (Providence, Rhode Island, 1970), 47.

40. *The Collected Sermons of Thomas Fuller, D.D., 1631–1659*, eds. J. E. Bailey and W. E. A. Axon, 2 vols. (London, 1891), 1:425. The

sermon was entitled "Jacob's Vow" and preached at St. Mary's, Oxford on 10 May 1644, before King Charles and Prince James.

41. See Millar Maclure, *The Paul's Cross Sermons, 1534–1642* (Toronto, 1958), *passim*.

42. William Barlow, *A sermon preached at Paules Crosse on the first Sunday in Lent, Martii, I, 1600. With a short discourse of the Earl of Essex his confession and penitence before and at the hour of his death* (London, 1601).

43. Maclure, *The Paul's Cross Sermons*, 244.

44. *The Letters of John Chamberlain*, ed. Norman Egbert McClure, 2 vols. (Philadelphia, 1939), 2:451.

45. Maclure, *The Paul's Cross Sermons*, 242–243.

46. Maclure, *The Paul's Cross Sermons*, 234.

47. Maclure, *The Paul's Cross Sermons*, 246.

48. See *The Works of William Laud, D.D.*, 9 vols. (Oxford, 1860) 1:185–212.

49. [*Remembrancia*] *Analytical Index* (London, 1878), 368, cited in William Gifford's article "Time and Place in Donne's Sermons," *PMLA*, 82 (1967): 388–398, to which I am much indebted in section 3 of this chapter.

50. See the *Diary of John Manningham* (Camden Society, London, 1868), 57–58, 69–70, and 85.

51. Donne, *Sermons*, 4:116, 127.

52. Thomas Playfere, *The Whole Sermons* (London, 1623), 117.

53. The first citation from Donne's Spital sermon comes from *Sermons*, 4:96, and the second from 4:101.

54. Thomas Goffe, *Deliverance from the Grave. A Sermon preached at St. Maries Spittle in London on Wednesday in Easter Weeke last, March 28, 1627* (London, 1627), 9.

55. Goffe, *Deliverance from the Grave*, 39–40.

56. Henry King, *Two Sermons Upon the Act Sunday Being the 10th of July, 1625. Delivered at St. Maries in Oxford. Psalm 133:1. Behold how good and pleasant it is for brethren to dwell together in unitie* (London, 1625), 32. With these sermons may be compared Dr. John Gauden's "Upon the Act Sermon" at Oxford on 11 July 1641. Its theme is the renewing of the mind in religion, and its text, Ephesians 4:23. The references to the audience are most elegant, and the classics and patristics are cited fully and frequently. Great respect for human reason is its dominant characteristic. For example, in criticizing the swearing of oaths Gauden urges that Christians should honor God

by refusing them, while "if you are an atheist, why take the name of God who does not exist in vain, it is folly and waste?" (*Three Sermons Preached Upon Severall Publike Occasions* [London, 1642], 105). Epigrammatic clarity is wedded to piety and learning.

57. Thomas Jackson, *Nazareth and Bethlehem, or, Israels Portion in the Sonne of Jesse. And, Mankinds Comfort from the weaker sexe* (Oxford, 1617), 36–37. Both were preached in St. Mary's Church, Oxford.

58. Hacket, *A Century of Sermons*, 962–963.

59. See the pseudonymous publication of the revised original sermon and the retraction sermon, *The Resurrection Rescued from the Souldiers Calumnies, in Two Sermons Preached at St. Maries in Oxon. By Robert Jones, D.D.* [actually Thomas Lushington, D.D.] (London, 1659).

60. See Christopher Hill, *The World Turned Upside Down: Radical Ideas during the English Revolution* (New York, 1972).

61. J. B. Leishman in "The Sermons of John Donne," *Review of English Studies*, N.S. 8 (1957): 434–443, argues that there are less differences in Donne's sermons to varying audiences than Evelyn Simpson finds. Her reply is found in "To the Editor," *Review of English Studies*, 9 (1958): 293–294.

62. Joan Webber, *Contrary Music: The Prose Style of John Donne* (Madison, Wisconsin, 1963), 58.

63. R. C. Bald, *John Donne: A Life* (London and New York, 1970), 447, makes this point.

64. Donne, *Sermons*, introduction to vol. 3:41.

65. Donne, *Sermons*, 6:92.

66. Donne, *Sermons*, 3:56.

67. Examples will be found in Donne's *Sermons*, 2:306–307; 3:184f. and 265; 5:77 and 190; and 6:305, among several others.

68. Donne, *Sermons*, 5:234.

69. Henry King, *An Exposition Upon the Lords Prayer. Delivered in certaine Sermons in the Cathedrall Church of S. Paul* (London, 1628), 26.

Chapter X

IMAGERY

T HE METAPHYSICAL DIVINES were almost all poets as well as preachers, and therefore makers of images. Their training in a classical curriculum at school and university required them to translate Latin and Greek poetry into English poetry. Similarly their training in the art of elocution demanded that they learn to move the hearts of their hearers to adore God, to imitate the example of Christ, and to show compassion for their indigent or ill neighbors. An essential for this task was the capacity to devise inspiring or minatory analogies as illustrations: in a word, images. This was particularly necessary for preachers because, like sacraments, sermons attempt to make the actions of the invisible God visible. Thus an eloquent preacher has only two alternatives: either he must make unforgettable images by creating them new from his observation and experience, or he must refurbish them and polish them from his chief literary source, the Bible. As in the Incarnation where the Word of God took flesh, so at a humbler level their words must take flesh too; otherwise their words will only be insubstantial abstractions, mere ghosts that fade in the memory and in the light of daily duty.

The function of images

The major function of images is to illuminate. They make concrete the abstractions of doctrine and behavior. As reasons are pillars, said Thomas Fuller in *The Holy State*,[1] so are images windows that let in the light. A subordinate function is to awaken interest by the surprise they create—a species of shock tactics. John Donne for example grips the attention of his reader by beginning a poem in a startling manner:

> Goe, and catche a falling starre,
> Get with child a mandrake roote,
> Tell me, where all past yeares are,
> Or who cleft the Divils foot.[2]

In a parody of the same technique, a popular clerical associate of Donne's starts a sermon with the same technique in prose. Adams' words are: "Goe, lead a Lyon in a single haire, send up an Eagle to the skie to picke out a starre, cope up the thunder, and quench the flaming city, with one widowes teares: if thou couldst doe these, yet *nescit modo lingua domari:* the tongue can no man tame."[3]

In a sermon entitled, "The Shot, or the Wofull Price which the wicked Pay for the Feast of Vanitie," Adams again uses shock tactics with a startling analogy. He tells of the guest of the Devil who "was madder than *Nero* in delights, *feare compasseth him on every side. He starts at his own shadow, and would not change firmnesse with an Aspen leafe.*"[4]

Bishop Brian Duppa is also a master of the surprising metaphor. Having caught our attention by the brilliant suggestion that the conscience is God's informer "sent by him as a spie into the soule," he drives home the point by the further question, "Dost thou know withall, that it is a Volume, which no *Jesuite* can corrupt, nor no *Index Expurgatorius* strike a Letter out of it; That it is the onely Book of all the Library that shall goe along with thee into the world to come?"[5]

A further use for a vivid and appropriate image is to etch it on the memory of the congregation. For example, Lancelot Andrewes wishes to make the point that, before any divine message can lodge in the soul, all trepidation must be allayed. He is commenting on the Nativity and the words of Luke 2:10,

"And the Angell sayd unto them: Be not afraid, for behold, I bring you good tidings of great joy." Andrewes comments:

> That the Message then may proceed, this *feare* must be removed. In a troubled water, no face will be seene: nor by a troubled mind, no message received, till it be setled. To settle them then for it; no other way, no other word to begin with, but *Nolite timere, feare not,* and that is ever the Angells beginning.[6]

The image of the troubled water is clear, concise, and apt—it conveys no reflection, and man (the recipient of God's message) is intended to reflect His image.

Elevating and diminishing metaphors

Other subordinate rhetorical purposes for which images can be used are for elevating the thoughts of the hearers by persuading them to accept lofty ideas and follow noble behavior, or the opposite—to denigrate an idea or action that the preacher considers despicable by the use of demeaning and debasing tropes. Puttenham, the English rhetorician, says that the "disabler" or demeaning trope is used "in despite to bring our enemies in contempt."[7]

An example of an image that elevates the thoughts of the hearers is Andrewes' analogy for the divine mercy which reigns over all. He has prepared us to recognize the importance of the meaning of the word by indicating that it lacks the depth of the Latin *misericordia,* which means compassion for misery, and that the Hebrew word is derived from the word for "womb," suggesting the more compassionate sex. Then comes the image of mercy: "It is not *above* onely, as an *Obelisk* or *Maypole,* higher than all about them, but have neither shadow nor shelter; no good they do." By contrast "*Mercie* hath a broad top, spreading it self *over all.* It is so above all, as it is over them, too. As the vault of this Chappell is over us, and the great vault of the Firmament over that. The *super* of latitude and expansion, no lesse then of altitude and elevation."[8] An obelisk at first suggests a grandiose monument suitably raised to commemorate a great person and so it might also celebrate God's majesty; a maypole on the other hand, suggests human merriment and is less suitable. But Andrewes makes the point vividly that God's mercy spreads its protection like the vault of the chapel itself, a microcosm of the macrocosm of the vast sheltering vault of heaven. His image therefore elevates the congregation's thoughts and illustrates the text, "The Lord is good to all: and His mercies are over all his workes."

Another example of an ennobling image is Donne's likening of Christ seeing the potential of apostolicity in the simple fishermen, to the stonecutter imagining the polished gem or the sculptor the statue concealed in the marble. The aptness consists in the prophetical quality in Christ and the artificers, and in the intrinsic value of the precious stones and marble which makes them worth the shaping and the polishing. Donne writes:

> In a rough stone a cunning Lapidary will easily foresee what his cutting and his polishing and his art will bring that stone to; A cunning statuary discerns in a marble-stone under his feet, where there will arise an Eye, and an Eare and a Hand, and other lineament to make it a perfect statue. Much more did our Saviour Christ . . . foresee in these fishermen an inclinableness to become usefull in that great service of his Church.[9]

Sometimes a decorative image may be used where a demeaning one would be more appropriate. Canon John Wall, for example, uses a richly barbaric image in reference to sin when it perhaps would have been wiser to use a contemptuous one, when he says, "we behold with pure eyes the tender bowels of his [God's] unspeakable love, to that Aethopian Queene, the blacknesse of our nature."[10] He is frequently gauche in his tropes. For example, when describing Christ's triumphal progress across the mountains of Transfiguration, of Calvary, of Olivet, and of Mount Sion he wishes us to admire Christ, but he inaptly uses active verbs, more suitable for deer or mountain goats than a holy procession. The result is bathos:

> These are the steppes and degrees of his royall pace and majestick procession, whilest hee comes leaping over the hills, and skipping over the mountaines, from mount *Tabor* where hee was transfigured to mount *Calvarie*, where hee was crucified, from mount *Calvarie* where hee was crucified to mount *Olivet*, where he was exalted to mount *Sion* where he lives and raignes for ever.[11]

It is not only an inappropriate image, but also exceedingly farfetched.

Sometimes Donne thinks he has slighted decorum as when he apologetically introduces a homely metaphor: "The Holy Ghost hath born further witnesse of this light, and, (if we may take so low a metaphore and so high a Mystery) hath *snuffed* this candle, mended this light in the *Reformation* of Religion."[12]

For an example of an appropriate diminishing figure we can also turn to Donne, as he rejects the divisions in the Church caused by sectarianism. For him they "are not bodies, they are but rotten boughes, gangrened limmes, fragmentary *chippes*, blowne off by their own spirit of turbulence."[13] The diminishing tropes are entirely suitable: as true believers are limbs of the body of Christ, so sectarians are cut off from the Body and are thus gangrenous. Similarly the boughs of a tree blown off by the wind are merely chips of wood lacking sap.

We have stated that the function of an image is to make the abstract concrete. This is particularly relevant for a preacher speaking about a deity who is invisible. The most commonly used image for God was that of kingship. The minds and devotion of the hearers would mount from the concept of the highest human authority, that of a monarch, to the King of Kings, Lord of Lords, the ascended and reigning Christ. It is also an appropriate figure in a court sermon to honor the highest magistrate, especially if one is preaching before the king. It is a common usage in the sermons of Donne.

Concise images

Later in this chapter we shall consider the various areas of observation and experience from which the preachers drew their images. Our immediate interest is in different types of images, and these may be classed broadly into four types: sharply concise images, extended images, catalogues of similes and metaphors, and highly ingenious images.

There are sharp arrowlike images that hit the bull's eye of the memory immediately and unforgettably. Playfere, for example, wishes to stress that worldly pleasures are transitory and insubstantial, so he thinks of the parallel with snowballs, delightful but dissolving. "You see," he observes, "little children what paines they take to rake and scrape snowe together to make a snow-ball." His moral is ". . . right so, they that scrape the treasures of this world, have but a snowe ball of it: as soone as the sunne shineth, and God breatheth upon it, and so entreth into it, by and by it comes to nothing."[14] Playfere also suggests that earthly treasures are but toys and the adults who collect them are merely children.

One of Donne's least complicated analogies suggests that saints, like pearls, are made slowly, drop by drop of grace:

> A drop of dew hardens and then another drop fals and spreads its selfe and cloathes that former drop and then another, and another, and because so many shels and films that invest that first seminal drop, and so (they say) there is a pearle in nature. A good soule takes first Gods first drop into consideration, what he hath shed upon him in nature, and then his second coate, what in the Law, and successively his other manifold graces and so many shels and films in the Christian Church, and so we are sure, there is a saint.[15]

The fitness of the image is in the preciousness of the pearl and of the saint, their slow maturation, and the reminder that

Jesus called the Gospel the pearl of great price, to gain which the merchant sold his all.

Our third example of a simple and relatively concise image is drawn from Archbishop Ussher. He finds a vinter's sipping of a variety of wines to be a suitable image for a superficial and merely temporary faith:

> He that can take a full draught of Christ crucified, he shall never thirst . . . but it shall not be so with him that doth but taste. The vintner goes round the cellar and tastes every vessel; he takes it into his mouth, and spits it out again, and yet knows by the tasting whether it will be good or bad; the wine goes but to his palate, it reaches not to the stomach. So a temporary believer tastes and feels what an excellent thing it is to have Communion with Christ, and to be made partaker of his glory; but he does but taste it.[16]

The strength of this analogy is twofold: it was drawn from a common experience; and it reminded the Christian that in Holy Communion he drinks from Christ's chalice, and that when Peter said that he would die with Christ, Jesus asked the apostle to consider if he was really able to drink Christ's cup of suffering. The mention of the wine cup sets off both secular and sacred reverberations in the listener's memory.

Extended images

When it comes to our second category of images, extended and elaborately detailed metaphors, we have the advantage of being able to compare three different metaphysical preachers. We can see how they develop images of Christ's Passion, expounded in two cases as medicine for humanity's sickness, and in the third case as a metaphorical sermon to heal mankind. Its expositors are successively Adams, Hacket, and Featley.

Adams developes the metaphor by contrasting Christ and humanity, the holy One as opposed to the sinful many:

Sinne which God so loathed, that he could not save his own elect because of it, but by killing his owne Son. It is such disease, that nothing but the bloud of the Sonne of God could cure it. He cured us by taking the receits [prescriptions] himselfe which we should have taken.

Then follow details of the treatment, which Adams elaborates with great ingenuity:

He is first cast into a *Sweat;* such a sweat as never man but he felt, when the bubbles were drops of bloud. Would not sweating serve? He comes to incision, they pierce his hands, his feet, his side; and set life it selfe abroach. He must take a potion, too, as bitter as their malice could make it; compounded of vinegar and gall. And lastly, he must take a stronger and stronger medicine, then all the rest; he must die for our sins.[17]

The meditation is reminiscent of devotional techniques, such as the Ignatian, calling for composition of place, and its ingenuity makes it apposite and memorable.

Hacket's treatment of Christ's Passion as bitter medicine for him to take for human healing is more concentrated than that of Adams. He writes:

Such wits as delighted in holy ingenuity, have applied the several parts of Christs merit, and sufferance, and passion unto us in the notion of *Physick* and *Chirurgery. Curavit non dietam cum jejunavit; per electuariam, quando corpus & sanguinem dedit in coena discipulis,* &c. He took upon him to cure us by the prescription of a diet when he fasted: By an *Electuary,* when he gave his body and blood to his Disciples in his last Supper: By a *Sweat* when drops of bloud trickled from him in the Garden: By an *Emplaster,* when his face was smeared with Spittle: By a bitter Potion, when he drank Vinegar upon the Cross: By cutting and lancination, when his feet and hands were pierced with nails, and his side with a Spear.[18]

This is in fact over-ingenious, for the "Emplaster," is not convincing, and the final blood-letting may be a cure for sinners, but surely not for the great Physician himself. Hacket may even, by his introductory reference to "holy ingenuity," have thought it was too witty to carry conviction.

Our final extensive metaphor for the Passion is also ingenious. Featley likens it to the delivery of a sermon, and so it incidentally tells a good deal about the structure of sermons in the mid-seventeenth century. In a devotional passage Featley addresses Christ:

> Let others goe on forward if they please; I will stay still at the *Crosse*, and take no other Lesson. For I desire no other *Pulpit* then that *tree*; no other *Preacher* then thy crucified body; no other *Text* then thy *death* and *passion*; no other parts [divisions of the sermon] then thy *wounds*; no other *amplification* then thy *extension*; no other *notes* then thy *markes*; no other *points* then thy *nailes*; no other *booke* then thy open side.[19]

Puns, such as "no other *amplification* then thy *extension*," and other examples of ingenuity were not thought by the metaphysical preachers to diminish the sincerity of the adoration in their devotions.

Donne of course is a master at using the exfoliating, extended image and no one employs nautical imagery more frequently or with greater precision than he. This has sometimes been explained as due to the experience of a terrifying storm,[20] but there are other reasons which would explain its frequency. Winfried Schleiner has argued[21] that life as a pilgrimage can be aptly envisioned as a journey which involves sailing through storms and past the rocks and shoals that wreck ships and lives. Certainly, the Christian life has frequently been viewed as a pilgrimage, or as a battle between the forces of God and Satan. But there is a double appropriateness in the dean of St. Paul's using marine imagery. He is preaching to members of an island nation—"this precious stone set in the silver sea"[22]—and furthermore, his cathedral looked on to a forest of masts in the port of London. Bishop John King made effective reference to this sight, to stir up London citizens to furnish the funds to mend the old Gothic St. Paul's, in a sermon of 1620:

> When I behold that forrest of masts upon your river for trafficke, and that more then miraculous bridge, which is the *communio terminus*, to joyne the two banks of that river. . . .[23]

As he went on to describe great buildings of London, including the Royal Exchange, the Halls of the Merchants' Guilds, the hospitals, orphanages, and churches, he must have held the vast congregation (including the king) in the hollow of his hand. So too Donne appealed to the pride of Londoners in their mariners, and to contemporary fascination for distant and daring voyages. Donne described life as a dangerous journey which had an eternal destination at its end, and had to be accomplished within a definite time limit. His use of marine images in describing this journey helped to dramatize its urgency.[24]

In Donne's farewell sermon at Lincoln's Inn, prior to his voyage to Germany, he viewed Christ's kingdom as a sea of mercy:

> Christ Jesus remember us all in his Kingdome, to which, though we must sail through a sea, it is the sea of his blood, where no soul suffers shipwrack; though we must be blown with strange winds, with sighs and groans for our sins, yet it is the Spirit of God blows all the wind, and shall blow away all contrary ends of diffidence or distrust in Gods mercy.[25]

He had also suggested in another sermon, "It is well with us if we can ride out a storm at anchour; that is, lie still and expect, and surrender ourselves to God, and anchor in that confidence until that storm blow over." In this extended image, he concludes that "He is a good Christian that can ride out, or board out or hull out a storme, that by industry as long as he can and by patience when he can do no more, over-lives a storm, and does not forsake his ship,"[26] despite the abuses and scandals of the state and Church he lives in. Here again we notice the precision of his nautical terminology as well as the practicality of his application.

On Whitsunday 1629, the dean preached a magnificent sermon on Genesis 1:2, "And the Spirit of God moved upon the face of the waters." In the course of this sermon the meaning of the imagery of the waters changes. It starts with the waters of the original chaos from which God creates the world, moves to the spiritual waters of Baptism, and finally to spilt water as the image of death and dissolution; and yet the Spirit of God brings life out of death in the waters.[27] No one can equal Donne in the extensions and the applications of his imagery.

It is only fitting that we should select another extended image from the only contemporary of Donne to rival him in popularity, namely Thomas Adams. Adams finds many parallels between the balm or balsam tree and the Word of God. One sermon uses the text Jeremiah 8:22, "Is there no Balme in Gilead? Is there no Physitian there? Why then is not the health of the daughter of my people recovered?" Here Adams is using the standard image of sin as disease and salvation as healing, as the title of the sermon indicates: *Physicke from Heaven.* Adams finds nine parallels between balm and God's revelation in Scripture. The balsam's leaves are white and God's Word is pure and spotless. Balsam's taste is biting, so is God's Word to the unregenerate. Balsam weeps a kind of gum, as the Word of God did for our sins. If the balsam tree is cut too deeply, it dies; so must God's Word be divided between reproof and encouragement. It was once according to Pliny confined to Judea, but now spreads over the world, as also God's Word. When balsam grew in Judea, it was found in the king's garden, and spiritual balm grows only in the garden of the King of Heaven. The balsam tree though it spreads wide yet the boughs support

themselves; similarly God's Word is self-supporting. The last
two points of the parallel may be given in the preacher's own
words:

> 8. Physitians write of *Balsamum*, that it is *paratu facile
> & optimum*, easie and excellent to be prepared. The spirit-
> uall Balme is prepared to our hands: it is but the adminis-
> tration that is required of us, and the application of you.
> 9. *Balme* is, *utilis ad omnium morborum expugnationem*, good
> against all diseases.[28]

However ingenious, this extended series of parallels seems contrived and is too far from common experience to be convincing.
Furthermore, the nine parallels are too many to be recalled.

Catalogues of similes

Another imagistic device to hold the attention of the congregation was to devise a catalogue of similes or metaphors, which
explode in the mind's eye like a series of cascading fireworks.
Devices of this type can be illustrated from the sermons of
Smith, Barlow, and Brownrig.

Henry Smith uses the catalog as a climax to a sermon on
covetousness on the text from I Timothy 6:6, "Godliness is a
great gaine, if a man be content with what he hath." This
greed he calls the Londoner's sin, and he provides biblical exemplars of covetousness. Then he contrasts the empty heart
of the miser with the coffers filled with gold:

> . . . So hee which is set on coveting, doth drink brine,
> which makes thirst more, and seeth no haven till he arrive
> at death; . . . and though his house be full, and his shop
> full, and his coffers full, and his purse full; yet his heart
> is not full, but lanke & emptie, like the disease which we
> call the Wolfe [Lupus], that is alwaies eating, yet keepes
> the bodie leane.[29]

Then there follows simile after simile, and a final diminishing
simile likening the covetous man to the most foolish of animals,
the ass:

The Ant doth eate the food which she findeth, the Lion doth refreshe him selfe with the praie that hee taketh; but the covetous man lyeth by his money, as a sicke man sits by his meate, and hath no power to take it, but to looke upon it, like the Prince to whom Elisha sayde, that hee should see corne with his eyes, but none should come within his mouth. Thus the covetous man makes a foole of him selfe, he coveteth to covet, hee gathereth to gather, he laboureth to labour, he careth to care; as though his office were to fill a coffer full of Angels; and then to dye; like an Asse which carrieth treasures on his backe all day, and at night they are taken from him, which did him no good but loade him.[30]

The most dramatic use of a series of similes is made by Bishop Barlow in a sermon on the Sunday following the discovery of the Gunpowder Plot. The succession of similes hammers home the great loss that would have ensued to the whole nation if Guy Fawkes and his fellow conspirators had been successful:

A *Realme* without a *Monarch* as the *Skie without the* Sunne, is a clowde of darkenesse, a darkenes of confusion.
A *Monarch* without *counsell*, as a *head without eyes*, obnoxious of it selfe to danger, and a burden to the members.
Counsell without *Wisdome*, as an *arrow out of a childes bow*, accidentally fortunate, but originally weake.
Wisedome without *Religion*, like *Tullies Offices*, politique but prophane.
Religion without *Learning*, like the *Athenian Altar*. Act. 17. superstitiously devout, but fundamentally unsound.
Learning not guarded with *Strength*, as *a rich Citie without wals, naked & unfenced.*
Strength without *Iustice*, as a *Lyon broke from his Cage*, furious and insatiable.[31]

Such a catalog can only be effectively declaimed. Its author was an able epigrammatist who piled image upon image to

443

convey what would have been overthrown in the debacle of the conspiracy.

Our final example of the cumulative effect of a series of images is taken from a sermon of Bishop Brownrig's, and the images provide its entire structure. The text is James 1:22, "But be ye doers of the Word, not hearers only." In a remarkable analysis he gathers and anatomizes several of the biblical images for Holy Scripture contained in the Bible. It is successively a Law, Seed, Meat, Looking-Glass, Physick of the Soul, Balm of Gilead, and the Counsel of God.[32]

Ingenious images

All our divines can on occasion produce arrestingly ingenious images, and the best preachers among them (like Smith, Donne, Adams, and Hacket) can do this frequently. As we have noted in another context, Henry Smith thinks of the tentative Christian as "an Owle peeps at the Sunne out of a barne, but dares not come to it, so we peepe at Religion and will not come neere it, but stande aloofe off, pinking and winking as though we were more afraid of GOD then the divell."[33] Even his homelier similes are ingeniously apt. Because we naturally love the world, Smith says God has given it an edge of bitterness to make us loathe it, "Like a Nurse which layeth Mustard upon her breasts to weane us from the dugge of the world."[34]

Donne is so ingenious that selection is difficult among so many strikingly appropriate and vivid images. A brief image of his is of the man who relies on his popularity, and in this respect resembles a stranded whale when the tide has ebbed away: "Therefore as *David* would say, *I will not be afraid of ten thousand men* . . . for they will change, and at such an ebbe, the popular man will lye, as a whale upon the sands deserted by the tide."[35] A far more thoughtful image of Donne's likens two types of theology respectively to sculptors and painters. The sculptor achieves his result by subtracting from the block of marble and this is the *via negativa* in theology: "Sometimes we represent God by Substraction, by Negation, by saying God is that, which is not mortall, not passible, not moveable."

The painter represents by adding colors, lines, light, and shadow to the canvas: "Sometimes we present him [God] by Addition; by adding our bodily lineaments to him, and saying that God hath hands, and feet, and eares and eyes; and adding our affections, and passions to him."[36] This is the way of the *analogia entis.* Donne's apt comparison makes sure that some highly abstract theological methodology is plain as daylight in a sermon on the Holy Trinity.

Moreover Donne's ingenuity provides not only visual but aural imagery. In the *Devotions* Donne had coined his most famous image: "Any mans *death* diminishes me, because I am involved in *Mankind;* And therefore never send to know for whom the *bell* tolls; it tolls for thee." The same image recurs in a sermon on the daily mercies of Divine providence, where Donne affirms:

God is a declaratory God. The whole yeare is to the Saints a continuall *Epiphany* one day of manifestation. In every minute that strikes upon the *Bell,* is a syllable, nay a syllo-gisme from God. And, in my *last Bell,* God shall speake too; that Bell, when it tolls, shall tell me I am going, and when it rings out, shall tell you I am gone into the hands of that God who is the God of the living and not of the dead.[37]

Thomas Adams catches our interest by saying that atheists are such as have "voluntarily, violently extinguished to themselves, the Sun-light of the Scripture, Moone-light of the Creature."[38] Illustrating the high calling and responsibility of a minister, Adams explains this by a contrasting image drawn from the stage:

The player that misacts an inferior and unnoted part, car-ryes it away without censure, but if he shall play some emperour or part of observation unworthily, the spectators are ready to hisse him off.

Adams continues by insisting that no one minds if an inferior role is miscast, but adds,

> The *Minister* represents no meane person, that might give toleration to his absurdities; but the Prince of Heaven, and therefore should be holy, as his Heavenly Father is.[39]

Bishop Hacket in a single memorable image combines wit, prophecy, and wisdom in his attack on the Puritans who want to change the liturgy and, implicitly, much else:

> At one hearing, the *Old Liturgy* castigated will give content: shortly nothing will serve but a new lump of Prayer, which hath no congruity with any that was before: in a while they will brook no set form at all. How many degrees hath the shadow run back from their Dial? 'Tis like a motion in the Ches-board, sometimes into a black chequer, sometimes into a white; but it is all one, so they may *check* the *King,* or move the *Bishop.* [40]

Other less renowned preachers among the metaphysicals were also ingenious image-makers. Such were Heylyn, John White, and Jasper Mayne. Heylyn makes effective use of a common phenomenon, the unnoticed movement of the shadow on a sundial, in order to show how heresies grow without being observed:

> . . . those errors as they came in privily, so they grew insensibly, like to 'he finger of a Diall, which we finde varied from the place where before it was, and yet we do not see it vary; so do private mens opinions, if they be but probable, gain by degrees we know not how, on the affection and good liking of particular persons. . . .

Thus, he says, paradoxes are accounted "School-points" and then "they are taken, or mistaken rather for the traditions of the Church and finally received as the Articles of the Christian Faith."[41]

Jasper Mayne vividly denounces deceivers and pretenders, likening them to "the Fish which blacks the *streame* in which it swimmes, and casts an *Inke* from its bowels to hide it selfe from being seen," while he accuses them of making "words which were ordained to reveale their *Thoughts,* disguise them. . . ."[42] Thus George Orwell's "doublethink" was anticipated over three centuries ago.

It was the ingenious images of the metaphysical preachers— so vivid, memorable, striking, surprising, and stimulating, often making a concord of initial discord (*concordia discors*)—that were the poetical contributions in their sermons.

The taste of the time was for bold and vigorous as well as didactic images, as can be seen in Robert Cawdrey's *A Treasurie or Store-House of Similies* (1600). In his dedicatory epistle the author insists upon the pedagogic value of images for the exposing of sins and vices and for the display of virtues "with due commendations, so lively and truly expressed, according to the plaine meaning of the word of God: that the godly Reader . . . will be mightily inflamed with the earnest liking and love unto them." He claims that the proof of their value is "that the holy Ghost hath so often used them." He insists, also, that their special use is "for Preachers profitable," and reminds us that Christ spoke in parables. Finally he adds, "the use of a Similie reacheth very farre: for it is used for ornament, for delight, for plainnesse & for gravitie."[43]

One example of the simple analogies available for preachers in Cawdrey's collection is the following simile taken from natural history (as others are culled from classical mythology). Its point is the moral importance of a good example:

As the yong crab-fish (being checked on a time of her elder, for going so crookedly), said, first go you straight before us, and then we will the straighter follow your steps.[44]

St. Augustine, centuries earlier, had insisted in *De Doctrina* that the preacher must *teach, delight,* and *move* (*ut doceat, ut*

447

delectet, ut flectat),[45] discarding only the *ut probet* of Cicero. The metaphysical preachers had learned that lesson well.

Individual preachers and the range of their images

Our concluding section will attempt to describe, if only in summary fashion, the range of images used by the leading metaphysical preachers.

Donne far excels the rest in the wide range of knowledge, varied experiences, in the esoteric reading disclosed in his images, and in the element of surprise found in several of them. These may be macabre, grotesque, repulsive,[46] or strangely out of context[47] in a sermon. The editors of Donne's sermons, Potter and Simpson, suggest that his imagery is gathered from four major fields: the law courts, the royal court, various trades, and from maritime life and explorations. In fact, his range is far more extensive. Images of a pharmaceutical, medical, and anatomical nature[48] abound in his sermons, and the latter group of images is used for the self-scrutiny that should lead to repentance.[49] Donne also often uses images from the visual arts, referring to art galleries, sculptors, and painters, as well as engravers.[50] It may be recalled that Donne owned a Leonardo da Vinci painting. As in his poetry, Donne was fascinated by geometrical images and maps: God is sometimes conceived as a circle, and sometimes as the centre through which all lines pass.[51] And some of his images come from the theatre, the gaming house, and even from the stews.[52]

Many of Donne's images are borrowed from the Church Fathers, and he especially raided the writings of Tertullian, Jerome, Gregory the Great, Gregory of Nyssa, Bernard of Clairvaux, and chiefly of Augustine. But his vividness of style and aptness of application made these borrowed images seem newly minted. We can however make two generalizations about his images. One is that he preferred dynamic and mobile images to static or quiescent ones, piling one upon another to show the relevance of his teaching to different members of his congregation. Secondly it seems that, as he delighted in using sacred images in his love poems, so in his sermons he reversed the process, using profane images for sacred topics.[53] The former characteristic gave his sermons vigor, and the latter a kind of surrealistic shock of surprise, as of a familiar object in an unusual setting, or a strange object in a conventional context.

Andrewes' appeal is more intellectual than emotional, and consequently his images are fewer and more restrained.[54] His chief illustrations are biblical exemplars of good and evil.[55] His images drawn from animals, birds, and insects are commonplace,[56] but at least he does not strain credence by using "unnatural" natural history as so many metaphysical preachers do. He likes musical and architectural images,[57] but there are also single images dealing with making wine,[58] conduits,[59] coinage,[60] upholstery,[61] and exploration.[62] His preference is for simple images in maxims, as, for instance, "And if Nature would have us *mowles*, Grace would *have us Eagles*. . . ,"[63] or "The Dove [The Holy Spirit] lights on no *carrion*. Into our Bodies, as a Temple, He is to come: as into a *stewes*, He will not."[64] His images are delivered in a brisk and businesslike manner.

Henry Smith's sermons, by contrast, are fuller of images than those of Andrewes, and of two kinds. One group seems to be derived from his observation of life at home and on farms, and the second group is derived from literary sources. Illustrating "It is not good for man to be alone," Smith argues that the single man is "like a Turtle, which hath lost his mate, like one legge when the other is cutte off, like one wing when the other is clipte, so had the man bene if the woman had not been ioyned to him."[65] Another simple and homely image illustrates how God knows better than we do what is good for us "as the Nurse knoweth better then the child when the milke is ready for it."[66] A divided heart is, according to Smith, like "a yong virgin which hath many suitors: some she fancieth for parentage, some for personage, some for wealth, some for wit, some for vertue, and after all, chooseth the worst of all."[67] Eager hearers of God's Word are likened to little birds with open beaks awaiting the return of their mother to the nest.[68] It is clear that the simplest or most inattentive soul in Smith's congregation could not fail to understand his message.

His literary illustrations are, however, meant to excite a sense of wonder and are chiefly drawn from Pliny and the like. Godliness, he claims, brings purity and peace into any house it visits, just "As the Unicorne dippeth his horne in the fountaine, and maketh the waters which were corrupt and noisome, cleare and wholesome upon the sodain."[69] On another occasion Smith tells of a Harpy (a bird with a man's face) who out of hunger will kill a man, but seeing his face in the water when she is about to drink, will pine with regret until she dies. The moral is: "What wilt thou doe then which hath not slain one like thy selfe, but thy selfe, thy verie selfe, with a cup of wine and murderest so many graces & vertues in an houre?"[70] Varied as his images are, Smith, like Andrewes, prefers to use a catalogue of biblical exemplars when possible, as the best illustrations of his sermons.[71]

Thomas Adams also had a gift for vivid and memorable images, but drawn from wider fields than Henry Smith. His aim was to have his words "pierce like a goad, be as sharp stroke to the conscience, that howsoever the smart is neglected, it leaveth a print behind it."[72] Sometimes a central analogy develops into a full allegory, as in an account of many spiritual dangers in the sermon "The Spiritual Navigator Bound for the Holy Land," or as in "The Soul's Sicknesse" where various physical illnesses are analogies for spiritual ailments. While he can provide homely similes,[73] he can also produce images of the highest literary quality, such as "The wounded conscience runs like a stricken deer with the arrows of death in her ribs, from thicket to thicket, from shelter to shelter, but cannot change her pain with her place."[74] His subtle inventory of images includes the use of characters,[75] as well as emblems,[76] historical narrations,[77] and fables.[78] And Adams, like Andrewes and Smith, likes catalogues of biblical personages.[79]

There is both mercy and condemnation in Adams' images. As we have earlier discussed, he has been called "Hell's local colorist" because his figures of hell sizzle and splutter sulphurously,[80] but he is also the preacher who most movingly pleads the cause of the poor.

We can conclude our appreciation of his imagery by citing an extensive pastoral passage which nicely illustrates his power of visualization:

> As in a faire Summers morning, when the Larke hath called up the Sunne, and the Sunne the Husbandman: when the earth had opened her shop of perfumes, and a pleasant wind fannes coolenesse through the ayre: when every creature is reioyced at the heart; On a suddaine the furious winds burst from their prisons, the thunder rends the clouds, and makes way for the lightning, and the spowts of heaven streame downe showers; a hideous tempest sooner dampes all the former delight, then a mans tongue can well expresse it: With no lesse content doe these guests of sinne passe their life, they eate to eate, and drinke to drinke, often to sleep, always to surfet: they caroll, dance, spend their present ioyes, and promise themselves infallible supply. On a suddaine, this *BUT* comes like an unlooked for storme, and turnes all into mourning, and such mourning (as *Rachell* had for her *children*) that will *not be comforted*, becaues their *ioyes are not*. [81]

The same gift is evident in the dramatic titles of his separately printed sermons, sermon titles which are as vivid as playbills.[82]

The last preacher whose images deserve detailed consideration is Bishop John Hacket, because his observation of life and his reading in Greek, Roman, and English history contributed greatly to his vividly illustrated sermons.

He exceeds all other metaphysical preachers in the number and aptness of his historical narrations. One tells of the emperor Trajan's appreciation of spontaneous applause because it is unfeigned,[83] another of devout Moslems putting out their own eyes after glimpsing Mecca,[84] a third decries excessive learning in religion by mentioning that those three learned men, Julian, Galen, and Porphyry, though eminent as emperor, doctor, and philosopher, were nevertheless all atheists.[85] Yet another celebrates the psychological shrewdness of Cardinal Pole,[86] a rare compliment after the usual anti-Roman philippics of the metaphysical preachers. Yet another of Hacket's exempla reports Camden's account of the Roman priest Sanders,[87] while others summarize stories from Sophocles[88] and Jerome.[89] He casts a very wide net, but is concerned for historical authenticity. This must be the reason for the almost complete absence of references to the mythical creatures of "unnatural" natural history[90] which flourished elsewhere in metaphysical preaching.

Metaphors and similes drawn from Hacket's own observation also cover a wide span. He uses animal and bird images—as of a kite for an ambitious man,[91] the devil as a mastiff that will not let its victim go,[92] and the servility of a dog.[93] The insatiability of concupiscence finds an analogy in a millhorse treading the same circular path unendingly,[94] while he uses artillery as a symbol for the cannon-shots of atheism directed at the faithful.[95] Clocks[96] and a game of cards[97] are also aptly used. For the Passion of Christ he uses medicine as an analogy.[98]

The shrewdness of Hacket's use of a demeaning figure is evident when he criticizes the folly of would-be Christians who give up heavenly riches for worldly gauds and trivia:

> You will smile at the Indian savages, that part with gold, and spices, and amber, for glass beads, and saffron brouches; yet whosoever sins for the mammon of iniquity, barters for a far more unequal merchandise; you change immortality for death, eternal joy for continual care, a certain treasure for uncertain riches, the most happy fruition of the *Creator* for less than the felicity of a dream. . .[99]

Like the other metaphysical preachers he can catch the congregation's attention with a biblical series of exempla,[100] riddles,[101] fables,[102] and emblems.[103] For example, how concisely and clearly he describes the emblem of a pious heart: "a firy coal washing away all the gross and earthly parts of it with the flame of divine love."[104] Metaphors flow from him: in a single paragraph Christ is viewed as Glass, Fountain, Ark, Pearl, Flower, Bread, and Light.[105] His devotion to his Redeemer is simply and perfectly expressed in the following, typically baroque, painter's image:

> As Painters and Guilders write the names of God in glass, or upon the walls with many rays, and flaming beames to beautify it about, so the name of Saviour is the great word in my Text; and all that is added beside in other circumstances is a train of golden beams to beautifie it.[106]

While strict Puritans might object to the elaborate ornamentation of most metaphysical sermons, it was used to clarify the message, delight the congregation, and honor God, the Creator of the snowflake and the rose. Dr. Daniel Price, a Calvinist chaplain to Prince Henry, James I, and Charles I, summarized the scriptural authority for imagery and its values in this way. He urged that Christ's seven parables of the Kingdom of Heaven are extended images, and that Jesus himself called fishermen to be disciples as an analogy for calling them to be fishers of men. From this ground he argued that Christ is

> herein shewing the Ministers of the Gospell their liberty left to them in performance of their calling, not only nakedly to lay open the trueth, but also to use helps of wit, invention, and art, good gifts of God, which may be used in Similitudes, Allusions, Applications, Comparisons, Proverbs, and Parables which tend to edification and illustrating of the word.[107]

Its purpose, he concluded, is "that so the weake may be comforted, the rude may be enformed, the drowsie may be awakened, the hard-hearted may be supled, the perverse overwhelmed, and so by al meanes God himselfe may be glorified & the hearers bettered."[108]

On the highest level of all it could be argued that the images of poets and preachers alike (and many were both) made them so many imitators of the supreme Artist, God.

NOTES

1. Cited in Arthur Pollard, *English Sermons* (London, 1963), 13.

2. Song, "Goe, and catche a falling starre," *John Donne: The Elegies and The Songs and Sonnets,* ed. Helen Gardner (Oxford, 1965), 29.

3. *The Workes of Tho: Adams* (London, 1629), 148. A sermon on the text, James 3:8.

4. *The Workes of Tho: Adams,* 234.

5. Brian Duppa, *The Souls Soliloquies* (London, 1648), 14.

6. Lancelot Andrewes, *XCVI Sermons* (London, 1629), 35. From a sermon preached before the king at Whitehall on 25 December 1610.

7. Cited in Winfried Schleiner, *The Imagery of John Donne's Sermons* (Providence, Rhode Island, 1970), 38.

8. Andrewes, *XCVI Sermons,* 962.

9. *The Sermons of John Donne,* ed. G. R. Potter and E. M. Simpson, 10 vols. (Berkeley, 1953–1962), 2:276. Sermon preached at the Hague, 19 December 1619, on Matthew 4:18–20.

10. John Wall, *Alae Seraphicae. The Seraphins Wings to raise us unto heaven. Delivered in Six Sermons, partly at Saint Peters in Westminster, partly in S. Aldate's in Oxford* (London, 1623), 4.

11. Wall, *Alae Seraphicae,* 39.

12. Donne, *Sermons,* 4:210. A sermon preached at St. Paul's, 13 October 1622, on the text John 1:8.

13. Donne, *Sermons,* 3:87.

14. Thomas Playfere, *Nine Sermons* (Cambridge, 1621), 40. The sermon is entitled "Glorie waighes downe the Crosse," preached before King James on 3 September 1604.

15. Donne, *Sermons,* 7:306. A Prebend sermon preached in St. Paul's, 28 January 1626, on Psalm 65:5.

16. *The Whole Works of the Most Rev. James Ussher. . . ,* 17 vols. (Dublin and London, 1847–1864), 13:235. This is sermon 15, preached on the text of Romans 5:1.

17. *The Workes of Tho: Adams,* 778. From a sermon entitled "The Foole and his Sport," preached on the text from Proverbs 14:9, "Fooles make a mocke at sinne."

18. John Hacket, *A Century of Sermons* (London, 1675), 240. From the third sermon on Christ's Temptations.

19. Daniel Featley, *Ancilla Pietatis* (London, 1625), 302.

20. Milton A. Rugoff, *Donne's Imagery* (New York, 1939), 191.

21. Schleiner, *The Imagery of John Donne's Sermons*, 85.

22. Shakespeare, *Richard II*, I.i.47.

23. John King, *A Sermon at Paules Crosse, on behalf of Paules Church. March 26, 1620* (London, 1620), 45.

24. Examples can be found in Donne, *Sermons*, 1:266, 3:111 and 743. See the naturalness with which he uses nautical imagery in a sermon on Genesis, I:26, "And God said, let us make man in our image, after our likeness," which proceeds thus: "By fair occasion from these words, we propose to you the whole compasse of man's voyage, from the lanching forth in this world, to his Anchoring in the next; from his hoysing sayle here, to his striking saile there," (*Sermons*, 9:69).

25. Donne, *Sermons*, 2:249.

26. Donne, *Sermons*, 3:184–185.

27. Donne, *Sermons*, 9: No. 3.

28. *The Workes of Tho: Adams*, 283.

29. *The Sermons of Maister Henrie Smith* (London, 1593), 209.

30. *The Sermons of Maister Henrie Smith*, 209–210.

31. William Barlow, *The Sermon Preached at Paules Crosse, the tenth day of November, being the next Sunday after the Discoverie of the late Horrible Treason* (London, 1606), sig. D1v-D2.

32. Ralph Brownrig, *Sixty Five Sermons* (London, 1674), 270–271.

33. *The Sermons of Maister Henrie Smith*, 932.

34. *The Sermons of Maister Henrie Smith*, 488.

35. Donne, *Sermons*, 8:324. Sermon preached at St. Paul's on the eve of the feast commemorating the conversion of St. Paul.

36. Donne, *Sermons*, 8:54. Sermon preached at St. Dunstan's, Trinity Sunday, 1627.

37. Donne, *Sermons*, 10:111. See another musical image in *Sermons*, 10:131, where the peace of God is depicted as harmony.

38. *The Workes of Tho: Adams*, 14.

39. *The Workes of Tho: Adams*, 300.

40. Hacket, *A Century of Sermons*, 819. From a sermon preached at Whitehall on Numbers 21:7; "Pray unto the Lord that he take the Serpents from us."

41. Peter Heylyn, *The Parable of the Tares expounded and applied in Ten Sermons* (London, 1659), 75–76. From a sermon preached at Whitehall, 28 January 1638.

42. Jasper Mayne, *A Sermon against False Prophets . . .* (London, 1646), 25.

43. Robert Cawdrey, *A Treasurie or Store-House of Similies* (London, 1600), sig. A4.

44. Cawdrey, *A Treasurie. . .* , 525–526.

45. Book IV, 12.

46. For example, "Confession works as a vomit; It shakes the frame, and it breakes the bed of sin, and it is an ease to the spirtuall stomach, to the conscience to be thereby disburdened," (Donne, *Sermons*, 9:304).

47. See Donne, *Sermons*, 3:17–21.

48. See Donne, *Sermons*, 6:116; 6:140; 8:45; and 9:396.

49. See Joan Webber, *Contrary Music. The Prose Style of John Donne* (Madison, Wisconsin, 1963), 108. She also points out that the legal images were useful in Donne's attempts at theodicy.

50. See Donne, *Sermons*, 2:237; 5:371; 7: sermon 3; and 8:54.

51. For example, in Donne's *Sermons*, 9:406–407. See Janel M. Mueller, *Donne's Prebend Sermons* (Cambridge, Mass., 1971), 222f. for an excellent note on Donne's use of the circle in his sermons and its antecedents.

52. See the examples given by Potter and Simpson, in Donne, *Sermons*, 1:98.

53. Joan Webber makes these generalizations, which my readings of all Donne's printed sermons confirm, in *Contrary Music*, 84f.

54. See Winfried Schleiner's comparison of the images of the Holy Ghost expanded by Andrewes and Donne in *The Imagery of John Donne's Sermons*, 182f.

55. Andrewes, *XCVI Sermons*, 210, 232, 781.

56. Andrewes, *XCVI Sermons*, 466, and the Spital sermon of 1588.

57. Andrewes, *XCVI Sermons*, 124, 128, 264, 828, 962.

58. Andrewes, *XCVI Sermons*, 573.

59. Andrewes, *XCVI Sermons*, 696.

60. Andrewes, *XCVI Sermons*, 837–838.

61. Andrewes, *XCVI Sermons*, Spital sermon, 1588.

62. Andrewes, *XCVI Sermons*, 515.

63. Andrewes, *XCVI Sermons*, 465.

64. Andrewes, *XCVI Sermons*, 647.

65. *The Sermons of Maister Henrie Smith*, 16.

66. *The Sermons of Maister Henrie Smith*, 219.

67. *The Sermons of Maister Henrie Smith*, 267–268.

68. *The Sermons of Maister Henrie Smith*, 655.

69. *The Sermons of Maister Henrie Smith*, 225–226.

70. *The Sermons of Maister Henrie Smith*, 593.

71. As for example the list of Bible characters whom God stopped in their proud tracks, in *The Sermons of Maister Henrie Smith*, 381f.

72. "The Sinner's Passing Bell" in *The Workes of Tho. Adams* (London, 1629), 256–257.

73. *The Workes of Tho: Adams*, 428. The hen who cackles where she has not laid an egg is like one who promises but does not perform. See also the image of the cock fighting, 781.

74. *The Works of Thomas Adams* (Edinburgh, 1860–1861), 1:240.

75. *The Workes of Tho: Adams*, 309, 324, 498f., 519f., 776, 927, and 995.

76. *The Workes of Tho: Adams*, 815, 817f., 886f.

77. *The Workes of Tho: Adams*, e.g. 647.

78. *The Workes of Tho: Adams*, 19, 420, 545, 925, and 1084f.

79. *The Workes of Tho: Adams*, 101, 154, and 195.

80. *The Workes of Tho: Adams*, 106–107, for a notable example.

81. *The Workes of Tho: Adams*, 220.

82. Such titles are: "Politike Hunting," "The Three Divine Sisters," "The Fatal Banket," "The White Devil," "The Black Saint," "The Spirituall Navigator Bound for the Holy Land," and "The Taming of the Tongue."

83. Hacket, *A Century of Sermons*, 67.

84. Hacket, *A Century of Sermons*, 93.

85. Hacket, *A Century of Sermons*, 259.

86. Hacket, *A Century of Sermons*, 717.

87. Hacket, *A Century of Sermons*, 289.

88. Hacket, *A Century of Sermons*, 177.

89. Hacket, *A Century of Sermons*, 131.

90. The one notable exception is found in Hacket, *A Century of Sermons*, 749.

91. Hacket, *A Century of Sermons*, 303.

92. Hacket, *A Century of Sermons*, 332.

93. Hacket, *A Century of Sermons*, 400f.

94. Hacket, *A Century of Sermons*, 95.

95. Hacket, *A Century of Sermons*, 264.

96. Hacket, *A Century of Sermons*, 67.

97. Hacket, *A Century of Sermons*, 819.

98. Hacket, *A Century of Sermons*, 240.

99. Hacket, *A Century of Sermons*, 347.

100. Hacket, *A Century of Sermons*, 334f.

101. Hacket, *A Century of Sermons*, 484, for one example.

102. Hacket, *A Century of Sermons*, 96, and in the ninth sermon on Christ's Temptations.

103. Hacket, *A Century of Sermons*, 199, 214, 836, and 893.

104. Hacket, *A Century of Sermons*, 199.

105. Hacket, *A Century of Sermons*, 110–111.

106. Hacket, *A Century of Sermons*, 50.

107. Daniel Price, *The Marchant. A Sermon Preached at Paules Crosse on Sunday the 24 of August, being the day before Bartholomew faire, 1607*, (Oxford, 1608), 2.

108. Price, *The Marchant*, 2.

Chapter XI

REVALUATIONS: WEAKNESS AND STRENGTH

THIS, OUR FINAL CHAPTER, will examine both the weakness and the strength of metaphysical preaching, in which I hope to account for its long popularity followed by a sudden drop in favor from which it never recovered. On the surface it looks as though the metaphysical mode was tied to the monarchy, the court, and the growing Arminian party among the prelates, and that the eventual victory of the opposing Parliamentarians, Puritans, and Calvinists, was associated with the eventual dominance of the plain and democratic style of preaching. But this is too facile an observation, for with the return of the monarchy at the Restoration there should have been a return to a metaphysical style of preaching. In actual fact the pulpit echoed the Royal Society's demand for "a close, naked, natural way of speaking; positive expressions; clear senses; a native easiness; bringing all things as near the mathematical plainness as they can: and preferring the languages of Artizans, Countrymen, and Merchants, before that of Wits, or Scholars."[1] It could be argued, with greater probability, that while Puritanism failed politically at the Restoration, its preaching style prevailed in the Church of England.

If a sermon is to aim at the edification of the congregation, to build them up in the faith, then the chief enemies of that aim are inevitably an unnecessary complexity and obscurity.

Metaphysical sermons unfortunately often exhibited both these defects in abundance. To begin with they had a propensity for designing discourses with multiple divisions and subdivisions; their sermons were often so fractured that no one could possibly grasp all the separate parts. The eighth Resurrection sermon of Andrewes has three major divisions, with seven subdivisions.[2] Barlow's Paul's Cross sermon of 10 November 1605, is on such a complex structure that the plan alone occupies three whole pages.[3] Brownrig's first sermon on the Inauguration of Charles I suffered from the same defect.[4] Perhaps the worst offender of all was Thomas Playfere who managed to devise a sevenfold division for as simple a text as Luke 23:28, "Weepe not for mee, but weepe for your selves."[5] And what could be more boring than John Wall's opening division of a sermon?

> That which I shall punctually distinguish unto you, is first the habit and ornament of the Church, that is, Christ and his righteousness implyed in the affixe of my Text; שׁמב *Put me, or set me.*
>
> Secondly, the Part and the Subiect to be adorned, that is, the heart and the arme: *Put me on thy heart and on thine arme.*
>
> Thirdly, the figure and semblance, that is, a seale or a signet. *Put me as a seale on thy heart, and as a signet on thy arme.*
>
> Last of all the superinduction, with a על in the Originall, which is upon, or the circumposition, with a Μερι in the Septuagint which is about. *Put me as a seale on thy heart, and a signet about thine arme.* All this is gathered, and recapitulated in that of *Paul* to the Romans, *Put ye on Christ Iesus. . . .*[6]

Such a division makes a simple text complicated to the point of meaninglessness.

Even more serious was the criticism of the obscurity of the metaphysical preachers. For learned and highly intelligent auditories, of course, the obscurity would be less a problem than for the man in the street, or the woman in the pew. But how could they be expected to understand the lengthy citations from the Fathers, the schoolmen, and the biblical commentators, not to mention the classical philosophers, moralists, poets, historians, fabulists, and tragedians quoted in the original Greek and Latin, often left untranslated? And why should the humble believers pretend an interest in Hebrew or Greek etymology, or in rabbinical nuances of hermeneutics? And even if the citations were reduced to Latin tags, such as Andrewes so often provided, what benefit were they to any but scholars? It seemed to many Puritan critics that this was nothing more than pedantic pride on the part of such preachers. Some sermons seemed as full of foreign citations as a Christmas pudding is of currants and raisins, and not half as easily digested. Indeed, they seemed more anthologies or chrestomathies than meditations on biblical themes, and far more suitable as lectures than sermons.

Canon John Wall is an example of a great offender in prolixity, obscurity, and pedantry. In a single sermon entitled *The Lion in the Lambe, Or, Strength in Weakness* (1628), he punishes the congregation with unnecessary paradoxes, "unnatural" natural history (he claims that sapphires reduce tumors and ulcers), a conjunction and possible confusion of classical and Christian images (visualising Christ as a dolphin), and historical narrations of Charles V and Ferdinand, King of Naples. We finally sink under the weight of his reading of folios: thirty references to fourteen authors. In short, like many metaphysical preachers, he loads our backs and our memories with a library of undigested reading.

Nor was he unusual in this respect. Heylyn referred to eighteen authors in a single sermon,[7] and Holyday cited seventeen different Fathers of the Church and three Reformation divines in one sermon.[8] Similarly in his first sermon upon Christmas Day,[9] Brownrig quoted Chrysostom and Gregory Nazienzen three times each, Basil twice, and Origen once in Greek citations, and Augustine thirteen times, Gregory the Great twice, and Ambrose, Aquinas, Bernard, and Salvian once each in full

Latin citations. In a sermon before Suffolk burgesses, prior to an election in 1661, on *Beatitas Britanniae; Or, King Charles the Second, England's Beatitude*, Willan included forty-three references to twenty-four different authors. Another preacher, Bishop Howson, larded his sermon with citations: in a Paul's Cross discourse of 1597 he included no less than sixty-six references to thirty-three different authors, eleven to Greek writers, nine to Latin Fathers, six to classical authors, and seven to other biblical commentators. In such quantities learning was an epidemic!

Many metaphysical preachers however controlled their quantity of citation and the length of them. Andrewes for example cited few, briefly, and usually translated them. His disciples Buckeridge, Cosin, Laud, and Wren followed his example faithfully. Donne's and Hacket's sermons were never overloaded with quotations. These men were exceptions however, and the majority freighted their sermons with overmuch curious learning.

A third defect noted in some metaphysical sermons was a tendency on the part of Andrewes and his disciples or imitators to crumble their texts into fragments, giving attention not only to each individual word, but sometimes even to individual syllables in a word. The most famous example of this device of word-splitting is to be found in Andrewes' Ninth Nativity Sermon on the text, Isaiah 8:14, *Ecce Virgo concipiet, & pariet filium, & vocabitur nomen Ejus IMMANUEL.* ("Behold a Virgin shall conceive, and beare a Sonne; and she shall call His name, Immanuel.") Of this name Andrewes observes: "He is not, cannot be named, without us: that when He is named, *Et nos una tecum Domine,* we also are named with Him. In *Immanu,* is *anu,* and that is we. This is not it; but this: That He hath set us in the fore-part of it; *Immanu* before *El, Nobiscum* before *Deus.*"[10] Aubrey reports the criticism of a Scottish lord who had heard Andrewes preach on the occasion of a royal visit to Scotland in 1617. "When King James asked him how he liked Bp. A.'s sermon said that he was learned, but he did play with his Text, as a Jack-an-Apes does, and then he takes up another, and playes

462

a little with it. Here's a pretty thing, and there's a pretty thing!"[11] Richard Baxter wrote "When I read such a book as Bishop Andrew's [*sic*] Sermons, or heard such a kind of preaching, I felt no life in it: methought they did but play with holy things."[12] Such a criticism refers not only to splitting up texts, but also to the puns and other forms of wit in the sermons of Andrewes. Gilbert Burnet, the bishop and historian of a later age, congratulates his contemporaries on having thrown off the fads of the metaphysical preachers: "The impertinent Way of dividing Texts is laid aside, the needless setting out of the Originals, and the vulgar Version [the Vulgate] is worn out. The trifling Shews of learning in many Quotations of Passages, that very few could understand, do no more flat the Auditory. *Pert Wit* and luscious Eloquence have lost their relish."[13] The chief criticism of Andrewes and his imitators was that he attempted to give his congregations the Bread of Life, but that the loaf always came in the form of crumbs.

We have noted that Andrewes was accused of "playing with holy things" and using "pert wit." Later in the seventeenth century both Isaac Barrow and John Eachard were highly critical of the facetiousness in the metaphysical preachers' sermons. Barrow attempts to define wit and the purpose in using it in the pulpit. It is a turning away from the simple, straightforward way of speaking, "which by a pretty surprizing uncouthness in conceit or expression doth affect and amuse the fancy, stirring in it some wonder, and breeding some delight thereto." He regards these farfetched conceits as mental juggling-tricks, and thinks that they are only justifiable if used infrequently, but are best kept "when sarcastical twitches are needfull to pierce the thick skins of men, to correct their lethargick stupidity, to rouze them out of their drowzy negligence." He finally concludes that "it is unworthy of a Christian . . . for him to be zealous about quibbles, for him to be ravished with puny conceits and expressions, 'tis a wondrous oversight, and an enormous indecency."[14]

Eachard offers devastating criticisms of both the conceits and the strained wit used by the metaphysical preachers, criticizing

their "Ridiculousness, phantastical Phrases, harsh and sometimes blasphemous Metaphors, abundant foppish Similitudes,
childish and empty Transitions, and the like so commonly uttered out of Pulpits, and so fatally redounding to the discredit
of the Clergy. . . ."[15] He later goes on to ask "Whether or no
Punning, Quibling, and that which they call Joquing, and such
other delicacies of Wit, highly admired in some Academick
Exercises, might not be very conveniently omitted?" Further,
he argues that anyone who has concentrated on developing
such wit thins his judgment, becomes prejudiced against sober
sense, that as soon as he gets hold of a text, "tossing it this
way and that . . . here catching at a word, there lie nibling
and sucking at an *and*, a *by*, a *quis* or a *quid*, a *sic* or a *sicut*;
and thus minces The Text so small, that his Parishioners, unless
he rendevouz it again, can scarce tell what's become of it."[16]
In this jeremiad Eachard is criticizing triviality, joking where
solemnity would be the appropriate religious response, and,
in particular, finding fault with the old method of dividing
sermons by Latin terms, a method used occasionally by preachers as popular and different as Playfere, Adams, and Donne.

Later Eachard criticizes what he calls "frightful metaphors"
by which he means similitudes used with reference to God
that are daring and irreverent, even blasphemous. He rightly
points out that the metaphysical preachers would introduce
such "unhallowed Expressions, to make amends, they'll out
you in, an *As it were*, forsooth, or, *As I may so say* . . . and
with their Reverence be it spoken."[17]

How justified are these serious charges, especially of producing "harsh and sometimes blasphemous Metaphors"? Playfere
certainly said of the apostles at Pentecost that "They (in a manner, if I may so say) had fingers upon their tongues, as well
as we have upon our hands."[18] It was equally farfetched, inappropriate, and even blasphemous of Jackson to use the image
of a polygamous Christ in the words: "so are the spouses of
this chaste and *holy one*, more in number then the wives and
concubines of luxurious *Salomon*."[19] Such metaphors were rare,
and as late as 1683 John Wallis rightly insisted "if we bar Meta-

phors, we must Exclude the greatest part of what is Sayd or Written." He even claimed that it was better to use vivid English metaphors rather than using "Exotick words of Latin or French Extraction."[20]

Eachard also criticized what he called "quibbling," by which he appeared to mean a fondness for puns and paronomasia. He infers that such word play implied an unsuitable levity in preachers, whose demeanor and speech should be marked by gravity. Certainly much of the punning was lighthearted and little the worse for that, and in some cases the puns added to the power of the sermon. This would seem to be the case when Donne emphasized that God's *ordinance* (preaching) was also the Divine *ordnance* (or artillery) for hitting the conscience, or when he found a parallel between the illumination cast by the *Sun* and Christ, God's eternal *Son* named the Light of the World. Similarly, Andrewes made a happy use of the term "mystery" to carry the meaning of a Christian sacrament and initiation into a guild. But punning could become merely superficial when it weakened the moral force of a criticism. When Andrewes speaks of hypocrites that "under the colour of a *long prayer*, now and then *prey upon the houses* and goods of a sort of *seduced widowes*. . . ."[21] We feel an unsuitability in the way that the point is expressed. Such an ignominious activity should not be mentioned in such bantering terms. Equally inept is Adams when he speaks of a Herodian feast at which John the Baptist's head was the last course.[22]

Even more outrageous however was the use of punning (or more frequently paronomasia) in foreign languages. In this matter Andrewes was a great offender, as were Thomas Adams and Hacket among others. It was outrageous because it combined two clerical temptations disadvantageous to the listeners, obscurity of meaning and pedantic pride. The idea behind the word-play was often an excellent one, as for example when Adams stressed the humility of the Magi, describing them as *petentes* (seekers or even beggars) rather than *potentes* (potentates).[23] But when the wit is strained the effect is pathetic, as when Adams tries to illustrate Paul's sense that wickedness is like a poison that robs hearts of all feeling, so that "Their body is no longer *Corpus* but *Morbus* . . . Neither can we say so properly of them, that they are sicke as that they are dead. *Non agroti, sed defuncti;* not *diseased,* but *deceased.*"[24] The two Latin tags are quite unnecessary; the meaning is clearer without them—Adams simply could not miss an opportunity of punning.

A further legitimate criticism of metaphysical wit in the pulpit was that it could, on occasion, be insensitive, and sometimes downright vulgar. Both Brownrig and Donne speak of vomit in their sermons. Brownrig indelicately found an analogy between vomit and the Resurrection which produces our own salvation "when the Stomach casts up that it cannot hold."[25] Donne saw a closer analogy between vomit and confession:[26] one cannot fault the appropriateness of the analogy, but its vividness has a counterproductive effect. Examples of indelicate analogies can be found in Laud's sermons as well as Donne's. Laud provides one example in the course of a sermon pleading for peace, preached before the Parliament in 1625. He mentions that the psalm from which his text is drawn was used at evensong for many years on the day of the Circumcision. It is an irenic psalm, "And that peace can neither be had nor held long" unless there be a "circumcision and a paring off round about of heated and unruly affections in the handling of differences."[27] Donne also provides an overripe metaphor in relation to Christ's circumcision: "Though then one drop of his bloud had beene enough to have redeemed infinite worlds, if it had beene so contracted, and so applyed, yet he gave us, a morning showre of his bloud in his Circumcision, and an evening showre after Sunset, in the piercing of his side."[28] Donne provides another indelicate and curious analogy in a sermon on Whitsunday, probably preached at Lincoln's Inn:

> They say there is a way of castration, in cutting off the eares: There are certain veines behind the eares, which, if they be cut, disable a man from generation. The Eares are the Aqueducts of the water of life; and if we cut off

those, that is, intermit our ordinary course of hearing, this is a castration of the soul, the soul becomes an Eunuch, and we grow to a rust, to a mosse, to a barrennesse, without fruit, without propagation.[29]

It can be stated, in extenuation of the use of these images of the male sexual organs, that they were employed for exclusively masculine congregations at Parliament or in Lincoln's Inn, and therefore possibly less offensive than if used in a mixed congregation.

Yet another criticism of the obscurity of the metaphysical preachers was of their overfondness for paradoxes. Their defense would have been twofold: that the Christian faith cannot be stated without paradox, and paradox is a way of indicating that faith, though not contrary to reason, transcends it through the divine miracles of revelation. The reply has considerable merit provided the paradoxes used by the preachers were the paradoxes of Christian doctrine and not of their own fanciful elaborations. Often Donne's penchant for paradox must have confused his hearers. His explanation that "Almighty God ever loved *unity*, but he never loved *singularity*; God was always *alone* in heaven, there were no *other Gods*, but he; but he was never *singular*, there was never any time, when there were not *three persons* in heaven,"[30] must surely have made the doctrine of the Trinity even more confusing to non-theologians in his congregation. It is equally obfuscating to be told that in the great marriage feast "whosover is a dish, is a ghest too . . ."[31] for here Donne is using two images, a net and a feast, and the dish is also a fish caught in the net of the promises of the Gospel. Yet one can argue that the metaphysical preacher is entirely in his rights in stressing the marvellous paradox of the Nativity of Christ. Again we can turn to Donne, who describes the Word of God as an unspeaking infant, and his mother a Virgin:

Immanuel est verbum infans . . . He is the ancient of daies, and yet in minority; he is the Word it selfe, and yet speech-lesse; he that is All, that all the Prophets spoke of, cannot speake: He addes more, He is *puer sapiens*, but a child, and yet wiser than the elders, wiser in the Cradle, then they in the Chaire: Hee is more, *Deus lactens*, God, at whose breasts all creatures suck, sucking at his Mothers breast, and such a Mother, as is a maid.[32]

Another serious criticism of the sermons of the metaphysical preachers concerned their content and exegesis rather than their style. Bishop Gilbert Burnet of Salisbury claims that the metaphysicals are repeating the errors of Origen in "the dry pursuing of Allegories," and he accuses them of bringing "a great deal of Art into the Composition of Sermons," so that "Mystical Applications of Scripture grew to be better liked than clear Texts."[33] How justified was this accusation? Certainly there are some admirable allegorical sermons. And it is also a defect in some Calvinist as well as some Arminian sermons. Thomas Adams, the Calvinist, has one sermon, *Eirenopolis: The Citie of Peace*, for which the text is only a pretext for an ingenious sermon using the four gates of the City of London as symbols of Christian virtues. The first gate is Innocence or Bishopsgate, the second is Ludgate or Patience, the third is Aldgate or Beneficence, and the fourth gate is Recompense or Satisfaction, Cripplegate "the lamest way to peace."[34] Several of Adams' sermons are extended allegories, as his "The Spirituall Navigator Bound for the Holy Land" and "Mystical Bedlam." Thomas Playfere is equally contriving in "The Pathway to Perfection" where he says his six points are as the six steps that King Solomon went up to his great throne of ivory.[35] However, more common than the use of an entire sermon as an extended allegory, was the inclusion of a typological element as illustration of parts of a sermon.

The latter was frequently the case in court sermons in which the preachers were invited to celebrate the delivery of the king and nation from the Gunpowder Plot, or the saving of the king from the Gowrie Plot. Preachers would frequently take a verse from a psalm as a text. They could then develop it, referring to the circumstances of King David (its presumed author), then of the contemporary King James, and finally of "great David's greater Son," Christ. This type of sermon was frequently preached by Lancelot Andrewes, Playfere, Cosin, Hacket, and Brownrig.

The single most impressive typological sermon is one preached by John Cosin in Paris on 16 April 1651 on the Octave of the Resurrection. His text was John 20:9, "For as yet they knew not the Scripture, that He must rise from the dead." The sermon includes an exegesis of Abraham's willingness to sacrifice Isaac as a foretelling of Christ's Passion and Resurrection. This is done by means of several striking parallels. Both Isaac and Christ were sons, and only sons, and only beloved sons, yet it was determined that both should be put to death. Both were alike in their obedience, and both were bound up for sacrifice, and the wood on which they were to be sacrificed was laid upon their shoulders. Both were led away to the mount of sacrifice, and Calvary and Mount Moriah were one and the same. The ram that was found in the thorns and was a substitute for Isaac's life was "the figure and pledge of Him that came forth with the crown of thorns, and offered up himselfe to save ours." Finally, the release of both, Isaac from death and Christ in the Resurrection, took place on the third day.[36] It is only in likening a ram in a thicket of thorns to Christ with a crown of thorns that the parallel becomes fanciful. The real gravamen of objection was to fanciful allegory which had only the flimsiest basis in Scripture. An equally impressive use of typology is provided by Bishop Brownrig in a sermon dealing with Old Testament foreshadowings of the Resurrection. These he finds in Enoch's translation to heaven, in Elijah's rapture and assumption in a fiery chariot, in Aaron's rod, in the renewing of the garments of the Israelites during forty years, in the three children preserved in the fiery furnace, and in Jonah being cast up from the belly of the fish on to dry land.[37]

A more just criticism of allegory might be made when the sermon departed not only from the text, but even from the context. Thomas Adams preached a sermon entitled "The Soules Sicknesse" which elaborated on nineteen different diseases from "head-ach and Braine-sicknesse" to "Short-windednesse and wearinesse of doing well" with a diagnosis of the cause and cure of each ailment.[38] Another sermon was entitled "A Generation of Serpents" where Adams speaks of eleven "Mystical Serpents" and strays not only from his text but far from his controlling image, since he includes salamanders, crocodiles, cockatrices, caterpillars, lizards, and last of all "the Great Red Dragon, the Devil."[39]

Another development in allegory was, of course, the allegorical character. It is found early in Henry Smith's account of "Contentation" or contentment:

Such a commander is Contentation that wheresoever she setteth foote, an hundred blessings waite upon her: in everie disease she is a Phisition, in everie strife shee is a Lawyer, in everie doubt she is a Preacher, in everie griefe she is a Comforter: like a sweete perfume, which taketh away the evill sent, and leaveth a pleasant scent for it.[40]

By the time of Thomas Adams' sermons the "characters" have developed in variety and vividness. This is his description of the allegorical character, Peace:

Peace is a faire Virgin, every ones Love, the praise of all tongues, the obiect of all eyes, the wish of all hearts; *Pacem te poscimus omnes.* She hath a smiling looke, which never frowned with the least scowle of anger: snowy armes, soft as Downe, and whiter then the Swannes feathers; always open to pious embracements. Her milken hand carries an Olive branch, the Symbole and Embleme of quietnesse.[41]

However ingenious the imagination of these "characters" was, they could all be faulted as being far removed from the text.

It seemed to many sermon critics that the original Reformation stress on the inadequacy of fanciful allegorical exegesis in order to return to the primary literal and historical sense of Scripture had been abandoned. It is intriguing to find John King, later to become bishop of London, strongly endorsing this conviction in an early sermon. He insists that the sickness of all the allegorists from the time of Origen was "in not contenting themselves with the literall and genuine sense of the Scripture, but making some mysterie of the plainest historie that ever was delivered and darkning the evident purpose of the Holy Ghost with the busie fansies of their owne heads, as if one should cast cloudes and smoke upon the sunbeames." Such allegorists, he maintains, "take the Scriptures as it were by the neck, and writhe them from the aime and intention of the holy Ghost."[42]

Yet another criticism of metaphysical preachers, especially on the part of Puritan parliamentarians, was their offensive obsequiousness to royalty. The charge is worth examining in detail. Certainly there is plenty of evidence of exaggerated deference, which went far beyond the call of loyalty and respect. Donne, who was not customarily obsequious, did occasionally become servile in his references to his sovereign. For example, in a Paul's Cross sermon of 1622, he exaggerated the religious knowledge and zeal of James I, by saying ". . . we have him now for a *father* of the *Church*, a *Foster-father*; such a father as *Constantine*, as *Theodosius* was; our posterity shall have him for a *father*, a *Classique father*; such a father as *Ambrose*, as *Austin* was."[43] In the same vein he referred to Charles I as "the greatest Master of Language and Judgement, which these times, or any other did . . . (that good and great King of ours)."[44] Yet Donne was acutely aware of the danger of flattery, declaring, "How often is that called a Sermon, that speakes more of Great men, then of our great God?"[45] and he was not afraid to preach a court sermon with blistering criticism of the court, as he did in a Lenten sermon before the king in 1629.[46]

Andrewes was mildly flattering in a sermon preached before Queen Elizabeth, claiming that she had always made a virtue of perseverance.[47] But in a Gowrie sermon of 1610 his reference to King James borders on blasphemy, and is certainly idolatrous. Commenting on the text I Chronicles 16:22, "Touch not mine anointed," he adds: "And then (from the nature of the word) not onely *His Annointed, Vncti Eius:* but CHRISTI *Eius, His* CHRISTS, which is the highest degree of *His Annointed:* for higher then that, ye cannot goe."[48] That surely was going too far.

Other popular royal preachers seem to have been less servile than Andrewes. Hacket, for example, when preaching a coronation sermon, offered a glowing testimonial to the king, saying, "you cannot deny but he is religious, pious, temperate, gentle, prudent, good in all respects as *David* was, but blemished with none of his vices." He went on to excuse himself from offering a "Cento of his deserved Praise" because "man is a changeable creature," desisting "partly because all *Encomiastick Exercises* are censur'd for flattery, and do soon prove scandalous to the Auditors; partly because the Temple is a place selected for the Praise of *God,* and not of Man. . . ."[49] This was an honest and courageous statement to make. It is significant that neither Hacket nor Donne ever preached a sermon on the divine right of kings.

Bishop John King offered a graceful but not obsequious tribute to King James, recently recovered from a serious illness, who came to Paul's Cross in order to second the appeal for funds to repair the cathedral.[50] Bishop Theophilus Field, who might have been expected to flatter excessively, was moderate in his praise of Charles I, calling him "our good King, who is first in place, hath also been formost in example, in the *Coryphaeus,* the first *proclaimer,* and in his own *person keeper of the solemne Fasts,* most *frequent* at prayers, a royall *praecentor* in *Gods* house and service."[51] Archbishop Laud, for his part, emphasized the necessary unity of God, the king, and the Church in his sermons, but expressed no servility in them.[52] The tendency to exaggerate the virtue of kings can be seen in a sermon by Bishop Morley delivered at a time when the temptation was most acute—at the coronation of Charles II. After referring to the miraculous preservation of Charles when Prince of Wales at the Battle of Worcester and his return to the throne without either bloodshed or bargain, this encomium follows:

And is not this as if God should have said to us in plain terms, *Behold the Man;* behold your *King;* Behold Charles the *Sufferer,* the Son of *Charles* the *Martyr;* the Grand-Child of *James* the *Wise* on the one side, and of *Henry* the *Great* on the other, and Heir to the several Excellencies of them both. . . .[53]

It is only a short step from such an eulogy to the canonization of a king, and the rash court preacher who took it was Barten Holyday, in describing the dead James I as "a Saint Iames, Saint Iames of Britaine."[54] During the last days of James I the flattery of kings had reached such a level that a letter, dated 25 April 1623, to a Cambridge divine, Joseph Mead, complained that "a main cause of all the misery and mischief in our land is the fearfullest of flattery of our prelates and clergy. The hope of a crosier staff or a cardinals hat could make many a scholar in England beat his brain to reconcile the Church of Rome and England."[55]

A further criticism levelled against the metaphysical preachers was the fondness of some of them for citing the differing opinions of commentators on obscure texts. This could lead to a sense of the vanity of learning or to a doubting of Scripture. Joseph Glanvill expressed it thus:

More vain are the recital of the different opinions of the Expositors and Commentators among such, and when they hear that learned men are of so many and of such disagreeing judgments about the sense of every Scripture, they are apt to conclude, either that learning is vain, or what is worse, that Religion is uncertain.[56]

How justified was this attack? We must recognize that while both Andrewes and Donne frequently quoted the Fathers on obscure passages, each had a different purpose. Andrewes would briefly review alternative meanings, settle on the one he considered the most probable, and proceed to illuminate that. Donne on the other hand rejoiced in multiple meanings and liked to

473

combine them if possible, as if they were the flashing facets of a single hermeneutical jewel. Andrewes asks why on Easter morning Jesus insisted that Mary Magdalene, his faithful disciple, was forbidden to touch him. To help him Andrewes cites with the utmost brevity the opinions of Chrysostom, Gregory the Great, and Augustine. The first interprets it as a rebuke to her over-eagerness, the second that it is to make her hurry to deliver the message of the Resurrection to the other disciples, and the third that Christ intended to teach the Magdalen to give up sensual touching for the spiritual touch of faith. Andrewes believes the third is the best interpretation.[57] This seems to be a justifiable use of different interpretations in sermons. Donne however is not above leaving his auditors very confused, as when he deals with the crux in I Corinthians 15:51, "Behold, I tell you a mystery: We shall not all sleep, but we shall all be changed." He says that Chrysostom means by this that we shall not all die, but the usual reading of the ancients is contrary, namely, that we shall all sleep, but we shall not all be changed. The Vulgate reads that we shall all rise again, but we shall not all be changed. Jerome and Augustine regard both readings as equally acceptable. Donne insists, after probably losing the attention of his cathedral congregation, that we may not all sleep, but we shall all certainly die.[58] Critics of the confusion created by different readings could certainly make their case from this summary of Donne's treatment of a crux.

Another criticism of metaphysical sermons was offered by Joseph Glanvill, namely that their applications were far too brief: "The other extream to be avoided, is too much Brevity in the Application, which being the directing and enforcing part, the life of a Sermon lies there."[59] James Arderne had anticipated Glanvill by his statement, "if you demand, which is the most useful and teaching method? I think, where the matter will bear it, it is that of Proposition, Confirmation, and Inference . . . all this in plain terms, no more than Doctrine, Reason, and Use."[60] This judgment Arderne owed to Bishop Wilkins' *Ecclesiastes* (1646), who accepted this, the Puritan preferred organisation of sermons. Its obvious advantage, apart from its insistence upon finding many scriptural proofs for its doctrines, is that it always ended with the practical concern of showing the relevance of the instruction to the Christian life. How just was this criticism of briefness of application to the metaphysical preachers?

Andrewes did not have long applications to his sermons, but brief ones were almost always appended. His sermon on Lot's wife begins the application wittily with these words: "Now, from her Storie, these considerations are yeelded, each one as an handfull of *salt*, to keepe us, and to make us *keepe.*"[61] The application is the need for perseverance. Similarly, there is a definite application in the fifth sermon on the Nativity in *XCVI Sermons* preached before the king in 1610. The true response to the good tidings brought to the shepherds by the angels, says Andrewes, is to hear Christ and to receive him in the Sacrament. Even though it is autobiographical, the following, from a sermon of Donne's, has a clear application to the congregation: "This is the conclusion for every humble Christian, no man is a greater sinner than I was, and I am not sure that I may fall to be worse then ever I was, except I husband and employ the Talents of Gods Graces better then I have done."[62] The commonest ending to Donne's sermons is mildly minatory but also petitionary. He prays that his congregation may, through Christ's atonement and their loyalty, attain to everlasting life:

> Keepe us Lord so awake in the duties of our Callings, that we may thus sleepe in thy Peace, and wake in thy glory, and change that infallibility which thou affordest here, to an Actuall and undeterminable possession of that Kingdome which thy Sonne our Saviour Christ Jesus hath purchased for us, with the inestimable price of his incorruptible Blood. Amen.[63]

The double warning and hope were both parts of a single application.

Other preachers also devoted considerable attention to applications in their sermons, and this is especially noticeable in the Calvinist preachers. In the very first of his sermons on the Incarnation, Bishop Hacket has a threefold set of lessons or "uses." The first was of the danger of resting amid pleasures and delights, the second of the transience of human life, and the third was to "learn from hence to condescend unto the Humility of Christ if you mean to ascend to his glory."[64] Bishop Brownrig's sermons too have ample applications as might be expected from one who defined religion as "not a matter of contemplation, but of action; 'tis an operative practick virtue. It is an art of holy living. It begets not a speculative knowledge swimming in the brain, but works devotion, and obedience in the heart and life."[65] Similarly, Henry Smith's sermons are full of applications, as in the conclusion to two sermons on Nebuchadnezzar: "Thus you have seen pride and humilitie, one pulling Nebuchadnezzar out of his throne, the other lifting him unto his throne, whereby they which stand may take heed lest they fall; and they which are fallen, may learn to rise againe."[66]

Thomas Adams has sermons with applications at the end and in the middle too. Nor can the irony in his application be missed, when in an Epiphany sermon he charges the congregation:

> Never thinke, ye miserable worldlings, *without opening your Treasures*, and *Presenting* the Lord with liberall *gifts;* ever with the *Magi* to see the face of the Lord *Iesus.* Goe home now, and make thy selfe merry with thy wealth, whiles Christ stands mourning in the streets: applaud thy Wardrobe, whiles he goes Naked: saturate thy self with thy Fatte morsels, whiles he begges (unrelieved) for the Crummes: . . . thy miserie is to come; thou shalt not behold thy *Saviour* in glory.[67]

The Arminian preachers too have applications in their sermons. Cosin, for one, stresses the implications of Epiphanytide as "the only way to be great is to be little, lowly before God, the only way to be accounted kings, to be servants to come and worship God."[68] In a marriage sermon he insists that its purpose is "the replenishing of the earth first with goodly inhabitants, and then of heaven with glorious saints. . . ."[69] The sermons of Jasper Mayne do not lack applications, and the only printed sermon of Bishop Matthew Wren that survives ends thus: "I charge the Consciences of all that this day heare me with, but TIME DEUM, FILI MI, ET REGEM, *Feare* GOD, *My Sonne, and the KING*; . . . *shew a due feare* of them Both, but yet both in that Order."[70]

The only sermons in which it would be difficult to provide long or new applications or "uses" for the congregation would be the secular commemorations of James I's escape from the plot of the Gowrie brothers, or the deliverance of the king and nation from the Gunpowder Conspiracy. These occasions required the preachers to ransack the Old Testament for obscure but apt texts, and the applications could be only two: a renewed pledge of loyalty to the monarch, and an expression of gratitude for Divine providence and protection. Such conventional applications had, in the nature of things, to be brief. Our conclusion must be that this defect of inadequate applications in the metaphysical preachers was an undeserved imputation. The most that can be admitted is that "exquisite pains were lavished on the exposition, but the application was not pressed home."[71]

The final charge levelled against the metaphysical preachers was that they became far too deeply involved with controversial and speculative matters, instead of confining themselves to the assurances of Scripture and the mandates of experience and reason. If we look at the sermons of Andrewes they have two striking characteristics: they are rarely controversial and even when they criticize they avoid name-calling; and they also avoid the discussion of speculative matters. However, it cannot be said that his imitators followed his example in these two respects.

Donne, as well as Hacket, and Brownrig, have extremely controversial passages in their sermons, as we have seen in their defense of the Anglican *via media*,[72] and their weapons more often resemble sledge hammers and axes than épées. The Calvinist metaphysical preachers seem to have taken greater delight in challenging Roman Catholicism, and the Arminians in criticizing Puritanism.

Nor can the metaphysical preachers be easily rescued from the charge that they often discussed speculative matters, a criticism that Arderne advised his young divines to avoid: "We ought not then to chuse obscure passages [of Scripture], or sublime controversies, or nice speculations to be propounded in publick, much less to the uncapable multitude."[73] Speculative preaching became such a nationwide problem that James I issued instructions that it was to cease. Ironically, one of its keenest practitioners, Donne, had to preach the official sermon on the prohibition from Paul's Cross in 1622.

Incidentally, a great deal of merely speculative material was contained in the often incredible illustrations in sermons drawn from Pliny and other sources of "unnatural" natural history. But the objection went deeper, to the discussion of matters on which there was no clear verdict in Scripture—attempting, as it were, to read the mind of God by breaking through the court into His presence in his bedchamber, as Donne had imaged it[74]—as in speculating on the doctrine of double predestination, or by discussing what Reinhold Niebuhr has called "the temperature of Hell or the furniture of Heaven." Hacket wisely desisted from "ouranography" (the architecture of heaven), and Donne was satisfied generally in indicating the quality of eternal life as peaceable, harmonious, well-ordered, restful, refreshing, joyful, and glorious, using the symbols of light and music and making use of the Book of Revelation. But he could not resist speculating on how a body in a thousand fragments can be resurrected:

> Does this trouble thee, says *Justin Martyr*, (and *Athenagoras* proceeds in the same way of argumentation in his Apology), does this trouble thee, *Quod homo a piscibus, & piscis ab homine comeditur*, that one man is devoured by a fish,

and then another man that eats the flesh of that fish, eats and becomes that other man? *Id nec hominem resolvit in piscem, nec piscem in hominem,* that first man did not become that fish that eate him, nor that fish become that second man, that eate it . . . both that man, and that fish are resolved in their owne elements, of which they were made at first.[75]

Donne continues by suggesting that even if one became a fish or a dog, or one's body was entirely annihilated, yet God created man originally from nothing, and so is faced at the General Resurrection with no greater a problem. He returns to the same problem of the disintegration of the body, and how is reintegration possible, in another sermon:

Where be all the splinters of that Bone, which a shot hath shivered and scattered in the Ayre? Where be all the Atoms of that flesh, which a *Corrasive* hath eat away, or a *Consumption* hath breath'd, and exhal'd away from our arms, and other Limbs? In what wrinkle, in what furrow, in what bowel of the earth, ly all the graines of the ashes of a body burnt a thousand years since? In what corner, in what ventricle of the sea, lies all the jelly of a Body drowned in the *generall flood?* What cohaerence, what sympathy, what dependence maintaines any relation, any correspondence, between that arm that was lost in Europe, and that legge that was lost in Afrique or Asia, scores of yeer between?[76]

Nor is this the end of Donne's speculation in the same sermon. He then goes on to ask how separated persons will recognize each other when they meet in heaven (the same question that Thomas Adams had also raised).[77] Donne answers his rhetorical question by saying that Adam, though asleep when Eve was made from his rib, yet knew her on his awakening to be "bone of his bone and flesh of his flesh." Even so, Donne urges that where faith is not bound to any direct place of Scripture his congregation is free to believe, as long as it exalts their devotion, and as long as they do not condemn those who believe otherwise.[78] Even though Donne knew that speculation in the pulpit was prohibited after 1622, yet in a sermon of 1629 he dared to ask and to answer the question of how many shall be saved. He suggested that since the good Christians will replace the fallen angels, and a third of the latter only fell, two thirds of the Christians shall gain entrance to heaven.[79]

Hacket occasionally speculates, but only briefly. He did, however, claim that the angels announcing the Nativity were joyful because those of their number lost at the fall of Satan will be made up through Christ's Incarnation and because of the success of the missionary work moving westward to America.[80] In another sermon he affirmed that guardian angels are not allocated one to an individual, but all assist the needy.[81] He also cited the Schoolmen at length, in an Easter sermon, on the properties of the resurrected,[82] and on another occasion mentioned all the guesses as to whose house contained the upper room in which the Last Supper was celebrated.[83]

Allegorizing led to speculation, and Barten Holyday speculates that the raven did not return to Noah's ark when the dove did, because it "sate upon some Carcasse, which he found floating."[84] His speculations are, however, more Donne-like when he wonders how those persons eaten by cannibals can regain their own bodies. He claims that "the unruly wit of Philosophie will here demand, how they shall rise with their owne bodies, who when they lived, had not bodies of their owne; being not only fed with the flesh of men, but descending also from parents nourished with the like horrible diet?"[85] A rigorous critic could argue that the Puritan preachers were as speculative in preaching the doctrine of double predestination—that *decretum horribile* as Calvin termed it—but they might have retorted that the doctrine was to be found both in the Book of Genesis and in St. Paul's Epistle to the Romans.

The criticism of metaphysical sermons by contemporary Puritans, as later by Restoration divines of the Church of England, was devastatingly negative, and seems to have been successful since this style was never imitated again. How could it possibly survive, when the preachers were accused of unnecessary complexity in sermon structure; obscurity and pedantry in development and citations; the use of fantastic conceits and images; a pert and facetious wit which in its levity employed puns and quibbles; a playing with or crumbling of the text; a preference for paradoxes that seemed more like contradictions; a fondness for allegory that departed from the literal or historical sense of the Scriptures; an offensive obsequiousness to royalty; applications to the congregation that were either nonexistent or brief; and a content, much of which was supposedly speculative and unscriptural? The sum total of the charges suggested that metaphysical sermons exemplified artificial eloquence designed to advertise the ingenuity, the wit, and the wide learning of the preachers, rather than being proclamations by servants of the Word of God. In brief, ultimately they lacked conviction.

What defense can be offered to this charge? One must admit that on occasion pride and ambition prevailed, and this might well have been the case when the preachers were at court and trying to impress King James I, who loved wit and learning. But no one who has seriously studied the sermons of the great metaphysical preachers, such as Lancelot Andrewes, John Donne, John Hacket, and Thomas Adams, can believe that they were other than dedicated servants of Christ. Behind all the text-crumbling and paradoxes of Andrewes there shines the holiness of a God-intoxicated preacher. In the superb eloquence of Donne we never lose sight of the fact that it is used for the glory of God, to chase souls out of the ambushes of deceit and the shadows of illusion in which they hide from the artillery and ordinance of God. Even behind Hacket's polemical thrusts at Rome and Geneva we detect a preacher who honestly believes that the Church of England, with its fidelity to the first six centuries of the Christian era and the reverence and beauty of its ceremonial, is to be preferred to the meretricious gaudiness of Rome or the grim nakedness of Puritanism. And Adams' fondness for creating "Characters," and for ingenious and witty sallies and illustrations, are attempts to woo and win his congregations to the *imitatio Christi,* and to rouse a compassionate concern for the poor in their midst.

How much poorer the annals of the English pulpit would be without the learning that drove the metaphysical preachers to study the texts in the original languages, to compare what light (or shadow) the Church Fathers and the medieval school-men and the near contemporary commentators, both Catholic and Protestant, had to shed on God's Word. Let Thomas Adams defend the use of learning in sermons in his own inimitably colloquial way, as he criticizes "sottish Enthusiastes":

> This is to tye the *holy Ghost* to a Pen and Inkhorne, &c. They must run away from their Sermons, as Horses with an emptie Cart. But now hee that will flye into Gods mysteries with such sicke feathers, shall be found to flagge low with a broken pineon: or soaring too high, without other direction, endanger himselfe. Barbarisme is grosse in an Orator, Ignorance in a Physitian, Dulnesse in an Advocate, rudenesse in a Minister.[86]

Earlier in the same sermon Adams had claimed:

> It is no small learning to illustrate obscurities, to clear the Subtilties of the *Schoole,* to open Gods mysteries to simple understandings, to build up the weake, and pull downe the confident in their owne strengths.[87]

Again, how dreary and dull would sermons be from which the gaiety and joy of wit had been totally excluded! John Donne recognized better than most the "extraordinary sadnesse, a pre-dominant melancholy, a faintnesse of heart, a chearlesnesse, a joylesnesse of spirit" in the people and so he rightly determined "therefore I returne often to this endeavor of raising your hearts, dilating your hearts with a holy Joy, Joy in the holy Ghost, for *Under the shadow of his wings,* you may, you should, *rejoyce.*"[88] Donne's chief delight as he contemplates his office is that he brings consolation to his people in sermons:

Chapter XI

Who but my selfe can conceive the sweetnesse of that salutation, when the Spirit of God sayes to me in a morning,
Go forth to day and preach, preach consolation, preach
peace, preach mercy, And spare my people. . . .[89]

Divine consolation should indeed be preached by a joyful man,
one whose eloquence sparkled with wit, as Donne's did.

Furthermore, what a grey and color-blind universe would
be presented to our eyes if sermons lacked all ornament, and
these poet-preachers left us entirely devoid of images and illustrations! To use Fuller's image, we should be living in churches
with ample and reasonable pillars, but inside walls without
windows. We can hardly conceive how uninteresting sermons
would be, which did not ransack reading, and observation, and
experience, to extend our knowledge and sensibility with historical examples, memorable maxims from thoughtful men, practical wisdom in proverbs, as well as the appeal to eye and ear
in images and emblems.

Finally, how unexciting would sermons be without the psychological insights which abound in the preaching of the less
conventional metaphysical preachers! This quality is very rarely
described in literature dealing with the metaphysical preachers,
and so it has been left to last to exemplify. This was Donne's
great gift, and Sidney Godolphin, who heard him, described
it perfectly:

> . . . thy one houre did treat
> The thousand mazes of the hearts deceipt;
> Thou didst pursue our lov'd and subtill sinne,
> Through all the foldings wee had wrapt it in.[90]

He uncovers the mixed motives that his congregation brings
to worship:

and whether *curiosity*, or *custome*, or *company*, or a loath-
somenesse to incurre the *penalties* of Lawes, or of the *cen-
sures* and observations of neighbours, bring thee thither,

483

though thou hadst nothing to do with *God*, in comming hither, God hath something to do with thee, now thou art here.[91]

He is acutely aware of the temptation of substituting natural causes for Divine Providence. This results in banishing God from earth to a distant and convenient heaven. As Donne insists, God sends calamities to alert the uncaring soul, and for "the deliverance from those calamities much more."[92] Donne shrewdly analyzes the three causes of unfaithfulness to God, the "three Enemies to that fixation and intireness of the Heart, which God loves: Inconsideration, when we do not Debate; Irresolution, when we do not Determine; Inconstancy, when we do not persevere."[93]

How cunningly Donne observes that the hearer delights in condemning the sins of others that he has no mind to commit: "We must not be glad, when our sins escape the *Preacher*. We must not say, (as though there were a comfort in that) though he have hit such a mans *Adultery*, and anothers *Ambition*, and anothers *extortion*, yet, for all his diligence, he hath missed *my sinne*." Then comes the sting in the tail: "for, if thou wouldest faine have it mist, thou wouldest faine hold it still."[94]

Andrewes did not know the labyrinthine ways of the human heart as well as Donne did. All the same he could assume the attitude of the worldling only to refute it the more effectively. In a court sermon he appears to make a digression: he imagines that a courtier objects beneath his breath, saying "Why goes he not to the point roundly?" To which Andrewes retorts that "The HOLY GHOST useth no wast words, nor ever speakes but to the point (we may be sure.)"[95] He demonstrates equal shrewdness in anticipating another objection, in an Easter sermon preached before James I in 1606. Here his point is that, fantastic as the Resurrection seems, yet "That is (ever) best knowen, that is most doubted of: And never was matter carried with more scruple, and slownesse of beleefe, with more doubts and difficulties, then was this of *Christs rising* . . . All this doubting was by them made, that we might be out of doubt, and *know, that Christ is risen*."[96]

Chapter XI

Three metaphysical preachers know that one of the subtler forms of self-delusion is to term vices euphemistically or to find excuses for sins. Bishop Francis White remarks: "And all we, *Adams* sinfull posterity, have worne this cloake of excuse even almost thred-bare by long usage of it, in palliating of our sinnes: And we cloake Drunkennesse with good fellowship; we cloake covetousnesse with good thriftinesse; wee cloake Pride with decency and comelinesse. . . ."[97] Bishop Joseph Hall makes a similar point: "The vice as well as the humour is diffusive of itself. How rarely have you ever seen a solitary drunkard! no, the very title which is misgiven to this sin is 'Good Fellowship'."[98]

Thomas Adams provides a very comprehensive analysis of the excuses offered for sins: Predestination, or God's will that I should do this wickedness, Ignorance, the sufficiency of my good deeds to weigh against my evil, the great mercifulness of God, the infinite satisfaction for sins offered by Christ's Atonement, and, finally, that "Repentance makes all even when it comes."[99]

Brilliant rhetoricians as the metaphysical preachers were, they proved themselves also to be outstanding physicians of the soul, both in their astute diagnoses and in their practical prescriptions. This included eager and obedient listening to God's Word from the pulpit and devout attendance at Holy Communion, as well as private and family prayers each day. But their great consolation was that they could always refer every case to the Great Physician, Christ Himself.

NOTES

1. Thomas Sprat, *The History of the Royal Society of London For the Improving of Natural Knowledge* (London, 1667), 113.

2. An Easter sermon preached at Whitehall on 18 April 1613.

3. William Barlow, *The Sermon Preached at Paules Crosse, the tenth day of November, being the next Sunday after the Discoverie of this late Horrible Treason* (London, 1606).

4. This is the first sermon in Ralph Brownrig, *Sixty Five Sermons* (London, 1674).

5. The sermon was Thomas Playfere, *The Meane in Mourning* (London, 1595), a Spital sermon.

6. John Wall, *Alae Seraphicae* (London, 1627), 5. Wren, too, could complicate a simple text by manifold divisions, as in *A Sermon Preached before the Kings Maiestie on Sunday the Seventeenth of February last, at White-hall* (Cambridge, 1627).

7. Peter Heylyn, in Sermon IV of *The Parables of the Tares Expounded & Applied in Ten Sermons* (London 1659).

8. Barten Holyday, *Of the Bread of Life. A Sermon* (Oxford, 1657).

9. Brownrig, *Sixty Five Sermons*, 75.

10. Lancelot Andrewes, *XCVI Sermons* (London, 1629), 77.

11. *Aubrey's Brief Lives*, ed. Oliver L. Dick, (London, 1949), 7.

12. Cited in F. J. Powicke, *A Life of the Reverend Richard Baxter* (London, 1924), 283.

13. Gilbert Burnet, *A Discourse of the Pastoral Care* (London, 1792), 216.

14. Citations in this paragraph are from Isaac Barrow, *Several Sermons against Evil Speaking* (London, 1678), respectively 45, 50, and 80.

15. John Eachard, *The Grounds & Occasions of the Contempt of the Clergy and Religion Enquired into. In a Letter written to R. L.* (London, 1670), 32.

16. Eachard, *The Grounds & Occasions . . .* , 33–34.

17. Eachard, *The Grounds & Occasions . . .* , 46–47.

18. Thomas Playfere, *The Whole Sermons* (London, 1623), 141. Donne was equally inept in referring to the need of ministers who "must have eyes in their tongues," so that they don't apply God's promises blindly to the presumptuous, nor His judgments to the brokenhearted,

(*The Sermons of John Donne*, ed. G. R. Potter and E. M. Simpson, 10 vols. [Berkeley, 1953–1962], 8:50). The image is confusing.

19. Thomas Jackson, *Nazareth and Bethlehem, or Israels Portion in the Son of Jesse* . . . (Oxford, 1617), 65.

20. John Wallis, *The Life of Faith. In two sermons to the University of Oxford* . . . (London, 1684), 38–39. I owe this reference to Rogers Miles, student and friend.

21. Andrewes, *XCVI Sermons*, 232. Adams uses the same pun in *The Collected Sermons*, ed. Thomas Smith (Edinburgh, 1861–1862), 972.

22. Adams, *Collected Sermons*, 169.

23. The citation reads: "Howsoever these *Magi* were *Potentes*, or no, they were *Petentes*. Though they were great men, yet they humbly seek the greatest of men, yea, the great God, *Iesus*" (*Collected Sermons*, 841.)

24. Adams, *Collected Sermons*, 888.

25. Brownrig, *Sixty Five Sermons*, 192.

26. Donne, *Sermons*, 9:304.

27. *The Works of* . . . *William Laud*, 9 vols. (Oxford, 1847), 1:72–73.

28. Donne, *Sermons*, 4:296.

29. Donne, *Sermons*, 5:53.

30. Donne, *Sermons*, 5:113.

31. Donne, *Sermons*, 2:309–310.

32. Donne, *Sermons*, 6:184. Christmas sermon of 1624 in St. Paul's.

33. Burnet, *A Discourse of the Pastoral Care*, 215.

34. Adams, *Collected Sermons*, 995–1015. The text is from II Corinthians 3:11, "Live in peace, and the God of love and peace shall be with you."

35. Playfere, *The Whole Sermons*, 125.

36. *The Works of* . . . *John Cosin*, Volume 1: *Sermons* (Oxford, 1843), 1:254.

37. Brownrig, *Sixty Five Sermons*, 209. The second Easter sermon.

38. Adams, *Collected Sermons*, 440f.

39. Adams, *Collected Sermons*, 888f.

40. *The Sermons of Maister Henrie Smith* (London, 1593), 228.

41. Adams, *Collected Sermons*, 995.

42. John King, *Lectures upon Ionas delivered at Yorke In the year of Our Lord 1594* (London, 1611), 11–12. This is a set of expository sermons.

43. Donne, *Sermons*, 4:280.

44. Donne, *Sermons*, 7:234.

45. Donne, *Sermons,* 4:307.

46. Donne, *Sermons,* 9:183.

47. Andrewes, *XCVI Sermons,* 308.

48. Andrewes, *XCVI Sermons,* 797.

49. John Hacket, *A Century of Sermons* (London, 1675), 689.

50. John King, *A Sermon at Paules Crosse, on behalf of Paules Church, March 26, 1620* (London, 1620), 50.

51. Theophilus Field, *A Watch-Word, or the Alarme, or, A Good Take Heed. A Sermon Preached at White-Hall in the open Preaching place last Lent before King Charles* (London, 1628), 48.

52. Laud, *Works,* 1: Sermons I and III, and especially p. 39.

53. George Morley, *A Sermon Preached at the Magnificent Coronation of the Most High and mighty King Charles the II*ᵈ . . . (London, 1661), 57–58.

54. An Ascension Day sermon, 1625, from Barten Holyday, *Three Sermons upon the Passion, Resurrection and Ascension of our Saviour, preached at Oxford* (London, 1626), 97.

55. Thomas Birch, *The Court and Times of James I,* 2 vols. (London, 1849), 2:392.

56. [Joseph Glanvill], *An Essay Concerning Preaching; Written for the Direction of a Young Divine* . . . (London, 1678), 44–45.

57. Andrewes, *XCVI Sermons,* 550–551.

58. Donne, *Sermons,* 4:74–75.

59. [Glanvill], *An Essay Concerning Preaching,* 53.

60. James Arderne, *Directions Concerning the Matter and Stile of Sermons,* ed. John Mackay (Oxford, 1952), 9. Originally published in 1671.

61. Andrewes, *XCVI Sermons,* 305.

62. Donne, *Sermons,* 1:318.

63. Donne, *Sermons,* 8:191. See similar endings at 7:278, and the last words he ever preached at the end of "Deaths Duell," Sermon 11 in vol. 10.

64. Hacket, *A Century of Sermons,* 8. Similarly, the eleventh sermon on the Incarnation in the division summarizes the lesson: "First, Blessedness offered us in Christs Incarnation. Second, Blessedness made complete in our own application," (78).

65. Brownrig, *Sixty Five Sermons,* 269. For some examples of applications, see also 37, 76, 91, 104, 137, 158, and 192.

66. *The Sermons of Maister Henrie Smith,* 425. For other examples, see 21f., 57, 67f., 130, 157f., 185, 202, 232, 259, 288f., 344, 401f., 451, 488, 505, 555, 589f., 642f., 657, 688, 717, 847, 862, 899, 954, 994f., and 1055.

67. Adams, *Collected Sermons,* 163–164 and elsewhere at 31, 63, 76, 120f., 132f., 140, 142, 154, 160, 166, 181, 202, 225, 245, 325, 348, 391, 413, 428, 477, 514, 557, 613, and 629. Another blunt conclusion can be found on 218.

68. *The Works of . . . Cosin,* 1:18.

69. *The Works of . . . Cosin,* 1:48–49.

70. Matthew Wren, *A Sermon Preached before the Kings Maiestie on Sunday the Seventeenth of February last at White-Hall* (Cambridge, 1627), 42.

71. F. E. Hutchinson, *The Cambridge History of English Literature,* 4:238.

72. See Chapter VII *supra.*

73. Arderne, *Directions Concerning the Matter and Stile of Sermons,* 3.

74. Donne, *Sermons,* 5:298. The exact quotation is "In his [God's] Cabinet, in his Bed-chamber, in his unrevealed purposes, wee must not presse upon him."

75. Donne, *Sermons,* 3:96–97.

76. Donne, *Sermons,* 8:98–99.

77. Adams, *Collected Sermons,* 746. He ingeniously argues: "Wee shall love the Saints. I may inferre wee shall know them. *Peter* knew *Moses* and *Elias* on the mount, whom yet before hee never knew: why then should we not know them in heaven?"

78. Donne, *Sermons,* 8:100.

79. Donne, *Sermons,* 8:270. Sermon for Easter Day, 1629.

80. Hacket, *A Century of Sermons,* 63. From the seventh sermon on the Incarnation.

81. Hacket, *A Century of Sermons,* 320. From the twelfth sermon on Christ's Temptations.

82. Hacket, *A Century of Sermons,* 573. From the second sermon on the Resurrection.

83. Hacket, *A Century of Sermons,* 643. From the first Whitsun sermon.

84. Barten Holyday, *Motives to a Good Life in Ten Sermons* (Oxford, 1657), 171.

85. Barten Holyday, *Three Sermons on the Passion, Resurrection and Ascension,* 64.

86. Adams, *Collected Sermons,* 297. From the sermon "Physick from Heaven."

87. Adams, *Collected Sermons,* 296.

88. Donne, *Sermons,* 7:69. From a prebend sermon preached on 29 January 1625.

89. Donne, *Sermons,* 7:133.

90. Cited in the introduction of Logan Pearsall Smith, *Donne's Sermons: Selected Passages with an Essay* (Oxford, 1919), xxxvii.

91. Donne, *Sermons,* 4:158. From a sermon preached at St. Paul's on Midsummer Day, 1622.

92. Donne, *Sermons,* 8:303. From a Christmas Sermon of 1621.

93. Donne, *Sermons,* 4:174. From a Lenten sermon preached before King Charles I at Whitehall on 12 February 1629.

94. Donne, *Sermons,* 3:363. From a St. Paul's Christmas sermon of 1621.

95. Andrewes, *XCVI Sermons,* 580. A sermon prepared to be preached on Easter, 1624.

96. Andrewes, *XCVI Sermons,* 385.

97. Francis White, *Londons Warning by Jerusalem. A Sermon Preached at Pauls Crosse on Mid-Lent Sunday last* (London, 1619), 36.

98. *The Works of . . . Joseph Hall,* Volume V: *Sermons,* ed. Philip Wynter (Oxford, 1863), 204.

99. Adams, *Collected Sermons,* 642. From the sermon "Mans Seede-Time and Harvest: Or, Lex Talionis."

INDEX

Aaron, 469

Abbot, Archbp. George, 33, 148, 168

Adams, Thomas: Calvinist, 2, 175; quantity of published sermons, 12; pity for poor, 13, 178, 361, 390; as prebendary, 28; link with Shakespeare, 42, 43; dissents from patristic interpretations, 53; uses allegorical interpretations, 64, 65; few festival sermons, 85, 87; misnamed a Puritan, 100; farfetched conceits, 100; Latin puns and paronomasia, 104–105; paradoxes, 108; popularity, 112; ingenious sermon titles, 112; striking starts, 116; uses of wit, 119, 174–180 passim, 465; eloquence, 176; clerical temptations, 176; images, 177f., 437f., 445, 464; proverbs, 290; fables, 292–293; critical of purgatory and Catholic ritual, 317, 319; on original sin, 354, 358; Godgiven joys, 355f.; on preferment, 360; use of "Characters," 361, 364; patience, 367; faith in adversity, 367; on the Incarnation, 370f.; on Crucifixion, 374; on Judgment Day, 385f.; on hell, 387f.; Paul's Cross and Spital sermons, 415–418; criticism of, 465–468; defense of learning, 452

Aesop, 56, 292

Alabaster, William, 7, 37, 44

Alciati, 75

Alexander of Hales, 164

Allegory: rejected in Protestant biblical interpretation, 63

Allen, J. W., 207

Amaziah, 408

Ambrose, St., 51, 53, 63, 164, 280, 281, 324, 330, 461, 471

Amos, 5, 62, 408, 420

Andrewes, Lancelot: Arminian, 2; as translator, controversialist, and patristics scholar, 21, 42, 62, 195, 196; wit, 22, 102–104; liturgical context of sermons, 66; use of Apocrypha, 81; Rabbinics, 81; paradoxes and oxymora, 108–112; compared with Donne, 195–198 passim; defects in preaching, 8, 196, 410, 471, 460, 463, 465; strengths, 291, 362, 363, 369, 371f., 404, 475, 484

Anne, Queen, 409

Anselm, St., 73

Aquinas, St. Thomas, 10, 80, 164, 237, 278

Aratus, 271

Arderne, James, 474

Arianism, 238

Aristotle, 158, 164, 235, 281

Arminian preachers: see chapter V; distinctive doctrines, 3, 307f., 353, 354; differences between them and Calvinists, 340–342 passim; English and Dutch forms of Arminianism, 135f.; backers, 33; Jacobean bishops, 206–214 passim; Caroline bishops, 214–227 passim; minor clergy, 227–254 passim; criticism of, 459–475; qualities of, 476–485

Ascham, Roger, 38

Athanasius, St., 54

Athenagoras, 478

Aubrey, John, 8

Audiences: see chapter IX, and under "Cathedral and Great church sermons"; "Court sermons"; "Oxford, Christ Church Cathedral"; "Paul's Cross sermons"; "St. Paul's Cathedral"; "Spital sermons"; "Westminster Abbey"; "University sermons"

491

Index

Classics, the: their impact on rhetoric of preachers, 36–39 passim;
cited, 51, 53–57 passim; historical
and literary references and Greek
and Latin citations, 62, 102, 139,
155; Prideaux's use of, 141; Hacket's, 144; Henry King's, 149, 162;
Barlow's, 158; Wren's, 218; Heylyn's, 230; Holyday's pedantic etymology from, 251
Clement of Alexandria, 158
Coke, Sir Edward, 148
Coley, Rosalie, 72
Conceits, 99–102 passim, 169, 177
Constantine, 58, 151, 414
Corbet, Bp. Richard, 7; wit, 31; at
Westminster School, 31; epitaph
on Donne, 48; maxims of, 106; ne-
glects diocese, 216
Coryate, Thomas, 284
Cosin, Bp. John: Arminian, 2; com-
piles *A Collection of Private Devotions*, 34; uses historical narration,
58; typological exegete, 64; complex sermon structure of, 66; liturgical context of sermons of, 66,
84; sufferings of, 214, 218–233 passim; lover of Anglican liturgy,
218; Master of Peterhouse, 219; on
the Incarnation, 221; wit, 221; on
overvaluation of preaching, 322;
critic of Puritans, 325; values reason, 354–355; strengths, 462–469
Court sermons, 4, 67, 90, 92, 93, 99,
111, 116, 128, 130–132, 150, 157,
197, 212, 217, 228, 259, 261, 283,
299, 303, 333–347, 350, 351, 369,
379, 393–399, 401, 404–414 passim;
defending status quo in Church
and State, 405, 407; summary of
needed qualities in, 414–415, 426–
428, 454, 486, 490. See also
"Gowrie Day sermons."
Coventry Cathedral, 374
Cowley, Abraham, 31
Cranmer, Archbp. Thomas, 337
Crashaw, Richard: sermons lost of,
9; supposed superstition of, 9;

Crashaw (*cont.*)
evaluation of poetry, 40; helps to
beautify Peterhouse chapel, 213
Croft, Bp. Herbert, 152, 239
Croll, M. W., 75
Cromwell, Oliver, 87, 148, 217
Cross, F. L., 343
Crum, Margaret, 37
Cyril of Jerusalem, St., 281, 331
Cyprian, St., 54, 281, 283, 330

Damascus, St. John of, 164, 331
Damien, Peter, 281
Danvers, Lady, 310, 396
Davenant, Sir William, 87
Docetism, 280
Donne, John: psychologist, 5, 13,
200f., 424, 484; macabre meditation of, 13, 383–384; Dryden on,
45; Corbet's epitaph, 4, 48; paradoxes of, 13, 203; patrologist, 52,
53, 230, 278, 280f., 330, 448; Rabbinic and Muslim lore, 81, 281–
282; sources of illustrations, 57,
59, 77, 81, 284, 288, 289, 423–425,
439–448; themes of: sacraments,
338–339, Church, 307, the Passion, 374, the Resurrection, 377–
378, Hope, 367f., Eternal Life,
307–308, Hell, 338–339; preaches
many Paul's Cross and Spital sermons, 415, 423–424; defends
learning in pulpit, 200; festival
preacher, 474, 478–480; weaknesses, 78, 79, 467, 471, 474, 475,
478f.; strengths, 8, 115–117, 202,
271, 341–342, 357f., 362f., 365, 374;
wit of, 117, 446, 482
Dort, Synod of, 133f.
Downame, George, 80, 418
Drake, Sir Francis, 284
Dryden, 37, 45, 175
Dublin: Trinity College, 27, 164
Duppa, Bp. Brian, 3; protege of
Laud, 35; beloved of Charles I, 35;
at Westminster School, 37; uses
maxims, 106, and metaphors, 432;
sermon analyses of, 223–226 pas-

Index